Sacramental
Shopping

BECOMING MODERN
New Nineteenth-Century Studies

SERIES EDITORS
Sarah Way Sherman
Department of English, University of New Hampshire
Janet Aikins Yount
Department of English, University of New Hampshire
Rohan McWilliam
Anglia Ruskin University, Cambridge, England
Janet Polasky
Department of History, University of New Hampshire

This book series maps the complexity of historical change
and assesses the formation of ideas, movements, and institutions crucial
to our own time by publishing books that examine the emergence of
modernity in North America and Europe. Set primarily but not exclusively
in the nineteenth century, the series shifts attention from modernity's
twentieth-century forms to its earlier moments of uncertain and often
disputed construction. Seeking books of interest to scholars on both sides
of the Atlantic, it thereby encourages the expansion of nineteenth-century
studies and the exploration of more global patterns of development.

For a complete list of books available in this series, see www.upne.com

Sarah Way Sherman, *Sacramental Shopping: Louisa May Alcott,
Edith Wharton, and the Spirit of Modern Consumerism*

Kimberly Wahl, *Dressed as in a Painting: Women and
British Aestheticism in an Age of Reform*

Hildegard Hoeller, *From Gift to Commodity: Capitalism and
Sacrifice in Nineteenth-Century American Fiction*

Beth L. Lueck, Brigitte Bailey, and Lucinda L. Damon-Bach, editors,
*Transatlantic Women: Nineteenth-Century American Women Writers
and Great Britain*

Michael Millner, *Fever Reading: Affect and Reading Badly
in the Early American Public Sphere*

Sacramental
Shopping

Louisa May Alcott,
Edith Wharton, and the
Spirit of Modern
Consumerism

SARAH WAY
SHERMAN

UNIVERSITY OF NEW HAMPSHIRE PRESS

DURHAM, NEW HAMPSHIRE

UNIVERSITY OF NEW HAMPSHIRE PRESS
An imprint of University Press of New England
www.upne.com
© 2013 University of New Hampshire
All rights reserved
Manufactured in the United States of America
Designed by Eric M. Brooks
Typeset in Bulmer by A. W. Bennett, Inc.

University Press of New England is a member of the
Green Press Initiative. The paper used in this book meets their
minimum requirement for recycled paper.

For permission to reproduce any of the material in this book,
contact Permissions, University Press of New England, One Court Street,
Suite 250, Lebanon NH 03766; or visit www.upne.com

The author gratefully acknowledges permission to reproduce the following:
"Sacramental Shopping: *Little Women* and the Spirit of Modern
Consumerism," by Sarah Way Sherman. *Prospects,* Volume 26 (2001),
pp. 183–237. Copyright © 2001 Cambridge University Press.
Reprinted with permission.

Library of Congress Cataloging-in-Publication Data
Sherman, Sarah Way.
Sacramental shopping: Louisa May Alcott, Edith Wharton, and the spirit of
modern consumerism / Sarah Way Sherman.
pages   cm. — (Becoming Modern: New Nineteenth-Century Studies)
Includes bibliographical references and index.
ISBN 978-1-61168-422-3 (cloth : alk. paper) —
ISBN 978-1-61168-437-7 (pbk.: alk. paper) —
ISBN 978-1-61168-412-4 (ebook)
1. Alcott, Louisa May, 1832–1888. Little women. 2. Wharton, Edith,
1862–1937. House of mirth. 3. Consumption (Economics) in
literature. 4. Civilization, Modern, in literature. 5. American fiction—19th
century—History and criticism. 6. American fiction—Women authors—
History and criticism. I. Title.
PS1017.L53S54   2013
813'.4—dc23   2013007237

5 4 3 2 1

To Jamie

Contents

Acknowledgments

This study began with a grant from my UNH English Department chair, the late Michael DePorte, to purchase books on consumer culture; they opened a whole new field of research to me. I am profoundly grateful for Mike's recognition of this project's promise and his faith in my ability to carry it through to the end. I am also grateful for the generous support of my UNH colleagues, especially Rachel Trubowitz, who has always been ready, sometimes at a moment's notice, to provide invaluable comments on a proposal, a chapter, or a possible revision. Douglas Lanier's graduate seminar on the ceremonial culture of early modern England laid the groundwork for my understanding of the Catholic/Protestant debates over the sacraments and their implications. Sean Moore talked with me about the new economist criticism. Brigitte Bailey read through my entire first draft and reassured me of its worth. Siobhan Senier and Paula Salvio affirmed the link between my research and present-day issues of over-consumption and sustainability. Lisa MacFarlane, Tom Newkirk, Ruth Sample, Diane Freedman, David Watters, and Michael Ferber were an enthusiastic audience for my ideas; they never seemed to lose faith that someday a book would actually appear. My former students Sharon Kehl-Califano, Sally Hirsh-Dickinson, and Jason Williams enriched my graduate seminars and taught me much.

And warm appreciation goes as well to the later chairs of my department — Rochelle Lieber, Janet Aikins Yount, and Andrew Merton — for their patience with my sometimes slow progress. Along with my college deans, Marilyn Hoskin and Kenneth Fuld, they also kept faith that this book would someday be done, and in doing so they helped me keep my own. I am also grateful to Harry Richards and the UNH Graduate School for a Summer Faculty Fellowship that gave me time to read those new books and jump-start my research. Burt Feintuch and the UNH Center for the Humanities awarded me a Senior Faculty Fellowship that provided me a semester off to reframe my study at a critical moment. Bruce Mallory and the Office of the UNH Provost named me a Faculty Scholar and freed me for another semester to complete the first draft. John Aber, as UNH provost, gave final approval for this book's publication. Even during difficult economic times, he continued to support the "Becoming Modern" series in which it appears. Lastly, Andrew Merton and the UNH English Department generously supplied last-minute help with book production costs. I have been very lucky to have received such strong and understanding support from my home institution.

I am grateful also for the recognition that has come from the larger scholarly community. June Howard and Carol Singley were early supporters of this project. Their appreciation of its larger implications meant a lot to me. They, along with my UNH colleague Lisa MacFarlane, helped secure the fellowships that allowed me to complete the book. I owe them all a great deal. Hildegard Hoeller, Rohan McWilliam, Doug Goldstein, and Megan Marshall offered much appreciated support along the way. Nickianne Moody and Julia Hallam provided the first chance to take my ideas public when they accepted my paper on *Little Women* and consumer culture for their conference "Consumption: Fantasy, Success, and Desire" at Liverpool John Moore's University in 1998. They later included this paper in their edited collection, *Consuming Pleasures: Selected Essays on Popular Fictions* (2000); it is reprinted here by their kind permission. A greatly expanded version of that essay, now chapter 1 of this book, was then accepted by Jack Salzman for *Prospects: An Annual of American Cultural Studies* (2001). My thanks to him and to Cambridge University Press for permission to reprint this material. I am also grateful to Derek Rubin and Hans Krabbendam for their acceptance of my paper "Religion, Consumer Culture, and the Body in Toni Morrison's *The Bluest Eye*" for their conference "Religion in America: European and American Perspectives." Subsequently published in their 2004 collection of conference papers, this essay allowed me to address a more contemporary writer and to demonstrate how my analysis of consumer culture could illuminate the construction of racial difference and its human consequences. And finally, thanks to Robert Lamb and G. R. Thompson for their inclusion of my essay "Mapping the Culture of Abundance: Literary Narratives and Consumer Culture" in their 2005 *Blackwell Companion to American Fiction, 1865–1914*. They gave me a welcome opportunity to apply the analytical approach used in this book to a broader overview of American writing.

I am extraordinarily grateful to Phyllis Deutsch at the University Press of New England. I could not have asked for a more intelligent and discerning editor. Always professional, yet always sympathetic and tactful, she guided an initially unwieldy manuscript to completion. My two peer reviewers, Elsa Nettels and Carol Singley, were exceptionally helpful as well. Their perceptive comments helped me to clarify and highlight crucial issues. Carol Singley, in particular, did me a great service by suggesting cuts that rendered the text more manageable and effective. Bronwyn Becker, my skilled and thorough copy editor, gave the manuscript its final polish. Finally, I would like to thank my family for its unwavering support of this project, especially my sister, Carrie Sherman, and my brother-in-law Terry Whiting, as well as my son, Peter Calderwood, who has become a lively intellectual colleague, and my husband, Jamie Calderwood, whose love, encouragement, and wise counsel have sustained me over years of research and writing. This book is dedicated to him.

Sacramental
Shopping

Introduction

sacrament, n. 1. *Eccles*. a. a visible sign of an inward grace.
b. a visible sign instituted by Jesus Christ to symbolize or confer grace.
The Random House College Dictionary

Consumption is governed by a form of *magical thinking* . . .
a primitive mentality . . . based on a belief in the omnipotence
of thoughts (though what we have in this case is a belief in the
omnipotence of signs). "Affluence" is, in effect, merely
the accumulation of the *signs* of happiness.

JEAN BAUDRILLARD,
The Consumer Society: Myths and Structures

In Childe Hassam's 1893 painting, "Street Scene, Christmas Morning," a lovely well-dressed woman walks toward the viewer. Surrounded by elegant shop windows and snow-filled air, she seems excited and happy, a mood expressed by the brilliant red flowers decorating her rakish black hat with its lacey veil. The scene is rendered with Hassam's lyrical impressionist brushstrokes, a full spectrum of whites and blues centered on a single object held in the woman's hands: a blue box tied with white ribbon. This box, the focal point of the painting, is a more arresting blue than all the other blues in the landscape. According to historian H. Barbara Weinberg, Hassam at this time was preoccupied with painting Fifth Avenue and its stylish women.[1] Given that this turquoise box matches the well-known trademark of one of New York's most prestigious stores, it is more than likely that we are looking at a portrait, not just of a fashionable woman, but also of her fashionable purchase: a Christmas gift from Tiffany's. By 1893 Tiffany's blue box was nationally recognized. First introduced in 1837, the store's packaging was trademarked and the color's formula carefully-guarded. The box soon became a marketing icon and potent symbol of social distinction and affluence.[2] For those privileged enough to receive it, as for those only able to dream of it, the Tiffany box was a coveted sign of happiness, a modern sacrament. In this painting of a joyous Christmas morning we see the eclipse of a traditional religious holiday by its emerging secular replacement: a celebration of materialistic hopes and desires.[3]

This book places two classic American novels at this historical intersection of modern consumer culture and older religious discourses on materialism and identity. It begins with Louisa May Alcott's *Little Women*, set during the Civil War and published in 1868 at the onset of the Gilded Age. The second novel, Edith Wharton's *The House of Mirth*, appeared a generation later in 1905, when the consumer culture emerging in Alcott's time had become fully dominant.[4] Both novels show their heroines grappling with the values of the elite group Thorstein Veblen named the "leisure class," defined by its conspicuous consumption and competitive display: Tiffany's target market.[5] Both books also reveal a deep concern with issues of materialism, moral development, and self-construction. And yet these texts, very dissimilar in style, have rarely, if ever, been compared. *Little Women* is a domestic novel written for children and shaped by an earlier generation of romantic and sentimental writers. *The House of Mirth* is known primarily as a work of realistic and even naturalistic fiction, influenced by Henry James, William Dean Howells, and Theodore Dreiser. In this study, however, I demonstrate how Wharton, who referred to Alcott in her autobiography as "the great Louisa" (her fastidious upper-class parents only allowed her to read the older writer's slangy books "because all the other children read them") drew on *Little Women's* core plot and themes for *The House of Mirth*.[6] Moreover, these commonalities help explain the enormous popularity of both books when first published and their continuing appeal to audiences today, as attested by the robust sales of the original texts and their successful adaptations through various plays and films.[7] These books still find readers in the twenty-first century because they speak so powerfully to the struggle to define identity and moral values in American consumer culture and, more specifically, because both speak to the especial difficulty of these struggles for women. However, while Alcott offers an idealistic and hopeful vision of how young women like the stylish figure in Hassam's Christmas painting might resist the seductions of the marketplace, Wharton's version of this story is more realistic and much darker. Directly addressing the limitations of Alcott's sentimental idealism in an increasingly materialistic world, Wharton's portrayal of her beautiful heroine Lily Bart's failure to survive materialism's destructive influence is sobering.

Central to my argument is how both Alcott and Wharton rework traditional Protestant discourses to interpret their heroines' struggle with modern consumerism. As Max Weber famously asserted in *The Protestant Ethic and the Spirit of Capitalism*, Puritanism advanced the rise of capitalism through a worldly asceticism that advocated amassing material wealth not for selfish gain but for the glory of God.[8] Orthodox Protestants saw themselves defined by their relationship to God, not by their earthly works or goods. Those works and goods were only signs of their favor in God's eyes; they were the stewards of wealth, not its ultimate owners. True identity and spiritual grace could only be gained through God; happiness rested in doing God's will. This worldly asceticism, which was deeply implicated in the material world while repudiating that world's ultimate significance, confronted new challenges during the period I am examining. As the capitalist economy shifted from scarcity to abundance, Americans were freshly tempted to rely on wealth and material goods for their identity and lasting happiness. As Colin Campbell has shown in his brilliant revision of Weber, *The Romantic Ethic and the Spirit of Modern Consumerism* (from which I take my own study's title), modern responses to this emerging consumer culture grew from the pietistic strand of Protestantism. This strand informs what Campbell calls the Romantic ethic with its emphasis on emotion, imagination, and interiority.[9] While drawing on Campbell's work, especially in my analysis of Romantic bohemians such as the Alcotts, my own approach to these novels emphasizes their return to traditional Protestant representations of materialism and idolatry, particularly their association of these dangers with non-Protestant religious discourses such as Roman Catholicism and, in Wharton's case, Judaism.

For example, the young women in both novels must traverse the dangerous terrain of a contemporary vanity fair, with direct reference to its model in John Bunyan's classic Puritan parable, *Pilgrim's Progress* (1678).[10] And, as in Bunyan's original Vanity Fair, danger often lies in temptations to materialist idolatry. For earlier Protestants, the prime example of such idolatry was the Roman Catholic doctrine of the sacraments, particularly the Eucharist or Lord's Supper. Where Protestants saw the bread and wine as only symbols of God's grace, a grace only God could bestow, Catholics saw them as conveyers of that grace. Similarly, Protestants saw Catholic veneration of religious iconography and sacred relics, not to mention the gorgeous ornamentation of vestments and cathedrals, as further evidence of idolatrous practices, a suspicion amplified by the extravagant secular displays of European aristocracy. In the nineteenth-century, Protestant suspicions about European Catholic culture informed a new critique of fashion and consumerism. As the radiant capital of an emerging consumer culture, Paris dictated whether an enormous range of goods were in fashion. According to historian Howard Mumford Jones, Americans were "following, often at second and third hand, the modes of a Gallic aristocracy." Their supposedly democratic and Protestant society had "yielded . . . abjectly to the universal domination of the French milliner and the French dress-maker."[11] Henry David Thoreau agreed: "We worship not the Graces, nor the Parcae, but Fashion. She spins and weaves and cuts with full authority. The head monkey in Paris puts on a traveler's cap, and all the monkeys in America do the same." His condemnation extended to the very stronghold of American Puritanism: "even in our democratic New England towns the accidental possession of wealth, and its manifestation in dress and equipage alone, obtain for the possessor almost universal respect. But they who yield such respect, numerous as they are, are so far heathen, and need to have a missionary sent to them."[12]

In *Little Women* and *The House of Mirth* we can see this new "heathen" worship as well as the missionary struggle to counter its appeal. In these novels Protestant anxiety over the interpretation of the sacraments has become modern anxiety over the use of consumer goods; Catholic belief in the power of consecrated bread and wine to grant grace is re-imagined as consumer faith in the power of commodities to confer the qualities they signify.[13] Evoking the Protestant belief that true identity and salvation are founded on one's inner relationship to God, Alcott and Wharton both stress the failure of fashionable consumer goods to deliver the happiness they promise. In both texts, however, the Protestant conception of authentic identity is subtly called into question as their authors grapple with problems raised by an increasingly secular society in which identity and self-respect seem less dependent on God than on the accident of social standing or the power of materialistic display. Confronted with the erosion of old certainties, these writers struggle to find a secular equivalent of the Protestant anti-materialistic discourse, one which would guide their heroines safely through the modern vanity fair.[14]

My study begins by exploring *Little Women* and Mrs. March's direction of her four young daughters on their "Pilgrim's Progress" to happiness as "little women." Chapter 1 discusses Alcott's Transcendentalist and sentimental influences, Victorian anxieties about consumption, and the centrality of the debate over the sacraments to questions of success and self-definition. The emerging consumer culture was particularly problematic for women because consumption was gendered female: shopping was women's work. Moreover, women were in danger of becoming consumer goods themselves.[15] With little access to well-paying jobs in the new industrial economy, particularly jobs that would preserve their respectability and status, middle and upper-class women were largely dependent on their fathers and husbands for financial security. In return for this security, women served the men who supported them as symbolic displays of male economic and social power. The elegantly dressed wives of the leisure class were as much trophies as their husbands' fancy carriages and imposing mansions.[16]

Alcott's critical response to this emerging culture drew on the waning discourses of Transcendentalism, that Romantic and individualistic descendant of Protestantism learned from her father, Bronson Alcott, and fellow Concord residents Ralph Waldo Emerson and Henry David Thoreau.[17] Mrs. March, modeled on Alcott's own mother Abby Alcott, teaches her daughters that they possess intrinsic worth, that they should marry for love, not money, and be valued for their inner moral qualities and creative gifts, not their surface material beauty. She would rather see them poor old maids than unhappy wives of wealthy men they do not love. Alcott's novel then updates the Protestant critique of Catholic idolatry by identifying the latter with a European-influenced devotion to fashionable self-presentation. In *Little Women* the leisure-class trophy wife is an idolatrous fashion slave who has ceded her selfhood, not to the Pope, but to her French dressmaker. However, the ironic, unintended outcome of Alcott's story is to moralize "sincere" shopping as self-expression. Although Amy March, Alcott's virtuous shopper, does not expect consumer goods to confer qualities she does not naturally possess, she is ultimately licensed to accumulate possessions as the "outward and visible signs" of her own "inward and invisible" style. Significantly, Alcott extends this association of a sincere style with moral character to literary narrative.[18] Jo March's achievement of an authentic writing style is linked to the successful development of her Protestant character. The supposed result is the first book of *Little Women* itself.

Thus, while this study examines how characters use consumer goods, it also looks closely at how this use is related to the way characters draw on various cultural frameworks or "representational economies" to construct a sense of self. Anthropologist Webb Keane has examined Protestantism itself as one such economy, which offers its followers not only an ethic but also a language and a way of seeing, a "Protestant gaze" that historian Jenny Franchot examines thoroughly in her study of the antebellum Protestant response to European Catholicism.[19] In earlier periods, orthodox Protestants believed that God's election and divine grace provided such guidance and a foundation for their identity. However, *Little Women's* depiction of moral development reflects the increasingly secular nature of a more liberal Protestantism. No longer relying on crisis conversion for enlightenment, Alcott's characters must learn their moral lessons through "Christian nurture." Although their spirituality and conscience are innate and God-given, bringing these potentialities to full awareness and development depends, not on a miracle, but on a human and social process.[20] For example, Mrs. March allows her daughters to experiment with the fashionable materialism of their neighbors, and when disappointment inevitably sets in, she is there to articulate the necessary moral. These dialogues are the heart of the novel.[21] By its end, the three surviving March sisters have absorbed their family's lessons and internalized its Protestant gaze. They have become reliable Protestant stewards of their worldly goods: selfless, anti-materialistic, devoted to their families and each other.

It is also important to point out that Christian nurture and sentimentalism, as historians Ann Douglas, Jane Tompkins, and (more recently) Mary Louise Kete have noted, represent an important revision of traditional Protestantism and its liberal, Romantic descendent, Transcendentalism.[22] In their emphasis on the family as the site and source of moral development, sentimental writers like Alcott explicitly critique the individualism of Emerson and Thoreau, as well as that of their precursors, Jonathan Edward and other orthodox Calvinists.[23] This intervention into Protestant discourses allows Alcott to forge a vision of identity that acknowledges the self as embedded in a social, material world, but also maps a path toward personal grace and true happiness through the material world's dangerous seductions. However, Alcott's vision, as I shall show, is not without its ironies and contradictions. For example, while *Little Women* stresses the "immanent" nature of spirituality, as embodied in the caring bonds of family, it also allows for a reassuringly anti-materialistic emphasis on divine justice and otherworldly salvation in its depiction of Beth March's Christ-like death, a death that is morally transformative for her sisters and offers transcendent consolation for her innocent suffering and untimely loss. By limiting its vision to the private domain, Alcott's novel also ignores the larger economic injustices that structure a system in which most women are denied access to a living wage and forced into economic dependency.[24] And, with its continued reliance on Protestant anti-materialism, it cannot fully address the very real pain that poverty and material deprivation cause.

Little Women thus presents an optimistic vision of individual moral development effected through the wise guidance of enlightened parents and books like itself, which substitute for scripture as sacraments of happiness and grace. It also quietly sidesteps the disturbing implications of its message for those who lack such crucial guidance in the modern vanity fair, an increasingly secular world in which Protestant anti-materialism is just one of several discourses circulating in the marketplace of faiths. However, these disturbing implications take center stage in *The House of Mirth*. Whereas *Little Women* offers itself as a map for young women in need of moral guidance, *The House of Mirth* is a cautionary tale of a young woman whose family neglects to give her such a map or teach her to read the signs that might direct her safely through modern materialistic culture.

The result is a startlingly contemporary story. Raised to value only wealth and social standing, Lily Bart, a beautiful gold-digging socialite, fails to snag a rich husband and runs into overwhelming debt through gambling and compulsive shopping. Bereft of money and status, the troubled heroine's dependence on luxury becomes an uncontrollable addiction to chloral hydrate, a replacement for the temporary comfort and renewal that luxury once provided. The novel ends with her death by drug overdose in a seedy New York boarding house, after saying farewell to her remaining designer dresses and the dreams of happiness they once signified.

In telling Lily Bart's story, Wharton also presents the self as social, shaped by discourses learned in the family and the wider social world. However, whereas *Little Women* shows us the four sisters moving inexorably toward identities stabilized through their attachment to family and their striving for Protestant virtue, Wharton gives us a heroine who is taught to honor materialistic goals and to value herself primarily as an expensive consumer good. Through her dawning romantic attachment to the young lawyer Lawrence Selden, Lily is then introduced to the power of the Protestant gaze. Selden's belief in an identity undefined by "material accidents" makes him eligible for membership in what he describes as a "republic of the spirit," a secular, highly individualist form of Enlightenment Protestantism. However, while Lily feels initially inspired and even liberated by her dialogues with Selden, his way of seeing has the ironic effect not of freeing her from her former materialism but of putting her in a constant state of conflict. She becomes torn between her recently acquired idealism and her old dependence on luxury. Unable to resolve this conflict, she is ultimately destroyed, as much by the demands of her newly formed conscience as by her need for financial security and material comfort. The lessons learned in her dialogues with Selden allow her to withstand the most morally damaging of her temptations, but they do not protect her from the pain and loneliness her conflicts create. Moreover, Selden's inflexible individualism prevents him from offering Lily the sympathy and forgiveness that in *Little Women* allow the March sisters to learn from their materialistic experiments. With their mother's help, they come to master as well as understand their desires. But as Lily's self-awareness and ability to narrate her own story grow, so does her anxiety. Never having "learned to live with her thoughts," and lacking the support that keeps the March sisters steady on their path, Lily repeatedly turns to various methods of emotional escape. The result is her addiction and death.

In addition to the conflict between the consumer "Catholic" and the upright Protestant, there is a new player in the drama of *The House of Mirth*: the figure of the predatory "Jew," represented by the successful businessman, Simon

Rosedale. Wharton's novel here reflects her own period's ethnic politics, partic-ularly its response to the influx of Jewish immigrants from Eastern Europe. In Rosedale, Wharton offers a new version of materialism's representational econ-omy and a new incarnation of the materialist idolater: one more skeptical, more modern, and, according to the logic of the novel, more dangerous. Unlike the consumer "Catholic," the "Jew" recognizes the difference between material ap-pearances and spiritual truths, yet knowingly rejects the latter when the former is more to his worldly advantage. Rosedale's offer to rescue Lily from poverty, an offer conditional upon her performing an act of blackmail, represents the greatest threat to Lily Bart's nascent Protestant identity. And yet, while Whar-ton's depiction of Rosedale underscores his moral corruption, it is also subtly sympathetic to his honesty about social ambition and acquisitive desire. In com-parison to Selden's judgmental gaze, Rosedale's acknowledgment of ugly social realities and their power is refreshingly realistic. He may be a materialist, but he is not a hypocrite. Among all the novel's characters, Rosedale is perhaps the most aware of Lily's struggle and, even when she resists his appeals, the most appreciative of her intrinsic value.

Finally, while Wharton's novel acknowledges and even affirms the insights of Alcott's Christian nurture, she also shows, disturbingly, that without such nur-ture, without the support and forgiveness of loving community, a divided soul like Lily Bart's can be irreparably damaged. For example, Gerty Farish, a social worker and friend of Lily, serves as the novel's representative of Alcott's senti-mental idealism. However, Gerty's compassionate efforts to heal Lily are ineffec-tual. She cannot reach her. The new helping professions, with their "therapeu-tic ethos," cannot replace the missing foundation of faith or family. Moreover, the anti-materialistic idealism of Protestantism, whether of the individualistic or the sentimentalist stripe, cannot account for Lily's very real material needs, es-pecially in a world where, without a wealthy husband or marketable skills other than the production of her own beauty, she has no place in the economic "ma-chinery" that would support her. And unlike Alcott, who in depicting Beth's death could still appeal to divine compensation for worldly injustice and suf-fering, Wharton withholds such reassurance. Her assessment of Lily's future is bleak.

The House of Mirth concludes by showing us the limitations not only of Rosedale's materialism but also of traditional Protestantism's individualism and Christian nurture's sentimentalism. Wharton's novel offers not a sacrament of happiness but a diagnosis of failure. That failure is not Lily's alone, but a whole society's. In *Little Women*, vanity fair is just one nouveau riche neighborhood; in *The House of Mirth*, it is Lily's entire world. Whereas Alcott once criticized her own *Little Women* and its literary progeny as "moral pap" for children, Wharton's novel serves up sterner fare for adults, "food for the full-grown," as her hero, Vance Weston, recalls the lines from St. Augustine's *Confessions* in her late novel *The Gods Arrive*.[25] The very title of *The House of Mirth* is taken from the biblical passage: "The heart of the wise is in the house of mourning, but the heart of the fool is in the house of mirth."[26] However, scripture also says that those who mourn shall be comforted. Wharton's novel may not promise happiness, but, as I hope to show, in its wise understanding of human frailty and its compassionate portrait of human loss, contemporary readers may still find a sacrament of consolation.

While this study's particular comparison of Alcott and Wharton is unique, it also offers a new critical framework, one that combines contemporary approaches to religious discourse, consumer culture, and identity formation. For example, in *Edith Wharton: Matters of Mind and Spirit* (1995), Carol Singley demonstrated the importance of the Protestant tradition to Wharton's writing; in *Displaying Women: Spectacles of Leisure in Edith Wharton's New York* (1998), Maureen Montgomery showed how Wharton represented the new culture of affluence and display; and in *Edith Wharton and the Making of Fashion* (2009), Katherine Joslin revealed how Wharton used dress to signify character and its social context.[27] Recent studies by scholars such as Gary Levine and Irene Goldman-Price have treated Wharton's possible antisemitism, its significance and sources, while Hildegard Hoeller and Lori Merish have analyzed Wharton's indebtedness to sentimentalism and its influence on *The House of Mirth*.[28] My project connects these apparently disparate areas of concern, in the process integrating current literary approaches not only to Wharton but also to Alcott. By tracing the influence of these various discourses on two important texts in the U.S. literary canon, I hope to reveal in turn how those texts illuminate modern consumer culture and its challenges to American identities and values.

This study also highlights how Christian nurture marks the beginning of a modern developmental psychology, ultimately leading to what we think of now as the "therapeutic ethos."[29] It is this appeal to the therapeutic that marks twenty-first century treatment of destructively materialistic behavior, including compulsive consumption (and addictive behaviors of all types). We can see this emergent ethos clearly in Alcott's *Little Women*, whose representation of childrearing and moral education parallels progressive approaches used today, especially in its advocacy of nonviolent discipline, its reliance on parent-child dialogues, and its concern with authenticity and self-expression. In addition,

Alcott's emphasis on the family's central role in developing and sustaining an individual's narrative of self anticipates present-day uses of personal narrative and therapeutic communities in the treatment of illness, trauma, and addiction.[30] At the same time, this study argues that *Little Women* is very much a transitional text, its modernity qualified by its reliance on otherworldly justice, providential interventions, and the notion of essential identity. By contrast, although Wharton keeps and even affirms many elements of the Christian nurture that we see in Alcott's classic, she also sharply critiques its optimism and remnants of otherworldly faith. While Wharton's characters struggle with the temptations of consumer materialism, they also must come to terms with the recalcitrant materiality of their lives: the inescapable economic and social constraints that no amount of idealism and sentimental optimism can loosen.

Finally, drawing on the wealth of existing Wharton scholarship to synthesize a fresh interpretation of *The House of Mirth*, this study also aims to resolve some long-standing debates about the much-studied novel. While critics have disagreed on the nature of the contradictions they see in the novel's last sections, they generally agree that the novel finally lacks coherence. For example, Lori Merish, like many critics before her, sees the novel slipping into anti-modern nostalgia, while Gary Levine, in his assessment of Wharton's antisemitism, finds the book a "nest of contradictions."[31] However, this study argues that *The House of Mirth* is not a novel compromised by its internal contradictions, but a novel that represents a *character* compromised, and ultimately destroyed, by her internal contradictions. Instead of closing with the unified identities that give Alcott's novel its happy ending, Wharton's darker, more ironic vision gives us a young woman riven by the competing discourses she has acquired in modernity's ideological marketplace. Rather than interpreting Wharton's conclusion as a retreat from a realist critique of Lily's society into a nostalgic evocation of lost domesticity, my analysis demonstrates how sentimental ideas of Christian nurture and Protestant moral instruction inform the novel from its opening pages. However, while Wharton shows us the healing power of love and care in the scenes just prior to Lily's death, she also shows us how that power fails to reach her troubled heroine when she needs it most.

In addition to this introduction, the book comprises five chapters. Chapter 1, "Raising Virtuous Shoppers: *Little Women* and the Marketplace of Morality," uses *Little Women* to present the study's core issues and show readers how the novel works as a developmental paradigm against which I will be measuring

Wharton's later novel. Here I also set up my theoretical framework concerning consumerism, Protestantism in its various forms, and idolatrous materialism. For example, I use theorists such as Mary Douglas and Baron Isherwood to define key terms such as "materialistic behavior," which ironically contrasts with the usual use of the term "materialist" insofar as consumer materialists do not value goods purely for their functionality. Rather, as Jay Mechling and Jackson Lears have noted, modern consumers tend to ignore the concrete, sensuous properties of objects in favor of their socially constructed symbolic properties, properties that promise to magically confer the happiness consumers seek.[32] The failure of this magic is also the source of what Colin Campbell and Grant McCracken term consumer "insatiability," the addictive nature of the consumer's quest for satisfaction.[33] Pierre Bourdieu's work shapes my discussion of consumer taste and its social formation, a process crucial to the March family's effort to give their girls a "taste" for morality, as opposed to fashionable dresses.[34] Warren Susman and Karen Halttunen contribute to my discussion of the rise of the modern concept of personality as a replacement for older notions of an essential self and the subsequent Victorian anxieties about the dangers of "confidence men and painted women" and the necessity for "sincerity" in one's performances of self.[35] Drawing on recent theorists on the dialogical formation of identity and the role of narrative in self-construction such as Ian Burkitt, Michael White, and David Epston, this chapter also lays out key concepts of Christian nurture, along with its origins in liberal Protestantism and its appearance in the developmental strategies employed in *Little Women*.[36] Here we see how the March family teaches its children the true sources of happiness and fulfillment, sources not found in expensive consumer goods (an insight seconded by recent work on materialistic behavior and "subjective well-being" by social psychologists Daniel Gilbert, Tim Kasser, Allen Kanner, and others).[37]

Chapter 2, "Lily Bart and the Pursuit of Happiness," begins by reviewing Wharton's upbringing and the hidden role that *Little Women* played in her imagination. It then provides an initial reading of Lily's character and the complex dialogue between *The House of Mirth* and its sentimental precursor. Critics have often noted the resemblance between Lily Bart's family background and Wharton's: the frivolous mother focused on consumption and social status, the depressed and financially exploited father, the lonely daughter, confused and emotionally neglected. "Lily" was actually one of Wharton's nicknames as a young woman. What has not been noticed, however, is the way key scenes in Alcott's novel provide ironic and sometimes surprisingly explicit parallels to Wharton's family history. While Wharton ultimately gained the self-awareness and intellectual strength to escape Lily Bart's fate, Lily's character draws on Wharton's own background and is constructed in revealing opposition to Alcott's "little women."

Most crucially, Lily is the product of an "anti-Christian nurture." Seeing her as a beautiful object and potential financial asset, her mother raises her daughter for sale on the marriage market, thereby setting her up for devastating emotional failure. Chapter 2 discusses Lily's perception of herself as a valuable commodity, a "jewel" immune to bodily disfigurement and mortality, in the context of Anne McClintock's study of Victorian anxieties about female labor, race, and class.[38] Drawing on Marx's analysis of how post-industrial society fetishizes commodities, McClintock extends his argument to the related devaluation and denigration of labor. Whereas the commodity fetish seems to emerge magically in the marketplace without benefit of human agency, workers and servants in this system are rendered dirty and their labor invisible: scandalous reminders of the sweat and bodily exertion behind the production of goods and the leisure necessary for their consumption.[39] In an explicit critique of this divide, the March family in *Little Women* works to demystify the commodity fetish for their daughters and, in turn, to ennoble labor. Moreover, they sustain the girls through experiences of loss and weakness not by promoting the acquisition of symbolic goods but by nurturing emotional acceptance and self-expression, qualities that Lily Bart conspicuously lacks. While *Little Women* shows us how the March sisters learn to resist consumerism's false promises, Wharton's novel makes it clear that, without the comfort and emotional support the young March women have, Lily seeks a substitute in luxurious surroundings and expensive clothing. The one thing she most fears is descending into the "dingy" life of servants and working women beneath her. And this dinginess is in fact the unacknowledged loneliness and human vulnerability that haunt her, as well as the morally disfiguring opportunities that tempt her, including the "dirty" work of prostitution and blackmail.

Chapter 3, "Lily at the Crossroads: Vanity Fair versus the Republic of the Spirit," analyzes Lily's developmental trajectory through book 1 of *The House of Mirth*, with special attention to her relationship to Lawrence Selden and her introduction, through him, to the representational economy of Protestantism. To define that economy and its inner contradictions more fully, I turn to anthropologist Webb Keane and his discussion of the body/spirit split in Protestantism and its implications for notions of an essential self free of social influence or material constraints.[40] This chapter also shows how Lily's emulation of Selden leads her to develop a "new" self, an inner double informed by anti-materialistic values that condemn her own behavior and goals. From this point on her story will be defined by these conflicting selves, informed by the competing discourses of consumer materialism and Protestantism. Among other topics this chapter discusses the question of the "real Lily" through its analysis of the novel's famous *tableau vivant*, in which Lily presents herself as the image of classical purity and authenticity, the embodiment of Selden's republic of the spirit, a moment which I compare to a scene in *Little Women* when Amy March costumes herself in similar classical dress. This chapter thus explores a central theme in the study concerning the social self and its sources, both in nature and nurture. Is there such a thing as a "real" or "essential" self? Is "sincerity" possible in a world governed by social performance? The chapter ends with an analysis of Lily's psychological disintegration following a threatened rape by a wealthy man she has been manipulating for money while withholding the sexual favors he expects. This incident, which closes book 1 of the novel, evokes Wharton's opening epigraph, "The heart of the wise is in the house of mourning, but the heart of the fool is in the house of mirth." My analysis connects this biblical reference to the relevant passages in *Pilgrim's Progress* when Christian is tempted to abandon his painful quest for self-awareness and salvation, a temptation with which Lily will continue to struggle throughout the novel.

Chapter 4, "Smart Jews and Failed Protestants," focuses on book 2 of *The House of Mirth* and looks closely at the figure of Simon Rosedale, the text's Jewish representative of modern materialism, examining his increasing influence on Lily and her agonizing vacillation between the competing claims of the worldly success he offers and the Protestant ethic she has internalized. In addition, this chapter, whose title refers to Sander Gilman's 1996 study *Smart Jews*, analyzes the text's possible antisemitism through Wharton's treatment of racial and ethnic identity. This discussion offers an overview of the history of Jews in New York society, as well as in Wharton's own life. Through the work of critics like Irene Goldman-Price, John Higham, Gary Levine, and Zygmunt Bauman, it explores how Jews were represented by scientific racists in the period as well as by elite Protestants in Wharton's social circle.[41] Read in this context, Rosedale begins the novel seeming like an antisemitic stereotype. Wharton's imagery even associates him with John Bunyan's original figure of the "Jew"—"Mr. Worldly Wiseman" — who attempts to leads Christian astray in *Pilgrim's Progress*. However, by the novel's end Rosedale becomes a complex and sympathetic character whose nominalist skepticism offers an important perspective on the issues troubling the novel's characters. For example, Selden's morally fastidious judgment of Lily's ethical lapses is founded on his individualism and anti-materialistic idealism, an idealism that is countered by Rosedale's growing empathy for Lily's struggle and its material foundation. In other words, it is partly through the character of Rosedale that *The House of Mirth* offers a significant critique of the Protestant gaze. Finally, contrary to some recent analyses of racial identity in the novel, I conclude that none of its central characters — Lily Bart, Simon Rosedale, even Laurence Selden — possesses a fixed, essential identity, racial or otherwise. All are divided selves, torn by competing values and allegiances.

Chapter 5, "Lily in the Valley of the Shadow," provides a close reading of the novel's final chapters. Here I explore how Wharton continues to draw on various sentimental precursors, as well as John Bunyan's *Pilgrim's Progress*, to structure her portrayal of Lily's inner conflicts and spiraling descent into addiction and death. In addition, this chapter focuses more closely on the role of narration in Lily's ultimate attempts at fashioning a sense of self. Drawing once more on recent work by Ian Burkitt on the social origins of selfhood, along with Michael White and David Epston on the importance of narration in the construction of identity, I argue that Lily is finally able to articulate a coherent and meaningful story of her life, one that takes account of her inner conflicts and could potentially help her surmount them by creating an integrated, imagined identity, what Burkitt would call not an "essential" but rather a "core" self.[42] However, without a compassionate audience to hear her, since Lawrence Selden does not initially respond to her heartfelt confession, Lily's self-awareness is simply too painful to bear.

Counterpointing her isolation and anxiety, Lily is briefly comforted by a young working-class woman she once helped. Nettie Struther had lost both her reputation and her will to live through being seduced and abandoned. And yet, unlike Lily, she finds acceptance from a man who is willing to marry her despite her past. This working mother's kitchen is hardly the dingy nightmare Lily fears. Rather, Wharton presents it as a "miracle of cleanliness," a domestic shelter from the vanity fair outside. Critics like Lori Merish see this scene as Wharton's retreat from realistic social criticism into anti-modern sentimentalism, and Nettie Struther's story is certainly worthy of Louisa May Alcott.[43] However, I show that Wharton's point is precisely the fragility of the Struthers' domestic "nest above the abyss" and its poignant inaccessibility for someone like Lily. This glimpse of domestic happiness only heightens Lily's despair and her need for the drug that has become the "only light" in the darkness around her. Like Bunyan's Christian traversing the Valley of the Shadow of Death, Lily is overwhelmed by her sense of moral weakness and inescapable mortality. Lacking not only religious faith but also human connection, terrifyingly alone, she turns to chloral hydrate for the love and forgiveness she craves but cannot find.[44] Wharton's conclusion is unsparing, even devastating, but clear-eyed. Profoundly modern in its rejection of the otherworldly hopes that sustain Bunyan's hero or console Beth March's sisters, her critique of the society that destroys Lily Bart is deeply felt, masterfully developed, and still relevant today.

CHAPTER 1

Raising Virtuous Shoppers

Little Women *and the Marketplace of Morality*

"Christmas won't be Christmas without any presents," complains Jo March in *Little Women*'s famous opening line. Her older sister Meg follows with a similar lament: "It's dreadful to be poor!" And the youngest sister Amy, with "an injured sniff," chimes in, "I don't think it's fair for some girls to have lots of pretty things, and other girls nothing at all." Only the third daughter, Beth, resists judging her condition according to her material possessions: "We've got father and mother, and each other, anyhow" (7). Beth's comment shifts the other girls' attention from material goods to emotional attachments. It is this divided allegiance that will shape the drama to come. Although critics have frequently observed that Louisa May Alcott's enormously popular *Little Women* (1868) is a novel of moral education, they have not addressed how, in an increasingly materialistic age, this is necessarily also a consumer education.[1] This chapter argues that *Little Women* engages the temptations posed by the emerging "spirit of modern consumerism" through traditional moral discourse, particularly Protestantism and its romantic/sentimental descendants.[2] With the possible exception of Beth, each of the four March sisters responds powerfully to the promises of wealth, material goods, and social status (defined in Jo's case as literary celebrity). Each is drawn by the ideologies of an emerging Gilded Age capitalism whose seductive appeal continually threatens to alienate them from the more wholesome pleasures of home and family. However, as close attention to key passages in the novel will show, Mr. and Mrs. March fight these influences by helping their daughters recognize the true sources of personal identity and fulfillment: in other words, by teaching them how to shop for happiness.

Little Women's first chapter, "Playing Pilgrims," sets up the book's central paradigm of Bunyan's Puritan narrative and demonstrates how these very modern young women's lives can be read according to its vision of Protestant salvation.[3] Moreover, chapter 1 displays how this drama, now secularized, plays itself out in relation to consumer goods and the Victorian marketplace. To return to the opening scene, the sisters' faces brighten once Beth reminds them of their parental and sisterly bonds and they consider this emotional wealth, but then darken as they remember that the wealth is jeopardized by their father's service as chaplain at the battlefront of the Civil War. After a moment of silence, Meg, "in an altered tone," tries to redirect her desire and dissatisfaction: "You know the reason mother proposed not having any presents this Christmas, was because it's going to be a hard winter for every one; and she thinks we ought not to spend money for pleasure, when our men are suffering so in the army." As Meg, prompted by the memory of her family ties, tries to repress her consumer desire, she also confronts the stubbornness of her own will: "We can't do much, but can make our little sacrifices, and ought to do it gladly. But I am afraid I don't" (7–8).

The rest of this opening chapter follows each girl's struggle with this moral conflict. Each has a dollar to spend. Meg wants "pretty things," Jo an edition of "Undine and Sintram," Beth some new sheet music, and Amy some Faber's drawing pencils. As they defensively proclaim their right to indulge themselves, they begin to quarrel and pick at each other. Their assertion of individualism seems to unleash a restlessness and irritability, and renders their sisterly loyalties fragile and unstable. Luckily, the hour comes for their mother's return. As Beth puts out a pair of slippers, "the sight of the old shoes" calms and brightens the girls, just as the memory of their father had earlier. Moreover, it strengthens the nascent altruism which had momentarily lost its hold on their wills. Seeing how worn the slippers are, Beth, always the least selfish, volunteers to use her dollar to buy new ones. Now all four compete to see who shall have the honor, and Beth again makes peace by suggesting that each of them use her dollar for their mother.

In the midst of this, Alcott's narrator stops the action momentarily to paint a picture of each girl, then adds, "What the characters of the four sisters were, we will leave to be found out" (11). In fact, those characters are clearly expressed in each girl's choices. For example, the Christmas gift each desires signifies her particular fantasy of success. As theorist Grant McCracken might put it, each of these objects is a kind of "bridge" to that idealized future.[4] In a later chapter, also taking its cue from *Pilgrim's Progress*, the sisters describe their "Castles in the Air" (significantly, although they begin by talking piously about "the Celestial City," their imaginations only catch fire with the castles they hope to inhabit in this world). Meg, who desired "pretty things" for Christmas, says her fantasy castle would be "a lovely house, full of all sorts of luxurious things: nice food, pretty clothes, handsome furniture, pleasant people, and heaps of money." Jo, who longed for "Undine and Sintram," wants "a stable full of Arabian steeds, rooms piled with books. . . . I want to do something splendid before I go into my castle . . . that won't be forgotten after I'm dead . . . . I think I shall write books, and get rich and famous" (178). Amy, who wanted drawing pencils, "has lots of wishes, but the pet one is to be an artist, and go to Rome, and do fine pictures, and be the best artist in the whole world" (178). As their friend Laurie comments, "every one of us, but Beth, wants to be rich and famous." As for Beth, who wanted new sheet music, her desire is simply to "stay at home safe with father and mother, and help take care of the family." She alone speaks in a "contented" tone and when prodded to confess at least *some* desire she explains, "Since I had my little piano I am perfectly satisfied. I only wish we may keep well, and be together; nothing else" (179).

If each girl's Christmas wish signifies her fantasized future and adult identity — in Baudrillard's terms, each gift becomes the "sign of happiness" as she imagines it — each girl's renunciation of this wish in order to honor her attachment to her mother reveals other qualities of her character.[5] Meg "announces, as if the idea was suggested by the sight of her own pretty hands, 'I shall give her a nice pair of gloves.'" Jo decides on "army shoes, best to be had!" Beth says she will give "some handkerchiefs, all hemmed." Finally, Amy says, "I'll get a little bottle of Cologne; she likes it, and it won't cost much, so I'll have some left to buy something for me" (12). Drawing on theories of gift exchange, we can see how each of these objects makes visible the quality of the relationship between each girl and her mother; more precisely, how each gift signifies a daughter's "reading" of her mother's desire through the lens of her own.[6]

Meg, for example, who is "rather vain of her hands" and worries about them becoming roughened through work, projects this concern onto her mother. Similarly, Jo, who had earlier expressed the wish to be a boy so she could go to war alongside her father, now substitutes army shoes for her mother's worn slippers. Beth's handkerchiefs are decidedly practical as well as feminine. She is only one of the four who actually makes her gift: she hems and embroiders the handkerchiefs herself. In a telling detail, she marks them with "Mother," instead of "M. March," a mistake that reveals Beth's difficulty imagining her mother outside her role *as* mother, outside the home that Beth herself fears to leave. Finally, Amy's choice demonstrates that her egocentricity is the strongest of all the daughters. She cannot quite sacrifice her own desire, and so she compromises. Her choice is the least practical, the most luxurious. Suggesting both the foreign and the aristocratic, her cologne is a marker of taste and femininity, as well as class — qualities that enter into Amy's character as the novel develops.

There is, as well, another dimension to these choices. Elsewhere in the novel, Meg notes that their mother taught them that a "real lady is always known by neat gloves, boots, and handkerchief," precisely the items her three oldest daughters choose for her (37). The fourth gift, Amy's cologne, is the final signifier of gentility and feminine class: the aura of luxury. If their renounced wishes represent "bridges" to their idealized futures, their gifts to their mother represent their contribution to the maintenance of her present identity as a middle-class lady, an identity threatened by their poverty and the absence of their father. And again, each envisages her piece of this codified identity through her own perspective. Jo's ambivalence toward her own assumption of "little womanhood," for example, is expressed in her substitution of army boots for feminine slippers.

Marmee's actual arrival prompts a consolidation of the girls' good intentions. She is described "as a stout, motherly lady, with a 'can-I-help-you' look about her which was truly delightful." The narrator pointedly stresses her difference from her daughters' fantasies of success: "She wasn't a particularly handsome person, but mothers are always lovely to their children, and the girls thought the gray cloak and unfashionable bonnet covered the most splendid woman in the world" (14). However, while the girls see their mother as "splendid" despite her "unfashionable" appearance, they cannot, as yet, assess their own identities according to these values. Nevertheless, as Marmee reads a letter from Father at the front, their better impulses are called into play: "I know they will remember all I said to them, that they will be loving children to you, will do their duty faithfully, fight their bosom enemies bravely, and conquer themselves so beautifully, that when I come back to them I may be fonder and prouder than ever of my little women" (16). At this, Amy sobs, "I *am* a selfish pig! But I'll truly try to be better, so he mayn't be disappointed in me by and by." Meg follows suit, "I think too much of my looks, and hate to work, but won't any more, if I can help it." Then comes Jo, "I'll try and be what he loves to call me, 'a little woman,' and not be rough and wild; but do my duty here instead of wanting to be somewhere else." Unassuming even in this, "Beth said nothing, but wiped away her tears with the blue army-sock, and began to knit with all her might, losing no time in doing the duty that lay nearest her" (17).

At this point Mrs. March introduces the story of *Pilgrim's Progress* and recalls to them how they had played out its plot as children.[7] When Amy says she would "rather like to play it again," Marmee remarks: "It is a play we are playing all the time in one way or another. Our burdens are here, our road is before us, and the longing for goodness and happiness is the guide that leads us through many troubles and mistakes to the peace which is the true Celestial City." When Amy, "who was a very literal young lady," asks where their "bundles" are, Marmee replies: "Each has of you told what your burden was just now, except Beth; I rather think she hasn't got any." And when Jo asks for her "roll of directions," as Christian had, her mother advises them "to look under their pillows, Christmas morning, and you will find your guide-book." True to her word, when Jo wakes she finds "a little crimson-covered book. She knew it very well, for it was that beautiful old story of the best life ever lived, and Jo felt that it was a true guide-book for any pilgrim going on the long journey" (20). Meg finds hers, with a green cover; Beth, with a dove-colored; and Amy a blue. While the girls immediately follow Meg's pious example and read from their new gifts, Amy can't resist saying, "I'm glad mine is blue" (21).

In her 1983 introduction to the novel, Madelon Bedell points to the brand names of the objects coveted by the girls as evidence of consumer culture's influence on their world.[8] The differentiation of these books by their color is further evidence. A marketing strategy facilitated by new manufacturing processes, the varied covers made them more appealing to shoppers eager to express their "personal style."[9] Moreover, the color coding here is very precise. Although Mrs. March gives the same story to each daughter, she matches the color of each book to the character and temperament of the girl who receives it. In Alcott's usage, "character" is not an honorific term, but a neutral, descriptive one. Individuals may have good or bad characters, mature or immature ones, conflicted or unified ones. Most importantly, although each girl's nature is essential and inborn, a unique mixture of temperament, talents, and propensities, these individual traits merely serve as the initial seeds, the potential for her future development, for better or for worse.

We can see these individual character traits signified in Marmee's color coding of each gift. Green, for Meg, is a color associated with both envy and fertility: the two poles around which her version of "Pilgrim's Progress" turns. Her vanity and her envy of wealthy friends like Sallie Gardiner comprise her "burden," but she will also be the first sister to marry and become a mother. Crimson is appropriate for Jo, whose passionate anger and overweening ambition jeopardize her relationships with others. However, this passion also informs her deep loyalty to those she loves as well as her literary talent. Her crimson reappears later in the thorny red roses that remind Laurie of Jo, and in the red ribbons that frame Jo's blushing face as she confesses her love for Fritz Bhaer. Amy's association with blue recurs through the book; she wears blue ribbons or handles her ponies with blue reins. The color signifies her tendency to selfishness and emotional coldness; she is the "snow-maiden" who needs thawing. However, it also suggests refinement and gentility, qualities to which she aspires and which she ultimately acquires. Finally, there is Beth's dove-colored book: the dove association signifies her saintliness, while the absence of color suggests her lack of desire and will. As Marmee comments, Beth appears to have "no burden." That is, in Puritan terms she appears to have no original sin, no pride, no "flesh." However, the lack of desire is also dangerous, for it makes Beth ultimately a martyr and a disembodied saint. She does not survive; her sisters do.

In the novel's vision of classic literature and authentic identity, each girl reads her own life in Bunyan's universal story, but does so through the colors of her given nature. Moreover, these color codes reveal the moral ambiguity or liminality of that nature in its original state. Nurture will make the difference in how these natures develop. Marmee's task is to guide each girl's intrinsic potential for genteel womanhood to its fruition. It is a task successfully accomplished, for by the final chapter, "Harvest Time," Meg, Jo, and Amy have each married and reproduced. Although their economic situations differ to some degree, each has found her own way to the "little womanhood" their father envisaged. Moreover, the styles of their adult lives express each girl's version of her maternal model. Even Beth has become a version of Marmee; her spirit, as we shall see, presides over the moral development of her sisters. She fails to mature biologically, but her life and death offer a dove-colored model of pious submission and maternal love of others.

Like the four Alcott sisters, on whose lives this story is based, the four March sisters do not begin life trailing clouds of glory. Rather they are undisciplined bundles of potentiality, for good and evil. While their quest for moral maturity is connected to earlier Puritan discourses like Bunyan's, their victories, as Richard Brodhead has noted, are not achieved through the orthodox Puritan conversion experience, but through the "Christian nurture" of emotional discipline, administered by that wise mother who intervenes at key moments in each girl's experiments with social life.[10] In this emphasis the novel reflects the educational theories of Alcott's reforming parents, Bronson and Abby Alcott, as well as the liberal Protestantism of theologians such as Horace Bushnell and sentimental writers such as Harriet Beecher Stowe.[11] In Puritan childrearing the child's will was seen as innately sinful and had to be broken to achieve at least the semblance of submission to divine authority. True submission could only be won through divine election and rebirth into a new moral life through God's grace. Enlightenment critiques of Calvinism argued that rather than being born in the grip of original sin, children were born innately good. Unitarians like William Ellery Channing, for example, believed all individuals were endowed with divine reason that enabled them to choose the good freely in their quest for a "likeness to God."[12] Transcendentalists like Emerson also believed that individuals had an innate moral intuition, a divine inner self that was corrupted not by original sin but by social conformity and fear. However, in the model of Christian nurture within liberal Protestantism, influenced by the German Romantic theologian Friedrich Schleiermacher and the American Horace Bushnell, children are seen neither as innately depraved nor as divinely innocent, but as morally undeveloped. All individual natures contain the potential to develop into full moral awareness and spiritual maturity; however, individual natures in their immature state also tend to selfishness and egocentricity. Human beings have natural passions and desires that need to be tamed and disciplined in order for their "better selves" to grow and thrive. Rather than being broken or converted, indulged or praised, their wills are to be educated.[13]

This developmental model is clearly depicted in *Little Women*. Amy March, for example, is not presented as having a sinful nature but as possessing an undisciplined temperament and immature character. Her egocentricity is not presented as total depravity, but as a kind of infantile self-interest that can be enlightened; she can learn that true happiness comes from affiliation to others. An important contribution of the novel, then, which was also a contribution of the Alcotts themselves and of liberal Protestants such as Bushnell and Schleiermacher, was the radical understanding that, in the absence of divine election, moral development was not only a social process but also an embodied one, a theological approach that came to be called "immanentism," since it saw spirituality and its expression primarily as immanent in the material world.[14] The Calvinist theologian Jonathan Edwards had believed that the will was tied to the "religious affections," but, reaffirming theological orthodoxy, he had also argued that the will could not freely choose the good unless divine grace detached the affections from their fleshly self-absorption and redirected them to their creator. Moreover, love of God, or, as Edwards put it, "Consent to Being in General," was the sacred fount from which all true virtue flowed. Human attachments were merely a refined form of idolatry if they competed with this central orientation. Hence the Puritan emphasis on acceptance of the death of loved ones as submission to God's will.[15] However, Alcott's novel modifies this ethic significantly, as can be seen in its treatment of grief.

For example, when the saintly Beth reveals she is dying of complications from scarlet fever, she manifests an orthodox spiritual submission and "like a confiding child . . . asked no questions, but left everything to God and nature, Father and mother of us all, feeling sure that they, and they only, could teach and strengthen heart and spirit for this life and the life to come." But when Jo rebels against this coming loss, Beth "did not rebuke Jo with saintly speech, only loved her better for her passionate affection, and clung more closely to the dear human love, from which our Father never means us to be weaned, but through which he draws us closer to Himself" (460). Passionate human love, far from being an idolatrous repudiation of God's authority, here becomes a female complement (albeit an un-capitalized complement) to Him: a maternal "nature" from whose breast we are never to be weaned, but through which we are drawn toward Him. This curious image shows how in this novel the instrument of spiritual education, even salvation, is the natural family itself. The gendering of these terms is also highly significant, since the female world of nature is clearly also the world of the sentimental, the bodily, and the material, through which, rather than against which, the spirit is to be educated.[16]

Here it is worth defining the term "sentimental" more precisely. "Sentimentalism" in this context refers to a broad cultural discourse growing out of liberal Protestantism and informing the moral pedagogy of Christian nurture. Unlike the more radical individualism of Emerson's version of Transcendentalism, sentimentalism emphasizes the social nature of the self and its development. Despite the common pejorative use of "sentimental" to disparage overwrought, "feminine" feelings and unrealistic optimism — the happy endings of popular literature — Mary Louise Kete explains that "sentimentality is not a genre, nor has it been, even in the eighteenth and nineteenth centuries, the peculiar province of women. Neither is it a sham display of emotion for the self-interested manipulations of others. It is not 'bad' Romanticism." Rather, sentimentality, as expressed across various literary genres, is the "written trace" of an important cultural discourse, based on "sentimental collaboration" and expressing a common faith that human identity is fully realized only through "the exchange of sympathy."[17] This is how I will be using the term, even though the writers I see as deeply influenced by the discourse of sentimentalism often use the term in the more common pejorative sense (usually to disparage the work of other authors).

Thus, if Alcott's representation of spiritual development differs significantly from that of orthodox Puritanism it also swerves from the Transcendentalism of her parents' generation in Concord. In "Transcendental Wild Oats," Alcott's sharply ironic account of her family's participation in the Fruitlands community, she suggests that such utopian solutions to the problem of modernity stumbled because they failed to take into account human embodiment and affective bonds. Experiments such as Fruitlands, or Brook Farm, presupposed withdrawal from society and purification of its influences.[18] Premised on the romantic notion of an authentic, pre-existing self, independent of social contexts, their radical individualism prevented them from conceiving solutions that would actually work within bourgeois consumer culture or that would take into account how identity and moral awareness developed within human relationships. While this is not the place to analyze the Fruitlands experiment in any detail, it is worth pointing out that Louisa's father, Bronson, entered the community open to the idea of a purified, celibate life, liberated from the constraints of familial ties and corporeal appetites. After a harrowing failure there, during which he attempted suicide by starvation and only accepted food for the sake of his four daughters and stalwart wife, Bronson affirmed a theory of spiritual development strikingly similar to that later represented by his daughter: one in which the "unit" of development is not the individual, but the family.[19]

But if genuine happiness and moral maturity, Alcott's versions of Puritan grace and true virtue, are developed through interaction with the material, social world, how to differentiate between the vanities of a corrupt society and true food for the soul? Under the wrong influences, the child's self-interest could be encouraged to ignore or renounce its connections to others and seek its satisfaction in unmitigated selfishness. In *Little Women*, the outcome of such uneducated desire and lack of emotional literacy is seen in fashionable bourgeois families like the Kings and the Moffats, whose members brandish multiple signs of happiness and success before the dazzled eyes of the March sisters. Yet, despite their French ball gowns, showy houses, and elegant carriages, the novel reveals that their emotional lives are ones of "quiet desperation," empty and governed by insatiable desire. For example, Meg bitterly envies the leisure of the wealthy King family, whose children she teaches. However, she subsequently learns that the oldest son has accumulated gambling debts and embezzled money from his father: a shame that no amount of money can undo. Similarly her friend, the stylish Sallie Gardiner, marries the socially prominent but unemotionally unreliable Ned Moffat. Their marital home, though far grander than Meg and John Brook's, is described as cold and cheerless. Sallie herself marvels at the warmth and satisfaction found in Meg's inconspicuous and unfashionable cottage, and cannot discover the "secret" of a happiness unheralded by the usual markers of status.

Alcott's antidote to this emotional emptiness and insatiable hunger is the sentimental family. That is, in the discourse of Christian nurture and liberal Protestantism, parents are responsible for the proper development of their children's moral awareness; they must teach them to avoid the temptations that destroy the "true" happiness of the Kings and Moffats. The crucial tool in this task is their children's affections. Through these sentimental attachments, egocentric as they may be, the parent delicately manipulates a child's love of others, her fear of their loss, and, finally, her awareness of their role in her own self-fulfill-ment. Thus while the girls in *Little Women* are drawn initially to the duplicitous signs of fashion and the selfish pleasures of consumption, they must be edu-cated through experience to prefer the counter-pleasures of work and love. Like Sylvester Graham's whole-wheat crackers, these pleasures offer genuine nour-ishment, unlike the craving and restlessness produced by the "poisoned sweets" of social status and material display.[20] However, while Alcott's novel demon-strates how an individual anchored by loving attachment to family can with-stand the false promises proffered by vanity fair, it also shows that attachment is not enough; the subject must be able to identify and make proper choices. The problem is still the will, but the will is here seen as capable of education, an education that, oddly enough, appears as a cultivation of taste.[21]

The novel offers immediate examples of this sentimental education in the opening chapters. One, which we have already seen, is the girls' decision to choose the pleasure of pleasing their mother over their own self-indulgence. This drama continues on Christmas morning as Amy slips out of the house secretly and hurries to the store. When her sisters, "surprised to see . . . that lazy Amy had been out so early," interrogate her, she says, "Don't laugh at me, Jo, I didn't mean anyone should know until the time came. I only meant to change the little bottle for a big one, and I gave *all* my money to get it, and I'm truly trying not to be selfish any more." Amy's next comment, however, reveals how subtle self-interest can insinuate itself into finest show of altruism: "You see I felt ashamed of my present, after reading and talking about being good this morning, so I ran round the corner and changed it the minute I was up; and I'm *so* glad, for mine is the handsomest now" (22–23). Despite its childish nar-cissism, Amy's pleasure at winning the competition for biggest gift represents a step upward in her willingness to affiliate her own interests with those others.

Marmee enters just after Amy's amusing story of attempted altruism, and after she accepts their thanks for their books and wishes of Merry Christmas, she initiates a far more challenging lesson in same virtue: "Not far away from here lies a poor woman with a little newborn baby. Six children are huddled around one bed to keep from freezing, for they have no fire. There is nothing to eat over there; and the oldest boy came to tell me they were suffering hun-ger and cold. My girls, will you give your breakfast as a Christmas present?" (23). These girls are, again, no angels: "They were all unusually hungry, having waited nearly an hour, and for a minute no one spoke." However, it is "only a minute, for Jo exclaims impetuously, — 'I'm so glad you came before we began!' " Following the narrative pattern Alcott then shows how each girl responds ac-cording to her own temperament: Beth "eagerly" asks, "May I go and help carry the things to the poor little children?" Meg immediately begins packing up the buckwheats, and Amy, in the spirit of her previous effort to achieve the biggest effect, "heroically gives up the articles she most liked": "*I shall take the cream and the muffins*" (23).

Marmee's request pits her daughters' desire for her approval over their desire for Christmas breakfast. The struggle is brief but real. Sacrificing their dollars for her gifts was motivated by their intimate attachment to her. Here the sacrifice is at one remove: they will give their feast to strangers, a choice crucially mediated by their need to rise to their mother's expectations. But that choice is rewarded by a new type of pleasure. Arriving at the tenement they find "a poor, bare, miserable room . . . with broken windows, no fire, ragged bed-clothes, a sick mother, wailing baby, and a group of pale, hungry children cuddled under one old quilt, trying to keep warm." The poor mother, "crying for joy," exclaims, "*Ach mein Gott!* It is good angels come to us!" " 'Funny angels in hoods and mittens,' said Jo, and set them laughing" (23–24). *These* angels have bodies and feel the cold. They start the fire and spread out the food, warming and feeding the children as if they were "hungry birds," and receiving their reward in the brightened faces and grateful cries of "*Das ist gute*" and "*Der angel-kinder!*" "The girls had never been called angel children before, and thought it very agreeable, especially Jo, who had been considered a 'Sancho' ever since she was born." Mrs. March's lesson is completely successful, for the individualistic pleasure they have sacrificed is now replaced by the satisfaction of altruism: "That was a happy breakfast, though they didn't get any of it; and when they went away, leaving comfort behind, I think there were not in all the city four merrier people than the hungry little girls who gave away their breakfasts, and contented themselves with bread and milk on Christmas morning" (24).

In her analysis of *Little Women* Nina Auerbach comments that Marmee's gift to her daughters in these opening Christmas scenes is "the gift of hunger."[22] This is a crucial insight into the novel's deepest issues and strategies, but one that needs refining. In fact, the novel opens with the girls *already* hungry; its first lines bespeak unsatisfied consumer appetites. Marmee's gift is not hunger itself, but how to discriminate between kinds of hunger, and kinds of pleasure. In a very real sense, helping the poor is a pleasure competing with other pleasures in the marketplace of bourgeois choices.[23] Marmee's task, which is the task of the moral family, is to cultivate a taste for this choice above others. Put another way, hunger in itself is not a pleasure, but hunger in relation to pleasure deferred or vicariously experienced is a powerful psychological tool, rather than simply a deprivation. It is a kind of spice, a heightener of other, more subtle and, the novel argues, more satisfying pleasures. Moreover, the hunger that is disciplined here is not purely physical hunger, since Alcott pointedly includes the fact that girls later "content themselves with bread and milk." Rather, it is the hunger for luxury that is disciplined; they give up their muffins and cream, but their stomachs do not go empty. To draw again on Baudrillard's phrase, their true sacrifice is to give up the holiday's material "signs of happiness," and substitute for those imagined pleasures other satisfactions signified by other signs: the name of "angel children."

In this, as in her other childrearing experiments, Mrs. March strives to teach her girls not to resist the temptations of pleasure but to recognize, name, and then to manipulate the sources of more lasting, more moral pleasures. In this task, she seems to fall squarely within Colin Campbell's description of the modern hedonist. In *The Romantic Ethic and the Spirit of Modern Consumerism*, Campbell argues that modern hedonism differs from traditional hedonism by shifting attention away from the material source of satisfaction to the imaginative experience of gratification.[24] Thus the category of pleasure is extended to include daydreaming about anticipated acquisitions — as we saw earlier in the "Castles in the Air" chapter — as well as the pleasures of benevolence and compassionate feelings. This view makes it possible to experience even apparently painful feelings, such as pity and sorrow, as sources of pleasure in that they are perceived as indicators of the subject's virtue and therefore as sources of self-esteem and congratulation. The key notion is the interiority of pleasure and its susceptibility to manipulation by the subject, whose mastery of pleasure is only limited by his or her mastery of imagination, including the moral imagination.

Campbell's complex analysis puts the imaginative pleasures of reading gothic novels and daydreaming about consumer purchases on the same continuum with the pleasures of empathic identification and benevolent feelings. It is a continuum whose source he finds in the neglected strand of Protestantism, the pietistic strand originally balanced in Calvinist Puritanism by the rationalist, disciplinary ethic described by Weber. As the rationalist strand moved toward utilitarianism, pietism split off, then found its fullest development in deism and the cult of sensibility, and finally in Romantic bohemianism. Campbell's thesis about Romantic bohemianism is that it unwittingly, and ironically, provided the patterns for modernism consumerism by endorsing a style of life focused on imagination, self-expression, and fantasy.[25]

If Abby and Bronson Alcott weren't Romantic bohemians, I'd be hard put to know who was. And I will argue here, ultimately, that Louisa May Alcott's resistance to the idolatrous materialism of mid-Victorian consumer culture ironically results in an acceptance, even validation of that culture. However, while my account of her route to that destination is similar to Campbell's, and draws on his insights, it also differs somewhat by focusing on the distinction not between the two strands of Protestantism but between Protestantism and its "other," Roman Catholicism. A key element in that differentiation, and therefore in Protestantism's own self-definition, was its concept of the sacraments, an issue which Campbell does not address in any detail. I would argue, however, that the core problem of sacramentalism—how one reads the outward and visible material signs of an inward and invisible spiritual grace—is also a core problem of consumerism. By examining this problem, in relation to both the Protestant and Romantic ethics, we can trace Alcott's resistance to consumerism, as well as her ironic and unwitting capitulation.

As Karen Halttunen argued persuasively in her 1982 study *Confidence Men and Painted Women*, Victorian anxieties abut identity and hypocrisy were prompted partly by the transition from an agrarian society based on small-town relationships and homogenous cultures to an industrialized and urban environment marked by social mobility and relative anonymity: a world of strangers.[26] The crisis of representation that she and numerous other historians see in the Victorian period stemmed from this social transition as well as from the instability of traditional belief systems challenged by contemporary scientific and historical inquiries. Given this newly urbanized society marked by increasingly diverse and complex codes of identification and interpretation, Halttunen's study traces a Victorian preoccupation with the threats of "confidence men" and "painted women" whose duplicitous self-presentation masked their true natures. The emphasis that ministers and other advisers of ambitious young men placed on personal "character" reflected this concern with how truly the outward performance of self represented the inward reality. Carefully detailing Victorian efforts to cope with these fears through calls for sincerity in dress and behavior, she links this phenomenon to Puritan attempts to cope with the problem of hypocrisy: the difficulty of judging internal states by external appearances.

The link can be most clearly in the Puritan doctrine of salvation by faith alone. Works or social acts could not redeem the sinner's soul, since the fallen will was so corrupted by original sin that it inevitably deflected every act away from God's glory toward self-interest. However, if grace could not be gained by good works, it nevertheless would result in them, since such fruits would follow inevitably from the saint's eagerness to fulfill God's will. Hence the difficulty of distinguishing the hypocritical sinner, doing good for social approval, from the genuine saint, doing good without thought of worldly rewards. The difference could only be found in the motivation of the act: its intentions, however unconscious. But, as the Massachusetts Bay minister and Puritan theologian John Cotton put the problem, the difficulty of sorting out the true lambs of God from the old goats of Satan could never be resolved in world. A human uncertainty would remain until the Revelation and Last Judgment. And yet, Cotton still believed there was a subtle difference in the "taste" of their behavior. The sincere acts of the saint had the sweet relish of young lamb, while the superficially similar deeds of the hypocrite had the gamy flavor of old mutton.[27]

The problem of hypocrisy also enters into the Puritan attitude toward the accumulation of wealth. As Max Weber famously argued, the worldly asceticism promoted by Protestantism created the conditions under which the money and goods necessary for the development of capitalism could be accumulated. Puritans were to live in this world for the sake of the next; their wealth was to be amassed not for their own glory, but for God's. Indeed, within the terms of the Puritan world view, the elect must be ever ready to give up their goods, since placing one's ultimate faith in the material world was idolatrous. Hence one way to separate the idolatrous materialists from the virtuous stewards of God's kingdom was to see how they responded to the loss of such goods. Saints should respond with equanimity, placing their faith in God, not in objects that rust could corrode and moths corrupt. And, passing this test, they might well be rewarded with further worldly success, as a sign of God's trust. However, as separation between the hypocritical capitalist and the righteous steward could not be finally achieved in this world, wealth remained an ambiguous sign: like works, it might be a sign of God's grace, but displaying the outward and visible sign did not guarantee the inward and invisible reality.[28]

Finally, this anxiety about idolatry can also be seen in the Puritan doctrine on the sacraments, one of the crucial points in their conflict with Roman Catholic belief. In the Puritan view, religious ritual did not convert the bread and wine of the Eucharist into Christ's actual body and blood. The material objects remained merely symbolic; they were not efficacious in themselves. The sacraments were only a remembrance of Christ. They were His signifiers, but there was a semiotic gap between them and their ultimate referent. To close this gap was, like closing the gap between the signifier of worldly wealth and the referent of God's election, idolatrous. That is, while receiving the sacrament might be a way to signify the inward and invisible presence of grace, it could not confer that grace. To take the bread and wine in the belief that they *could* confer such qualities was to ascribe to them a power that, the Puritan argued, belonged only to God. Hence such belief was, at its core, idolatrous.[29]

There is a link, I would argue, between these Puritan anxieties about the idolatrous use of the sacraments and Victorian anxieties about the materialistic use of consumer goods. Let me first draw on the historian Jay Mechling's relatively recent definition of the *materialism*, a definition that is surprisingly similar to what we see in Alcott's text. Mechling uses Mary Douglas and Baron Isherwood's breakthrough study *The World of Goods* to set up a model of the normal or healthy use of consumer goods. In this model, goods function like language to articulate cultural meanings and make them visible. Note that this description focuses not on the sensuous or functional qualities of these material objects but on the symbolism they carry. As a map describes a territory, goods display the social identifications and interrelationships of a given group. Mechling then differentiates between this "normal" use of consumer goods and a materialistic one. In the latter, the materialist confuses the map with the territory, a mistake Mechling compares to the schizophrenic's literal reading of metaphors. That is, the materialist mistakes the material signifier for the quality it signifies. In Mechling's normal use of goods, clothes cannot make the man, merely represent him. The materialist, however, mistakes the props of identity for identity itself. And in so doing, he or she ascribes to consumer goods the power to confer qualities that they only symbolize. Thus, as the Puritans argued about the sacraments, Mechling argues about goods: there must be a semiotic gap between the material signifier and what it signifies, an "as if" understanding of their difference. Without that gap, we have materialism, or consumer culture idolatry.[30] It is precisely this gap that Marmee teaches her girls to recognize.

The world of *Little Women* is very much the one Halttunen describes. The Marches, with their shabby gentility, belong to the once ruling, now residual, class of the older, pre-industrial and agrarian order. Mrs. March is the daughter of a distinguished patriot, and her husband, who serves as chaplain to the Union forces in the Civil War, lost his fortune when his business partner embezzled funds and he scrupulously repaid them to his own family's detriment. Once recognized within a tightly knit community of families with similar values and backgrounds, the Marches find themselves in a transitional society increasingly ruled by the nouveau riche families of industrialists and tycoons like the Kings and Moffats. Mr. March's integrity and benevolent occupation no longer have a secure place within this urban marketplace, and his daughters' social position, extended to them by virtue of their family's past, is correspondingly tenuous.

In this new social context, the opposition between the true virtue of the Puritan saint and the idolatry of the Roman Catholic is revived in the guise of the tension between the sincere style of authentic self-expression and the fashionable artifice of hypocritical materialism. "Fashion" here becomes the secular equivalent of the Roman Catholic Church. Indeed, adherents of this faith are almost always presented in Alcott's work as under the spell of French culture.[31]

As a social institution, fashion promises that it can confer happiness and desirability, even identity itself, through the objects it mediates. By surrendering their freedom of consumer choice to fashion, the individual abandons the difficult process of discovering his or her own internal nature, in exchange for the false promise that happiness and identity can be conferred simply by purchasing objects stamped with their socially constructed marks. Thus, just as the Catholic worshipper is seen as dependent on the priest and his "magic" rituals, so the "fashion slave" is dependent on the French seamstress and her magazines *à la mode*. The more this dependency takes hold, the more the fashion slave neglects the cultivation of the true sources of happiness, satisfying work, and fulfilling human relationships. She mortgages her individuality and emotional preferences — the only authentic sources of identity and contentment — for artificial substitutes. And, like an addiction, the process is cumulative and self-perpetuating. As the true sources of happiness are neglected, the internal need grows more insistent and the consumer is urged toward new promises made by new goods. As each object, once obtained, fails to delivers on its promise, yet another in the chain of linked consumer signifiers beckons over the horizon: If only I can have that magical thing, my happiness will be complete.[32]

Marmee's educational strategy is to allow her daughters to experiment with idolatrous desires but then, at the moment of inevitable disappointment, to intervene by articulating materialism's failure and redirecting attention to the true sources of happiness and identity. In the process she is helping them develop their emotional literacy, an ability to read the subtle signs of their own desires, feelings, and moral intuitions. This analysis might suggest that Alcott, like her mentor Henry David Thoreau, was attempting to purge consumer goods of their symbolic power, negating their status as commodity fetishes and returning them to some state of pure, non-signifying functionality.[33] However, Alcott deviates from the Thoreauvian solution to materialism and moves toward a complex reworking of the interrelationship between identity and goods. While her characters must learn to abstain from the idolatry of fashionable materialism, they also consistently express their distinctive natures through their own particular style of consumption. Indeed, as the novel demonstrates repetitively, even obsessively, individuals cannot *help* expressing their natures through their every action, hence their every object. Their choice of Christmas gifts, their style of letter-writing, their approach to party-going, their efforts at storytelling — each and every action in the world displays its actor's true nature: style is as innate and essential to the individual as fingerprints. As Emerson wrote: "A man is only one half himself; the other half is his expression."[34]

Just as the problem with the sacraments is not in the bread and wine, but the soul of the celebrant, so the problem with shopping is not in the goods, but the spirit of the shopper. Submission to the dictates of fashion represents an effort to escape identity by assuming the style of another. However, just as hidden sinfulness perverts the hypocrite's effort to do good, so innate character also subtly and unconsciously inflects the individual's every act and gesture. This unconscious subversion of fashion's intentions can be seen in Alcott's rather snobbish portrayal of the newly rich Mrs. Moffat. Represented as essentially vulgar and "uncultivated," Mrs. Moffat dresses herself like an aristocrat in silk and lace. However, her attempt to appropriate the identity of gentility fails miserably for, as the narrator comments, she "lumbers like an elephant" in her finery (108). As John Cotton pointed out in his discussion of saints and sinners, although their superficial costume may seem the same, the discerning observer can taste the difference in its effect. Moral maturity, according to this analysis, lies in recognition and acceptance of the true self and its free expression through the cultivation not of fashion but of style. In *Walden* Thoreau comments that "every day our garments become more assimilated to ourselves, receiving the impress of the wearer's character, until we hesitate to lay them aside, without such delay and medical appliances and some such solemnity as even our bodies."[35] But such "assimilation" should flow only one way: from the "sacred fount" of internal nature outward, never the reverse.

The first daughter to be challenged by separation from home and exposure to the temptations of the fashionable world outside is Meg. If hunger and disillusionment are necessary to demystify consumer fetishism, so separation and loss are necessary to awaken consciousness of emotional attachment. In the first, gaining the longed-for consumer object reveals its inability to satisfy. In the other, losing the taken-for-granted emotional object reveals its ability to fulfill. This double movement marks the developmental rhythms of the novel and educates the taste of the girls as they make choices that will shape their adult lives. Separation becomes an important tool to awaken appreciation for affiliation. As Marmee tells Jo, who is preparing to live alone in New York, enjoy your freedom, until you learn there is something "sweeter" (408). Here again we see the language of taste, which is refined and cultivated through experience.

Meg's original castle in the air was a beautiful house, filled with luxury and servants to do her bidding. Her bridge to this fantasized future was the "pretty things" she sacrificed for Marmee's new gloves. Her moral trial occurs in a chapter actually entitled "Meg Goes to Vanity Fair," in which she is invited to her friend Annie Moffat's luxurious mansion and allowed to enjoy its borrowed pleasures. The chapter opens with Meg packing to leave. Her very simple out-fit initially seems "nearly perfect." It includes some things from Mrs. March's treasure chest, where she keeps "a few relics of past splendor, as gifts for her girls when the proper time came." Meg sighs over a violet silk dress that had belonged to her mother, but there isn't time to make it over and so she must con-tent herself with her old tarleton. Although she longs for a set of old-fashioned pearls, her mother says that "real flowers are the prettiest ornaments for young girls."

However, as the sisters begin to imagine Meg's clothes in their new setting, new limitations appear. Although Amy reminds Meg that she "has the tarleton for the big party, and you always look like an angel in white," Meg complains that "it isn't low-necked, and it don't sweep enough, but it will have to do." Now she sees that her "silk saque isn't a bit the fashion" and "her bonnet don't look like Sallie's." Finally, she admits that although she didn't like to say anything, she was "dreadfully disappointed" with her umbrella: "I told mother black, with a white handle, but she forgot, and bought a green one, with an ugly yellowish handle. It's strong and neat, so I ought not to complain, but I know I shall feel ashamed of it beside Annie's silk one, with a gold top." Although Meg admits its use-value, the umbrella's expressive values disappoint her. Jo simply advises, "Change it," but Meg replies, "I won't be so silly, or hurt Marmee's feelings, when she took so much pains to get my things. It's a nonsensical notion of mine, and I'm not going to give up to it." Just a line or two later, however, she is ask-ing Beth to sew blue and pink ribbons on her nightcap, to match Annie Mof-fat's. Jo's answer is again prompt and decisive, "No, I wouldn't; for the smart caps won't match the plain gowns, without any trimming on them. Poor folks shouldn't rig." At this, Meg says impatiently, "I wonder if I shall *ever* be happy enough to have real lace on my clothes, and bows on my caps." Beth quietly comments, "You said the other day that you'd be perfectly happy if you could only go to Annie Moffat's." Now even Meg can see the problem: "So I did! Well, I *am* happy, and I *won't* fret, but it does seem as if the more one gets the more one wants, don't it" (107).[36]

If, as Baudrillard argues, the meaning of consumer objects is constructed through systems of linked signs, each sign signifying happiness, yet each draw-ing the consumer inexorably from one purchase in the chain to the next, we can see Meg drawn into a complex system of fashionable goods.[37] The fashion sys-tem, moreover, is tyrannical in its demands and brooks no compromise: smart caps "don't go" with plain gowns. As Grant McCracken argues in his essay, "The Diderot Effect," the stylization of goods encourages their being assembled into representations of whole ways of life. Meg's outfit may be "nearly perfect" in the context of the March's home and history, but it represents a world very different from the one she will find at the Moffats.[38] And so Meg, with her burden, sets out for Vanity Fair, where her resolve to overcome her "nonsensical notions" will be sorely tried.

Although the Moffats are clearly very fashionable, Meg soon feels, "without understanding why, that they were not particularly cultivated or intelligent people, and that all their gilding could not quite conceal the ordinary material of which they were made." Despite this intuition, Meg begins to envy and imitate her friends. She discusses fashion "as well as she could" and uses "French phrases," details that link the Moffats' social climbing and materialism to their aping of aristocratic European manners, along with their neglect of old-fashioned democratic and Protestant virtues. Meg's resolve is particularly tried the night of the first, smaller party. Her poplin suit, she finds, just won't do, and when she brings out the tarleton she had saved for best, she thinks it "older, limper, and shabbier than ever." As the other girls look her over, Meg is nearly overcome with embarrassment. But just then flowers arrive from her family's wealthy neighbors and friends, the Laurences. Remembering Marmee's advice that real flowers are a young girl's best ornament, and remembering as well the affection behind the gift, Meg momentarily loses her feeling of inadequacy. When she descends to the party she sees a "happy, and bright-eyed face in the mirror." However, her happiness is short-lived for she overhears a disturbing conversation. Prompted by the flowers, a gathering of ladies speculate about the romantic possibilities for Meg and sixteen-year-old Laurie: "It would be a great thing for one of those girls wouldn't it? Sallie says they are very intimate now, and the old man quite dotes on them." Mrs. Moffat chimes in, "Mrs. M. had laid her plans, I dare say and will play her cards well, early as it is. The girl evidently doesn't think of it yet." Yet another voice counters, "Poor thing! She'd be so nice if she was only in style. Do you think she'd be offended if we offered to lend her a dress for Thursday?" The group then decides to ask Laurie to the ball as well: "We'll have fun about it afterward."

These words "open a new world" to Meg, whose pride is wounded and whose sensibilities are disgusted by what she hears. Nevertheless, when the evening of the ball arrives, Meg accepts Belle Moffat's offer to dress her in style, as if they were "Cinderella and her godmother." Between Belle and her French maid, Hortense, Meg becomes the image of "a fine lady": "They crimped and curled her hair, they polished her neck and arms with some fragrant power, touched her lips with coralline salve, to make them redder." (Meg refuses the maid's attempt to rouge her cheeks.) Then they "laced her into a sky-blue dress, which was so tight she could hardly breathe, and so low in the neck that modest Meg blushed at herself in the mirror." Further ornamented with silver jewelry and shod with a "a pair of high-heeled blue silk boots" that "satisfied the last wish" of Meg's heart, she is surveyed by Belle "with the satisfaction of a little girl with a newly-dressed doll." Now the mirror tells Meg that she is "a little beauty." As her friends repeat the phrase, she stands viewing herself "like the jackdaw in the fable, enjoying her borrowed plumes, while the rest chattered like a party of magpies."[39]

But the effect of these clothes is more complicated than Meg anticipates. She confesses to Sallie, "I'm afraid to go down, I feel so queer and stiff, and half-dressed." Her friend replies, "You don't look a bit like yourself, but you are very nice. I'm nowhere beside you, for Belle has heaps of taste, and you're quite French, I assure you. Let your flowers hang; don't be so careful of them, and be sure you don't trip." Sallie's final comment highlights an important aspect of these fashionable goods. Rather than expressing the body's movements, they constrict them. The tight dress gives Meg a cramp, the train keeps getting under her feet, and she is in "constant fear lest her ear-rings should fly off, and get lost or broken" (116). In fact, Meg's efforts to be fashionable often result in her being physically hurt, as when she sprains her ankle trying to dance in high-heeled shoes or burns her hair attempting to curl it. The queer, stiff feeling results from her new role as a mannequin for Belle's taste, not her own.[40] Moreover, the French style displays her body in an overtly sexual way, disturbing Meg's own "innate" modesty. Given the conversation she has overheard, these clothes represent the values of a culture that displays marriageable young women as commodities. Mrs. Moffat and her set are the American equivalents of those French aristocratic families who arranged marriages for their *jeunes filles* purely for considerations of property and status. Meg's new clothing makes her an icon designed to attract prosperous husbands as buyers. Indeed now that her appearance has been reconstructed to signify qualities more desired by this particular market, Meg notices a disturbing change in others' responses to her, for "there is a charm about fine clothes which attracts a certain of people and secures their respect." These people now court her attention and even rename her. She becomes "Daisy," instead of Margaret, and Mrs. Moffat goes so far as to reinvent her family's history, promoting Mr. March from a simple chaplain to "a colonel in the army — one of our first families, but reverses of fortune, you know."

The arrival of Laurie further complicates Meg's experience. He says he comes for Jo's sake, who wants to know how her sister looked, but then adds, "I shall say I didn't know you; for you look so grown-up, and unlike yourself, I'm quite afraid of you." When Meg asks why he dislikes her transformation, "he glanced at her frizzled head, bare shoulders, and fantastically trimmed dress, with an expression that abashed her more than his answer . . . 'I don't like fuss and feathers.'" Although Meg is offended, she turns away only to hear Laurie's judgment confirmed by another voice. A Major Lincoln passes by and comments to his mother, "They are making a fool of that little girl; I wanted you to see her, but they have spoilt her entirely; she's nothing but a doll tonight." Unlike the Moffats, who view her through the lens of fashion, Laurie and Major Lincoln assess Meg through a deeply Protestant gaze, similar to the gaze of those touring Americans that historian Jenny Franchot describes dubiously appraising Catholic Rome's idolatrous arts.[41] Differently interpreted according to the values of two opposing cultures, Meg is thoroughly confused. Although she admits that she is "uncomfortable and ashamed" and was "a goose" to wear the tight dress which is "the plague of her life," nevertheless she cannot resist playing the part for which she has been costumed. When Laurie's gaze disturbs her again, she tells him, "with an affected little laugh": "I'm not Meg, to-night; I'm 'a doll,' who does all sorts of crazy things. To-morrow I shall put away my 'fuss and feathers' and be desperately good again."

When tomorrow comes and Meg is back at home, she feels the need to confess. As if to signal her resumption of home values, she sits herself on Beth's stool, then tells how she was made into a fashion-plate, how she drank and flirted and "was altogether abominable." Finally, she reveals the gossip concerning her mother's plans to marry her daughters off for money. The last confession stirs Mrs. March the most deeply: "I was very unwise to let you among people of whom I know so little; kind, I dare say, but worldly, ill-bred, and full of these vulgar ideas about young people. I am more sorry than I can express, for the mischief this visit may have done you." Meg, however, promises that she will learn from the experience not to be dissatisfied: "I'll stay with you till I'm fit to take care of myself. But it *is* nice to be praised and admired, and I can't help saying I like it." Reassuring her that such desires are "natural" and "harmless, if the liking does not become a passion, and lead one to do foolish or unmaidenly things," Marmee confirms the lesson Meg had already gleaned from Major Lincoln's comment: "Learn to know and value the praise which is worth having, and to excite the admiration of excellent people, by being modest as well as pretty." Then, in one of the novel's key passages, Mrs. March explains that she does have plans, although they differ from Mrs. Moffat's: "My dear girls, I *am* ambitious for you, but not to have you make a dash in the world, — marry rich men merely because they are rich, or have splendid houses, which are not home, because love is wanting." Careful to differentiate her aversion to materialism from her appreciation for the material, she concludes, "Money is a needful and precious thing, — and, when well used, a noble thing, — but I never want you to think it is the first or only prize to strive for. I'd rather see you poor men's wives, if you were happy, beloved, contented, than queens on thrones, without self-respect and peace" (123).[42]

Here we see how Marmee's analysis intervenes at the crucial moment when the consumer, having actually obtained the commodity fetish, discovers that the dreams displaced onto it evaporate with its possession, or else prove disconcertingly different than imagined. Meg's fashionable costume presents her with two materialistic problems. First, it is an outward and visible sign that does not truly represent her inward and invisible qualities. Second, this slippage engenders Meg's interrogation of the now-perceptible gap between costume and self. How is one recognized by others? How is the self presented in the social world? Marmee does not tell Meg, anticipating Erving Goffman or Michel Foucault, that she has no authentic self, but then neither does she tell her, following Emerson or Thoreau, that the self is to be discovered only in the woods, far from the performance of crippling roles and the bondage of limiting relationships.[43] Instead, Marmee's counsel throughout the book is that one's true character is discovered and developed in relationship to family and friends. This intimate context is the one mirror in which identity can be reliably recognized. Here, Meg is not a socially constructed doll in costume, but a human being in emotional relation. Her familial judges believe themselves able to recognize authentic expression of identity in dress, just as romantic poets believed themselves able to recognize spontaneous expression of emotion in language. Thus the family and its affiliates now play the role of those Congregational saints once charged with assessing the sincerity of potential church members' narratives of personal conversion, although distinguishing the authentic from the hypocritical perhaps remains as problematic for a Romantic bohemian family like the Marches as it was for orthodox Puritans of an earlier time. However, while Alcott's novel asserts that mature identity develops out of a pre-existing, essential self, twenty-first-century readers might see the self reflected in this familial mirror as contextual, historical, and dialogical. In fact, I would argue that this tension between the essential, pre-existent, and individual self of Protestantism — whether of the Puritan, Unitarian, or Transcendentalist stripe — and the social self of modern and even postmodern theory lies at the heart of this novel and remains unresolved to its end. In many ways, this tension reveals *Little Women* to be a kind of historically transitional text, one shaped by unacknowledged contradictions that Edith Wharton will later confront directly in her own treatment of female development and consumer culture.

We can see the effect of Meg's moral education in the costume she chooses for her wedding to John Brooke, a poor man who meets with the March family's approval. Her identity now clearly defined within the context of family bonds, and her desire now firmly attached to her husband, Meg "looked very like a rose herself; for all that was best and sweetest in her heart and soul, seemed to bloom into her face." Now her desirability comes from internal sources, immaterial qualities animating her features and giving them a "charm more beautiful than beauty." Correspondingly, Meg resists the temptation to borrow desirability from external sources: "Neither silk, lace, nor orange flowers would she have." As she explains, "I don't want to look strange or fixed-up to-day . . . I don't want a fashionable wedding, but only those about whom I love, and to them I wish to look and be my familiar self" (307). She "makes her wedding gown herself, sewing into it the tender hopes and innocent romances of a girlish heart." Her hair is not frizzled, but braided by her sisters, and "the only ornaments she wore were the lilies of the valley which 'her John' liked best of all the flowers that grew." When Amy cries, "You *do* look just like our own dear Meg, only so very sweet and lovely, that I should hug you if it wouldn't crumple your dress," Meg replies, "Then I am satisfied. But please hug and kiss me every one, and don't mind my dress; I want a great many crumples of this sort put into it to-day." This dress does not restrict nor objectify. It does not impress its imperatives onto the body and spirit of the wearer. Rather Meg's emotions are sewn into this gown's very textures, and those she loves leave their marks on its fabric as remembrances of their attachment to her. Even Mrs. Moffat is moved to wonder, "That is the prettiest wedding I've been to for an age, Ned, and I don't see why, for there wasn't a bit of style about it" (313).

And yet, significantly there *is* a style about it. As Meg makes her bridal journey — not a trip to Switzerland or Paris, but a "quiet walk with John, from the old home to the new" — she looks like "like a pretty Quakeress, in her dove-colored suit and straw bonnet tied with white."[44] *These* clothes, the text argues, are the appropriate signifiers of Meg's true nature. This passage suggests that, while the novel gives readers a mother determined to inoculate her daughters against the pathology of idolatrous materialism, in the end it shows those readers how negotiation of consumer culture's temptations can, like Christian's journey through the vale of earthly life, actually lead to moral development, as expressed, ironically, in an authentic consumer style. Meg's choice of her demure wedding dress and "Quaker" suit are presented as creative acts of self-expression, as true reflections of her mature inner self.

The analogy between artistic creativity and consumer self-expression becomes even clearer, and more complex, in Alcott's portrayal of Amy's development, for it is Amy who achieves the luxurious, even fashionable life that Meg had envied and longed for. Moreover, Amy, to the annoyance of many readers, assumes this worldly life without apparent moral censure from the narrator or, even more disturbingly, from her mother.

In Amy, the youngest of the sisters, we see Meg's social climbing and vanity combined with Jo's aggressiveness and artistic ambition. Her Christmas wish was not for pretty things but for drawing pencils, tools of self-expression. Her gift for her mother was the bottle of cologne, a signifier of the luxurious and the European. Finally, her color, blue, suggests emotional coolness and narcissism, as well as a longing for refinement. Forced to wear hand-me-downs from her cousin, whose "mama hadn't a particle of taste . . . Amy suffered deeply at having to wear a red instead of a blue bonnet, unbecoming gowns, and fussy aprons that did not fit. Everything was good, well made, and little worn; but Amy's artistic eyes were much afflicted, especially this winter, when her school dress was a dull purple, with yellow dots, and no trimming" (54). A running source of humor in the novel is Amy's effort to appropriate the manners and language of the fashionable society that she, like Meg, longs to enter. Her speech is peppered with amusing malapropisms and mispronounced French phrases, markers of her efforts to assume a linguistic costume that also does not quite fit. Her desire to be part of fashionable society is highlighted in one of the book's early chapters, "Amy's Valley of Humiliation."[45]

Here we see Amy attempting to "keep up" with a group of wealthier girls at her school. The chapter opens with her explaining to Meg that she is "dreadfully in debt" because she "owes at least a dozen pickled limes, and I can't pay them, you know, till I have money, for Marmee forbid my having anything charged at the shop" (84). Although Meg struggles to keep a straight face, she also empathizes: "Tell me all about it. Are limes the fashion now? It used to be pricking bits of rubber to make balls." Looking "grave and important," Amy explains the fashion system that rules her school: "Why, you see, the girls are always buying them, and unless you want to be thought mean, you must do it, too. It's nothing but limes now, for every one is sucking them in their desks in school-time, and trading them off for pencils, bead-rings, paper dolls, or something else, at recess." If the social relations between the various girls are the territory, their exchanges of pickled limes are the map that displays it: "If one girl likes another, she gives her a lime; if she's mad with her, she eats one before her face, and don't offer even a suck. They treat by turns; and I've had ever so many, but haven't returned them, and I ought, for they are debts of honor, you know." The Marches' status anxieties are at work once more. Amy is evidently appreciated for qualities that mark her for membership in her friends' particular fashionable group. However, like Meg, she cannot afford the consumer goods necessary to display and consolidate such membership.[46]

Now fortified with Meg's money, Amy arrives at school the next day with a "moist brown paper parcel" that she cannot "resist the temptation of displaying, with pardonable pride." Immediately "the rumor that Amy March had got twenty-four delicious limes (she ate one on the way), and was going to treat, circulated through her 'set,' and the attentions of her friends became quite overwhelming." One girl invites her on the spot to her next party, another lends her a watch until recess, and another, "Jenny Snow, a satirical young lady, who had basely twitted Amy on her limeless state, promptly buried the hatchet, and offered to furnish answers to certain appalling sums." However, Amy "had not forgotten Miss Snow's cutting remarks about 'some persons whose noses were not too flat to smell other people's limes, and stuck-up people, who were not too proud to ask for them." (One of Amy's chief concerns is that her nose is too flat to look truly classical.) From her exalted position Amy feels free to crush Miss Snow's hopes with a "withering telegram": "You needn't be so polite all of a sudden for you won't get any."

Alas, the snubbed Miss Snow has her revenge: she informs on her rival to Davis, the headmaster, who has outlawed pickled limes altogether. Stern and unrelenting, he forces Amy to retrieve all the limes from her desk and toss them out the schoolroom window: "Scarlet with shame and anger, Amy went to and fro twelve mortal times." Her pride finally fallen, the agents of her temptation become even more seductive as she parts with them: "As each doomed couple, looking, oh so plump and juicy! fell from her reluctant hand, a shout from the street completed the anguish of the girls, for it told them that their feast was being exulted over by the little Irish children, who were their sworn foes." Access to pickled limes not only displays the social territory within the school, but marks the boundary between the privileged girls within and the impoverished immigrants without. As the cries of the Irish children are heard, the girls "all flash indignant or appealing glances at the inexorable Davis, and one passionate lime-lover bursts into tears" (87).[47]

The headmaster completes Amy's humiliation by striking several blows on her hand with a ruler, then making her stand exposed on a platform before the class: "During the fifteen minutes that followed, the proud and sensitive little girl suffered a shame and pain which she never forgot. . . . for during the twelve years of her life she had been governed by love alone, and a blow of that sort had never touched her before." Marmee's response is to withdraw Amy from the school: "I don't approve of corporal punishment, especially for girls. I dislike Mr. Davis' manner of teaching, and don't think the girls you associate with are doing you any good." But when Amy begins to exult, "That's good! I wish all the girls would leave, and spoil his old school," then gives a martyr's sigh, "It's perfectly maddening to think of those lovely limes," Marmee refuses her sympathy: "I am not sorry you lost them, for you broke the rules and deserved some punishment for disobedience." As she explains, while she would not have chosen to disgrace Amy before the whole school, she isn't sure the experience "won't do you more good than a milder method." Now comes the lecture: "You are getting to be altogether too conceited and important, my dear, and it is quite time to set about correcting it. You have a good many little gifts and virtues, but there is no need of parading them, for conceit spoils the finest genius." Here the Marches' faith in their intrinsic "quality" comes through, for as Marmee explains, talent and virtue are rarely overlooked but are "always seen and felt in a person's manner and conversation, if modestly used." Moreover, unlike the Moffats, who are made of only "ordinary materials," the Marches' finer qualities are not mere "gilding." As Marmee further explains to Amy, the "consciousness of possessing and using" such qualities well should satisfy one, even if they go temporarily unrecognized by a society blinded by fashionable display.

The incident forcibly demonstrates that Amy's overwhelming desire for limes is not linked to some essential desirability in the limes themselves, but to the socially constructed symbolism they carry. Yesterday it was rubber balls; today it is limes; tomorrow it will be something else. The object itself is arbitrary. Marmee's impatient dismissal of Amy's desire cuts to the heart of the matter. The problem is not in the limes but the spirit of the lime-eater. Her lecture emphasizes the gap between the subject's intrinsic qualities and the display of those qualities. Amy's lesson, however, is subtly different from Meg's. Meg attempted to assume another identity: that of the doll whose style was not her own but Belle Moffat's. Amy wishes to express her own style; to display her own qualities and yet still have them recognized by fashionable society. Meg, for all practical purposes, withdraws from the fray of fashion; she chooses the moral safety of sewing her own clothes and ignoring, as best she can, the appraising eye of the Gardiners and Moffats. But Meg's mistake, Amy's experience suggests, is to assume that she can only participate in the fashion system on its own terms: a idea we see demonstrated later when Meg is tempted to emulate her friend Sallie Moffat's luxurious appearance by buying yards of violet silk that she and John cannot afford.[48] Even after her marriage, Meg still can be seduced into believing that material goods can confer the qualities she longs for. However, Amy, as I shall show, comes to a more sophisticated conclusion. If consumer goods only *carry* meanings — if they are merely the bearers of a fantasy that has been displaced onto them or the signifiers of an identity that stands ultimately apart from them—then the goods themselves are not important. What is important is producing the signifying effect. Amy, rather than an idolatrous materialist, becomes, finally, a dream artist.[49]

First, however, Amy must learn how to shape her inner character to fit the outer role she aspires to play. Striving to become a gentlewoman worthy of social respect, aware of the danger of hypocrisy, Amy studies to match her internal, moral identity to her outward self-presentation. Like the ambitious young men counseled by the ministers Karen Halttunen describes, Amy must avoid the temptation to become a confidence man (or painted woman); her performance of self must be sincere. In the chapter "Consequences" she is invited to oversee the art table at Mrs. Chester's elite charity fair. However, May Chester is jealous of Amy's greater popularity, and the night before the fair, Mrs. Chester decides that the art table, being the most prominent, should belong to her own daughter by rights. Amy will be relegated to the flower table, situated in a far corner. Hurt and resentful, Amy first responds by removing all of her drawings and illustrated books from the table now occupied by May, a table that consequently loses much of its charm. At home that evening Jo demands why Amy doesn't simply take her things out of the fair altogether. But Amy answers, "I hate such things; and though I think I've a right to be hurt, I don't intend to show it. They will feel that more than angry speeches or huffy actions, won't they, Marmee."

This is a far cry from the Amy who once revengefully burnt her sister's manuscript because she hadn't been taken to the theater. Of course, Marmee approves: "That's the right spirit, my dear; a kiss for a blow is always best, though it's not very easy to give, sometimes." The next day, as Amy arranges her table she looks at a favorite illuminated text. There, "framed in brilliant scroll-work . . . were the words, 'Thou shalt love they neighbor as thyself.'" Amy's first response is "I ought, but I don't." Then she sees May's unhappy face, and gathers up her drawings and carries them back to their original place. While Amy wonders whether virtue will have to be its own reward, she soon discovers that her generosity restores the cooperative spirit all around and prevents this particular vanity fair from degenerating into destructive competition. As a result, both tables are a success, and, "when May bid Amy 'good-night,' she did not 'gush,' as usual, but gave her an affectionate kiss, and a look which said, 'Forgive and forget.'" Even Jo, usually skeptical of Amy's motives, is impressed. Amy's response reveals both her progress and its model: "I only did as I'd be done by. You laugh at me when I say I want to be a lady, but I mean a true gentlewoman in mind and manner . . . I'm far from it now, but I do my best, and hope in time to be what mother is" (379–80).

Amy's reward is a trip to Europe with her wealthy Aunt Carroll. Her sacrificial gesture has proven her a worthy steward of a gentlewoman's privileges. When Laurie, who has been rejected as suitor by Jo, comes upon Amy in Nice he discovers a young lady whose French is "improved in quantity if not in quality" and whose manners have received a "foreign polish" without spoiling her "native frankness."[50] As the narrator carefully discriminates, although "she had a gained a certain *aplomb* in both carriage and conversation, which made her seem more of a woman of the world than she was . . . her old petulance now and then showed itself, her strong will still held its own" (467). The text suggests, in fact, that Amy's strong will and native frankness are the tough inner qualities that allow her to "take a foreign polish" without losing her inner character, in sharp contrast to Meg whose more docile temperament submits to the dictates of others. And, unlike the Moffats, whose surface gilding disguises the vulgar material below, Alcott suggests that Amy's new surface sheen is really a refinement of the essentially superior substance of which she is made.

We can see the contrast between Meg and Amy most forcibly in a Christmas ball that is a virtual replay of Meg's experience at the Moffats. Amy has no more money at her disposal than her older sister had, and she also longs to cut a desirable figure before people wealthier than herself. But there the resemblance ends. This particular evening, she has only another hand-me-down to wear, one of her cousin's Florence's "old white ball dresses." However, Amy transforms it with an inexpensive froth of white tulle, "out of which her white shoulders and golden head emerged with a most artistic effect." Then, rather than "frizzle, puffing or braiding as the latest style commended," she simply twists her thick, wavy blond hair "into a Hebe-like knot at the back of head." As she explains, this simpler style is "not the fashion, but it's becoming, and I can't afford to make a fright of myself." Finally, "having no ornaments fine enough for this important occasion, Amy loops her fleecy skirts with rosy clusters of azalea, and frames her white shoulders with delicate green vines." Significantly, her choices echo those Marmee had originally advised for Meg on the eve of the Moffats' ball: the simple white dress, the demure hairstyle, the fresh flowers. But Amy has mastered these materials to produce the impression of her own style: the refined, mature expression of her own intrinsic nature. And she has produced these effects not through expensive goods, but through imagination and artistic skill. When Laurie sees her, his greeting, "good evening, Diana," is fully appropriate. The allusion marks Amy's classical style as transcending fashion, just as Emerson believed the classic work of literature sublimely ignored the merely fashionable tastes of its time to express its author's unique but somehow universal self.[51]

On this occasion, unlike that of the Moffat party, Laurie's gaze is not critical, but appreciative: "You look like Balzac's '*Femme piente par elle meme.*'" For reply, Amy merely says, "my rouge won't come off," then she "rubs her brilliant cheek, and shows her white glove, with a sober simplicity that makes him laugh outright." Next he fingers the light tulle of her dress, "What do you call this stuff?" Amy, with the confidence of a woman who has indeed "painted herself," answers: "Illusion." Laurie, increasingly aware of her unsuspected power, asks openly, "Where did you learn this sort of thing?" "Knowing perfectly well what he means," she nevertheless challenges him to "describe what is indescribable." Now he laughs again and flounders, and finally draws on the new word to frame his question: "Well — the general air, the style, the self-possession, the — the — illusion — you know." That new word, "illusion," is of course exactly what is indescribable: the aura of desirability, of happiness, of self-possession. Amy replies simply, "Why tulle is cheap; posies to be had for nothing, and I am used to making the most of my poor little things." While Amy's mastery of illusion refers to both fabric and effect, the last phrase betrays the struggle behind the art, and Amy immediately regrets it, fearing it isn't "in good taste." However, "Laurie likes her the better for it, and finds himself both admiring and respecting . . . the cheerful spirit that covered poverty with flowers" (476).

And yet the last phrase also reveals that Amy is, in fact, not so cheerful about her poverty. Her letters home make it clear that she has set her sights on Fred Vaughan, son of a prominent English family: "Now I know mother will shake her head, and the girls say, 'Oh, the mercenary little wretch!' but I've made up my mind, and, if Fred asks me, I shall accept him, though I'm not madly in love." As she explains rather lucidly, they get along; he's likable, good-looking, clever, and, most important, even richer than the Laurences. She extols the wealth of the Vaughan property: "I've seen the plate, the family jewels, the old servants, and pictures of the country place with its park, great house, lovely grounds, and fine horses. Oh, it would be all that I should ask!" And finally, she comes to the main point, "I may be mercenary but I hate poverty, and don't mean to bear it a minute longer than I can help. One of us *must* marry well; Meg didn't, Jo won't, Beth can't, yet, — so I shall, and make everything cosy all round" (393).

Part of Amy's determination stems from the failure of her own artistic dreams. Seeing the wonders of Rome revealed the meagerness of her own skill and destroyed her hopes of a brilliant career. Her new goal is to "polish up my other talents, and be an ornament to society, if I get the chance." As Laurie astutely comments, this is where Fred Vaughan comes in. Although Fred has not yet proposed, Amy admits that if he does, she will very likely accept. When Laurie probes further, asking if she really is fond of him, Amy can only answer,

"I could be if I tried." Laurie quickly senses a lack, "But you don't intend to try until the proper moment? Bless my soul, what unearthly prudence! He's a good fellow, Amy, but not the man I fancied you'd like." Amy, "trying to be quiet and dignified, but feeling a little ashamed of herself," explains: "He is rich, a gentleman, and has delightful manners." And Laurie picks up the thread: "I understand — queens of society can't get on without money, so you mean to make a good match and start in that way? Quite right and proper as the world goes, but it sounds odd from the lips of one of your mother's daughters."

Laurie once more represents the March family values, values that he himself has come to share, for he suddenly feels himself serious and disappointed. But if Laurie can look at Amy with the eyes of home, Amy can do the same. Nettled, she asks if he wants to know what she honestly thinks of him. When he answers, "Pining to be told," she says, "Well, I despise you." Her reasons? "Because with every chance for being good, useful, and happy, you are faulty, lazy, and miserable." She completes her lecture by showing him two portraits she has drawn of him: one done earlier at home that shows him energetic and purposeful, the other done in Europe that shows him passive and listless. Again, the contrast with Meg's experience at the Moffats' is interesting. While Meg ultimately submitted meekly to Laurie's critique, Amy gives as good as she gets. Her revived Protestant gaze is just as sharp and searching as Laurie's.

The exchange, much like the opening Christmas dialogue in which the sisters renounce their materialistic wishes in favor of their altruistic bonds, reconnects both Amy and Laurie to their "better selves." When Laurie takes his leave of Amy, he tries to kiss her hand in European fashion, but Amy stops him, "No; be yourself with me, Laurie, and part in the good old way. I'd rather have a hearty English hand-shake than all the sentimental salutations in France" (507). He leaves to rehabilitate his self-respect, while Amy has time to reflect on the pleasures their intimacy provided despite, or more likely because of, its painful honesty. When Fred Vaughan does come with his marriage proposal, "her courage failed her, and she found that something more than money and position was needed to satisfy the new longing that filled her heart so full of tender hopes and fears." She keeps remembering Laurie's disappointment and her words, "I shall marry for money." Now she wishes to take those words back; they sound "so heartless and worldly." Being a queen of society now seems much less desirable than being "a lovable woman."

Beth's illness completes Amy's moral maturation by making her even more aware of the value of emotional intimacy and family bonds. As she reads the letters about Beth's slow decline, "her heart was very heavy — she longed to be at home; and every day looked across wistfully across the lake, waiting for Laurie to come and comfort her." When the news of Beth's death finally arrives, Laurie is in Germany, but leaves immediately to be with her in Vevey. As he approaches, Amy is sitting in an old garden, "leaning her head on her hand, with a home-sick heart and heavy eyes, thinking of Beth, and wondering why Laurie did not come." For his part, Laurie stands unseen, "looking at her with new eyes, seeing what no one had ever seen before — the tender side of Amy's character." Her appearance now declares her emotional transformation: "the blotted letters in her lap, the black ribbon that tied up her hair, the womanly pain and patience in her face; even the little ebony cross at her throat seemed pathetic to Laurie, for he had given it to her, and she wore it as her only ornament." When she catches sight of him, Amy runs to Laurie, spontaneously crying out his name in longing.

Despite Madelon Bedell's comment that Amy is the true princess of the fairy tale embedded in *Little Women*, it is worth nothing that this courtship is not conventionally romantic.[52] Although Laurie himself had imagined it would hap-pen "in the chateau garden by moonlight," instead "the matter was settled on the lake, at noonday, in a few blunt words." As Laurie rows their boat, Amy offers to take an oar, "and, though she used both hands, and Laurie but one, the oars kept time, and the boat went smoothly through the water." Amy comments, "How well we pull together, don't we." Laurie, "very tenderly," replies: "So well, that I wish we might always pull in the same boat. Will you, Amy?" This cou-ple will be a team, a partnership. Their bond is based not on fantasies of the loved one's magical qualities, as if the lover were yet another consumer fetish, but on shared labor, intimate knowledge, and emotional attachment. Alcott here resists a crucial aspect of the modern hedonism described by Colin Campbell.[53] According to his analysis, modern romantic love operates serially, like consump-tion. As each desired love is consummated, its aura of fantasy dissolves, leaving the realistic, and arguably unsatisfying, relationship revealed — and setting the stage for another romantic and mysterious lover to beckon from the horizon. Alcott deliberately undercuts this pattern. In this novel, friendship or even fa-milial relations are the best models for marriage — a pattern in Alcott's work that often verges on the incestuous.

Some young readers complain bitterly that Amy, who begins the novel as the most selfish and narcissistic, should, in effect, get it all: the money and Laurie too. And yet Alcott attempts to show that Amy has done the developmental work necessary to deserving it all. First, Amy can safely wear the fine French dresses Laurie now buys her because she is no materialist. She is true to her own sense of style but knows that the power of clothing lies not in the material goods, but in the character they signify. Second, she will be a worthy steward of the money now entrusted to her because she has proved her ability to sacrifice wealth and social position for love. She will use her new wealth not for her own self-aggrandizement but for the greater good. After their marriage she persuades Laurie to set up an endowment to help poor girls with artistic ambitions get the training they deserve. Finally, Amy is now capable, following her separation from her family and the loss of Beth, of valuing her relationships to others. She has overcome her narcissism, and by the end of the novel has herself become the mother of a daughter she names Beth, after the sister whose death helped bring her to moral awareness and maturity. Amy is the March sister who can best handle the dangerous materials of European and Catholic culture without being mastered by them. Strong-willed but finally tender-hearted, she turns those materials to her own uses without sacrificing her own American and very Protestant integrity. Situated between Alcott's images of the semi-savage Irish children who scramble for discarded limes in the dirt and the hyper-civilized French girls whose mamas arrange their marriages, Amy represents the American vision of combining the wisdom of the serpent with the innocence of the dove.[54] In the books that follow *Little Women*, Amy does become a virtual queen, not of Fred Vaughan's aristocratic English society, but of her own New England "city on a hill."

Of all the sisters, Jo has received the most critical attention, partly because she is the character based upon Alcott herself and partly because she seems the most resistant to the ideology of womanhood to which the others so enthusiastically subscribe. This resistance is clearly displayed in Jo's relationship to material goods in the novel. Her gift of army shoes to her mother reveals her ambivalence toward the conventions of female dress, a resistance which is also entertainingly displayed in her tendency to tear, burn, or mangle every piece of clothing she touches. She fries Meg's bangs to "little black pancakes," she scorches her party dress, she "smashes" her coral bracelet. Given a choice, she much prefers functionality to fashion. Despite the amusement of others, she wears an enormous sun hat to one party, and throughout the novel she wars with voluminous Victorian dresses that signify propriety and elegance but hamper walking and running. Her sublime indifference to public opinion echoes Thoreau's dictum that the only true purpose of clothing is to preserve the "vital heat."[55] All this suggests that Jo is also indifferent to the consumer temptations that so trouble her sisters, Meg and Amy. However, I would argue that in Jo's case these temptations simply come from another quarter.

Jo's own castle in the air is a library full of wonderful books, over which she presides as a famous author, assured of immortality. However, just as Amy has to overcome her childish vanity and egotism, Jo has to master her own temper-amental burdens: her overweening ambition and her sometimes blinding rage. The chapter from Bunyan's parable that Alcott chooses for Jo's trial by rage is aptly named "Jo Meets Apollyon," after the hellish giant that Bunyan's Christian must face down on his journey. Analyzing this particular trial, based on Alcott's own struggles as a child and young woman to discipline her anger and aggres-sion, reveals even more clearly the dynamics of the March family's moral peda-gogy, a pedagogy closely modeled on that of the Alcott parents themselves. Just as Amy's childish consumption and distribution of the forbidden pickled limes demonstrate issues with which she will continue to struggle until her ultimate maturity, so Jo's behavior in these scenes reveal the weaknesses and passions that threaten the development of her "better self."

The chapter begins with Meg and Jo resisting Amy's appeals to take her with them on a trip to the theater with Laurie. Amy was not invited, they argue, and her presence would cause all kinds of complications. Amy is not appeased, and while her sisters are out enjoying themselves, she secretly takes a handwritten manuscript on which Jo has labored for years and throws it into the fire. When Jo returns, she soon discovers her little sister's revenge, and her response is fierce and violent. As the narrator explains of the two sisters: "Although the oldest, Jo had the least self-control, and had hard times trying to curb the fiery spirit which was continually getting her into trouble; her anger never lasted long, and having humbly confessed her fault, she sincerely repented, and tried to do better" (94). This time, however, her anger is not easily calmed, but flares out dangerously: "Jo's hot temper mastered her, and she shook Amy till her teeth chattered in her head; crying, in a passion of grief and anger, — 'You wicked, wicked girl! I never can write it again, and I'll never forgive you as long as I live'" (96).

When Marmee returns in the evening, she takes Amy aside and persuades her of the harm she has done her sister. Now Amy is willing to beg Jo's for-giveness and genuinely regrets her act. But Jo is not satisfied; her manuscript "was the pride of her heart, and was regarded by her family as a literary sprout of great promise." The destruction of her final and only copy of a dozen fairy tales "seemed a small loss to others, but to Jo it was a dreadful calamity, and she felt that it could never be made up to her." Although Marmee advises: "My dear, don't let the sun go down upon your anger; forgive each other, help each other, and begin again tomorrow," Jo refuses: "She wanted to lay her head down on that motherly bosom, and cry her grief and anger all away; but tears were an unmanly weakness, and she felt so deeply injured that really *couldn't* quite forgive yet" (97). The next day, Jo's bitterness and alienation from her sister has hardened. In a repeat of the theater incident, Jo goes off to skate on the river with Laurie, leaving Amy behind. Eager to join in, Amy follows them at a distance. Once on the river, Jo hears Laurie, up ahead, warn her that the ice is thin toward the center. Aware that Amy is still on the shore and perhaps too far away to hear Laurie's warning, "Jo glanced over her shoulder, and the little demon she was harboring said in her ear, — 'No matter whether she heard or not, let her take of herself.'" With this she skates off, only to turn back just in time to see Amy falling through the broken ice. Laurie then takes command, and working blindly under his direction, Jo struggles to bring Amy out of the freezing water and home. Once Amy is safe, Jo breaks down to her mother "in a passion of penitent tears, telling all that had happened, bitterly condemning her hardness of heart, and sobbing out her gratitude for being spared the heavy punishment that might have come upon her." Despairing, Jo cries to Marmee, "You don't know; you can't guess how bad it is! It seems as if I could do anything when I'm in a passion; I get so savage, I could hurt anyone and enjoy it. I'm afraid I *shall* do something dreadful some day, and spoil my life and make everybody hate me. Oh, mother! Help me, do help me!" (100–101).

In this scene we see Jo's shame, her sense of intrinsic unworthiness and agonizing exposure, gently converted into guilt, an acknowledgment of natural frailty that can be mercifully forgiven and remedied through personal effort and humane support. First, there is the important act of sincere confession, a humbling of Jo's pride and a call for help. Marmee's response, which accords with the precepts of Horace Bushnell's Christian nurture, is not to confirm Jo's passionate self-condemnation as a necessary recognition of her innate and total depravity, only to be remedied by complete surrender of self to the saving grace of God. Rather, Marmee's first gesture is to draw Jo to her and to kiss her tear-stained cheek, a gesture that prompts even more tears from the girl whose hard, resistant surface has now entirely broken down. Then, when Jo cries out for help, Marmee, surprisingly, informs her, "Jo, dear, we all have our temptations, some far greater than yours, and it often takes all our lives to conquer them. You think your temper is the worst in the world; but mine used to be just like it" (101). Rather than taking the position of an authority above her daughter, Marmee uses this opening into Jo's troubled spirit to connect with her daughter. Of her own temper, Marmee says, "I've been trying to cure it for forty years, and have only succeeding in controlling it. I am angry nearly every day of my life, Jo; but I have learned not to show it; and I still hope to learn not to feel it, though it may take me another forty years to do so" (101). Jo is not punished for her confession, but rewarded by having her mother talk to her like a peer, a fellow human being who has also struggled. The result is greater closeness and greater sympathy between them: "The knowledge that her mother had a fault like hers, and tried to mend it, made her own easier to bear, and strengthened her resolution to cure it; though forty years seemed rather a long time to watch and pray, to a girl of fifteen" (101).

In the conversation that follows, Marmee explains how when her daughters were young and money was short, she had often lost her temper with them. With her husband's help, she learned to curb her harsh words. More, "a startled or surprised look from one of you, when I spoke sharply, rebuked me more than any words could have done" (102). When Jo asks her mother if the gesture she had seen of her father putting his finger to his lips while looking at his wife was a sign that he was encouraging her to control herself, Mrs. March tears up. Jo responds, "Was it wrong to watch and speak of it? I didn't mean to be rude, but it's so comfortable to say all I think to you, and feel so safe and happy here." Marmee's reply sums up her goal in these dialogues with each daughter: "My Jo, you may say anything to your mother, for it is my greatest happiness and pride to feel that my girls confide in me, and know how much I love them" (103). It would be easy, and has been easy for many critics, to see this conversation as evidence of the March parents' insidious effort to weaken Jo's strong personality, to socialize her into womanly submission.[56] Certainly, the image of Mr. March silencing his wife with a single gesture seems chilling. However, it is worth pointing out that Jo's rage really was violent and dangerous and that her sister's life really was jeopardized by Jo's disavowal of their bond. And Marmee's memory of anger as a young struggling wife and mother suggests that she really did startle and frighten her children with her frustration and temper. So is her advice for her tempestuous daughter stunting and inhibiting? Or is it encouraging Jo to master, not stifle, her strong passions? I would argue for the latter: that this scene is about fostering self-awareness and self-control in Jo, about nurturing a passionate nature so it becomes both strong and morally responsible.

Evidence for this interpretation can be seen in a chapter that shortly follows the previous scene: "Camp Laurence." The four March sisters have been invited to picnic with Laurie, his tutor, and some well-to-do guests from England. As the chapter opens, Jo has just received a letter from her mother: "I write a little word to let you with how much satisfaction I watch your efforts to control your temper. You say nothing about your trials, failures, or successes, and think, perhaps that no one sees them but the Friend whose help you daily ask, if I may trust the well-worn cover of your guide-book. *I*, too have seen them all, and heartily believe in the sincerity of your resolution, since it begins to bear fruit. Go on, dear, patiently and bravely, and always believe that no one sympathizes more tenderly with you than your loving MOTHER" (150).

The "friend" of the guidebook is Alcott's version of the Christian savior, humanized and divested of institutional trappings. But what's equally important is that this divine friend is not the only one watching; the human mother is too. While, again, this might seem like intrusive surveillance, a kind of maternal panopticon always on guard, Jo's response is predictably positive: "That does me good! That's worth millions of money and pecks of praise. Oh, Marmee, I do try! I will keep on trying, and not get tired, since I have you to help me" (150). The central idea here is that moral development is a social process; it's dialogical, not individual. It unfolds over time and through repeated learning experiences, not through a single crisis. Moreover, Jo needs her mother's recognition to follow through on this process and to stabilize her new behaviors; she needs to see herself as a moral subject in that sympathetic human mirror. Equally important, she needs that self to be articulated, to be narrated, and to have that narration heard and understood. This support is especially important in the minor drama that shapes the chapter.[57]

In the course of the day's entertainments, the group plays croquet. The Americans, in a kind of patriotic and even chauvinistic spirit, line up against the Brits. Jo ends up competing with the young Englishman, Fred Vaughan, who slyly takes the opportunity to nudge his ball, lying on the wrong side of the wicket, into a more favorable position and through the wicket. Jo spies him and calls him on it, but he denies what he has done. When Jo retorts, "We don't cheat in America; but *you* can, if you choose," Vaughan replies in nationalistic kind: "Yankees are a deal the most tricky, everybody knows." With that, he "croquets her ball far away." Rightly provoked, "Jo opened her lips to say something rude; but checked herself in time, colored up to her forehead, and stood a minute, hammering down a wicket with all her might, while Fred hit the stake, and declared himself out, with much exultation" (156). Jo then goes off to find her ball in the bushes, where she remains for some time until she can get her temper back under control. When she returns, she manages by "a clever stroke" to win the game after all, telling Vaughn as she does so, that "Yankees have a trick of being generous to their enemies . . . especially when they beat them" (157). Laurie and Meg both tell Jo privately that they knew how unfairly she had been treated, how provoked she must be have been, and how well she had held her temper. Here also it might seem that the moral of the story is never to lose your temper, never try to get even, but rather to submit, even to injustice. But a little later in the afternoon, Jo finds the opportunity to even the score and gleefully takes it. The young people propose a game of "Truth." When it is Fred's turn to answer the group's questions, Laurie whispers to Jo, "Let's give it to him." They ask him point blank if he cheated earlier at croquet, and he instantly confesses. Rather than explode and escalate the bad behavior that Fred Vaughn initiated, Jo finds a way throughout the chapter to maintain her poise, defuse the situation, and, most importantly, assert her rights. She is in control not only of her temper but of the entire situation. This is not a story about a young woman learning to forego power, but about her learning to use it effectively.

While Jo's struggles to manage her aggression are largely successful, she still has to master her enormous hunger for artistic success. After all, it was her pride in her literary production that led to her rage at Amy's burning of her manuscript. Only when her anger threatened her sister's life did she learn how important that relationship was to her and how the lost manuscript could never replace it. As Jo matures, she too will have to deal with the seduction of the materialistic world outside the March home. However, while vanity fair for Meg and Amy comes in the form of the marriage market, for Jo it appears as the literary market. Just as Meg is tempted to dress like Belle Moffat and Amy is tempted to marry Fred Vaughan, Jo is tempted to write like Mrs. S. L. A. N. G. Northbury and sell to *The Weekly Volcano*.[58] She discovers Northbury (a thin disguise for the real Victorian author E.D.E.N. Southworth) in a pictorial sheet specializing in "that class of light literature in which the passions have a holiday, and when the author's invention fails, a grand catastrophe clears the stage of over one-half the *dramatis personae*, leaving the other half to exult over their downfall" (330). When she encounters a young boy eagerly consuming one of Northbury's tales, Jo first sees the story as merely trash, but when its admiring reader tells her what a good living the author makes, she looks "more respectfully at the agitated group and thickly sprinkled exclamation points that adorned the pages." As the boy helpfully explains, "She knows just what folks like, and gets paid well for writing it." Soon Jo's powers of invention are at work. Earlier in the novel Alcott had shown Jo and her sisters concocting melodramatic home theatricals; now these skills are put to new use. Eager to whet her readers' appetites, she fills her story with as much "desperation and despair as her limited acquaintance with those uncomfortable emotions enabled her." New England, of course, won't do for a setting. Lisbon provides the exotic locale, with an earthquake for appropriate climax.

The gratifying result is a letter containing a promise of publication and a check for $100 that falls into Jo's lap, where "for a minute she stared at it as if it had been a snake." Despite the portentous image, Jo is relieved; at last she can make her way in the marketplace.[59] Although her idealistic father tells her, "You can do better than this, Jo. Aim at the highest, and never mind the money," a young Amy characteristically regards "the magic slip of paper with a reverential eye" and comments, "*I* think the money is the best part of it. What *will* you do with such a fortune?" Jo's answer shows how her desire is divided between fame and family love: "Send Beth and mother to the sea-side for a month or two." When Beth protests, Jo explains: "That's what I tried for, and that's why I succeeded. I never get on when I think of myself alone, so it will help me to work for you." And so, like Louisa May Alcott herself, Jo begins her career as a sensation writer in earnest. And again like Louisa's, her success makes her "a power in the house; for by the magic of a pen, her 'rubbish' turned into comforts for them all . . . . 'The Duke's Daughter' paid the butcher's bill, 'A Phantom Hand' put down a new carpet, and 'The Curse of the Coventrys' proved the blessing of the Marches in the way of groceries and gowns" (333).[60]

However, despite her success as a sensation writer, Jo, much like Louisa, soon becomes ambitious for artistic recognition. After copying her fourth draft of a high-minded novel (a version of Louisa's early book *Moods*), she sends it out to three publishers, one of whom finally accepts it on the condition that she "cut it down one-third, and omit all the parts which she particularly admired."[61] The choice is clear, as Jo explains in a family council: "I must either bundle it back into my tin-kitchen to mould, pay for printing it myself, or chop it up to suit purchasers, and get what I can for it. Fame is a very good thing to have in the house but cash is more convenient." The family's response is mixed. Mr. March advises against revision: "Don't spoil your book, my girl, for there is more in it than you know, and the idea is well worked out. Let it wait and ripen." As Jo well knows, "he practiced as he preached, having waited patiently thirty years for fruits of his own to ripen, and being in no haste to gather it, even now, when it was sweet and mellow." The latter reflection, however, works against his advice, for his reluctance to market his wisdom is largely the reason the family is in such financial straits. Amy, again his foil, advises doing what the editor requires: "He knows what will sell, and we don't. Make a good, popular book, and get as much money as you can. By and by, when you've got a name, you can afford to digress, and have philosophical and metaphysical people in your novels." The ailing Beth's response, however, carries the day: "I should so like to see it printed *soon*."

"So, with Spartan firmness, the young authoress laid her first-born on her table, and chopped it up as ruthlessly as any ogre. In the hope of pleasing every one, she took every one's advice; and . . . suited nobody" (335). Although Jo receives $300 for her effort, she also gets "plenty of praise and blame, both so much greater than she expected that she was thrown in state of bewilderment, from which it took some time to recover." Like Meg at the Moffats, her appearance in print is not the "real" Jo, but an assemblage of other people's opinions and styles. The violent language and maternal metaphors describing the revisions suggest the intimacy of the link between literary self-presentation and bodily self-presentation. The novel may be at a remove from the body, but only as a child from its parent. And the literary marketplace makes demands on the body even more violent than Meg's high-heeled shoes and tight bodice. As with Meg, Jo's bewilderment offers an opportunity for beneficial disillusionment, although in Jo's case the process is more protracted. For the moment, she remarks that she "has the joke on her side, after all; for the parts that were taken straight out of real life, are denounced as impossible and absurd, and the scenes that I made up out of my own silly head, are pronounced 'charmingly natural, tender, and true'" (336). Just as Meg's experience opened up the possibility that identity is a social construction, unstable and contextual, Jo's experience opens up the possibility that literary identity is equally malleable: that sincerity can be misread and that hypocrisy can pass successfully for truth. While the problem lies largely with a reading audience lacking discerning taste, responsibility also lies with Jo, who has not only failed to protect her own integrity but sacrificed it in the marketplace.

That temptation becomes even greater when Jo moves to New York to live in a boarding house and work as a teacher. Jo now sees that "money confers power; money and power, therefore, she resolves to have; not to be used for herself alone, but for those whom she loves more than self." Telling no one, "she concocts a 'thrilling tale,' and boldly carries it herself to Mr. Dashwood, editor of the 'Weekly Volcano.'" Here the narrator emphasizes Jo's capitulation to the gaze of the marketplace: "She had never read *Sartor Resartus*, but she had a womanly instinct that clothes possess an influence more powerful over many than the worth of character or the magic manner."[62] Having had no desire to win the approval of the Kings or the Moffats, Jo is now eager to please, and she dresses herself in her best clothes and hesitantly climbs the stairs to the decidedly masculine editorial offices. After reading her story, Mr. Dashwood agrees to take it, if she's willing to accept "a few alterations." Handing over her pages, he explains, "People want to be amused, not preached at, you know. Morals don't sell nowadays." The shocked Jo "hardly knows her own MS. again, so crumpled and underscored were its pages and paragraphs; but feeling as a tender parent might on being asked to cut off her baby's legs in order that it might fit into a new cradle, she looks at the marked passages, and is surprised to see that all the moral reflections, — which she had carefully put in as ballast for much romance, — had all been stricken out" (428). The imagery is again violent. This "baby" has been mutilated and crippled, been defaced and rendered unrecognizable. However, when Jo hears that she'll get "from twenty-five to thirty for things of this sort," she swallows her compunctions and trims her imagination to its new cradle.

As in her first sensation story, Jo "goes abroad for her characters and scenery, and banditti, counts, and gypsies, nuns, and duchesses appear on her stage, and play their parts with as much accuracy and spirit as could be expected" (429). She reassures herself that such writing is harmless and "sincerely means to write nothing of which she should be ashamed, and quiets all pricks of conscience by anticipation of the happy minute when she should show her earnings and laugh over her well-kept secret." However, the narrator explains that, in her quest to keep her audience excited and attracted, Jo has to delve into the "tragic world which underlies society." She has to "introduce herself to folly, sin, and misery, as well as her limited opportunities allowed." But "imaginary though it was" the influence of this "bad society" affects her. Compared to the wholesome nourishment she had been given at home, "she was feeding heart and fancy on dangerous and unsubstantial food, and was brushing the innocent bloom from her nature by a premature acquaintance with the darker side of life, which comes soon enough to all of us" (430–31).[63]

Just as Laurie's Protestant gaze recalled Meg and Amy to their "better selves," it takes a man to represent the home values to Jo. In this case it is Fritz Bhaer, a widowed German professor, middle-aged and somewhat stout, who lives in the same New York boarding house as Jo. Alcott's construction of Professor Bhaer's character, as has been pointed out many times, draws heavily on Bronson and Abby Alcott, as well as the fictional March parents. Like Mr. March, Bhaer is a philosopher, deeply conversant with German Romantic poetry and idealist philosophy. Like Mrs. March, he is warm and sympathetic with children. We first see him romping on the floor with his nephews, for whom he has assumed responsibility after his sister's death. Most important, German culture in this novel is often contrasted favorably with French. For example, when Laurie first catches sight of Meg, in her simple party dress, he says she reminds him of the German girls, who are simple and fresh and unassuming. Bhaer himself later says that the Germans are more "sentimental" than the English, warmer and more expressive in their personal relationships. He begs Jo to use the personal "thou" with him, rather than "the cold English 'you.'" In the other books in the March family series, Bhaer's German culture is praised for its love of family rituals and folk practices. Its men are seen as more domestic, more home-loving. In a key scene in *Little Women*, John Brooke asks the English aristocrat Kate Vaughan to read Schiller's *Mary Stuart*. Her translation is correct but cold. When Meg tries the passage, her German is by contrast more halting, but her reading is suffused with feeling. The true European soul mate of the democratic and Protestant American is not the English aristocrat nor the French Catholic, but the German Romantic.[64]

At first this affinity puzzles Jo. Fritz Bhaer "was neither rich nor great, young nor handsome, — in no respect was he what is called fascinating, imposing, or brilliant, and yet he was as attractive as a genial fire, and people seemed to gather about him as naturally as about a warm hearth." This description clearly parallels the novel's opening description of Marmee as an unfashionable woman with a "can-I-help-you look." In both cases, the source of their charm, Jo decides, is "benevolence." Significantly, Fritz Bhaer is even more resistant to fashionable self-presentation than Mrs. March. Indeed, "his very clothes seemed to partake of the hospitable nature of the wearer. They looked as if they were at ease, and liked to make him comfortable; his capacious waistcoat had a social air, and the baggy pockets plainly proved that little hands often went in empty and came out full" (435). In fact, Bhaer is so unselfconscious and unaccustomed to checking his appearance that on one occasion he remains totally unaware, during the entire length of a lesson on Schiller's "The Death of Wallenstein," that he's wearing a child's soldier-cap, left over from play with one of his small students.

In this unworldliness Bhaer also resembles Mr. March, whose role he takes in his response to the *Weekly Volcano*'s literary productions. When he denounces its stories as trash, more dangerous to children than gunpowder, Jo, without openly revealing her complicity, argues that it may be "only sillyness . . . and if there is a demand for it, I don't seem the harm in supplying it. Many very respectable people make an honest living out of what are called sensation stories." But Bhaer is not appeased: "There is a demand for whiskey, but I think you and I do not care to sell it. If the respectable people know what harm they did, they would not feel that the living *was* honest." This form of literary consumption, like the Moffats' fashion consumption, is addictive and even poisonous: "They haf no right to put poison in the sugarplum, and let the small ones eat it." Developing children should be fed more truly nourishing narratives like those parables Marmee tells her four daughters, or Bunyan's allegory, or the story of "the greatest life ever lived" with its four differently colored covers. Professor Bhaer here gives voice to contemporary anxieties about the compulsive reading of gothic thrillers, anxieties that were, according to Colin Campbell's history of the emergence of modern consumerism, linked to similar fears about unbridled shopping for consumer goods. Like whisky and opiates, both activities were seen as potentially addictive: weakening the will and opening the imagination to dangerous influences and insatiable desires.[65]

Subjected to the professor's judgmental gaze, Jo's own vision shifts: "Being a little short-sighted, Mr. Bhaer sometimes used eye-glasses, and Jo had tried them once, smiling to see how they magnified the fine print of her book; now she seemed to have got on the Professor's mental or moral spectacles also, for the faults of these poor stories glared at her dreadfully, and filled her with dismay" (438). Now she thinks: "They *are* trash, and will soon be worse than trash if I go on." And, in a curious parallel to Amy's initial burning of Jo's fairy tale manuscript, Jo burns her own stories, nevertheless thinking, "I almost wish I hadn't any conscience, it's so inconvenient. If I didn't care about doing right . . . I should get on capitally. I can't help wishing, sometimes, that father and mother hadn't been so dreadfully particular about such things." But this, of course, is the crux of the story: the March parents' battle against the ideology of the marketplace, with Jo's allegiance in the balance.

Jo, determined to do good, now obediently reviews the works of Mrs. Sherwood, Miss Edgeworth, and Hannah More and produces an intensely moral tale more akin to a sermon. However, "her lively fancy and girlish romance feels as ill at ease in the new style as she would have done masquerading in the stiff and cumbersome costume of the last century." The result is dismal, and decisively rejected. A try at children's stories doesn't fare any better. The only editor who will pay is dedicated to converting his readers to his own religious beliefs. After refusing to meet his stipulation that fictional boys "be eaten by bears or tossed by mad bulls, because they did not go to a particular Sabbath-school," Jo "corks up her inkstand" and admits "in a fit of very wholesome humility, 'I don't know anything; I'll wait until I do before I try again'" (440).

Earlier the narrator had suggested that Jo's experimentation was harmful because it was premature, a trifling with the darker side of life "which comes soon enough to all of us." This darker side now presents itself through Beth's illness and death. And, just as it does for Amy, this loss completes the process of Jo's maturation and self-discovery. When Jo goes home to nurse Beth, she comes to appreciate the quiet virtues that made her sister the conscience of the family and its unassuming anchor. Now dying, Beth becomes, like Little Eva or Paul Dombey, an "angel in the house." The threat of her loss awakens Jo's consciousness of what this bond has meant to her, and how dependent she has been on Beth's counsel and moral integrity. In Bunyan's *Pilgrim's Progress*, Christian is accompanied by his companion, Faithful, who never makes it to the final river crossing, but is instead martyred at Vanity Fair. More steadfast in his vision than Christian, he is more Christ-like; his death is exemplary and redemptive, as is Beth's. The chapter in which Beth contracts the scarlet fever that ultimately takes her life is entitled "Little Faithful." Moreover, her initial illness is a direct result of her sisters' more selfish and immature characters. She is the only one to fulfill her mother's instructions to visit the impoverished Hummels; the others are too preoccupied with their own affairs. But she is also the only one, besides Amy, who has not had scarlet fever. Meg and Jo could have visited the ailing

Hummels without consequences, but they, unlike Beth, ignore the duty their mother placed on them.

Now, as she cares for her sister, Jo comes to see the value of a life spent in service to others. In a poem that Beth discovers, Jo asks Beth's spirit to

> Give me, for I need it sorely,
> Of that courage, wise and sweet,
> Which has made the path of duty
> Green beneath your willing feet.
> Give me that unselfish nature,
> That with charity divine
> Can pardon wrong for love's dear sake —
> Meek heart, forgive me mine!

However, true to the novel's larger patterns, Jo also sees this grief as necessary to her own maturation:

> My great loss becomes my gain.
> For the touch of grief will render
> My wild nature more serene,
> Give to life new aspirations —
> A new trust in the unseen.

Beth's reading of this poem strengthens her as well, for it reveals that her life has been neither insignificant nor wasted. She tells Jo she must take her place within the family, especially to their parents: "They will turn to you — don't fail them; and if it's hard work alone, remember that I don't forget you, and that you'll be happier in doing that, than writing splendid books, or seeing all the world; for love is the only thing that we can carry with us when we go, and it makes the end so easy" (513). "Then and there," in a moment that many critics have found disturbing, "Jo renounces her old ambition, pledges herself to a new and better one, acknowledging the poverty of her other desires, and feeling the blessed solace of a belief in the immortality of love."[66]

In the days that follow Beth's death, Jo discovers a new closeness with her parents through their sharing of intense grief. Almost unconsciously she takes up the role that Beth left empty: "Brooms and dishcloths never could be as distasteful as they once had been, for Beth had presided over both . . . As she used them, Jo found herself humming the songs Beth used to hum, imitating Beth's orderly ways, and giving little touches here and there that kept everything fresh and cosy, which was the first step toward making home happy, though she didn't know it" (532). She rediscovers her sister, Meg, and comes to value her new happiness and wisdom in marriage. Meg even counsels Jo that marriage would do her good as well: "You are like a chestnut-burr, prickly outside, but silky-soft within, and a sweet kernel, if one can only get at it. Love will make you show your heart some day, and then the rough burr will fall off" (533). Jo counters the idea lightly, "Frost opens chestnut burrs, ma'am. Boys go nutting, and I don't care to be bagged by them." But, as the narrator swiftly suggests, "Grief is the best opener for some hearts, and Jo's was nearly ready for the bag; a little more sunshine to ripen the nut, then, not a boy's impatient shake, but a man's hand reached up to pick it gently from the burr, and find the kernel sound and sweet." The boy's impatient shake is, of course, Laurie's — who tries before Jo's loss has opened her heart. The man's hand is Fritz Bhaer's.

Significantly, the process that ripens and opens Jo's heart also ripens and opens her talent. But first she discovers just how hard taking Beth's place can be. Jo, the narrator explains, is not "the heroine of a moral story, but only a struggling human girl." Her childish ambition was to do something splendid; now that ambition has shifted from literary fame to family happiness. Her castle in the air has changed, but her temperament remains the same, despite its education through experience: "If difficulties were necessary to increase the splendor of her the effort, what could be harder for a restless, ambitious girl, than to give up her own hopes, plans and desires, and cheerfully live for others." Jo may be trying to take Beth's place, but unlike Beth, she is not an angel in the house. Marmee, once more, comes to the rescue. She suggests that Jo write again, and when Jo replies, "I've no heart to write, and if I had, nobody cares for my things," Marmee answers simply, "We do; write something for us, and never mind the rest of the world." Reluctantly, Jo begins, and although "she never knew how it happened . . . something got into that story that went straight to the hearts of all who read it."

The story, of course, is the highly autobiographical part 1 of *Little Women* itself.[67] Although the narrator writes that it was only a small thing, "it was a great success; and Jo was more astonished than when her novel was commended and condemned all at once." As her father explains, "There is truth in it, Jo — that's the secret; humor and pathos make it alive, and you have found your style at last. You wrote with no thought of fame or money, and put your heart into it." Jo's reply suggests that family is not only the best audience for her art, but also the "sacred fount" of the emotion that animates it: "If there *is* anything good or true in what I write, it isn't mine; I owe it all to you and mother, and to Beth." Now Jo's relationship to her literary productions has entirely shifted: "Taught by love and sorrow, Jo wrote her little stories, and sent them away to make friends for themselves and her, finding it a very charitable world to such humble wanderers, for they were kindly welcomed, and sent home comfortable tokens to their mother, like dutiful children whom good fortune overtakes." Jo has become a good mother to her literary children. Rather than mutilating them for sale, she nurtures them until they have found their true forms and are ready to seek their place in the wide world. The money they earn, like the money earned by dutiful Puritans, is a "comfortable token" of an intrinsic worth recognized by "good fortune" and a discerning Providence.

Moreover, like the Puritan capitalist whose wealth supposedly came not from his dependence on the market but from his stewardship of a higher good, Jo is rewarded with literary fame only when she abandons her search for celebrity and writes out of love for her family. Rather than penalizing moral honesty, the market rewards it lavishly. Here also we see the Romantic idea of literary composition: to write out of true feeling, spontaneously, is to write authentically and with one's own "genius." To quote Emerson's "The Poet" once more: "The man is only half himself, the other half is his expression." To adopt the style of another, to construct a style according to fashion, is to write like Emerson's nemesis, Edgar Allan Poe, whom he contemptuously called "the jingle man." The style of Jo's last book, like the style of Meg's wedding dress or of Amy's ball gown, represents the achievement of mature authenticity, made visible through its material expression.

However, here we can also see the unresolved tensions in Alcott's work, for while the text celebrates Jo's new authenticity, the novel also shows us how that authenticity, far from being intrinsic and spontaneous, is the fruit of a social process. As an achievement, it is product of nurture as much as nature. Jo may have "have found her style at last," but her own narrative shows us how she acquired the words and plots that shape it: from Bunyan's moral parables, from Marmee's comforting letters, from the nameless friend of her guidebook with its passionate red cover. Sociologist Ian Burkitt, drawing on Mikhail Bakhtin and other theorists, would describe Jo's mature identity as a "core self," as opposed to an intrinsic self: one that is not given at birth, but developed through dialogue with others and through internalizing the discourses circulating in her cultural milieu, the "representational economies" of Protestant New England and Gilded Age America. Moreover, Jo creates that core self not spontaneously, but through what psychologists Michel White and David Epston would define as a process of self-narration: fashioning her own story, and therefore her own identity, by adapting, editing, and recomposing the narratives she has heard throughout a lifetime.[68]

Finally, Jo's artistic and personal development reveals that writing, like dressing, can be both false and idolatrous. But then, as Amy's aesthetic development also reveals, dressing, like writing, can be both moral and creative. The text subtly blurs the line between production and consumption. It suggests that as long as shoppers respect the semiotic gap between inner self and outer dress, they may safely enter stores in quest of fitting symbols. Like the elect amassing wealth not to aggrandize themselves but to make God's kingdom visible, moral shoppers acquire goods not to construct false personae or to proclaim their own superiority but to make visible those admirable inner qualities that could not otherwise be articulated. Their choices are made in the free spirit of creative self-expression. It is, I believe, Alcott's faith in this creative consumerism that partially accounts for the deep, continuing appeal of the novel. While *Little Women* speaks eloquently to young girls of the dangers of vanity fair, it also suggests how they may avoid its temptations without forsaking its pleasures.

Thus, as Jo moves from the fashionable constructions of the marketplace to the authentic, sincere style of home, she writes the first book of *Little Women*, the story we have just read. With its recasting of *Pilgrim's Progress*, her narrative becomes another version of that supposedly universal plot. In distributing those original Christmas books, Marmee selected the differently colored covers, but the narrator withheld their common title. She identified it only as "the story of the best life ever lived," a sly move, anticipating that the book she was narrating would take its place: mothers would soon be placing *Little Women*, not *Pilgrim's Progress*, under their daughters' pillows. Their purchase of *Little Women* would seem itself a moral act — a sign of enlightened taste — and their daughters' reading of it would be a rehearsal of the development it describes. In the book's narrator, girls would discover their own portable Marmee; in the three sisters, their choice of pilgrims with whom to identify; in the martyred Beth, a redeemer who shared their age and gender. Hence the significance of the book with different covers but no name: it is every girl's story, wrapped in the colors of her own character and consumer choice.

The final chapter of *Little Women* is "Harvest Time," set five years after Jo's marriage to Fritz Bhaer. Jo has inherited a mansion, Plumfield, from her Aunt March and, with her husband, transformed it into a progressive school for boys, loosely modeled on Bronson Alcott's own ill-fated Temple School. Its experimental quality is also signaled in its name, which echoes the utopian Fruitlands. The novel's last scenes take place in the school's orchards on the occasion of the apple harvest and Mrs. March's sixtieth birthday. All three surviving daughters are present, each with her spouse and progeny. Jo has her two sons; Meg her twins, Daisy and Demi; and Amy, her daughter, Beth. In many ways these passages are designed to bring the book full circle; in a kind of reproductive cycle, they recall the opening gift-giving scenes, but now it is the sisters' own children who are presenting Mrs. March, the "queen of the day with various gifts, so numerous that they were transported to the festive scene in a wheelbarrow" (599). With the significant exception of Amy's child, each offers something handmade: "Funny presents, some of them, but what would have been defects to other eyes were ornaments to grandma's — for the children's gifts were all their own." To complete this vision of exchange outside the commodity system, "the Professor suddenly began to sing. Then, from above him, voice after voice took up the words, and from tree to tree echoed the music of the unseen choir, as the boys sung, with all their hearts, the little song Jo had written, Laurie set to music, and the Professor trained his lads to give with the best effect" (600).

Finally, the mother and her daughters are alone "under the festival tree." Jo is first to speak: "I don't think I ought ever to call myself 'unlucky Jo' again, when my greatest wish has been so beautifully satisfied" (as she fishes her littlest son's hand out of the milk jug). When Amy reminds her of how different their lives are from the ones they had pictured in their youthful "castles in the air," Jo replies, "Yes, I remember; but the life I wanted then seems selfish, lonely, and cold to me now. I haven't given up the hope that I may write a good book yet, but I can wait, and I'm sure it will be all the better for such experiences, and illustrations as these," whereupon she gestures toward her mother, "sitting enthroned among her daughters, with their children in her lap and at her feet, as if all found help and happiness in the face which could never grow old to them" (601). Next, Meg reflects, "My castle was the most nearly realized of all. I asked for splendid things, to be sure, but in my heart I knew I should be satisfied, if I had a little home, and John, and some dear children like these. I've got them all, thank God, and am the happiest woman in the world;' and Meg laid her hand on her tall boy's head, with a face full of tender and devout content" (601).

And, lastly, Amy: "My castle is very different from what I planned, but I would not alter it, though, like Jo, I don't relinquish all my artistic hopes, or confine myself to helping others fulfill their dreams of beauty. I've begun to model a figure of baby, and Laurie says it is the best thing I've ever done. I think so myself, and mean to do it in marble, so that whatever happens, I may at least keep the image of my little angel" (601). As the narrator explains, "her one well-beloved daughter was a frail little creature, and the dread of losing her was the shadow over Amy's sunshine." And yet, "this cross was doing much for mother and father, for one love and sorrow bound them closely together. Amy's nature was sweeter, deeper and more tender; Laurie was growing more serious, strong and firm, and both were learning that beauty, youth, good fortune, even love itself, cannot keep care and pain, loss and sorrow, from the most blest." When Marmee advises her not to despair, Amy replies, "I never ought to, while I have you to cheer me up, Marmee, and Laurie to take more than half of every burden. . . . In spite of my one cross, I can say with Meg, 'Thank God, I'm a happy woman'" (602).

Despite the "unromantic" facts that her husband is turning gray and stout, they will never be rich, and she herself is growing "thin as a shadow, and am over thirty," Jo concludes that she has "nothing to complain of, and was never so jolly in my life." When Mrs. March remarks, "Yes, Jo, I think your harvest will be a good one," Jo impetuously replies, "Not half so good as yours, Mother. Here it is, and we never can thank you enough for the patient sowing and reaping you have done." Amy joins in, "I hope there will be more wheat and fewer tares every year," and Meg adds, "A large sheaf, but I know there's room in your heart for it, Marmee dear." At this, "touched to the heart, Mrs. March could only stretch out her arms, as if to gather children and grandchildren to herself, and say, with face and voice full of motherly love, gratitude, and humility, — 'Oh, my girls, however long you may live, I never can wish you a greater happiness than this!'" And so, one of the most popular novels ever published ends.

The theme, unrelentingly stressed, is the achievement of happiness, and not only happiness but a kind of ultimate satiation. The fulfillment of the sisters' dreams is paralleled with the gathering of the harvest, a moment of ultimate ripeness that overflows ecstatically like Abraham Maslow's vision of a peak experience at the top of the pyramid of self-realization.[69] This moment's realization, a secular version of the Puritan saint's grace and true virtue, depends upon Marmee's wise guidance of each girl through vanity fair toward her own celestial city, a castle in the air finally grounded in family love. In the process, those castles have been transformed; each girl's vision of future happiness and identity has shifted to make this coincidence of dream and reality possible. This vision is Alcott's solution to what many theorists of modern consumer culture have seen as its central problem and puzzle: consumer insatiability. To return to Colin Campbell, the daydreaming and pleasure-seeking characteristic of modern "self-illusory hedonism" follow a course in which consumers attach their dreams of pleasure to objects they imagine gaining in some vague future. Once obtained, however, those objects provide not satiation or fulfillment but disillusionment. Unlike Alcott, however, Campbell argues that no change of object can alter this course, for no real object or experience can ever match the perfection we can imagine. For human beings, the greatest pleasure lies in anticipation, not acquisition, and unsatisfied desire is the modern hedonist's chronic condition.[70]

Campbell's rueful vision is shared by many twentieth-century writers. For example, in *Sister Carrie*, Theodore Dreiser vividly describes his heroine's consumer dreams: "She wanted pleasure, she wanted position, and yet she was confused as to what these things might be. Every hour the kaleidoscope of human affairs threw a new lustre upon something, and therewith it become for her the desired — the all. Another shift of the box and lo, some other had become the beautiful, the perfect."[71] Carrie in her rocking chair "longed and longed and longed. It was now the old cottage room in Columbia City, now the mansion up on the Shore drive, now the fine dress of some lady, now the elegance of some scene. She was sad beyond measure and yet uncertain, wishing and fancying."[72] However, Dreiser, like Campbell, believes that reality can never outstrip the human capacity to dream, for as Carrie "hummed and hummed" in her rocking chair, she was "therein as happy, though she could not perceive it, as ever she would be." He closes with this paradox: "Carrie! Oh Carrie! Ever whole in that thou art ever hopeful, know that the light is but now in these his eyes. Tomorrow it shall be melted and dissolved. Tomorrow it shall be on and further on, still leading, still alluring, until thought is not with you and heartaches are no more."[73]

Another classic novel of consumer desire closes with a similar image. The final lines of F. Scott Fitzgerald's *The Great Gatsby* evoke its hero's "infinite capacity for hope" and his bruising, ultimately fatal, collision with the material world, a world that, once his dream has shattered, seems merely disillusioned dust, "material without being real."[74] Gatsby, Fitzgerald writes, "believed in the green light, the orgastic future that year by year recedes before us. It eluded us then, but that's no matter — tomorrow we will run faster, stretch out our arms farther. . . . And one fine morning — So we beat on, boats against the current, borne back ceaselessly into the past." In the novel's powerful final vision, its narrator Nick Carraway evokes the "fresh, green breast of the new world" whose "vanished trees . . . had once pandered in whispers to the last and greatest of all human dreams."[75] Louisa May Alcott's novel resists this modernist, even postmodernist current. Here the "fresh green breast" of the material world offers real nourishment. Her trees do not pander to ultimately insubstantial dreams, but lift her characters aloft like "featherless birds" to sing their unique song. Their gifts, overflowing the wheelbarrow, are as much a part of nature as the apples they replace. Moreover these gifts are pointedly not perfect, as the lives that they express are not perfect, and yet Meg, Jo, and Amy have been educated to appreciate the sweetness of a material reality animated by love, despite its mortality and inevitable flaws. In Arthur Miller's *Death of a Salesman*, yet another twentieth-century treatment of consumer desire, Biff Loman laments his father's failure and suicide at the play's conclusion, a conclusion virtually the polar opposite of Alcott's triumphant saga of successful parenting. Willy, Biff says, "had the wrong dreams. All, all, wrong."[76] Marmee has taught her daughters to dream the right dreams, and now they have come true.

According to *Little Women*'s deeply sentimental and significantly antimodernist vision, love of home and family is like the Puritan's love of God, a center to which all refers, a source which generates material signs, but is not generated by them. Unlike the simulacrum described by Baudrillard or the insubstantial spectacle analyzed by Guy Debord, this object of desire delivers on its promise of ultimate happiness.[77] The novel's utopian premise is that longing for the future will be foreclosed by perfect satisfaction in the present. A liberal Protestant solution to the insatiability of consumer capitalism, it attempts to control materialistic behavior through education within the private sphere. Moreover, it extends this vision of moral consumerism to a vision of larger social reform. Reminiscent of *A Christmas Carol* by Charles Dickens, a writer Alcott emulated all her life, *Little Women* portrays a voluntary movement of social action, a "trickle down" benevolence powered by rings of influence moving outward from men and women of good will.[78] These rings of influence form a kind of secularized providential system. When the March girls give up their Christmas buckwheats to the starving Hummels, their wealthy neighbor, Mr. Laurence, is moved by their example to send them a Christmas supper much more sumptuous than the breakfast they sacrificed. When Meg gives up her violet silk to buy her husband a much-needed winter coat, she is rewarded a paragraph later with a happy marriage and twin babies. Amy gives up Fred Vaughan and her mercenary ambition, then is rewarded with Laurie, who may not be as rich as Fred, but is certainly rich enough and much more charming. Jo gives up sensation thrillers and is rewarded by the rebirth of her talent and genuine success. And while the death of their sister might suggest that true morality is not always rewarded, the text reassures readers that, as Jo believes, the saintly Beth is now "well in heaven." Although the miracle of crisis conversion no longer stabilizes moral identity, the promise of an eternal afterlife and divine justice still underpins the novel's optimism and faith in the ultimate utility of moral behavior.

In Alcott's final chapter we see this vision of voluntary benevolence and its expanding rings of social influence in the founding of the Plumfield School. The taste for charitable deeds prompts Amy and Laurie to contribute some of their capital to the project. Even Aunt March's legacy shows the influence of others' good deeds. Having once deprived the antisocial Jo of a trip to Europe, she rewards her newly docile niece with a mansion in which to house her school and marriage. The school itself serves as a kind of "city on a hill," a model community centered on the principles taught by the March family. While the bulk of students are boys from wealthier families, their tuition subsidizes the rescue of poorer boys, damaged by their experience in the wider world. At Plumfield rich and poor together will receive the nurture that guided the moral development of the March sisters themselves.

Family love can apparently cure virtually everything, not only restlessness and insatiable desire, but also the evils of acquisitive and capitalist society. Like Harriet Beecher Stowe, who told readers of *Uncle Tom's Cabin* anxious to end slavery that they should begin by "feeling right," Alcott bypasses more systemic solutions to the social problems of modernity to advocate internal changes of heart, moral education, and a "thousand points of light." One problem with this vision of private reform is, of course, its very emphasis on family and consequent neglect of larger social structures responsible for conditions of inequality and injustice. In fact, her critic and biographer Charles Strickland acknowledges that Alcott was herself surprisingly unsympathetic to the welfare of the "undeserving poor." Her focus on parental, particularly maternal, responsibility can be linked to popular bouts of nineteenth-century mother-blaming and lack of careful attention to other, perhaps more intractable, factors for immoral and materialistic behavior.[79]

A second problem with Alcott's visionary solution is that it naturalizes the "good taste" of established social groups as a sign of their moral superiority. That is, Alcott's reassuring conclusions are founded on a belief that the March sisters' mature taste reliably represents their true natures. However, if consumer taste unconsciously consolidates class identifications and shores up class interests, as Pierre Bourdieu argues in his study *Distinction*, then *Little Women* can also be seen as a strikingly successful attempt to figure the socially constructed taste of white middle-class New England Protestants as the heroic achievement of the authentic and the morally mature.[80] The styles privileged here were not uncoincidentally recognized as the proper heritage of New England's old moneyed families, families such as that of the fictional Mrs. March and real-life Abby Alcott.[81] The neoclassical outlines of Amy's dress suggest the Colonial revival mansions still dotting exclusive New England townships, and Meg's demure wedding clothes recall Boston Brahmin fondness for the "chaste" and functional forms of Quaker meeting houses and Shaker furniture. By linking their consumer tastes to their moral authority, the novel reaffirms the cultural prestige of a group anxious about being elbowed aside by new money and new citizens.

However, as liberal Protestants like the Alcotts moved from the stricter, more orthodox practices of Calvinism — away from crisis conversion toward the developmental model of Christian nurture, away from the disciplinary rationality of early capitalism toward the modern hedonism of its later forms — their own practices brought them uncomfortably close to the "others" they feared. For example, the Alcotts' Orchard House parlor, like the parlor of many middle-class Protestant Victorian homes, included the reproduction of a Raphael Madonna and child.[82] In the novel the young Amy is advised by her aunt's French Catholic maid to set up a similar reproduction for contemplation and comfort while her mother is away. When Marmee hears of this she does not disapprove; Amy was not worshipping Mary in the Catholic manner, but merely "remembering" her mother through the idealized figure of the Madonna. And yet, the problem and the presence of the painting suggest the tension that was held at bay. Within each of these Protestant girls lies the bud of a Catholic, and it is only a mother's careful nurture that prevents its flowering. *Little Women* asserts the superiority of the Marches' gentility, a word closely aligned in this case with *gentile*. Their distinction sets the standard against which all other pretenders to respectability could be measured: a taste test that presumed to separate the idolatrous social climbers from the true moral elite. The novel can be seen as another contributor to the nineteenth-century project of constructing a national identity, although in this case religious and ethnic oppositions shape the imagined struggle to sustain the nation's purity in the face of changes wrought by urbanization, immigration, and an emerging capitalist consumer culture.

And yet it is worth noting this 1879 *Boston Daily Advertiser* description of Alcott at a literary reading: "In dress and appearance she was the typical showwoman. She wore a short, green-stuff gown with a narrow, ruffle around it, pink stockings, laced slippers, a red shawl worn mantle-wise, a collar almost wide enough to be a cape, and a bonnet which was enough to throw a modern milliner into convulsions. It was of green silk lined with pink, a feather stood assertively upright, and [nodded] emphasis to all her words."[83] This theatrical image of the author's own highly eccentric taste underscores a crucial irony. Jo's "sincere" book is, we are led to imagine, the first half of *Little Women* itself; however, a look at Alcott's own biography reveals that the book's conditions of production were far different from those it portrays. In a journal entry for May 1968, Alcott describes how the publisher Thomas Niles had approached her with a request for a "girls' story." Her mother and sisters approved the plan to go ahead, and so, Alcott writes, "I plod away, though I don't enjoy this sort of thing. Never liked girls or knew many, except my sisters; but our queer plays and experiences may prove interesting, though I doubt it."[84] When readers of part 1, published separately, clamored to have Jo married off to Laurie, Alcott initially resisted — she preferred her heroine as a happy spinster — but she finally capitulated in part 2 by pairing Jo off with Fritz Bhaer, a middle-aged figure she purposely set at odds with readers' romantic expectations.

The spectacular success of the story (the first edition sold out almost immediately, and three thousand copies were sold between publication in October and the new year) and the pressing financial needs of her family motivated Alcott to produce more of the same. But, after manufacturing a string of similar books, she openly expressed her resistance in a July 1884 letter to Thomas Niles about *Jo's Boys*, the anticipated third novel dealing with the March family: "I wish I was inspired to those dreadful boys; but rest is more needed than money. Perhaps during August, my month at home, I may take a grind at the old mill."[85] Her exhaustion shows in the novel. Jo is now not only headmistress of Plumfield but also a celebrity author who, like Alcott herself, is constantly harassed by inconsiderate fans. She has become, she complains, merely "a literary nursemaid" producing "moral pap" for the young. In the conclusion the narrator confesses that "it is a strong temptation to the weary historian to close the present tale with an earthquake which should engulf Plumfield and its environs so deeply in the bowels of the earth that no youthful Schliemann could ever find a vestige of it." Then, apparently recalling her literary duty, she hastily adds, "But as that somewhat melodramatic conclusion might shock my gentle readers, I will refrain, and forestall the usual question, 'How did they end?' by briefly stating that all the marriages turned out well. The boys prospered in their various callings; so did the girls."[86]

Little Women, like the sister novels that followed, was not a spontaneous expression of domestic sentiment, but a commercial product written to order, and reluctantly at that. It was less the outpouring of an Emersonian poet than the construction of a Poe-esque jingle woman, who carefully crafted its tidy plot to market specifications and delivered it on time for the Christmas selling season. Moreover, its author was not only bored by its unrelentingly earnest narrative, but preferred the supposedly artificial gothics written earlier in her career. In an interview, she once confessed, "I think my natural ambition is for the lurid style. I indulge in gorgeous fancies and wish that I dared inscribe them upon my pages and set them before the public." But then, she reflected, "How should I dare interfere with the proper grayness of old Concord? The dear old town has never known a startling hue since the redcoats were there. Far be it from me to inject an inharmonious color into the neutral tint." As for her favorite "sensational" characters, "suppose they went cavorting at their own sweet will, to the infinite horror of dead Mr. Emerson, who never imagined a Concord person but as walking a plumb line stretched between two pearly clouds in the empyrean." Her self-analysis concluded on a despairing note, "To have had Mr. Emerson for an intellectual god all one's life is to be invested with a chain armor of propriety. . . . And what would my own good father think of me . . . if I set folks to doing the things that I have been longing to see my people do? No, my dear, I shall always be a wretched victim to the respectable traditions of Concord."[87]

Alcott's comments suggest that, although apparently as sincere as Meg's wedding gown, *Little Women* was yet another socially constructed costume worn to please and appease. Further, as critics have noted, those shocking potboilers that Alcott published pseudonymously allowed their author to release the desires and aggressions her idealistic upbringing and respectable image forced her to repress. Her evocation of Emerson's benevolent myopia and her father's looming disapproval are telling. Bronson Alcott, for example, often figured his tempestuous daughter through the very "Catholic" traits that *Little Women* eschewed: as dark, passionate, and theatrical, even in one instance, demonic.[88] Louisa's struggles to discipline these traits and earn her parents' approval were poignantly recorded in her childhood journals and continued throughout her life. Although the traditions of Concord, with its neutral tints and Protestant plain-living, forced her to sacrifice the sensational writing that thrilled her, in retrospect, we can see how the brilliant fashions of her gothic villainesses, like the "assertive feather" of her outrageous bonnet, displayed qualities within this "show-woman" that otherwise would have remained invisible, even unspeakable. While *Little Women* offers us a comforting assertion of stable identity, Alcott's own history suggests that there is no single mirror in which to read its mercurial author, no reliable representation, only multiple and even contradictory performances driven by competing discourses and desires.

Finally, despite *Little Women*'s compelling assertions of realism, the relationship between this novel and the women on whom it was based is deeply ironic. Elizabeth, the model for Beth, did die at young age from scarlet fever, contracted from an immigrant family Mrs. Alcott had helped. However, while Anna Alcott, the model for Meg, married her unassuming young man, he died at the age of thirty-seven, leaving his wife with two little boys to raise alone. May, the model for Amy, went to Europe to study art, with her literary sister's financial blessing, and there found love with a young Swiss, Ernest Nieriker. However, her story ended in tragedy, not wealth and wedded bliss; she died from complications following childbirth in 1879, after barely a year of marriage. Her infant daughter was sent home to be raised by Louisa, who took on yet another familial responsibility, in addition to her nephews and aging parents. As for a comparison of Louisa with Jo, the blissfully replete matriarch of Plumfield, Alcott herself consciously chose not to marry, and seems, from letters and journals, happiest when she could escape from her Concord home to a hotel in Boston, a city in whose cosmopolitanism, theatricality, and anonymity she reveled. In the end, this example of "duty's faithful child," who fed and clothed her family and sent her sister to Europe, was rewarded for her voluntary sacrifice and hunger with a literary celebrity that constantly plagued her and an intestinal cancer that fatally weakened her.

And yet, while Alcott's own history undercuts *Little Women*'s realism and its representation of authentic, integrated identity, this very impurity fuels the novel's fascination for contemporary critics, who in a postmodernist age relish rather than reject its contradictions. Similarly its ironic way of moralizing consumption while simultaneously moralizing *about* consumption may actually contribute to its continuing popularity, for, as Jean Baudrillard notes, "Just as medieval society was balanced on God *and* the Devil, so ours is balanced on consumption and its denunciation."[89] Lastly, we might also agree with Alcott herself that, by directing young readers to fit their futures to middle-class expectations, *Little Women* is merely "moral pap," the literary equivalent of the porridge Marmee serves her daughters on Christmas day. But by promising that such domesticity could satisfy her readers' deepest desires, Alcott sugar-coated this moral pill with middle-class culture's sweetest dream: a seductive vision of marriage and reproduction that she herself deliberately resisted. Whether the final literary product is a yet another "poisoned sugarplum," even more insidious than the gothic thrillers Professor Bhaer condemned, is a question that still inspires lively debate. In fact, the only thing *not* in question about this text may be its enduring appeal. Reproduced in innumerable editions, its female pilgrims displayed in coloring books and doll catalogs, *Little Women* has itself become an important sacrament of modern consumer culture, a much-desired "sign of happiness," however elusive such happiness might be.

CHAPTER 2

Lily Bart and the
Pursuit of Happiness

Edith Wharton, who noted that she read the "great Louisa" as a child, often asserted her break from the domestic women's tradition that Alcott represented.[1] However, Wharton's 1905 bestseller, *The House of Mirth*,[2] nonetheless reveals a hidden affiliation with *Little Women*, one with its origins in Wharton's disavowed identification with the earlier novel's characters as well as her preoccupation with its thematic concerns. Like Alcott, Wharton seems to frame her heroine Lily Bart's developmental story with a concern for Protestant authenticity, Anglo-American purity, and the moral development of national womanhood. In fact, as critic Carol Singley points out, *The House of Mirth* also refers explicitly to *Pilgrim's Progress*, filtered through Nathaniel Hawthorne's nineteenth-century parody of modern materialism, "The Celestial Rail-Road."[3] While I agree with Singley's analysis of the link between the novel and Bunyan's religious parable, I would argue that *Little Women*, which was explicitly modeled on *Pilgrim's Progress*, is an equally plausible, and more immediate, source for *The House of Mirth*, especially since Alcott adapted the Christian hero's religious quest so skillfully to the moral terrain encountered by nineteenth-century female readers. Yet while *Little Women* was a parable designed to guide young readers past the temptations of vanity fair through successful courtship to their ultimate happiness as middle-class wives, Wharton's very adult version of a similar quest is the story of Lily Bart's failure to negotiate that same moral terrain. Through Lily's doomed struggle with materialistic desires, Wharton critiques the very attitudes the March family feared: status seeking, conspicuous consumption, and the mistaking of consumer goods for the emotional and spiritual qualities they signify. If *Little Women* gives us the successful nurture of the March sisters and their ultimate realization of their dreams of Protestant womanhood, *The House of Mirth* gives us a parable of failed parenting and a cautionary tale of idolatrous materialism and its consequences. Ultimately, there is no happy ending for Lily Bart.

However, *Little Women* is not simply a novel about materialism, as chapter 1 demonstrated. It is also a novel about the development of individual identity and moral awareness within a materialistic society. And this makes its intertextual relationship to Wharton's best-selling novel especially revealing. Reading *The House of Mirth* against *Little Women* lets us see the various discursive strands that form the figure in the later novel's carpet. Moreover, tracing each strand's contribution to the pattern allows a fuller, more complex portrait of Lily Bart to emerge. Critics drawing on individual discursive strands — sentimentalism, commodification, antisemitism — have been highly successful in identifying particular versions of Lily, but as Wharton reveals in the novel's central *tableau vivant*, Lily is quite capable of inviting multiple and even contradictory interpretations, largely, this study argues, because she herself is multiple and riven by contradictions. While *Little Women* shows us young women who appear triumphant in their final achievement of an integrated self, as evidenced by their happy marriages, *The House of Mirth* shows us Lily's failure, a failure that I will argue is precipitated by her failure to achieve a similar integration, as well as by her society's failure to support her in that effort. As Wharton famously wrote about her conception of the novel, "In what aspect could a society of irresponsible pleasure-speakers be said to have, on the 'old woe of the world,' any deeper bearing than the people composing such a society would guess? The answer was a frivolous society can acquire dramatic significance only through what its frivolity destroys. Its tragic implication lies in its power of debasing people and ideals. The answer, in short, was my heroine, Lily Bart."[4] Analyzing that debasement of people and ideals, along with the conflicting discursive strands woven into Lily Bart's character, reveals both the complexity of Wharton's central figure and its larger significance. But first, a quick look at the novel's historical context and biographical background.

Like *Little Women*, *The House of Mirth* has some strong biographical roots.[5] However, the old New York into which Edith Newbold Jones was born in 1862 was a very different place from the Transcendental and bohemian New England that Louisa May Alcott knew. In her memoirs, both published and unpublished, Wharton emphatically distinguished the society in which she grew up from the Puritan-influenced world of Boston and Concord. She herself was, she said, too fashionable for Boston and too intellectual for New York, which suggests that the more relaxed, pleasure-loving Anglican community of wealthy New Yorkers lacked the moral rigor and intellectual emphasis that characterized the world in which Louisa May Alcott grew up. As Wharton explained in her memoir *A Backward Glance*, "Milder manners, a greater love of ease, and a franker interest in money-making and good food, certainly distinguished the colonial New Yorkers from the conscience-searching children of the 'Mayflower.'"[6] The benefit of this particular religious background, Wharton believed, was the Episcopalian emphasis on ritual and the Book of Common Prayer: "May not the matchless beauty of an ancient rite have protected our ancestors from what Huxley called the 'fissiparous tendency of the Protestant sects,' sparing them sanguinary wrangles over uncomprehended points of doctrine, and all those extravagances of self-constituted prophets and evangelists which rent and harrowed New England?"[7] Of her own family's attitudes, she wrote in her memoir "Life & I," a never-completed work that remained unpublished until 1990: "The Christian sense of an abstract law of conduct, of any religious counsel of perfection, was completely absent from their talk, & probably from their consciousness. My mother's rule of behavior was that we should be 'polite'—my father's that one should be kind. Ill breeding—any departure from the social rules of conduct—was the only form of wrong-doing I can remember being condemned."[8] The residual traces of Puritan worldly asceticism can be seen only in the family's dictum, "Never talk about money, and think about it as little as possible," a rule that seems to assume elect status as a matter of course.[9] As illustrated in her 1920 novel *The Age of Innocence*, Protestantism in old New York had become more a set of traditions and social rituals, an opportunity for displays of class and taste, than a crucible of moral and religious development.[10]

While Wharton grew up among New York's elite, its members were never, she hastened to point out, truly "aristocratic" in the European sense of the world. Her ancestors were bankers, lawyers, and merchants (although later generations excluded as a matter of course anyone involved in retail trade from highest levels of society). And yet, as Carol Singley explains, "over time, these enterprising bourgeois colonials and their republican descendants transformed themselves into a social aristocracy—financially comfortable, insular, and static."[11] By the turn of the century, however, this "insular" society was changing radically. The Gilded Age of the post–Civil War period brought the immensely wealthy robber barons to the city: Vanderbilts, Rockefellers, and Carnegies. Waves of immigrants poured into New York in the late nineteenth and early twentieth centuries and eventually established their own enclaves: the Lower East Side, Little Italy, and Chinatown. The Vanderbilts and others like them desperately wanted to enter old New York's closed society, but soon the newer ambitious entrepreneurs established their own social circles, disregarding the traditions and values of Wharton's ancestors. While elite New York ladies at the turn of the century still ordered their dresses from Paris, or had them sewn by seamstresses with French names, the burgeoning consumer culture that was transforming the rest of the nation was turning the rapidly growing city into a center for shopping and display. The "Ladies' Mile," twenty-eight blocks between 18th and 24th Streets, was home to gigantic, visually compelling stores such as Lord & Taylor, B. Altman, Arnold Constable, Best & Co., W. J. Sloane, and Bergdorf Goodman. Broadway and Fifth Avenue, so often painted by the American impressionist Childe Hassam, became showcases for parades of fashionable women. In a parallel development, the world of publishing shifted its center from Boston to New York, a move heralded by William Dean Howells's move from *The Atlantic Monthly* to *Cosmopolitan* in 1891. The proliferation of illustrated newspapers and magazines, filled with advertisements, created a new culture of publicity and celebrity very different from the 1870s society Wharton depicted in *The Age in Innocence*, in which one upper-class mother, planning her daughter's bridal procession outside a Manhattan church, worries that journalists "might take a photograph of my child *and put in the papers!*"[12]

Edith Jones entered this world as the third child of George Frederic Jones and Lucretia Rhinelander Jones; her two brothers being much older, she was raised virtually as an only child. Despite a relatively brief financial struggle when she was a girl, a time during which her family moved to Europe to economize, Edith's family was well-off. Wharton describes herself as a precocious and sensitive child, highly self-conscious and often shy. Although she could recall no pressure from her parents to adhere to any strict and punitive moral code, especially given their rather easy attitude about religious observances in general, Wharton recalls an early period of intense moral self-scrutiny, manifested in a strict, "Puritan" conscience that convicted her of the slightest attempt at falsity. A particularly traumatic incident occurred when the family was in Europe. Young Edith, who had an unconquerable aversion to any kind of "ugliness," commented to a fellow dancing-school student that the instructor's mother looked like an "old goat." Immediately stricken with remorse, she confessed her fault to the instructor only to be met with a cold reception; at which point, she went to her mother, whose response was, if anything, even colder and much the opposite of reassuring: "Nothing I have suffered since has equally the darkness of horror that weighed on my childhood in respect to this vexed problem of truth-telling, & the impossibility of reconciling 'God's standard of truthfulness' with the conventional obligation to be 'polite' & not hurt any one's feelings." Although Wharton absolved her parents of inculcating this kind of self-scrutiny, "It is difficult to imagine how the sternest Presbyterian training could have produced different or more depressing results. I was indeed 'God-intoxicated', in the medical sense of the word." And so, "between these conflicting rules of conduct I suffered an untold anguish of perplexity & suffered alone, as imaginative children generally do, without daring to tell any one of my trouble, because I vaguely felt that I *ought* to know what was right, & that it was probably 'naughty' not to." Most important for the young Edith's psychological development, including her intense sense of moral obligation and anxiety, was Lucretia Jones's unsympathetic response to her daughter's anxious questions, "At any rate, for years afterward I was never free from the oppressive sense that I had two absolutely inscrutable beings to please — God & my mother — who, while ostensibly upholding the same principles of behavior, differed totally as to their application. And my mother was the most inscrutable of the two."[13]

In "Life & I" Wharton comments: "Happily I had two means of escape from this chronic moral malady. One was provided by my love of pretty things — pretty clothes, pretty pictures, pretty sights — & the other by my learning to read."[14] Her love of beauty, especially beautiful clothing, houses, and gardens, remained with her all her life and resulted in her design and decoration of several extraordinary houses and gardens, accompanied by books such as her first full-length publication, with Ogden Codman, *The Decoration of Houses* (1897). It also influenced her great sensitivity to aesthetic style and language, a sensitivity also encouraged by her family's strict policing of English usage by their children and their monitoring of Edith's reading, which she began, virtually self-taught, at a very young age.[15] While neither of her parents was by any means intellectual, they were educated according to the fashion of their class and time: "My mother read nothing but novels & books on horticulture; my father read sermons, & narratives of Arctic exploration. But at that time every gentleman, whether he was a reader or not, possessed what was known as 'a gentleman's library'; that is, a fair collection of the 'standard' works in French & English."[16] Despite her young age, Edith was given free access to the library shelves: "my mother's rule being that I must never read a novel without asking permission, but that 'poetry & history' (her rough classification of the rest of literature) could do no harm." Wharton adds that "having been thus put on my honour, I never once failed to observe the compact, & never read a novel without asking leave until the day of my marriage."[17] This library, lovingly described in her memoirs, would prove a safe refuge and source of solace for her, one she would reproduce in several of her novels as a similar refuge for her male characters.

Most importantly, the books she found there provided the guidance she found lacking in her inscrutable mother. For example, she recalls her excitement on reading Coleridge's "Friend":

Let no one ask me why! I can only suppose it answered to some hidden need to order my thoughts, & get things into some kind of logical relation to reach other: a need which developed in me almost as early as the desire to be kissed & thought pretty! It originated, perhaps, in the sense that weighed on my whole childhood — the sense of bewilderment, of the need of guidance, the longing to understand *what it was all about*. My little corner of the cosmos seemed like a dark trackless region "where ignorant armies clash by night", & and I was oppressed by the sense that I was too small & ignorant & alone ever to find my way about in it.[18]

Similarly, after finding an abridged edition of William Hamilton's *History of Philosophy*, she was deeply reassured: "Oh, thrice-blest discovery! Now I was going to know all about life! Now I should never be that helpless blundering things, a nice 'little girl' again! The two little black cloth volumes, with their yellow paper & small black type, were more precious to me than anything I possessed."[19]

The other solace Wharton found as a child sprang naturally from her reading: "But meanwhile I had found a new refuge from the outward miseries — I had begun to write! My earliest efforts date from my tenth year, & are in the form of poems and stories."[20] While there is no space to discuss these early writings in any detail here, it is worth noting one of her very first publications was a poem about the suicide of a young boy put in solitary confinement. His loneliness and despair lead to his death.[21] Her other early writing included sermons (she later wrote that she might have made a powerful preacher), influenced in part by her father's collection and by her childish romantic interest in the minister of the First Calvary Church, which she attended with her father not only once but twice on Sundays: "The service was 'low,' the music indifferent, and the fuliginous chancel window of the Crucifixion a horror to alienate any imaginative mind from all Episcopal forms of ritual; but the Rector, the Reverend Dr. Washburn, was a man of great learning, and possessed of a singularly beautiful voice — and I fear it was chiefly to hear Dr. Washburn read the Evening Lessons that my father and I were so regular in our devotions."[22] Although Wharton later turned away from her young "God-intoxication," becoming much more secular in her beliefs (until an interest in Catholicism at the end of her life), R. W. B. Lewis notes that as an adult she had more books devoted to religion than to any other subject.[23]

What then of "the great Louisa"? In *A Backward Glance* Wharton writes, "my mother, herself so little of a reader, was exaggeratedly scrupulous about the books I read; not so much about the 'grown-up' books as those written for children. I was never allowed to read the popular American children's books of my day because, as mother said, the children spoke bad English *without the author's knowing it.*"[24] Nevertheless, "I remember it was only with reluctance, and because 'all the other children read them' that my mother consented to my reading 'Little Women' and 'Little Men' and my ears, trained to the fresh racy English of 'Alice in Wonder-land,' 'The Water Babies' and 'The Princess and the Goblin', were exasperated by the laxities of the great Louisa."[25] Clearly Wharton read Alcott, but just as clearly, she wished when older to disavow any influence from the book or identification with its characters. She does not recall this immensely popular book with the reverence she held for Coleridge or the *History of Philosophy*, books which validated her mature intellectual tastes. However, if we look more closely at Wharton's family background as described in her memoirs, an important connection to Alcott's *Little Women* appears. It begins with the history of Wharton's mother, Lucretia Rhinelander.

Like the March sisters, the four Rhinelander sisters, including the eldest, Lucretia, were born into a family whose father was missing: the March girls because their father was off serving as a chaplain in the Union Army, the Rhinelander daughters because he had died young, at the age of thirty, leaving them comparatively poor, in a state of "shabby gentility" similar to that of the real-life Alcotts. As Wharton explains, "his young widow and her children continued to live at the country place at Hell Gate, lived there, in fact, from motives of economy, in winter as well as summer while the children were young; for my grandmother, whose property was left to the management of her husband's eldest brother, remained poor though her brother-in-law grew rich." Although "the little girls were taught needle-work, music, drawing, and 'the languages' (their Italian teacher was Professor Foresti, a distinguished fugitive from the Austrian political prison)," their clothing left something to be desired: "In winter their 'best dresses' were low-necked and short-sleeved frocks, of pea-green merino, with gray beaver hats trimmed with tartan ribbons, white cotton stockings and heelless prunella slippers. When they walked in the snow hand-knitted woolen stockings were draped over this frail footgear, and woolen shawls wrapped about their poor bare shoulders." As a result they not only endured the ugly "pea-green merino," but "suffered, like all young ladies of their day, from chilblains and excruciating sick-headaches" (although Wharton also notes that they "all lived to a vigorous old age").[26]

While the economic and social parallel between the four Rhinelander sisters and the four March sisters seems significant on its own, its relevance to Wharton's sense of her mother's history is confirmed by this description of Lucretia's social debut: "When the eldest (my mother) 'came out', she wore a home-made gown of white tarlatan, looped up with red and white camellias from the green-house, and her mother's old white satin slippers; and her feet being of a different shape from grandmamma's, she suffered martyrdom, and never ceased to resent the indignity inflicted on her, and the impediment to her dancing, the more so as her younger sisters, who were prettier and probably more indulged, were given new slippers when their turn came."[27] Lucretia's "coming out" dress is virtually identical to that worn by Meg March to the party at the wealthy Moffat household in Alcott's chapter "Vanity Fair": the home-made white tarlatan, limp and out-of-fashion, decorated only with the greenhouse flowers (provided in *Little Women* by the rich neighbors, Mr. Laurence and his grandson, Laurie). The hand-me-down shoes are the final indignity that Lucretia endures, and as her daughter notes, she never ceased to resent them. In *Little Women*, Meg's similar humiliation results in her allowing herself to be dressed up in the height of French fashion by her hostess, Belle Moffat. After her evening performance in her new identity as "Daisy" March, Meg returns home to confess her discomfort and embarrassment at having betrayed the values of her family and passed for the fashionable "doll" that the Moffats had made her. Most importantly, she realizes that the Moffat family sees her as a kind of gold-digger, angling to marry the wealthy family friend, Laurie. After having been rigged up as a commodity on the nouveau riche marriage market, she returns home to the safe haven of nonmaterialistic values, patiently explicated by a forgiving and understanding mother. Later, Meg is tempted once more, and she overspends her young husband's money on fashionable clothing and accessories, culminating in her purchase of yards of expensive purple silk. When her husband, tutor to Laurie's family, confronts her, she recognizes the difficult financial burden her consumer desires have placed on him and returns her purchase, thereby ensuring a happy marriage (soon "blest" by twins).[28]

As Wharton shows, the outcome of Lucretia Rhinelander's experience of fashionable humiliation was quite different. Like Meg she married a kind and slightly bookish husband, George Frederic Jones, "a young man of twenty, handsome, simple and kind," who was "madly in love" with her. George Frederic lived a "little lower down the Sound," and his parents "thought him *too* young to marry; perhaps they had other ambitions for him; they bade him break off his attentions to Miss Rhinelander of Hell Gate." However, when his "stern papa" refused to give him a sailboat, perhaps to discourage the developing courtship, George Frederic "was not to be thwarted. He contrived to turn an oar into a mast; he stole down before dawn, his bed-quilt under his arm, rigged it to the oar in guise of a sail, and flying over the waters of the Sound hurried to his lady's feet." Just as happens at the close of the first book of *Little Women*, when the similarly young Meg and John win the approval of the March parents, "devotion at last overcame paternal opposition, and George and 'Lou' were married when they were respectively twenty-one and nineteen." Luckily, unlike John Brooke, who struggles to make a living, George Frederic Jones had a father who "was rich, and must have made his sons a generous allowance; for the young couple, after an adventurous honeymoon in Cuba (of which [George] kept a conscientious record, full of drives in *volantes* and visits to fashionable plantations) set up a house of their own in Gramercy Park, then just within the built-on limits of New York, and Mrs. George Frederick took her place among the most elegant young married women of her day."[29] Her parents' social success continued to consume them well into Edith's childhood, often, she suggests, to her own detriment, since they had little attention to spare for her: "My father and mother entertained a great deal and dined out a great deal; but in these diversions I shared only to the extent of hanging over the stair-rail to see the guests sweeping up to our drawing-room or, conversely, my mother sweeping down to her carriage, resplendent in train, aigrette, and opera cloak."[30]

But for Lucretia this social triumph was sweet. "At last," Wharton writes, "the home-made tarlatans and the inherited satin shoes were avenged, and there began a long career of hospitality at home and travels abroad."[31] However, Lucretia did not learn the lessons that make Meg and Amy March into such responsible Protestant stewards of their husbands' wealth. Wharton's memoirs are sharply critical of her mother's lifelong need to avenge that early indignity, a need that she implies ultimately took a terrible toll on her father. In her late essay, "A Little Girl's New York," she meticulously describes George Frederic's study, including "a monumental writing table, "where I imagine little writing was done except the desperate calculations over which I seem to see my poor father always bent, in the vain effort to squeeze my mother's expenditure into his narrowing income." This memory comes from a period of particular financial difficulty for the nation, and "once the unhappy consequences of the Civil War had worn off, prosperity returned to us, as it did to the great number of old New Yorkers. To New York, in especial, it came with a rush; but in the difficult years between my father must have had many anxious hours." The reason was Lucretia: "My mother was far worse than a collector—she was a born 'shopper'; and the born shopper can never resist a bargain if the object is in itself a 'good value,' no matter how little the purchaser may need it. Perhaps it was for this reason that my mother's houses were always unfinished and that, for instance, a stately conservatory, opening out of the billiard-room in our twenty-third street house, remained an empty waste, unheated and flowerless, because the money gave out with the furnishing of the billiard-room."[32]

Lucretia's consumer desire was especially focused on fashion. Wharton imagines her parents' travels in Europe shortly after their marriage, when they happened to witness, in February 1848, King Louis Philippe and Queen Marie Amélie fleeing the Tuileries in Paris. And yet, "though my mother often described this scene to me, I suspect that the study of the Paris fashions made a more vivid impression on her than the fall of monarchies. The humiliation of the pea-green merino and the maternal slippers led to a good many extravagances; among them there is the white satin bonnet trimmed with white marabout and crystal drops in which the bride made her wedding visits, and a 'capeline' of *gorge de pigeon* taffetas with a wreath of flowers in shiny brown kid, which was one of the triumphs of her Paris shopping."[33] This was the maternal atmosphere in which the young Edith was raised: "All this happened years before I was born; but the tradition of elegance was never abandoned, and when we finally returned to live in New York (in 1872), I shared the excitement caused by the annual arrival of the 'trunk from Paris', and the enchantment of seeing one resplendent dress after another shaken out of its tissue-paper." These influences inevitably provided Edith with a model to emulate. For example, she remembered vividly how, when still a small girl, "my beautiful and serious-minded Aunt Mary Newbold, asked me, with edifying interest: 'What would you like to be when you grow up?' and on my replying in all good faith, and with a dutiful air, 'The best-dressed woman in New York,' she uttered the horrified cry: 'Oh, don't say that darling!' to which I could only rejoin in wonder, 'But, Auntie, you know Mamma *is*.'"[34]

Recalling the family's move to Europe when she was four, Wharton reflects, "I believe we went because my father's income was reduced by 'bad times' (& also, probably, by bad management of his property), & he wished to economize for a time, & to let his newly-built country-house at Newport, & our town house as well." This is one of the moments when Wharton suggests that Lucretia's tastes and spending habits were especially burdensome: "I imagine that the expense of these two establishments weighed rather heavily on him, & that my mother, who was a very indolent woman — though she could be spasmodically active when anything amused her for the moment — preferred the drifting European life to the care of two houses & the obligations which my father's taste for society laid upon her when they were at home."[35] By contrast, Wharton's affection for her father shines through her memoirs; *A Backward Glance* opens with her small child's hand securely held by her father. As Hermione Lee explains, "The handsome blue-eyed father whose hand she is holding in her first memory, whose chief rule of conduct was to be kind, whose appetite for travel took her on her excited early journey to Spain while they were in Europe, and with whom, in the year before his death, she shared Ruskin-ian explorations of Italy, is presented in her autobiography as benign but ineffectual: worrying over bills, taking second place to his wife." Despite these perceived weaknesses, Lee continues, "he gave his daughter affection and he gave her her first serious form of education through his 'gentleman's library.' It was only a younger son's collection, and she implies that he had not read all that much of it himself. But by her teens she knew it by heart. . . . It is a mark of her attachment to her father and his books that so many of the titles she names in *A Backward Glance* as formative reading, remained in her library all her life."[36]

However, a darker note in Wharton's portrait of her father and his marriage emerges in her discussion of George Frederic's nascent interest in poetry: "The new Tennysonian rhythms also moved my father greatly; and I imagine there was a time when his rather rudimentary love of verse might have been developed had he had any one with whom to share it. But my mother's matter-of-factness must have shriveled up any such buds of fancy." Without his wife's sympathy and encouragement, George Frederic, according to his daughter, led a suppressed, even stunted life: "In later years I remember his reading only Macaulay, Prescott, Washington Irving, and every book of travel he could find. Arctic explorations especially absorbed him, and I have wondered since what stifled cravings had once germinated in him, and what manner of man he was really meant to be. That he was a lonely one, haunted by something always unexpressed and unattained, I am sure."[37] Hermione Lee captures the poignancy of Wharton's father's death in 1882: "George Frederic Jones died young, at sixty-one, of an illness that began in exhaustion and nervous prostration and ended with a stroke, when Edith was twenty. She remembered all her life his expression on his deathbed. There was something he wanted to say to her, and he never managed it."[38] When *The House of Mirth* appeared with such great success in 1905, Wharton wrote to a family friend, "I often think of Papa and wish he could have been here to encourage me with my work."[39]

Wharton's later portraits of men trapped in unhappy, restrictive marriages to uncongenial or even explicitly selfish women clearly draw on these deep autobiographical sources: Newland Archer in *The Age of Innocence* and Ralph Marvell in *The Custom of the Country* are two examples. However, Wharton reserved her most vitriolic criticisms of Lucretia Jones for "Life & I," the autobiographical sketch that remained unpublished until long after her death. In this essay, she reproduces dialogues with her mother in which Lucretia coldly rejects and misdirects her daughter's emotional and sexual life (and the sexual element of these conversations is probably the reason that they remained unpublished). In the first incident, following Wharton's description of how she discovered such solace in the books of her father's library, she recalls that "all the while Life, real Life, was ringing in my ears, humming in my blood, flushing my cheeks & waving in my hair—sending me messages & signals from every beautiful face & musical voice, & running over me in vague tremors when I rode my poney, or swam through the short, bright ripples of the bay, or raced & danced & tumbled with 'the boys.'"[40] By "Life" Wharton seems to mean the life of the body: its blood, its emotions, its desires and inclinations, particularly its sexual inclinations, what she would later call "the blind motions" of Lily Bart's "mating-instinct"—blind because they were, to Lily and to the young Edith, unnamed, unspoken: "And I didn't know—& if, by any chance, I came across the shadow of a reality, & asked my mother 'What does it mean?' I was always told 'You're too little to understand', or else 'It's not nice to ask about such things' . . . Once, when I was seven or eight, an older cousin had told me that babies were not found in flowers, but in people. This information had been given unsought, but as I had been told by Mamma that was 'not nice' to enquire into such matters, I had a vague sense of contamination, & went immediately to confess my involuntary offense."[41] As in the incident of the French dance instructor's mother, when Edith had gone to her mother for help, Lucretia failed to provide it: "I received a severe scolding, & was left with a penetrating sense of 'not-niceness' which effectually kept me from pursuing my investigations farther." Even more disturbingly, Wharton explains that "this was literally all I knew of the processes of generation till I had been married for several weeks—the explanation which I had meanwhile worked out for myself being that married people 'had children' because God saw the clergyman marrying them through the roof of the church!"[42] The throwaway line that this was all she knew about sexual reproduction until weeks *after* her marriage suggests just how disastrous Wharton's sexual education, to use Gloria Erlich's term, was.[43]

But there is more. Wharton goes on to describe her anguished attempt once more to elicit help and sympathy from the forbidding Lucretia: "A few days before my marriage, I was seized with such a dread of the whole dark mystery, that I summoned up courage to appeal to my mother, & begged her, with a heart beating to suffocation, to tell me 'what being married was like.' Her handsome face at once took on the look of icy disapproval which I most dreaded."[44] Like the inscrutable Calvinist God to which Wharton once compared her, Lucretia repudiates her daughter's now desperate attempt at dialogue. The failed attempt is worth reading in full:

"I never heard such a ridiculous question!" she said impatiently; and I felt at once how vulgar she thought me.

But in the extremity of my need I persisted. "I'm afraid, Mamma — I want to know what will happen to me!"

The coldness of her expression deepened to disgust. She was silent for a dreadful moment; then she said with an effort: "You've seen enough pictures & statues in your life. Haven't you noticed that men are — made differently from women?"

"Yes," I faltered blankly.

"Well, then — ?"

I was silent, from sheer inability to follow, & she brought out sharply: "Then for heaven's sake don't ask me any more silly questions. You can't be as stupid as you pretend!"

This dreadful moment was over, & the only result was that I had been convicted of my stupidity for not knowing what I had expressly been forbidden to ask about, or even to think of! . . . . I record this brief conversation, because the training of which it was the beautiful & logical conclusion did more than anything else to falsify & misdirect my whole life. . . . And, since, in the end, it did neither, it only strengthens the conclusion that one is what one is, & that education may delay but cannot deflect one's growth. Only, what possibilities of tragedy may lie in the delay![45]

Many critics and biographers have discussed Wharton's deeply troubled relationship to her mother. Cynthia Griffin Wolff sees Wharton's life as an ultimately successful struggle to overcome her mother's "domination." Gloria Erlich sees Lucretia Jones's coldness and emotional rejection as playing a decisive role in shaping Wharton's personality and that of characters like Lily Bart. And Hermione Lee writes, "Wharton's version of Lucretia Jones is one of the most lethal acts of revenge ever taken by a writing daughter. The fictional materials were inexhaustible — Wharton was still 'doing' her in her seventies — and Lucretia remained unforgiven."[46] But if Lucretia's "frivolous," repressive, and domineering ways delayed Wharton's growth, they did not deflect it. The results were not tragic in her case, as they would be in that of Lily Bart, whose fictional mother, as we shall see, closely resembles Lucretia. And although Wharton's marriage, in 1885, to Teddy Wharton was deeply unhappy and unfulfilling, she did experience a measure of sexual and sensuous happiness during her brief affair with Morton Fullerton from 1908 to 1910, and her sensitive portrayals of love and marriage, however thwarted and unhappy, show that she was not blinded like those young women of old New York she described in *The Age of Innocence*: young women whose eyes had been bandaged by their mothers and grandmothers to prevent them from seeing the truths of human sexuality, their eyes covered so long that once the bandages were removed they could no longer see.[47]

The dialogues between Wharton and her mother offer an important and striking contrast to those in Alcott's novel, which, because of the age of their readers and the time in which they are written, necessarily skirt the explicitly sexual issues about which Wharton so anxiously questioned Lucretia. Marmee's conversations with her daughters show us girls and young women whose concerns are addressed by their mother with sympathy and forthright explanation, in which emotions are named and her daughters' eyes opened to their meaning of their experience.[48] If Edith Jones measured her own mother against the idealized parent in Alcott's classic, Lucretia would have come up devastatingly short. One of the repeated ironies found in *The House of Mirth* is Lily Bart's lament that she has no mother to manage her negotiations on the marriage market and maneuver her into the kind of loveless marriage to a wealthy man that Marmee explicitly advises her daughters to avoid. The irony, of course, lies in the reader's growing recognition that what Lily needs is someone to guide her on the opposite path than the one her mother has taught her to take.

As scholars like Katherine Joslin have shown, Wharton took intense interest and pleasure all her life in elegant clothing, houses, and gardens.[49] Fashion and the sense of beauty were great sources of consolation for Wharton, a way to assuage her loneliness and emotional confusion. For her, as for Lily Bart, a lovely, luxurious room could seem "to open almost human arms" when her heart was "uncomforted by human nearness" (118). However, her piercing critique of her mother's obsessive and destructive shopping shapes the themes of both *The House of Mirth* and the later, even more sharply satirical, novel, *The Custom of the Country*. These novels reveal that Wharton was deeply aware of the dangers of relying on acquisition to provide a sense of identity and fulfill emotional needs. Material objects, however powerfully symbolic, were not, in the end, adequate substitutes for "human nearness." Although Wharton's love of material beauty was lifelong, it was her other source of consolation, reading, to which she finally turned for guidance and human connection. Despite there being no wise mother or father to guide that reading, Wharton's intellectual interests and forays into literary authorship slowly but surely began to link her to what Susan Goodman has described as her "inner circle" of congenial friends, colleagues like Walter Berry and Henry James, who provided her with support for a new self-awareness, a blossoming of her identity as a thinker and a writer.[50] With the publication of her first collection of stories, *The Greater Inclination*, in 1899, she "felt like some homeless waif who, after trying for years to take out naturalization papers, and being rejected by every country, has finally acquired a nationality. The Land of Letters was henceforth to be my country, and I gloried in my citizenship."[51] And yet, despite this new citizenship, her writing, as critics have shown, is filled with images of homelessness and what Wendy Gimbel has called "orphancy."[52] With people she did not know well and with whom she felt incompatible, Wharton would always retain a chilly reserve, perhaps disturbingly similar to her mother's. She found " 'unsought demonstrations of affection repugnant' and was called cold and inexpressive."[53] However, with her close friends, she was extraordinarily warm, as many testified. This circle of friends, female as well as male, provided her with inner sanctum of friendship that was, like the her father's study, a sustaining and healing space, a space to which her reading and writing gave her access; it is a space her heroine, Lily Bart enters at key, formative moments, but never owns.[54]

The process of disengaging from old New York began, according to Wharton's lifelong friend Sara Norton, soon after her father's death. One of the most important influences in this process was Walter Berry, Wharton's literary mentor and confidant until the end of his life in 1927. According to Lee, Berry was "the first person to encourage and criticize her writing, and one of the first with whom she shared her reading enthusiasms — which at the turn of the century were for Stevenson's letters, or *The Turn of the Screw* or Whitman's poetry. He gave her an intellectual example which speeded her on her move away from everything the Reverend Washburn and Calvary Church stood for."[55] As Wharton shed the Calvinist-inflected Protestantism of her youth, she turned toward the new evolutionary theories influenced by Charles Darwin's work. As scholars like Claire Preston, Nancy Bentley, Carol Singley, Sharon Kim and others have documented, Wharton, initially guided by her friend Egerton Winthrop, gave herself an intense course of study in evolutionary theory, anthropology, and secular philosophy beginning in the 1890s. Authors included not only Darwin, but Ernest Von Haeckel, T. H. Huxley, George Romanes, Max Weber, and Herbert Spencer, along with anthropologists such as Paul Topinard and Edvard Westermarck. She read Thorstein Veblen and James George Frazer.[56] Sharon Kim has persuasively explored Wharton's continuing interest in the theories of Jean-Baptiste Lamarck, whose ideas on acquired traits, although in conflict with Darwinian ideas on natural selection, continued to inform many of the theorists Wharton consulted.[57]

According to Carol Singley, as Wharton recovered from the Calvinist "God-intoxication" of her childhood, she found the skepticism and emphasis on determinism in evolutionary theory compatible with her own vision of life, which was considerably less optimistic than that of the educated elite in New York, who saw Spencerian Darwinism as a sunny philosophy confirming their own evolutionary success.[58] Wharton's intellectual questioning ultimately led her to reject traditional Christian beliefs almost entirely, while keeping a secular core of moral insights. As Singley writes, "Wharton's argument with Christian, and particularly Calvinist, doctrine reached its peak at midlife," when she wrote this *cri de coeur* to Sara Norton: "There are times when I *hate* what Christianity has left in our blood—or rather, one might say, out of it—by its cursed assumption of a split between body & soul."[59] According to Singley, the "seeds of her discontent were sown even earlier, as early as 1898, when she copied the following lines from Whitman's 'Song of Myself' into her commonplace book: 'I think I could turn and live with animals, they are so placid and self-/contain'd . . . They do not lie awake in the dark and weep for their sins,/They do not make me sick discussing their duty to God,/Not one is dissatisfied, not one is demented with the mania of owning things."[60] The reference to Whitman is particularly telling. Well-brought-up ladies were not allowed to read the sexually explicit and uninhibited poet, whose work Wharton remembered being kept under lock and key in gentlemen's libraries. Introduced as a young adult to his work by Walter Berry, Wharton found an inspirational example in Whitman for the rest of her life. R. W. B. Lewis notes that he appeared on her 1898 list of favorite books.[61] The title of her 1933 memoir refers to Whitman's own "A Backward Glance O'er Travel'd Roads." Wharton's 1924 novella *The Spark* even includes Whitman as a character; he appears as a Civil War nurse caring for the protagonist, who never recognizes the kindly older man as a great poet. And in 1907, just after the success of *The House of Mirth*, Wharton began to sketch a critical essay on Whitman, which remained unfinished and unpublished, but which shows again her deep love of the poet. While that love might appear inexplicable in a writer who seemed to so many to be "cold and inexpressive," to those friends, including Henry James, who knew Wharton's inner warmth and passionate, emotional core, it made perfect sense.[62]

Moreover, her love of Whitman shows her close ties to the Transcendentalism that originally inspired the poet: the philosophy of Emerson and Bronson Alcott, albeit transformed by Whitman's own radical vision. However, although Wharton professed a great appreciation for Emerson's philosophy, she was also keenly aware of its shortcomings, particularly the limitations of its individualism. In the character of Lawrence Selden she critiques that individualism for its failure to take account of the social nature of identity and the human need for emotional connection. While she found affirmation of this critique in Whitman, another important source of support may have come from contemporary philosophers like William James and George Herbert Mead, whose pragmatic approach to the truth of ideas and emphasis on the social sources of identity paralleled her own portrayal of human development, a connection Jill Kress has studied with much insight.[63]

Closely related to the Transcendental influence of Emerson and Whitman was Wharton's lifelong love of Plato's Dialogues. Like Bronson Alcott and Friedrich Schleiermacher, whose Romantic, German idealism shaped liberal Protestantism in the nineteenth century, Wharton saw her copy of the Dialogues, a five-volume 1875 set, as among her most treasured books. Further, as Carol Singley notes, "her personal library contained not only classical poetry and plays but books about Greek religion and philosophy, including J. P. Mahaffy's *Greek Life and Thought*, G. Murray's *Four Stages of Greek Religion*, E. Westermarck's *The Origin and Development of the Moral Ideas*, G. L. Dickinson's *The Greek View of Life*."[64] That Greek philosophy was on Wharton's mind in 1905 when she was composing *The House of Mirth* is revealed by a letter to Sara Norton that year in which she writes that she is 'in the mood for the Hellenic" and has been reading the Dialogues.[65] Her commonplace book includes this passage from Plato's "Phaedrus": "Beloved Pan, & all ye other gods . . . give me beauty in the inward soul; and may the outward & the inward be one."[66] In 1888 she spent funds from an inheritance on an Aegean cruise. This experience was among the happiest in her marriage and early adulthood and accorded with her lifelong interest in classical literature and philosophy. Her similar pleasure and interest in Italian history and culture led to her books on Italian gardens and her first novel, *The Valley of Decision*, a two-volume study of eighteenth-century Italy, where aristocratic feudalism, Roman Catholicism, and Enlightenment skepticism compete for the allegiance of its hero, a young Italian nobleman.[67]

While this is only the briefest of sketches, I have noted some of the lines of influence that I see intersecting in *The House of Mirth*: Wharton's early self-doubt and fearful "Puritan" conscience, her turn to Darwin and Lamarck for an alternative vision of human nature, her love of Plato and interest in the transformative power of dialogue, her association with Henry James and the forces of "modern" thought about consciousness and identity, and finally, her love of Walt Whitman. In addition to these, there was her experience of the increasing diversity and materialism of American life, particularly the changes in the New York society in which she was born and raised: the rise of "new money" and "robber barons," and especially the exemplars of the new ideology of wealth and success, the Jewish entrepreneurs and businessmen who were trying to move into the closed circles of gentile Anglo-American society. Then there was the increasingly complex and pervasive culture of consumption and display described by Wharton's contemporary Thorstein Veblen and most recently by critic Maureen Montgomery: the world of enthralling, carnivalesque department stores with their dreamlike displays and the intricate, theatrical social performances enacted on the urban stage of opera boxes, horse shows, elaborate dinner parties, and gala events such as the *tableaux vivants* that figure so prominently in *The House of Mirth*. Amy Kaplan has also detailed the emergence of a culture of publicity and the "crowded spaces" of modern social life. Where in all this would the influence of a writer like Alcott fit?[68]

Later in life, Wharton, as noted earlier, explicitly disassociated herself from sentimental writers like Alcott and Alcott's female contemporaries. Wharton's disavowal of these associations has been much studied by critics such as Donna Campbell and Deborah Lindsay Williams and deservedly so, since Wharton also carefully distanced herself from the happy endings and moral optimism of these writers.[69] "A material monist," as Sharon Kim described her, Wharton had no faith in a supreme being, divine justice, or otherworldly recompense for earthly suffering. While there are other ways to assess her literary place, her much-discussed realism also rests on this anti-foundational foundation: a modern skepticism that stoically faced suffering and mortality without the aid of traditional religious reassurances. And yet critics such as Hildegard Hoeller, Jeanne Boydston, and Lori Merish have nonetheless traced an important strand of influence from sentimentalist writers and domestic novels through Wharton's work, an influence the author denied but that is still visible and even central, as I will argue.[70] And there were strong, hidden reasons why Alcott's novel would have appealed to the young Edith Jones. In fact, I believe that this appeal was more than superficial, more than a simple, childish identification of her mother (and herself) with the struggling March sisters. Not only did *Little Women* have affinities with Wharton's own life, its dramatization of Christian nurture in action had a sustained influence on her vision of materialistic values and the social sources of selfhood. In other words, while Wharton disavowed what Mary Louise Kete has called the literary mode associated with sentimentalism — that stereotypical style marked by religious optimism, didacticism, and heightened emotion — she also drew heavily on the broad cultural discourse of sentimentalism to represent her characters' psychological and moral development.[71]

By 1904, Wharton's interest in architecture, interior design, and gardening had led not only led to her first full-length publication, *The Decoration of Houses* (1897), but also to the construction of the Mount, her elegant house with its French and Italian gardens in Lenox, Massachusetts. Wharton spent many summers at the Mount from September 1902, when it was finished, to 1911, when it was sold. It was there that she wrote portions of *The House of Mirth* in the fall of 1904, while Henry James was visiting — Wharton writing during the days and James reading aloud from Whitman's *Leaves of Grass* in the evenings.

Just as the March parents had advised Jo, then grieving over her sister's death and confused about her artistic identity, to write about her own life, so James, after the publication of *Valley of Decision*, had advised Wharton to turn away from eighteenth-century Italy and "Do New York!" The result was *The House of Mirth*. Like the first volume of *Little Women*, *The House of Mirth* proved to be its author's first great literary success, perhaps because, like Alcott's classic, it drew on such deep wells of feeling and experience.

And, as for *Little Women*, initial sales were overwhelmingly strong. The chapters were first serialized from January to November 1905 in *Scribner's Magazine*, with illustrations by A. B. Wenzell.[72] Once out in book form, according to Hermione Lee, "it sold 30,000 copies in its first three weeks of publication (the most paid sales of any Scribner publication up till then) and 140,000 copies in its first year. Alongside macho realist epics like Frank Norris's *The Pit* or Upton Sinclair's *The Jungle*, it was one of the biggest 'serious' best-sellers of the turn of the century."[73] However, if the sales were comparably successful, the audience response to Wharton's novel was decidedly different from that accorded *Little Women*. Wharton's story, written for an adult audience of sophisticated readers, was much less reassuring about the prospects for a young, unguided woman navigating the new, more ruthless world of materialism and consumer culture than Alcott's had been. Moreover, the reading audience in 1905 was no longer as receptive to the anti-materialistic message of Alcott's bestseller (coupled as it was with a seemingly paradoxical message that shopping could also be both moral and self-expressive). Karen Halttunen's study of mid-nineteenth-century advice books, discussed in chapter 1, describes their prescription that young men carefully balance inner moral character with persuasive, but sincere performances of self designed to win friends and influence people in the new urban marketplace.[74] As Halttunen explains, this tension had its source in Protestant concerns about hypocrisy: its demand that the "works" of one's outward appearance truly reflect one's inner moral reality. It is a demand that also seems to inform Wharton's own childhood conflict between her mother's requirement that she be "polite" and the moral requirement that she be "honest." And while Wharton's "Puritan conscience" eased in later years, her interest in the prayer from Plato's "Phaedrus" — "Beloved Pan, & all ye other gods . . . give me beauty in the inward soul; and may the outward & the inward be one" — reflects her lifelong concern with issues of sincerity and hypocrisy, the sacramental relationship between outward and visible signs and the inward and invisible realities they represent.

However, Wharton's concerns may have been out of step with those of her audience. According to Amy Blair's careful archival research, by the turn of the century advice books were more preoccupied with persuasive performances of self and less with whether those performances were sincere or hypocritical.[75] Rising upward, like Horatio Alger's young heroes, was still key, but maintaining one's inner "respectability" was no longer the central issue that it was for the bootblack turned office clerk of Alger's *Ragged Dick*, an observation that accords with historian Walter Susman's analysis of the shift from sincerity and "character" to performativity and "personality" in American ideas about identity. Susman's analysis, which also underpins Halttunen's discussion of the earlier period's emphasis on character, describes the century's increasing focus on managing one's outward appearance and reputation. Moreover, reading was seen by many turn-of-the-century advice writers not as a way to improve one's moral awareness and character but as a way to acquire the cultural capital required for class mobility.[76] As Amy Blair notes, the authors of these later advice books recommended literature as way to "read up": not to resist the temptations of a materialistic society, but to master them. For readers looking for such mastery, Lily's failure and death seemed a blow to their hopes, a disconfirmation of their dreams of happiness.

Blair's research into the extensive critiques and letters that appeared in *The New York Times Saturday Review of Books* immediately following *The House of Mirth*'s publication (from November 1905 through January 1906) reveals how surprisingly controversial the novel was. Blair finds that, rather than condemning the "frivolous society" that destroys Wharton's heroine, readers tended to misread the novel and to blame Wharton herself for Lily's unhappy fate: accusing the author of cruelty to her character, a perverse refusal to grant her the social and material success they themselves longed for.[77] Apparently some twentieth-century readers have had the same response. For example, according to Stephanie Harzewski, Candace Bushnell, the author of the "Sex and the City" newspaper columns in mid-1990s New York, cites Wharton as an important influence. However, Bushnell's reading of Wharton's work seems as misguided as those Amy Blair cites. As Harzewksi explains, drawing on a personal interview with Bushnell, the author "and a girlfriend read *The House of Mirth* in their early thirties and found Lily Bart's demise harrowing. Its unnerving similarities to their own social situation in late-twentieth-century Manhattan galvanized them to adopt dating tactics that would ensure a more prosperous fate."[78] Rather than resist and reject the frivolity that destroys Lily Bart, Bushnell was moved to invent strategies that would turn that frivolity to her financial advantage. One can only imagine what Wharton's response would have been to the adventures of Bushnell's New York heroines in their various television and film incarnations, but perhaps we need only look to her devastatingly satirical novel,

The Custom of the Country (1913), whose heroine Undine Spragg seems even more single-minded in her pursuit of fashionable clothes and wealthy husbands than Bushnell's Carrie Bradshaw.[79] And with that, it is time to turn to *The House of Mirth* itself.

Like Wharton's own mother, Lucretia Rhinelander Jones, Lily Bart might well be the daughter of Mrs. Moffat in *Little Women*, a sister to Belle and Ned. She is raised, as many critics have noted, as a commodity for the marriage market.[80] Moreover, the society in which she develops is not the transitional Gilded Age of Alcott's girls, in which the older tradition of the Protestant gentry still held some authority, but one in which the values of new capitalists like the Moffats now dominate. The novel opens in media res. Unlike Alcott, who begins at the beginning with the sisters' childhood and immature characters, Wharton first shows us a twenty-nine-year-old Lily: apparently fully formed and self-assured. As the novel will reveal, however, she is inwardly as "malleable as wax," as wavering as a "water plant in the flux of tides" (44). Without the careful moral instruction of a mother like Mrs. March, Lily's character has remained undeveloped, stunted, in an arrested state of bewildered childhood.[81] The reasons for this arrest are reviewed in the narrator's brief review of Lily's adolescent history. In *Little Women*, we see how Marmee carefully clips the buds of her girls' latent materialism in order to cultivate their moral "tastes" and ultimate blooming as hardy Protestant matrons. In *The House of Mirth* we see virtually the opposite: the buds of any latent identity besides the crowning rose of Lily's ornamental beauty are ruthlessly pruned. While the March sisters painfully learn to adjust outward appearance to inner reality, and to fit their dreams to their material means and emotional needs, Lily is taught that outer appearance is all, and that if her grandiose dreams require grandiose materials means, she must do whatever it takes to get them.

The novel is set in New York at the turn of the nineteenth century. The Barts are related to one of the reigning New York families, the Van Alstynes. Given this connection, along with her father's relative financial prosperity, Lily begins life in a highly favorable social position. Wharton represents New York in a state of financial well-being and moral sickness. Like Alcott's Boston, its upper reaches are dominated by two groups: old money and new. The old-money families include the Van Alstynes and Lily's aunt, Mrs. Peniston, along with the Van Osburghs and Gryces. More recently rich families include the Trenors and the Dorsets. Then there are the upstart newcomers like the Brys and the Gormers, or the financier, Simon Rosedale, a successful Jewish businessman who is making his steadfast attempt to break into this society's closed ranks when the novel opens.

The residual culture of old New York is embodied in Lily's aunt, Mrs. Peniston, who later takes Lily on as a dependent after the death of her parents. In *Little Women*, we see "stuffy" old Boston in Aunt March, who eventually softens enough to leave her mansion Plumfield to the impetuous Jo (Lily will not be so lucky in her legacy from her guardian). Wharton portrays Mrs. Peniston and the old New York she represents in unsparingly critical terms. This is not Puritan Massachusetts, but Episcopalian New York. Nevertheless, the codes of these ruling families are as rigidly moralistic as any found on Beacon Hill. However, Wharton is careful to show that this moralism is one that has lost its genuine ethical content. These are people governed not by a deep, spiritual understanding of the meanings underlying moral behavior, but rather by an idolatrous reverence for the appearance of morality. Take, for example, Mrs. Peniston's annual rites of return.

Since her youth, fashionable society had reliably left the country for town in October, "therefore on the tenth day of the month the blinds of her Fifth Avenue residence were drawn up, and the eyes of the Dying Gladiator in bronze who occupied the drawing-room window resumed their survey of the deserted thoroughfare" (77). The ensuing two weeks "represented to Mrs. Peniston the domestic equivalent of a religious retreat. She 'went through' the linen and blankets in the precise spirit of the penitent exploring the inner folds of conscience; she sought for moths as the stricken soul seeks for lurking infirmities." In this material substitute for moral renewal, "the topmost shelf of every closet was made to yield up its secret, cellar and coal-bin were probed to their darkest depths and, as a final stage in the lustral rites, the entire household was swathed in white and deluged with expiatory soapsuds" (78). If moral purity and respectability are signified by material cleanliness, their opposites are signified by material dirtiness, the pollution of domestic spaces by the sights, smells, and sounds of embodied life and its processes. Mrs. Peniston, for example, responds to gossip about "fast" girls with the shudder of revulsion she reserves for unsightly garbage. Indeed, "the mere idea of immorality was as offensive to Mrs. Peniston as a smell of cooking in the drawing-room: it was one of the conceptions her mind refused to admit" (100).

Again, appearance is all. In this rigidly structured society, as Thorstein Veblen so famously observed, leisure-class status is signaled by freedom from labor.[82] The immaculate condition of one's person and one's rooms displays to the world one's liberation from the degrading activities of cooking food, washing clothing, and scrubbing floors. Wharton is careful to note, however, that it is Mrs. Peniston's steely attention to these activities as performed by others that guarantees that her domestic self-presentation will be unimpeachably free of the marks of this work. The public space of her drawing room possesses a "glacial neatness," theaterlike in its controlled design, while the apparatus that produces this effect is carefully hidden. Most importantly, material cleanliness is taken as the outward sign of inward moral purity.

Wharton's assessment of this social paragon is unusually tart. Mrs. Peniston belongs "to the class of old New Yorkers who have always lived well, dressed expensively, and done little else; and to these inherited obligations Mrs. Peniston faithfully conformed. She had always been a looker-on at life, and her mind resembled one of those little mirrors which her Dutch ancestors were accustomed to affix to their upper windows, so that from the depths of an impenetrable domesticity they might see what was happening in the street" (31–32). This suggestion of a person who exists only through and for social conventions, who cannot think for herself but only mirrors the judgments of an outer world, is reinforced in the narrator's analysis of Mrs. Peniston's motives in taking her niece, Lily Bart, after her parents' death. Since Lily already had a reputation as a fashionable and free-spending young woman, no other relatives offered her shelter. Mrs. Peniston accepts responsibility out of "a kind of moral *mauvais honte*, which makes the public display of selfishness difficult, though it does not interfere with its private indulgence" (31). According to Elizabeth Ammons, *mauvais honte* can be defined as "false shame; a desire for things to appear a certain way to avoid embarrassment or censure, rather than because one cares about the underlying reality."[83] Given her emotional coldness, Mrs. Peniston would doubtless have turned away from her orphaned niece had there been no one to witness the rejection, "but with the eyes of her little world upon her she took a certain pleasure in her act" of apparent generosity (31).

This portrait of Mrs. Peniston is unmistakably one of hypocrisy both thorough and thoroughly unconscious. In the Puritan theologian John Cotton's terms, Mrs. Peniston should be herded up with the tough old goats of the church, not the succulent, true lambs of God. However, John Cotton also noted ruefully that as long as the goats successfully imitated the behavior of the lambs, there was no way to purge them from the ranks of the faithful. The subtle taste of their acts might distinctly convey the essential selfishness of their motives, just as the gamy flavor of old mutton could be distinguished from the relish of young lamb, but as long as the appearance of those acts conformed to standards of morality, they could not be questioned.[84] Mrs. Peniston's apparent magnanimity in assuming Lily's care conforms to her society's idea of charity, but its motive is purely a desire for social approval. Later in the novel, when Lily encounters a severe crisis, the narrator comments, "Lily had no heart to lean on. Her relation with her aunt was as superficial as that of chance lodgers who pass on the stairs" (118).

Wharton is equally critical of other members of New York's old guard. For example, there is Mrs. Gryce, a wealthy old New Yorker possessed of a marriageable son. "A monumental woman with the voice of a pulpit orator and a mind preoccupied with the iniquities of her servants," she "came sometimes to sit with Mrs. Peniston and learn from that lady how she managed to prevent the kitchen-maid's smuggling of groceries out of the house" (20). And like Mrs. Peniston, she is moved to charity only when it results in increased social capital: "Mrs. Gryce had a kind of impersonal benevolence: cases of individual need she regarded with suspicion, but she subscribed to institutions when their annual reports showed an impressive surplus" (20). Mindful of the dangers of self-indulgence, "she never allowed herself many pleasures. Once, however, she had had a special edition of the Sarum Rule printed in rubric and presented to every clergyman in the diocese; and the gilt album in which their letters of thanks were pasted formed the chief ornament of her drawing-room table" (20).[85] The material display of this album — gilt no less — serves in this society as evidence of moral worthiness. Mrs. Gryce's nurture of her son, Percy, is what one might expect from "so excellent" a woman: "Every form of prudence and suspicion had been grafted on a nature originally reluctant and cautious, with the result that it would have seemed hardly needful for Mrs. Gryce to extract his promise about . . . overshoes, so little likely was he to hazard himself abroad in the rain" (20). Prudish about appearances and frightened of innovation, Percy is taught primarily to obey conventions. When her son reaches adulthood and inherits the fortune of his father, made from a "patent device for excluding fresh air from hotels" (a particularly damning detail), "Mrs. Gryce thought that what she called his 'interests' demanded his presence in New York . . . where he was initiated with becoming reverence into every detail of the art of accumulation" (21). This is the Protestant ethic emptied of ethics.

Wharton's portrayal of New York as mindlessly conformist and unconsciously idolatrous is sharpest, and most amusing, in her description of a Sunday at the Trenors' country estate, Bellomont. First, there are the old-guard guests, the Wetheralls, with their Bunyan-esque name: "The Wetheralls always went to church. They belonged to the vast group of human automata who go through life without neglecting to perform a single one of the gestures executed by the surrounding puppets" (43). Although the narrator acknowledges that some guests at Bellomont neglect this duty, other guests equally important did not: "and Mr. and Mrs. Wetheralls' circle was so large that God was included in their visiting-list" (43). Yet the fact that the others at Bellomont manage not to attend Sunday services suggests that for a significant portion of New York's high society attitudes toward conventions had by this time subtly changed, a change that can be seen most clearly in Bellomont's hosts, the Trenors.

While Mrs. Peniston and Mrs. Gryce are presented as unconsciously hypocritical, the Trenors are presented as frankly so. Rather than being slavishly obedient to convention, they are openly manipulative of it: cultivating the appearance of moral behavior only as it serves them. For example, while the Wetheralls scrupulously attend church in their puppetlike, automatic way, the Trenors make only the weakest attempt to display interest: "The observance of Sunday at Bellomont was chiefly marked by the punctual appearance of the smart omnibus destined to convey the household to the little church at the gates. Whether any one got into the omnibus or not was a matter of secondary importance, since by standing there it not only bore witness to the orthodox intentions of the family, but made Mrs. Trenor feel, when she finally heard it drive away, that she had somehow vicariously made use of it" (42).

Bellomont appears to be the very "house of mirth" of the novel's title, and the seat of this society's uproarious vanity fair. Fashionable and sensuous, life at Bellomont is designed for the pursuit of pleasure and the display of status. Its mistress, Judy Trenor is "a tall fair woman," whose "rosy blondness had survived some forty years of futile activity without showing much trace of ill-usage except in a diminished play of feature." Like Mrs. Peniston and Mrs. Gryce, she identifies herself not by some inward sense of individual character but by her outward conformity to social expectations: "It was difficult to define her beyond saying that she seemed to exist only as a hostess, not so much from any exaggerated instinct of hospitality as because she could not sustain life except in a crowd" (34). She is generally kind to her friends, but not out of any compassionate understanding. In fact, "she knew no more personal emotion than that of hatred for the woman who presumed to give bigger dinners or have more amusing house-parties than herself" (34). Since, the narrator explains, "her social talents, backed by Mr. Trenor's bank-account, almost always assured her ultimate triumph in such competitions, success had developed in her an unscrupulous good nature toward the rest of her sex" (34).

This "unscrupulous good nature" also marks Judy Trenor's efforts to square the somewhat lax behavior of Bellomont with the more severe expectations of old New York. Her hypocrisy is frankly displayed in her complaints about Lady Cressida, a guest from England, whom they expected to have the same sort of easygoing attitude as themselves. However, as she explains ruefully to Lily, "you can never tell in those English families. They are so big that there's room for all kinds, and it turns out that Lady Cressida is the moral one—married a clergy-man and does missionary work in the East End. Think of my taking such a lot of trouble about a clergyman's wife, who wears Indian jewelry and botanizes!" (35). Reflecting on the difficulties of being a hostess, Mrs. Trenor concludes, "The worst of it is that she would have been so useful at the right time. You know we have to have the Bishop once a year, and she would have given just the right tone to things. I always have horrid luck about the Bishop's visits . . . last year, when he came, Gus forgot all about his being here, and brought home the Ned Wintons and the Farleys—five divorces and six sets of children between them!" (36).

The Trenors and their set still take the trouble to invite the Bishop to visit, and Judy Trenor still has enough respect for social convention to be chagrined, not by her friends' multiple divorces, but by the appearance of immorality they display to His Eminence. In other words, life at Bellomont is a delicate nego-tiation between the maintenance of respectability and the acceptance of self-indulgence. Gambling at bridge is openly enjoyed, while more serious breaches of the moral codes, such as adultery, are tacitly accepted, provided the perpe-trators manage the affair with discretion. Part of that discretion is never forcing witnesses to acknowledge the activity. Just as Mrs. Trenor manages to believe that her family is actually attending church every Sunday, she manages to avoid admitting that her friend Bertha Dorset is having an affair. While the old guard represses the desire for transgression as well as the act, the new guard represses neither the desire nor the act, but only its public naming.

If Bellomont is Wharton's version of Bunyan's Vanity Fair, its church-bound omnibus is, as Carol Singley has persuasively shown, her version of Hawthorne's "Celestial Railroad." In Hawthorne's updated version of Bunyan's allegory, his nineteenth-century pilgrims accept a satanic railroad conductor's promise to ease their journey to the celestial city. He happily relieves them of their sinful burdens, promising that they will be conveyed safely in the baggage car, while the pilgrims enjoy their ride, unlike faithful Christian, who struggles heroically on foot, his burden firmly on his back. (Needless to say, the lazy pilgrims' ulti-mate destination turns out to be hotter than they expected.)[86] At Bellomont, the Trenors seem to believe that they don't need to make the journey at all: just buy-ing an omnibus ticket will do the trick, while they stay comfortably in bed. Even the Wetheralls take advantage of the omnibus's convenience, perhaps signifying their willingness, as spiritual "puppets," to let others do their introspective work for them. Of all the guests, the only one willing to make the mile-long walk to church is the scorned Lady Cressida, the one who does missionary work among London's poor, and even she is finally convinced to take the omnibus, despite her initial disapproval of its self-indulgence. After all, it's only sociable.

Lady Cressida represents an important niche in this cultural ecology: the Christian reformer and social activist. Wharton was certainly aware of the most famous American version of this type: Jane Addams, the wealthy socialite who was influenced by British social reform movements and founded Chicago's Hull House.[87] In *The House of Mirth* she portrays this alternative to the dominant values of New York society through Gerty Farish, Lily Bart's friend and foil. Gerty seems a direct descendant of Alcott's March sisters. Like them, she might be described as "shabby genteel," a young woman of "good" family and little money. Her response to her situation mirrors the values inculcated by Mrs. March. Rather than seeking a wealthy husband or attempting to display herself as the equal of her economic superiors, she makes do with what she has, and finds satisfaction in the pleasures of doing good. Gerty's affinity with the values of *Little Women* is especially apparent in her work among the poor. Able to identify compassionately with those whose lives differ sharply from her own, Gerty serves on the governing committee of an association whose object is "to provide comfortable lodgings, with a reading-room and other modest distractions, where young women of the class employed in down town offices might find a home when out of work, or in need of rest" (70).[88] Like the March sisters after their Christmas visit to the starving Hummel family, Gerty has experienced a "sharpening of the moral vision which makes all human suffering so near and insistent that the other aspects of life fade into remoteness" (119–20).

Gerty manifests her unconventionality through unusual self-sufficiency; she maintains her own little apartment and has a cook, who also does her washing. Although her means are meager, Gerty, like Amy in Europe, manages to produce the effect, if not of luxury, then at least of style. Although her rooms are so small that guests must be fitted into them like pieces into puzzle, when her cousin, Lawrence Selden, comes for dinner, Gerty's "little sitting-room sparkled with welcome . . . Its modest 'effects,' compact of enamel paint and ingenuity, spoke to him in the language just then sweetest to his ear. It is surprising how little narrow walls and a low ceiling matter, when the roof of the soul has suddenly been raised" (122). The meal also has its charming surprises, including caramel custard made with Gerty's own hands and an improvised dinner cooked in a chafing dish. This is the good old Alcott philosophy: it is not the material house that matters, but the spirit that inhabits it. Imagination and emotional expressiveness sweeten this simple meal and illuminate the face of its ordinarily plain hostess. (That much of her radiance comes from an undeclared love for Selden is part of the story, and his failure to perceive it is another.)

However, unlike *Little Women*, where Meg is invited to the Moffats' version of vanity fair, in Wharton's novel, Gerty Farish is too socially peripheral to merit an invitation to Bellomont. That honor falls to Lily Bart, our heroine, whose values are more in tune with the pleasure-loving Trenors and their bridge-playing friends. While the Moffats suspect Meg, and her mother, of manipulating social opportunity for a chance to win a wealthy husband—a suspicion that shocks and scandalizes the unworldly Meg—that is exactly Lily's intention. While Gerty makes do with her slender means and her clothing in "useful" colors, Lily eagerly reaches for the chance to experience the pleasures of wealth. On that fall weekend at Bellomont, she ponders her choices in life and concludes they come down to whether she should "be herself, or a Gerty Farish." Her response to her luxurious surroundings provides the answer: "As she entered her bedroom, with its softly shaded lights, her lace dressing-gown lying across the silken bedspread, her little embroidered slippers before the fire, a vase of carnations filling the air with perfume, and the last novels and magazines lying uncut on a table beside the reading lamp, she had visions of Miss Farish's cramped flat, with its cheap conveniences and hideous wallpapers" (23). Unable to read the homely "effects" of Gerty's life sympathetically, since the spiritual roof of her own soul remains stubbornly low, Lily draws the obvious conclusion: "No; she was not made for mean and shabby surroundings, for the squalid compromises of poverty. Her whole being dilated in an atmosphere of luxury; it was the background she required, the only climate she could breath in" (23).[89]

Lily is, as the narrator tells us several times, a "specialized product," a "hothouse flower," able to thrive only in the artificial conditions of wealth. She cannot imagine herself except as a decorative bloom throwing out scent in luxurious drawing-rooms. If, as Baudrillard asserts, affluence is "merely the accumulation of the *signs* of happiness," then Lily not only finds herself unable to breathe unless surrounded by such signs, but identifies herself as such a sign: an expensive commodity, a beautiful object displaying the affluence of its possessor. As we have seen earlier, however, possessing the sign of happiness is not at all the same as possessing happiness itself. With her fervent faith that the proper material surroundings will grant her this gift, Lily is another version of the idolatrous consumer encountered in Alcott's novel. Like Amy going into debt to purchase her coveted pickled limes, or Meg squandering her household budget to acquire her fashionable purple silk, Lily gambles with her slender means in hopes of buying happiness, along with membership in the elite society to which she aspires. Enfolded by the luxurious furniture of the Trenors' guest bedroom, Lily's "whole being dilates." That this luxury is, in fact, owned by others only accentuates its effect on her, for, as Colin Campbell pointed out, consumer desire is fueled by anticipated possession of the signifying object. Actual possession is apt to produce disappointment in the object's ability to deliver the happiness it promises—a happiness that is then projected onto the next object on the consumer's horizon.[90] Lily, like Dreiser's Carrie, is possessed by deep and insatiable longing, a hunger for happiness that sees its future fulfillment in the revolving objects of consumer desire. Wharton's analyses of this hunger's sources and its idolatrous goals are more subtly presented than Alcott's, but share many of the earlier author's diagnoses.[91]

In *Little Women* the four daughters are initially presented as immature and therefore egocentric and morally unaware. Realizing the inevitability of their children's exposure to an increasingly materialistic society, the March parents carefully nurture their daughters' characters by allowing them to experiment with their longings for status and consumer goods, and then helping them to articulate their consequent disappointment and dismay. Through skillfully managed family dialogues, the girls are taught to interpret their own desires and emotions. Most importantly they are taught to look for their "true" selves in the intimate mirror of their familial relationships, rather than in the public mirror of fashion and status. As pointed out earlier, this is a double process. On the one hand the girls are given the wholesome nourishment of family love and support; on the other they are allowed to gorge themselves on the "poisoned sweets" of social display. When the latter makes them sick, they are gently made aware of the nutritious meal they have scorned. As the death of Beth demonstrates, it sometimes takes the shock of losing an intimate attachment to recognize its value, just as it sometimes take the shock of disappointment in a commodity to recognize its inability to provide the happiness it promised. Guiding them through this delicate developmental process, Marmee listens to her daughters' rueful confessions, absolves them of their materialistic sins, and provides them with a language and a moral map for their pilgrimage.

Lily Bart's upbringing is diametrically opposed to this vision of a calm, wisdom-dispensing home. Indeed, Wharton makes her central character a virtual experiment in materialistic upbringing; the nearly perfect product of an anti-Christian nurture. Lily's first memories are of "a house in which no one ever dined at home unless there was 'company'" (25). A parade of changing servants, including nurses and footmen, fills the house with quarrels, while the

family's life alternates between financial extravagances and consequent economies. "Ruling the turbulent element called home was the vigorous and determined figure of a mother still young enough to dance her ball-dresses to rags,
while the hazy outline of a neutral-tinted father filled an intermediate space between the butler and the man who came to wind the clocks" (25). Mr. Bart seems
even to Lily's infant eyes an old man, gray and tired, while her mother, fueled by
an unflagging desire for pleasures and social approval, appears young and energetic. And yet this energy is not directed toward the nurture of her daughter, but
rather to impressing the outer world with her brilliant displays.

Throughout Lily's adolescence, the Barts follow their "zig-zag broken course
down which the family craft guided on a rapid current of amusement, tugged
at by the underflow of perpetual need — the need of more money" (26). This
constant call for more money is generated by Mrs. Bart, despite her having the
reputation among her friends as "a wonderful manager." Unlike Mrs. March,
known for her frugal but comfortable homemaking, "Mrs. Bart was famous for
the unlimited effect she produced on limited means, and to the lady and her
acquaintances there was something heroic in living as though one were much
richer than one's bank-book denoted" (26). All is abruptly halted one fateful day
when Lily is nineteen years old. Her father comes home from his office looking
even grayer and more tired than usual, and announces to his unsuspecting wife
and daughter that he is ruined. He then begins to die. From the moment of his
announcement, Mr. Bart "no longer counted" for his wife: "He had become
extinct when he ceased to fulfill his purpose, and she sat at his side with the
provisional air of a traveler who waits for a belated train to start" (28).

To her credit, "Lily's feelings were softer: she pitied him in a frightened ineffectual way. But the fact that he was for the most part unconscious, and that his
attention, when she stole into his room, drifted away from her after a moment,
made him even more of a stranger than in the nursery days when he had never
come home till after dark" (28–29). Such a loss might, in the world of *Little
Women*, be the opportunity for a spurt of moral development. The small bud
of emotional attachment might begin to grow into a strong, mature tendril, and
even yield a blossom of new awareness. However, Lily's connection to her father
is so slight, so lacking in deep roots, that she can only respond with a sense of
helplessness: "She seemed always to have seen him through a blur — first of
sleepiness, then of distance and indifference — and now the fog had thickened
till he was almost indistinguishable" (29). Wharton's analysis of this failed opportunity is sharp, if concise: "If she could have performed any little services
for him, and have exchanged with him a few of those affecting words which
an extensive perusal of fiction had led her to connect with such occasions, the

filial instinct might have stirred in her" (29). However, this filial instinct withers not only because it lacks strong roots, but also because Lily's mother actively thwarts it: "Her pity, finding no active expression, remained in a state of spectatorship, overshadowed by her mother's grim, unflagging resentment. Every look and act of Mrs. Bart's seemed to say: 'You are sorry for him now—but you will feel differently when you see what he has done to us'" (28–29). Given an environment hostile to more compassionate responses, Lily feels only relief upon her father's death.[92]

Consumed with rage against her deceased husband, who worked himself to death trying to meet her financial demands, Mrs. Bart now turns to Lily's beauty for consolation. She studies it "with a kind of passion, as though it were some weapon she had slowly fashioned for vengeance" (30). This beauty becomes "the last asset in their fortunes, the nucleus around which their life was to be rebuilt. She watched it jealously, as though it were her own property and Lily its mere custodian; and she tried to instill into the latter a sense of the responsibility that such a charge involved" (30).[93] Wharton's analysis of this maternal relationship is matter-of-fact but deeply disturbing. Lily's mother has made her into a commodity whose value can be only realized through sale to a wealthy male buyer. In *Little Women*, Mrs. Moffat assumed that Mrs. March was maneuvering to marry her daughter Meg off to her rich neighbor's grandson. However, Mrs. March would never think of such a thing, for as she explains to Meg and Jo, although money is "needful" and even, "when well used, a noble thing," marrying for money alone would deprive her daughters of their "self-respect and peace." She would rather see them married to poor men, as long as they were "happy, beloved, and contented" (123). This is far from Mrs. Bart's philosophy. Rather than wholesome parables fostering moral awareness and self-acceptance, she feeds her daughter a steady diet of poisonous stories about beauties who managed to capitalize on their physical assets by marrying men of means, alongside tales of other, equally handsome women who failed to realize the earning potential of their gift: "To Mrs. Bart, only stupidity could explain the lamentable denouement of some of her examples. . . . she inveighed so acrimoniously against love-matches that Lily would have fancied her own marriage had been of that nature, had not Mrs. Bart frequently assured her that she had been 'talked into it'—by whom, she never made clear" (30–31). One could argue that Mrs. Bart's excessive interest in Lily's future is evidence of maternal involvement and intimacy. And so it is, but of an overwhelmingly narcissistic type. Mrs. Bart sees Lily only in light of her use; Lily "remembered how her mother, after they had lost their money, used to say to her with a kind of fierce vindictiveness: 'But you'll get it all back—you'll get it all back, with your face'"

(25). Valued only for her outer appearance, Lily receives maternal approval only insofar as she furthers her mother's selfish aims. Lily's own happiness in this process is never considered, unless one counts the unexamined assumption that wealth will bring fulfillment as a matter of course. Love, compassion, friendship, vocation: none of these are considered worthy of cultivation; none of these are seen as capable of bringing happiness.[94]

Coupled with this intense desire for material success is an equally intense fear of material poverty, figured first by Mrs. Bart and later by Lily as "dinginess." The exact referent for this signifier is vague and shifting. "Dingy" refers to those people who, according to Mrs. Bart "live like pigs" because their clothes and houses are shabby, but it can also refer to those whose belongings simply fail to meet her standard of fashionable display. In fact, some of these people who live like pigs are the Barts' own relatives, "who inhabited dingy houses with engravings from Cole's Voyage of Life on the drawing room walls, and slatternly parlour-maids who said 'I'll go and see' to visitors calling at an hour when all right-minded persons are conventionally if not actually out" (26–27). Although neither Lily nor her mother can come up with an alternative interpretation of this way of life, "the disgusting part of it was that many of these cousins were rich, so that Lily imbibed the idea that if people lived like pigs it was from some choice, and through the lack of any proper standard of conduct" (26–27).[95]

Lily is taught that her own standard of conduct, expressed primarily in a vigorous taste for "splendor," is a mark of her essential superiority. To compromise this taste is accordingly viewed as a self-destructive defeat. Since Lily's identity is centered entirely on her outward appearance, and the approval of that appearance in the mirror of fashion, failure to maintain a socially constructed standard of display can only be interpreted as a devastating loss. She has no other values by which to measure her human worth. Moreover, she has no other idea of where to turn. Her "whole being dilates" not when she is embraced by the arms of those who love her but when she is enfolded by the atmosphere of wealth and luxury. French dresses and elegant upholstery provide the only comfort she knows. In their company, she feels, at least temporarily, complete and secure. Viewing exquisite jewelry at a society wedding, Lily responds much as she did in the Trenors' guest bedroom: "The glow of the stones warmed Lily's veins like wine. More completely than any other expression of wealth they symbolized the life she longed to lead, the life of fastidious aloofness and refinement in which every detail should have the finish of a jewel, and the whole forming a harmonious setting to her own jewel-like rareness" (71–72).

An understanding of how commodities work illuminates the dynamics of

Lily's response. As a specialized product designed for a rarified, upper-class market, Lily's distinction is affirmed only in the presence of other such goods for, as Baudrillard notes, consumer goods accumulate and display their meanings through systems of associated objects. To explain the workings of this effect, Grant McCracken draws on Diderot's amusing essay "On My Dressing Gown."[96] Just as a modern consumer might feel driven to upgrade her living room to "match" a new purchase, the French philosopher felt obliged to replace all his possessions to meet the higher standard set by the gift of a luxurious silk dressing-gown. The dressing-gown made everything else he owned seem "dingy" by comparison. Lily sees herself as such a gift, a precious object signifying the rare and the distinctive. But to keep this meaning alive, and ensure that potential purchasers read her value properly, she must be seen within the context of other such objects. Perhaps even more importantly, to feel she *is* herself, she must see herself within that context. In *Little Women*, Meg experiences the "Diderot Effect" upon her transition from the Marches' comfortable home to the Moffats' mansion. In that splendid setting, her once adequate tarlatan dress seems "limp" and "shabby," and Meg, suddenly ashamed of her material poverty, gives herself up to Belle Moffat to be made into stylish "doll." Along with her original identity, she loses her self-respect. Only when she remembers that she is valued by her family for her internal character, not for her outer appearance, does Meg regain her familiar sense of self. Lily has no such memories of familial acceptance and love, no reassurance of an internal character apart from her outward appearance.

Wharton's portrait of Lily, however, includes dimensions besides her commodification. There is, for example, an uncultivated idealism that manages to survive her mother's strenuous attempts to clip its developing tendrils. The narrator suggests that this "vein of sentiment" stems from the discarded Mr. Bart, who had himself sheltered such leanings, the dwindling intellectual capital of a residual culture, manifested in the small library of poetry auctioned off after his death.[97] Lily thus tempers the ruthlessness of her mother's ambition by thinking "of her beauty as a power for good, as giving her the opportunity to attain a position where she should make her influence felt in the vague diffusion of refinement and good taste" (30). Moreover, despite her mother's injunctions, Lily "would not have cared to marry a man who was merely rich; she was secretly ashamed of her mother's crude passion for money" (30). Fond of pretty flowers and sentimental fiction (which in this context refers to romantic tales with conventionally happy endings), Lily believes these tastes ennoble her desire for worldly success. Her notion of lofty aspiration includes marriage to an English aristocrat, whose political ambition she could further, or to an Italian prince, whose ancient traditions she could uphold. Such romantic fantasies manage to soften and even obscure the financial motives of her marital ambitions.

Coupled with this vague idealism is Lily's strong aesthetic sensibility. Confronted at lunch with decaying roses left over from the previous night's party, Lily suggests replacing them with fresh lilies-of-the-valley: "Mrs. Bart stared. Her own fastidiousness had its eye fixed on the world, and she did not care how the luncheon-table looked when there was no one present at it but the family" (27). Beauty for Mrs. Bart is an investment whose profit is social advancement, not personal pleasure. Coolly pragmatic, she explains that the cost of lilies-of-the-valley, which are out of season, is prohibitive, especially since nothing is to be gained by their purchase. Lily, "who knew very little of the value of money," is not impressed by this logic (27). Lily's intense hunger for beauty could have been directed to artistic expression, as Amy's similar hunger is directed in *Little Women*. Instead, at her mother's urging, it is directed to her self-production as a commodity. However, her own motives for this production are significantly mixed. Other potential identities, for better and for worse, remain latent, only lacking the proper environment and encouragement to grow. For example, her success as a consummate figure of fashion suggests a nascent artistic talent, but since the only artistic product she is able to produce is herself, she is faced with significant problems.[98]

Take Lily's vision of herself as a jewel in a splendid setting. Achieving this vision is dependent upon marriage to a man able to provide that setting, but her role in this marriage is to be "fastidious" and "aloof." In other words, she is to be a beautiful but impenetrable object, a work of sculpture, a kind of elegant mannequin. This is not a living being whose organic surfaces respond to time and experience with the indelible marks of age. Lily may aspire to the condition of inorganic stone, but she is still mortal, subject to decay and death. She may be an artist, but she is like a sculptor assembling figures out of fruit. Unlike marble or granite, her medium will betray her: its pristine lines must eventually soften and dissolve. Moreover, the conditions of this particular sale involve other uses besides display. While she may "dilate" in anticipation of elegant furniture, her husband will no doubt respond to more carnal desires. Whether or not Lily faces the fact — and we will see her struggle to keep this aspect of her imagined future veiled — once married she will be touched, opened, and sexually enjoyed by the man who purchases her.

In sum, Lily's self-production demonstrates her potential to develop into an artist who works not for money but for the pure enjoyment of beauty and self-expression. However, it also suggests her potential to develop into a prostitute who cynically sells her body for social status and economic power.[99] Further, her marketing of herself reveals a keen psychological ability to read a man's character and a theatrical ability to arouse his desire. While her performances demonstrate Lily's potential to develop into an actress who aims at artistic expression, they also suggest her tendency to operate as a confidence woman who focuses only on financial gain. Significantly, Lily's divided motives seem destined to lead her into life that would be considerably more painful than that of an outright prostitute or con woman, for at least a prostitute can take her pay and escape her customer, and a con woman can drop her mask once she's fleeced her mark. Since Lily's overt goal is to *marry* her mark, if successful she faces of lifetime of sex with a man she does not love: the endless performance of a persona designed to please another, not herself.[100]

At the moment the novel opens, Lily's divided motives and lack of self-awareness have resulted in her repeated failure to achieve her stated goal. At twenty-nine years old, she is still unmarried. At first, her failure could be laid to her father's failure and the family's reduced circumstances. Mrs. Bart does her best to make use of her daughter's beauty, but "her visions of a brilliant marriage for Lily had faded after the first year" (30). The problem is simple. They don't have enough money to live where Lily can be properly displayed. She is like a Tiffany necklace for sale at Woolworth's. No one who can afford her shops there. As Mrs. Bart laments, "People can't marry you if they don't see you — and how can they see you in these holes where we're stuck?" (30–31). Mrs. Bart dies "after two years of hungry roaming . . . died of a deep disgust. She had hated dinginess, and it was her fate to be dingy." As with Lily's father, there is no redemptive deathbed scene. Rather, this mother's "last adjuration to her daughter" is that she must escape the dinginess if she can: " 'Don't let it creep up on you and drag you down. Fight your way out of it somehow — you're young and can do it" (31).

At first, with Lily's adoption by Mrs. Peniston, it does seem as if Lily will fight her way out. She is now brought back into the elite public's eye, given enough funds to dress herself "decently," and provided a stage for her performance as a desirable wife-to-be. However, even with these new opportunities, Lily cannot close the deals she so cleverly initiates. As she explains to Lawrence Selden, she had several early opportunities, but somehow failed to reach her goal. Reflecting on Lily's repeated failures, despite her acknowledged beauty and subtle manipulative skills, another friend, Carry Fisher remarks, "Sometimes . . . I think it's just flightiness — and sometimes I think it's because, at heart, she despises the things she is trying for. And it's the difficulty of deciding that makes her such an interesting study" (148).

As we shall see, Lily's failure to close the deal seems to arise from an almost instinctive recoiling when she comes to the moment of commitment. During the early phases of each chase, she seems guided by visions of future luxury and comfort, of respite from financial worry and escape from the threatening dinginess. But as success appears more likely, the reality of marriage also looms larger. Once her financial future seems secure, her usual anxieties begin to subside and the price of this security thrusts itself upon her consciousness. There is the tedium of playing a never-ending role, and the physical submission of her body to a man she has chosen only for his money. Lily never seems to picture this future sexual act fully to herself. Wharton shows us only her emotional repulsion, as if her heroine could not bear to pull the bedroom curtain aside in her own imagination. The irony, which pervades the book, is that despite Lily's deliberate, even desperate intention to marry for money, she cannot bring herself to sacrifice her lilylike purity on the idolatrous altar of financial gain. And this inability, which Alcott's Mrs. March would see as a triumph of moral character over materialistic temptation, Lily sees as an inexplicable failure of will.

And here, curiously, we come back to the Puritan's favorite problem of moral behavior: the freedom of the will. Like Alcott, Wharton adapts the Edwardsian notion of the will as determined by human "affections."[101] Also like Alcott, Wharton has reshaped this problem to fit a more secular world, and a more overtly psychological understanding of the human psyche and its motives. Both authors see these affections, not as shaped by original sin and divine election, but as cultivated through human interaction. For example, Hermione Lee quotes Wharton as commenting that she didn't believe in God, but she did believe in his saints.[102] Thus Wharton's vision resolutely turns away from otherworldly solutions to human failings and losses, including mortality itself. In her work, moral behavior, even that of saints, is a human, not a divine, achievement.[103] However, since Lily is given a virtually anti-Christian nurture, her last-minute rejections of materialistic temptations can seem mysterious, almost anomalous, especially without any otherworldly influence to account for them. John Cotton and the Massachusetts Bay Colony were concerned primarily with moral hypocrisy: with those sinners who worked hard to display themselves as saints, but who couldn't help subtly revealing their true selfish natures through their uncontrollable gestures and unconscious slips. Lily's problem is the opposite. She has been deliberately trained to be a hypocrite, trained to take selfish advantage, but there is a latent idealism in her, an undeveloped, unconscious moral sense that betrays her worst intentions.

In John Cotton's and Jonathan Edwards's world, human nature was either damned or saved; one was either a sinner or a saint, no gray areas. In Alcott's world, human nature is more mixed, more malleable, more subject to human intervention. And so it is in Wharton's. Lily may have the potential for a higher level of moral development than she is initially taught to achieve, but it remains to be seen if that potential will ever receive the encouragement it needs to grow. Wharton several times describes Lily's character as containing a "wild" streak; she compares her to a dryad or wood nymph. The image suggests that there is some component of Lily's complex nature that is "natural," "uncultivated," something almost instinctual. It is this streak of wildness that Lawrence Selden believes gives her artificiality such savour, and perhaps it is that which intrigues her friend Carry Fisher. The key is that this streak *is* uncultivated, and is therefore also inarticulate, beneath the threshold of consciousness, and therefore beneath the threshold of control.

In *Little Women*, Mrs. March painstakingly guides her daughters across this threshold: carefully teaching them through those family dialogues how to recognize and name their own emotions and thereby to discipline their impulses, both good and bad. Confessions of fault, as when Jo confesses her rage against Amy or Meg confesses her vanity at the Moffats, result in maternal forgiveness and daughterly expiation. This process leads eventually to self-knowledge and moral awareness. However, Lily has never, Wharton writes, been taught "how to live with her thoughts." She has never been encouraged to express, let alone name or accept her emotions. Mrs. March's most potent educational tool is her daughters' deep attachment to her. Through this bond she is able to guide their awareness and to cultivate their taste for moral pleasures. Never having had the experience of intimate attachment, Lily is strangely unable to name it or to value it. If anything, she has taken her mother's injunctions against love-matches too much to heart, and seems genuinely frightened at overtures of affection, even those given in friendship. Impulsiveness and passion imply loss of control, a threat Lily's mother has repeatedly warned her against. As Lily's friend Gerty recalls, "once, when we were children, and I had rushed up after a long separation, and thrown my arms about her, she said, 'Please don't kiss me unless I ask you, Gerty,'—and she *did* ask me, a minute later; but since then I've always waited to be asked'" (211).[104]

Lily's lack of emotional literacy and fear of physical intimacy have a powerful influence on her behavior and choices, an influence that I believe reveals important links between her upbringing and her materialistic values. They are worth a closer look.

Here I would like turn to Lily's vision of herself as a rare jewel, a valuable and distinguished commodity. The achievement of this jewel-like status appears as the opposite of the material dinginess she fears. Analyzing this persistent opposition more deeply brings us to some of the sources of Lily's dread and reveals the links between her materialism and her fears. In her study, *Imperial Leather: Race, Sex, and Gender in the Colonial Contest*, Anne McClintock explains that the Victorians' "dirt fetish" was the complement to their romance with commodities.[105] Citing Mary Douglas's anthropological analysis of dirt as a cultural category, McClintock writes, "Nothing is inherently dirty; dirt expresses a relation to social value and social disorder. Dirt . . . is that which transgresses a social boundary. A broom in a kitchen closet is not dirty, whereas lying on a bed it is. Sex with one's spouse is not dirty, whereas conventionally the same act with a prostitute is. In Victorian culture, the iconography of dirt became deeply integrated in the policing and transgression of social boundaries."[106] The social boundaries particularly in need of such policing were those between the working classes, whose labor produced the commodities of the new capitalism, and the middle- and upper-class consumers like Lily, who identified themselves through the possession and display of those commodities.

Drawing on Marx's classic analysis of the commodity fetish, McClintock argues that "in Victorian culture, the bodily relation to dirt expressed a social relation to labor." McClintock explains the complementary opposition this way: "If as Marx noted, commodity fetishism flamboyantly exhibits the *overvaluation* of commercial *exchange* as the fundamental principle of social community, then the Victorian obsession with dirt marks a dialectic: the fetishized *undervaluation* of human *labor*."[107] Commercial exchange, the "invisible hand" of the marketplace, creates the surplus value of the commodity and lifts it above its mundane origins as a made object with a practical use value. Elevated in the human imagination, it becomes, as we have seen earlier, a symbol of human hopes and longings, a virtually transcendent object promising to deliver ineffable satisfactions. As the commodity fetish assumes this role in the marketplace, its humble birth in factory and workshop becomes a scandal to be hidden: Tiffany's elegant blue box, the artful department store display, the vivid advertising image, and the copyrighted brand name — all suggest that the commodity came into existence magically full-grown, independent of human work.

In order to maintain the commodity's ascendance, McClintock argues, the dirt of production must be hidden and discounted at all costs: "Smeared on trousers, faces, hands, and aprons, dirt was the memory trace of working class and female labor, unseemly evidence that the fundamental production of industrial and imperial wealth lay in the hands and bodies of the working class, women and the colonized." And given the status anxieties of the emergent middle classes, dirt was particularly threatening since it revealed the tension between the magic of the marketplace and the reality of the workshop: "Dirt, like all fetishes, thus expresses a crisis in value, for it contradicts the liberal dictum that social wealth is created by the abstract, rational principles of the market and not by labor."[108] This tension was particularly evident in the middle- and upper-class home, where a wife was charged with validating her husband's financial power and her family's class status through the conspicuous display of leisure. Her supposed freedom from labor and her home's immaculate, dirt-free condition both testified to her family's elevation above the sweat of the working classes. But, as McClintock points out, the wife's display of leisure was itself an arduous labor, a calculated, ritualized performance demanding "the skilled erasure of every *sign* of her work" and supported in the domestic theater by a hidden, almost invisible cast of servants.[109]

Just as dirt is the complementary hidden other of the commodity, so the devalued servant is the complementary hidden other of the leisured lady. And here as well, the hidden side of the equation concerns devalued labor: "While contemporary historians have noted the *symbolic value* of the serving class in the formation of middle-class identity, few have acknowledged the *economic value* of the domestic serving class as labor."[110] A keystone of the Victorian world view was the supposed separation of spheres: the public world of men, work, and money versus the private world of women, leisure, and consumption.[111] And just as the wife's role was leisured display, the servant's role was invisible labor. However, as McClintock explains, the separation of the private from the public was achieved only by paying working-class women for domestic work that wives were supposed to perform for free: "Female servants thus became the embodiment of a central contradiction within the modern industrial formation . . . the figure of the paid female servants constantly imperiled the 'natural' thresholds of private and public, home and market, working and middle class . . . servants brought into the middle-class home the whiff of the marketplace, the odor of cash."[112] As a result, domestic workers "embodied a double crisis in historic value: between men's paid labor and women's unpaid labor and between a feudal homestead and an industrial wage economy."[113] Female servants in the home thus carried the burden of Victorian culture's contradictions. Since their very presence transgressed social boundaries that their society preferred to see as closed, female servants "came to be figured by images of disorder, contagion, disease, conflict, rage and guilt. For this reason, domestic space became racialized as the rhetoric of degeneration was drawn upon to discipline and contain the unseemly spectacle of paid women's work."[114]

Wharton maps this cultural territory with precision, beginning in the opening chapter of the novel. There, Lawrence Selden's vision is arrested and "refreshed" by the sight of Lily Bart emerging from the crowds outside New York's Pennsylvania Station. Having gallantly offering to escort her, "he led her through the throng of returning holiday makers, past sallow-faced girls in preposterous hats, and flat-chested women struggling with paper bundles and palm-leaf fans. Was it possible that she belonged to the same race? The dinginess, the crudity of this average section of womanhood made him feel how highly specialized she was" (6). Lily herself is well-aware that she is a "specialized product"; moreover, she is well aware that her production is dependent on the labor of others, in particular those "dingy" working-class women who provide the background against which her artful figure is so arrestingly displayed: "She had always accepted with philosophic calm the fact that such existences as hers were pedestalled on foundations of obscure humanity. The dreary limbo of dinginess lay around and beneath that little illuminated circle in which life reached its finest efflorescence, as the mud and sleet of a winter night enclose a hot-house filled with tropical flowers" (119). Lily's complacency stems from her deep sense of entitlement, her belief in her essential superiority: "All this was in the natural order of things, and the orchid basking in its artificially created atmosphere could round the delicate curves of its petals undisturbed by the ice on the panes" (119). Wharton's irony, of course, is that this "philosophic calm" is simply ignorance, interrupted at moments by panic when the hothouse flower feels a draft.

As Lawrence Selden gazes upon this spectacle of elegant femininity, it prompts a series of reflections: "As she moved beside him, with her long light step, Selden was conscious of taking a luxurious pleasure in her nearness: in the modelling of her little ear, the crisp upward wave of her hair — was it ever so slightly brightened by art? — and the thick planting of her straight black lashes. Everything about her was at once vigorous and exquisite, at once strong and fine" (7). As numerous critics have pointed out, Selden's appreciation evokes a manufactured object, a mannequin or doll whose eyelashes have been "planted" and whose hair has been "brightened by art."[115] These implications are made more explicit in the next lines: "He had a confused sense that she must have cost a great deal to make, that a great many duller and ugly people must, in some mysterious way, have been sacrificed to produce her." Here Selden seems dimly aware that Lily's elegance is not only a product of labor, but a product of *other* people's labor: the nearly invisible army of workers who sew Lily's dresses, trim her hats, bleach her linens, wash her sheets, and swab her commode. His "confused" sense of their sacrifice is even more to the point, as the capital that buys this elegant creature's costumes can be traced back to its source in the labor of those dingy people who blur into the background behind and beneath her.

These thoughts lead Selden next to the question of Lily's difference from those on whose backs she is "pedalstalled": "He was aware that the qualities distinguishing her from the herd of her sex were chiefly external: as though a fine glaze of beauty and fastidiousness had been applied to vulgar clay. Yet the analogy left him unsatisfied, for a coarse texture will not take a high finish; and was it not possible that the material was fine, but that circumstance had fashioned it into a futile shape?" (7). Is Lily essentially different from the working women who are sacrificed to make her? Or is her difference only a matter of surface appearance? Perhaps this surface only masks their shared human identity and she, like the women who serve her, is made of clay. Dust to dust, ashes to ashes. Fate has allowed her a more luxurious fate and given her an external shimmer, but internally she is made of the same earth. But here Selden pauses, and questions this assumption of human equality. In *Little Women*, Mrs. March distinguishes between the gilding that disguised the ordinary materials of which the Moffats were made and the refined polish of her own daughters' intrinsically superior nature. Now Selden also wonders if such a refined polish as Lily Bart's might require an equally refined material. Perhaps Lily *is* made of better stuff than the tired women who trudge beside her. In Selden's opening vision of her, she seems nearly "another species"—a description that suggests a racializing of those dingy working-class women who form such a contrast to her fastidious lily-whiteness. However, if she is in fact made of better stuff, then that stuff has been given, he thinks, a "futile" shape.[116]

Here, I think, Selden is reflecting on Lily as a commodified spectacle, a product without a practical use, a waste of superior materials on a merely ornamental object. Moments later, as he prepares her tea in his apartment, his observation echoes his initial perception: "They both laughed, and he knelt by the table to light the lamp under the kettle, while she measured out the tea into a little tea-pot of green glaze. As he watched her hand, polished as a bit of old ivory, with its slender pink nails, and the sapphire bracelet slipping over her wrist, he was struck with the irony of suggesting to her such a life as his cousin Gertrude Farish had chosen" (8). Lily is again identified by her polish and her ivory-whiteness. Now her body appears as a refined, elegant piece of jewelry, a product of empire: ivory with an "old" line of descent. The twist is that this privileged identity appears also as a kind of slavery, a life that she never chose and that she cannot escape: "She was so evidently the victim of the civilization which had produced her, that the links of her bracelet seemed like manacles chaining her to her fate" (8).

And yet, to Lily, the links of her bracelet are a life-line suspending her above the encroaching tide of dinginess below. Lily's fear of dinginess is in part a realistic fear of falling from her high status into the working class. As she explains frankly to Selden, "If I were shabby no one would have me: a woman is asked out as much for her clothes as for herself. The clothes are the background, the frame, if you like: they don't make success, but they are a part of it. Who wants a dingy woman?" (12–13). Like Amy's pickled limes, Lily's expensive clothes display her right to enter the territory of the wealthy and well-connected.[117] When Selden suggests that Lily might live more independently, like his cousin, who maintains her own apartment, Lily is disparaging; his example does not apply because Gerty is not "marriageable," her unconventional life has disqualified her, "and besides, she has a horrid little place, and no maid, and such queer things to eat. Her cook does the washing and the food tastes of soap. I should hate that, you know"(8). Lily's objections are revealing. Gerty's whole life represents a rejection of the class boundary on which Lily's identity depends: not only does she spend her time and slender funds aiding young working women, but in her own little home the performance of leisure has broken down, and the separation of kitchen from drawing room has been broached. When Lily, in desperation, spends the night there, she wakens to an unfamiliar sight: her dress from the night before: "Finery laid off is as unappetizing as the remains of a feast, and it occurred to Lily that, at home, her maid's vigilance had always spared her the sight of such incongruities" (133).

While Lily's Aunt Peniston seems dedicated to the double-life that Anne McClintock describes — a hidden labor of housekeeping coupled with a public display of leisure — Lily seems to believe in the fiction of elite women's freedom from work and all its signs. Although she actually works hard to produce her own charming performances, she seems to believe that wealth will ultimately free her from this burden too. Lily's stationery seal is a flying ship in full sail, with the single word "Beyond." Lily's longing for transcendence, for an ineffable "beyond," oftentimes appears to be the consumer's longing for the ineffable happiness promised by the commodities that beckon to her. In this promised dream world, wishes will be transformed instantly into realities by invisible hands. Given a choice, Lily would prefer to remain in her hot-house drawing room, undisturbed not only by the cold outside her windows, but also by the consciousness of the labor that creates her comfort. Her response to Mrs. Peniston's expensive, clean home is very revealing: not only does Lily not "dilate" as she enters it, but she actively recoils "from the complacent ugliness of Mrs. Peniston's black walnut, from the slippery gloss of the vestibule tiles, and the mingled odor of sapolio and furniture-polish that met her at the door" (78). Here, as in Gerty's apartment, her distaste arises in part from the promiscuous mingling of public and private: the taste of soap in the food, the smell of cleaning in the vestibule.

The other contributor to her distaste is style. At Mrs. Peniston's house Lily is forced to surround herself with objects that reflect her aunt's taste, not her own. Like the young Amy forced to wear her cousin's unfashionable hand-me-downs, Lily experiences a kind of psychic torture. As she explains to Selden, after apologizing for disparaging Gerty, "We're different, you know: she likes being good, and I like being happy. And besides, she is free and I am not. If I were, I daresay I could manage to be happy even in her flat. It must be pure bliss to arrange the furniture just as one likes, and give all the horrors to the ash-man. If only I could do over my aunt's drawing-room I should be a better woman" (8). In what sense she would be a "better woman" is not entirely clear, but it appears that Lily believes that commodities, well-chosen, can provide not only happiness, but moral worth. For her aunt, the mark of such worthiness is cleanliness; for Lily the mark is beauty. Both are materialistic beliefs, for both marks are only the material signifiers of nonmaterial qualities, not the qualities themselves. Lily may believe that an artfully arranged drawing room will magically confer the qualities it signifies, but she is making the consumer idolater's mistake. The commodity can only symbolize the qualities associated with it; it cannot confer them. There is an unbridgeable gap between signifier and signified. In the course of the novel, Lily will have to learn, painfully, how a beautiful appearance can hide an ugly character and how material wealth can mask moral poverty.

Finally, it is important to note that Lily's own embodiment threatens her with dinginess. Her ambition to make herself into a beautiful, jewel-like object is an ambition to transcend her own mortality, to go "beyond" her own immanence into a realm of transcendent beauty. Lily's dream of success is, among other things, a dream of ultimate control and self-sufficiency. Her emotional and physical needs seem impediments to this achievement. Feminist scholars such as Susan Bordo, Sherry Ortner, and Simone De Beauvoir have argued that, in Western culture at least, women's bodies have been perceived as more burdened by natural immanence than men's.[118] Hence the cluster of cultural images that associate women with mortality and pollution: the archetype of the whore. Hence also a related and complementary cluster of images of women who magically transcend this "earthiness": the archetype of the virgin. In the context of Wharton's novel, this opposition between virgin and whore, clean and dirty women, is played out in the opposition McClintock describes between leisured ladies and the devalued women who serve them. For Lily to fall from her privileged social position is not only to lose her sense of her identity as a valuable object, but to be dirtied beyond recognition, psychically disfigured, even destroyed. The compensations of embodiment — sexual pleasure, emotional care, human intimacy — are unknown to her, even unnamed.

Here again a comparison with *Little Women* is instructive. Alcott resolves the contradiction described by McClintock by breaking down the boundary between these two opposed images: woman as "pure" commodity and as "dirty" laborer. Mrs. March purposefully initiates her four daughters into the reality of labor, and teaches them to honor the work that produces their tidy (but not immaculate) home and wholesome meals. The family cook and housekeeper, Hannah, is a visible presence, valued and acknowledged. In one entertaining chapter Mrs. March deliberately allows her four girls to enjoy a completely leisured "vacation," which results in their increasing dissatisfaction with life and themselves. The lesson, she explains to them, is that leisure is only sweet in relation to labor.[119] In the concluding chapter, "Harvest Time," the three surviving daughters find ample compensation for their embodiment and labor in their family attachments. Compared to the comfort of their children's affections, marital satisfactions, and maternal loyalties, their graying hair and wrinkles are a small price to pay. The marks of physical aging are not seen as irretrievable losses of personal capital or descents into disfiguring immanence, but as outward signs of inward experiences, an embodied and honored history. As Alcott's narrator comments, Marmee's beloved face "could never grow old" to her daughters.[120] In *Little Women* transcendence is achieved not by rejecting the body and its natural fate, but through an acceptance, even an embrace of it. The family provides a love that does not deny suffering or loss, but that turns such events into opportunities for moral instruction and emotional development. Grief, tempered by faith in divine justice and resurrection, is the "cross" that awakens compassion and teaches the value of care.

Lily, however, has no notion of such compensations. For her, aging can only represent loss. Her anxious scanning of her face in various mirrors throughout the novel testifies to her growing panic. If she sees herself as a commodity, it's one with a limited shelf life.[121] Unmarried at twenty-nine, she finds her age cruelly close to an expiration date. Her fear of dinginess is not only a fear of poverty, but a displaced fear of mortality, for which material poverty is a signifier, just as material wealth is a signifier of transcendence. Yet poverty is more than just a signifier of mortality; it can also be its agent. As Abraham Maslow points out, physical security is a prerequisite for all other aspects of human development, but while such security may be a required condition for happiness and self-realization, it is a not a sufficient one. Wealth is no guarantee of happiness, and it cannot save us from the death all human beings face.[122] It is this existential threat that *Little Women*'s characters learn to counter, not with money and goods, but with the solace of human connection, love, and forgiveness. However, the only way Lily knows how to deal with frailty, loneliness, guilt, and vulnerability, as well as the deeper fear of death itself, is not through expressing these emotions and sharing them with a compassionate listener, but through acquiring the commodified signs of happiness. This consumer fantasy is a dream of transcendence achieved through mastery of the material world, including mastery of death as signified by dirt and decay. Thus the word "beyond" becomes ambiguous in this text; it could signify transcendence of the material world, but it could also signify an imagined escape *into* it: "beyond" the dingy and into an imagined paradise of material wealth. We can see a similar idolatrous faith in the young Jay Gatsby's wonder at Daisy Fay's expensive house and magical beauty. As the "wicker of the settee squeaks fashionably" on her elegant porch, "bright with the bought luxury of star-shine," Gatsby kisses Daisy's cool lips. Suddenly, he becomes "overwhelming aware of the youth and mystery that wealth imprisons and preserves, of the freshness of many clothes and of Daisy, gleaming like silver, safe and proud above the hot struggles of the poor."[123]

What critic Judith Fetterley has called Lily's temptation to be a beautiful object is thus also a temptation to escape the human condition.[124] As material comforts and aesthetic pleasures become insidious substitutes for love and human kinship, they act as a kind of narcotic, which cannot ever fully satisfy, but only mask deeper needs and fears.[125] These are escapist pleasures, more "poisoned sugarplums" — dangerous and addictive substitutes for the "real thing." Hence the meaning of Wharton's title, taken from Ecclesiastes 7:4: "The heart of the wise is in the house of mourning, but the heart of fools is in the house of mirth." Lily's one chance to learn from loss, her father's death, is missed. Instead of learning that love can alleviate suffering and survive even death, she witnesses Mrs. Bart's callous abandonment of her husband, a fate that may be in store for her should she fail to live up to her mother's expectations. It is hard to imagine a character more distrustful of human relationships, more out of touch with emotional needs, more alone than Lily Bart. If Meg, Jo, Beth, and Amy are fortified on their "Pilgrim's Progress" with their mother's love and advice, along with their personalized books of instruction, Lily faces the road before her alone and unguided. It should therefore not be surprising that she often strays from the right path, or cannot even recognize the right path when she sees it. Toward the close of book 1, Wharton writes, "Miss Bart had in fact been treading a devious way, and none of her critics could have been more alive to the fact than herself; but she had a fatalistic sense of being drawn from one wrong turning to another, without ever perceiving the right road till it was too late to take it" (101). In the next chapter, I turn my attention to Lily's pilgrimage and her progress, such as it is.

CHAPTER 3

Lily at the Crossroads

Vanity Fair versus the Republic of the Spirit

Given Lily's character, it might be surprising to find her on that Sunday morning at Bellomont fully intending to attend church. She has selected a gray dress of the properly devotional cut and even asked her hostess for a prayer book to bring with her, along with the two Trenor daughters, who have agreed to drag themselves from their slumbers to keep her company. The mystery is solved, however, when one takes into account the presence at Bellomont of Percy Gryce, the wealthy unmarried son of the housekeeping paragon described earlier. Lily has cased her mark astutely and is now crafting an appropriate persona to hook and reel him in. First of all, Gryce is a rather shy and sheltered young man, out of place in the racy Bellomont circle. Indeed, "Mr. Gryce "thought it a very materialistic society; there were times when he was frightened by the talk of the men and the looks of the ladies" (43). Lily knows exactly how to allay his anxieties, so much so that that "he was glad to find that Miss Bart, for all her ease and self-possession, was not at home in so ambiguous an atmosphere. For this reason he had been especially pleased that she would, as usual, attend the young Trenors to church on Sunday morning" (43).

Skillfully assuming the role of *la jeune fille à marier*, Lily has put away her cigarettes and avoided gambling at the bridge table, at least for the duration of her campaign. Discovering that Mr. Gryce has inherited a famous collection of Americana, she pumps the literate Lawrence Selden for information on rare books. When she encounters Gryce on the train to Bellomont, she flatteringly turns the conversation to his newly acquired inheritance. Here we get see how adroit she is at psychological manipulation: "Most timidities have such secret compensations, and Miss Bart was discerning enough to know that the inner vanity is generally in proportion to the outer self-deprecation. With a more confident person she would not have dared to dwell so long on one topic, or to show such exaggerated interest in it; but she had rightly guessed that Mr. Gryce's egoism was thirsty soil, requiring constant nurture from without" (20).

Lily's campaign is even more desperate than usual because of the gambling debts she has run up at bridge. In fact, reviewing her finances at Bellomont, Lily is disturbed to find how reduced they are, at the same time her face in the mirror appears more tired and more lined than usual. The evidence that time and funds are running out prompts a moment of rebellion; she even considers "dropping out of the race" and trying to make an independent life, away from the wealthy people whose standards she, for the moment anyway, despises. But "she was too intelligent not be honest with herself." The kind of life she could afford is not a life she would be willing to live: "She had barely enough money to pay her dress-makers' bills and her gambling debts; and none of the desultory interests which she dignified with the names of tastes was pronounced enough to enable her to live contently in obscurity." That recognition steels her resolve: "She knew that she hated dinginess as much as her mother had hated it, and to her last breath she meant to fight against it, dragging herself up again and again above its flood till she gained the bright pinnacles of success which presented such a slippery surface to her touch" (33).

Lily is well aware of the difficulties facing her. Given his maternal training, Gryce will no doubt resist some of her marital plans: "She knew that Mr. Gryce was of the small chary type most inaccessible to impulses and emotions. He had the kind of character in which prudence is a vice." And yet Lily is confident of her ability to manipulate even so dense a medium: "Such a guarded nature must find one huge outlet of egoism, and she determined to be to him what his Americana had hitherto been: the one possession in which he took sufficient pride to spend money on it." Lily's analysis draws on her own maternal training, and she seems to be unconsciously seeking to reproduce in Gryce the kind of narcissistic attachment she knew in Mrs. Bart: "She knew that this generosity to self is one of the forms of meanness, and she resolved so to identify herself with her husband's vanity that to gratify her wishes would be to him the most exquisite form of self-indulgence." Intelligent enough to realize that her strategy "might first necessitate a resort to some of the very shifts and expedients from which she intended it would free her," nevertheless, "she felt sure than in a short time she would be able to play the game in her own way" (41).

Increasingly certain of her ultimate success, by Saturday morning Lily finds her face looking fresh and unlined in her morning mirror. Her beauty now seems less ephemeral, more a well-armored and irresistible weapon; it seems to have a kind of "permanence." She can see her future as Gryce's wife: "Her vulgar cares were at end. She would be able to arrange her life as she pleased, to soar into that empyrean of security where creditors cannot penetrate." She will have more stylish gowns than Judy Trenor, and give more successful parties. No longer in danger of being exiled from their charmed circle, she now sees her companions at Bellomont bathed in a rosy glow: "Society is a revolving body which is apt to be judged according to its place in each man's heaven; and at present it was turning its illuminated face to Lily" (41). Under the pressure of her anxieties, these very companions had seemed "brutal" and "self-engrossed"; now they seem almost admirable: "She liked their elegance, their lightness, their lack of emphasis: even the self-assurance which at times was so like obtuseness now seemed the natural sign of social ascendancy. They were the lords of the only world she cared for, and they were ready to admit her to their ranks and let her lord it with them" (41–42). Lily's flexibility, her dependence on her material setting, and her lack of stable inner values leaves her vulnerable to whatever influence is most dominant at the moment.

At the same time, a nagging awareness begins to grow. By Saturday evening, when it seems as if the campaign is about to be won, Lily allows some of her more rebellious thoughts to enter her consciousness: "She had been bored all the afternoon by Percy Gryce—the mere thought seemed to waken an echo of his droning voice—but she could not ignore him on the morrow, she must follow up on her success, must submit to more boredom, must be ready with fresh compliances, and adaptabilities, and all on the bare chance that he might ultimately decide to do her the honour of boring her for life" (23). By Sunday morning, when her demure gray dress and prayer book arrive in time for her church-going performance, the spark of rebellion "flashed a long light down the years." She imagines herself forced to attend the most expensive church in New York every Sunday, seated in the family pew next to an increasingly stout Percy Gryce, who would contribute handsomely to the parish and eventually become a warden. Lily has no illusions about the spiritual quality of these activities: "Once in the winter the rector would come to dine, and her husband would beg her to go over the list and see that no *divorcées* were included, except those who had shown signs of penitence by being re-married to the very wealthy." Admittedly, "there was nothing especially arduous in this round of religious obligations; but it stood for a fraction of that great bulk of boredom which loomed across her path" (47). In other words, perhaps she won't be able to control the game after all.

Despite her plan to close the deal and elicit a marriage proposal from Mr. Gryce that very morning on the way back from church, Lily impulsively invents an excuse, and ducks out of her commitment. Instead of taking the omnibus, she decides to give in to that "streak of sylvan freedom" in her and walk—not in the direction of Sunday services, but into the beautiful fall woods. While her decision is consistent with her past history of sabotaging her own best-laid places for capturing husbands, this time it is given special impetus by Lawrence Selden's arrival at Bellomont the night before. That arrival occurs as a surprise to Lily, just when she is at the peak of luxuriant security, newly appreciative of her friends' fine qualities. His entrance on the scene has much the same effect that Laurie's similar entrance has at the Moffats' ball in *Little Women*. In the chapter titled "Vanity Fair," Meg is also submerged in the rosy glow of a luxury she had longed for. Laurie's critical gaze reminds her of the March family's values, values she has temporarily forgotten, and her own vision adjusts accordingly. Similarly, Jo during her stay in New York finds that conversation with Professor Bhaer results in an abrupt change in her vision, as though she had put on his glasses. Through those glasses, her ambition to gain fame as a writer of lurid adventures stories suddenly appears tawdry and morally suspect.

Lawrence Selden has the same effect on Lily when he appears at her version of vanity fair, an effect that Wharton describes through carefully linked images of light and vision: "His presence shed a new light on her surrounding" and had a "way of adjusting her vision" (45). Whereas only moment earlier, Lily had seen her friends through a "rosy glow," turning her eyes from Selden she finds "herself scanning her little world through his retina: it was as though the pink lamps had been shut off and the dusty daylight let in" (45). Now Judy Trenor looks like "a jeweller's window lit by electricity" and Gus Trenor "with his heavy carnivorous head sunk between his shoulders," seems to "prey" on the jellied plover before him. Between their host and hostess the guests now appear as "dreary and trivial," a "long stretch of vacuity" (45). The implications of this shift in vision are not lost on Lily; she even smiles at the difference. Her friends have gone from brilliant to dull; she now sees the "poverty of their achievement" beneath of the glitter of their display, and she feels a certain shame at recollecting the way she had surrendered to their standards: "Then they had symbolized what she was gaining, now they stood for what she was giving up" (45).

As it had with Percy Gryce, the foreknowledge of the price Lily will have to pay for approval suddenly intrudes on her sense of renewed security: "She had closed her eyes an instant, and the vacuous routine of the life she had chosen stretched before her like a long white road without dip or turning: it was true she was to roll over it in a carriage instead of trudging it on foot, but sometimes the pedestrian enjoys the diversion of a short cut which is denied to those on wheels" (45–46). The metaphor here is again that of the pilgrim who chooses the leisure of riding over the effort of walking. Like Thoreau, who argued that the traveler who walked to Boston gained more in the end than the man who took the comfortable train but earned his ticket through soul-killing labor, Lily is realizing that luxury may have unforeseen costs, including the rich possibilities of life itself.[1] That this uncomfortable insight should be prompted by Lawrence Selden is appropriate, for Selden, like his cousin Gerty, represents the values of the old Protestant tradition, the values extolled in Alcott's novel. Since Selden's gaze opens the book, and his presence is a key to Lily's divided intentions, it is worth looking more closely at his character and its implications.[2]

While Lily's professed goal is to marry, Selden's is to avoid marriage. As Wharton explains, this is not from "any poverty of feeling, but because, in a different way, he was, as much as Lily, the victim of his environment" (120). Just as Lily's motives are profoundly mixed, so are Selden's, though with significant differences due to gender as much as upbringing. Like Lily's, Selden's means are slender. A lawyer by profession, he can afford a shabby but comfortable flat, filled with books he has managed to purchase not because of their rarity and investment value, as is the case with the Gryce collection, but because he loves the writing within their covers. Although, as Lily complains, "no one wants a dingy woman," a relatively shabby single man is acceptable, as long as he has the requisite cultural and social capital: a good education, a respectable profession, and some entertaining conversation. Selden enjoys his access to the Dorsets' elite circle, all the while treasuring his freedom from economic dependency. A wife with expensive requirements would jeopardize that freedom. And yet, while a sensible, "nice" girl might be someone he could support on his small income, he confesses to his cousin Gerty that he can't bring himself to marry one. He prefers elegant hot-house flowers like Lily, whose tastes he cannot afford, or Bertha Dorset, with whom he has had a clandestine affair but whose marriage to the wealthy George Dorset keeps her safely beyond his reach. His gaze in the opening pages is that of a disciplined consumer window-shopping on Fifth Avenue. While he can look and even sample the goods, he knows he cannot buy.

His preference for the luxury of a charming woman is one ingrained by family history. As Wharton's narrator explains, "it had been Selden's fate to have a charming mother: her graceful portrait, all smiles and Cashmere, still emitted a faded scent of the indefinable quality. His father was the kind of man who delights in a charming woman: who quotes her, stimulates her, and keeps her perennially charming" (120). Like the real Abby Alcott, who prided herself on her excellent taste while criticizing others for their flashy display, neither of Selden's parents "cared for money, but their disdain of it took the form of always spending a little more than was prudent" (120). Also like the Alcotts, the Seldens appear to be models of the Romantic bohemian, a type the historian Colin Campbell described in *The Romantic Ethic and the Rise of Modern Consumerism*.[3] Their disdain for materialism is coupled with a conscious pride in their distinction, expressed in their impeccable taste: "If their house was shabby, it was exquisitely kept; if there were good books on the shelves there were also good dishes on the table. Selden senior had an eye for a picture, his wife an understanding of old lace; and both were so conscious of restraint and discrimination in buying that they never quite knew how it was that the bills mounted up" (120).

As Campbell explains, the Romantic bohemian emphasis on consumption as self-expression, as opposed to idolatrous materialism or invidious competition, resulted in a moralizing of shopping, a new understanding of consumer goods as material symbols of authentic internal character.[4] Just as Amy's essential distinction is signaled by her ability to express her exquisite style within her meager means, the Seldens assert their freedom from vulgar materialism without surrendering their right to a setting reflecting their refined sensibility. Although they might seem poor compared to the families of Selden's friends, they live in an "atmosphere where restricted means were felt only as a check on aimless profusion: where the few possessions were so good that their rarity gave them a merited relief, and abstinence was combined with elegance in a way exemplified by Mrs. Selden's knack of wearing her velvet as if it were new" (120). However, while Alcott applauds Amy's progress from the little girl who squanders her sister's money on pickled limes to the young lady who "makes do" with inexpensive tulle, as well as Meg's self-discipline in forgoing her expensive purple silk in deference to her husband's limited means and hard work, Wharton's assessment of the Seldens is more qualified. Despite their sense of righteous restraint, those bills keep mounting up. Financial discipline and tasteful self-expression are not so easy to reconcile after all, as the real-life Abby Alcott discovered. Wharton, unlike Alcott, is not so sure that economic and material needs can be transcended through imagination and right thinking.

Just as Lily's awareness of life's possibilities is shaped by her mother's view, so Selden's "views of womankind in especial were tinged by the remembrance of the one woman who had given him his sense of 'values'" (120–21). While the result is straightforwardly positive in Alcott's world, the consequences for Selden are more complex and divided. From his mother he has "inherited his detachment from the sumptuary side of life; the stoic's carelessness of material things, combined with the Epicurean's pleasure in them. Life shorn of either feeling appeared to him a diminished thing; and nowhere was the blending of the two ingredients so essential as in the character of a pretty woman" (121). Whether he can find a female version of his own Romantic bohemianism remains, of course, to be seen. Lily, as we know, is not an Amy March: a young lady capable of painting her party shoes to resemble the blue satin she cannot afford.

And yet something in Lily responds strongly to Selden's presence. As Wharton explains, "the peculiar charm of her feeling for Selden was that she understood it; she could put her finger on every link of the chain that was drawing them together" (52). Those links belong, of course, to a very different chain than that of her jeweled bracelet, those "manacles" that tie her tight to the fate her mother ordained for her. These links connect to other impulses: to perceptions less cultivated and feelings less articulate. There is Selden's reputation as a literate and educated man: "Lily, who prided herself on her broad-minded recognition of literature, and always carried an Omar Khayyam in her traveling-bag, was attracted by this attribute, which she felt would have had its distinction in an older society" (53). Then there is his height, which seems to lift him above the crowd and to make his mental superiority materially visible. And his "keenly-modelled dark features which, in a land of amorphous types, gave him the air of belonging to a more specialized race, of carrying the impress of a concentrated past" (53). As the narrator puts it rather dryly, "It was . . . one of his gifts to look his part" (53). In the phrase of sentimental romance, Selden is tall, dark, and handsome.[5]

Finally, there are Selden's manners and style: "Everything about him accorded with the fastidious element in her taste, even to the light irony with which he surveyed what seemed to her most sacred. She admired him most of all, perhaps, for being able to convey as distinct a sense of superiority as the richest man she had ever met" (52–53). Given what we know of Lily's respect for wealth, this is high praise indeed. However, Selden is able to project this superiority, this aura of what Pierre Bourdieu calls "distinction," without a display of wealth, without the conventional material signs. This is again the mark of the Romantic bohemian.[6] As Mrs. March explains to the young Amy March, true quality does not need to be displayed through status symbols because people whose respect is worth having will inevitably recognize it. Inner character cannot help but shape outer style, whatever one's material means. As we have seen, Alcott's novel seems to say that distinction in an inborn, intrinsic characteristic: one that can be nurtured and refined, but not acquired wholesale.

While Wharton's views on the sources of distinction (nature or nature?) are more qualified than Alcott's, as my later discussion of less elite characters such as Simon Rosedale and Nettie Struther will demonstrate, the affinities between Lily and Selden seem clear. Both appear to be of a "specialized race": their sensibilities are more refined, their tastes more sophisticated than those of the merely rich. However, Lily cannot help being seduced by the signs of happiness displayed by the affluent society in which she lives. Her acquired faith in wealth's ability to make her happy, and her fear of any emotional attachment that would sever her links to that wealth, make her attraction to Selden deeply problematic. Nonetheless, Selden's very opposition to the values by which she was raised is part of that attraction. It is not that he is exceptionally brilliant or successful; "in his own profession he was surpassed by more than one man who had bored Lily through many a weary dinner." Rather, it is his attitude toward their common society that draws her: "He had preserved a certain social detachment, a happy air of viewing the show objectively, of having points of contact outside the great gilt cage in which they were all huddled for the mob to gape at. How alluring the world outside the cage appeared to Lily, as she heard its door clang on her!" And yet Lily also knows that the door is never really shut, but that "most of the captives were like flies in a bottle, and having once flown in, could never regain their freedom. It was Selden's distinction that he had never forgotten the way out" (45). All of this suggests that Lily, perhaps unconsciously, senses in Selden the thwarted values and ambitions she once felt in her father, the source of that streak of "latent idealism" her mother had so strenuously tried to eradicate. Like Lily's father (and Wharton's), Selden, with his own library of treasured books, carries "the impress of a concentrated past"; he has been shaped by an older culture now being rapidly eclipsed.[7]

In sum, if the central thread of Wharton's plot is the romantic attraction of these two people, it is a tangled thread. Although Lily and Selden have much in common, one element of that commonality is their ambivalence, their divided natures. And much of the novel's tension is whether they will resolve the inner conflicts that keep them apart. As the novel's readers know, they do not succeed, but this study's task is not only to analyze why they fail, but what effect their relationship has on the novel's heroine. Lily does not find the happy ending, the earthly celestial city that Meg, Jo, and Amy find at *Little Women*'s close. She will not end her pilgrimage with marriage validating her moral maturation. And yet, Lily does develop, does grow in response to Selden, and it is Wharton's strength as a writer not to make this growth a simple matter. Rather, it is painful, even tortuous: a product and a source of suffering, not mirth.

The opening scene in Selden's bachelor apartment sketches the dynamic between them. First, there is Lily's unconventional decision to accompany him there in the first place. Young marriageable women risked their reputations by this kind of behavior, as Lily well knows. Her agreeing to do so is impulsive, a product of her wild, sylvan streak. Then, there is Lily's equally unconventional decision to appeal to him as a confidant. This seems strangely out of character for Lily, who has been trained to control her self-presentation at all times. However, Lily's attitude toward Selden is mixed. On the one hand, she is attracted to him. On the other hand, she has rejected him as a potential husband. Although she may recognize his superiority, that recognition is not enough to make him marriageable. Her allegiance is still to the wealth she believes she needs to survive. Having ruled Selden out as an eligible buyer, Lily can drop her mask and stop selling herself.[8]

The result is a conversation that appears unprecedented for her. "Don't you see," she says, "that there are men enough to say pleasant things to me, and that what I want is a friend who won't be afraid to say disagreeable ones when I need them? Sometimes I have fancied you might be that friend — I don't know why, except that you are neither a prig or a bounder, and that I shouldn't have to pretend with you or be on my guard against you" (9). Her appeal is a confession of her emotional isolation and moral confusion: "You don't know how much I need such a friend,' she said. 'My aunt is full of copy-book axioms, but they were all meant to apply to conduct in the early fifties. I always feel that to live up to them would include wearing book-muslin with gigot sleeves" (9–10).[9] Selden, unsurprisingly, appears at first not to take this request seriously. However, Lily closes her appeal by presenting herself in an entirely new guise: "Her voice had dropped to a note of seriousness, and she sat gazing up at him with the troubled gravity of a child" (9).

This appearance of the troubled child in Lily is a response to her instinctive trust in Selden — her confidence that he is "neither a prig nor a bounder," but a person whose judgment and kindness she can depend on. The true beginning of the novel, this moment marks the long-delayed initiation of Lily's painful growth toward self-awareness. Her interaction with Selden somehow coaxes the "troubled child" her mother denied into the open. Through their dialogue that child begins to speak. With Selden's gentle, nonjudgmental encouragement, Lily begins to voice opinions and feelings she has never articulated before. As we saw in *Little Women*, similar dialogues, the keystone of Bronson Alcott's educational philosophy, are fundamental to Mrs. March's guidance of her daughters' development. By the time Meg, Jo, and Amy are old enough for courtship, they are at least partially self-aware, able to articulate their emotions, their values, and even their inner conflicts. While the men to whom they are attracted — Laurie, John Brooke, and Professor Bhaer — occasionally have to remind them of their better selves, at least they come to their adult relationships with prior training. Not so Lily. At twenty-nine years old, she appeals to Selden as much for the parenting she needed as a child as for the love she desires as an adult.[10]

Significantly, she confesses her own confusion to him, much as Meg confessed to Marmee after her own foray into vanity fair. Despite her mother's insistence that she seek a wealthy husband, Lily admits her failure and frustration with her quest. Selden's response shows his understandable reluctance to play the role she has assigned him: "Isn't marriage your vocation? Isn't it what you're all brought up for?" When she sighs and says, "I suppose so. What else is there?" he refuses to provide an alternative: "Exactly. And so why not take the plunge and have it over?" Again, she asks him to show her an alternate path: "You speak as though I ought to marry the first man who came along." Selden, however, still can't treat her appeal with entire seriousness: "I didn't mean to imply that you are as hard put to it as that. But there must someone with the requisite qualifications." At this Lily seems to drop her mask entirely, "She shook her head wearily. 'I threw away one or two good chances when I first came out—I suppose every girl does; and you know I am horribly poor—and very expensive. I must have a great deal of money'" (10). Lily's self-description is extraordinarily honest and strikingly self-deprecating: she admits she has made herself a commodity, and accepts responsibility for the choice. Compared to her performance as a *jeune fille à marier* for Percy Gryce, her confession shows how willing she is to let Selden behind the curtain.

While this initial conversation is inconclusive, it establishes their nascent attachment, and Lily's dawning dependency. It is not surprising therefore that Selden's arrival at Bellomont should shift Lily's perceptions and lead her to change her Sunday plans. Instead of performing the church-going young lady for Percy Gryce, she chooses a different path: into the Emersonian woods, free of confining and false social roles. Enjoying her solitude in nature is something to which Lily is not accustomed, and after a while, despite the beautiful weather and scenery, "she felt a stealing sense of fatigue as she walked; the sparkle had died out of her, and the taste of life was stale on her lips. She hardly knew what she had been seeking, or why the failure to find it had so blotted the light from her sky: she was only aware of a vague sense of failure, of an inner isolation deeper than the loneliness about her" (50). Then she encounters Selden. What is significant here is that Lily appears unconscious that she was seeking him. The effect of his presence is immediate. When he asks her to accompany him on a walk in the Bellomont woods later in the day, she agrees. When Lily joins him that afternoon, although she maintains the appearance of calm, "she was throbbing inwardly with a rush of thoughts" (52). As the narrator explains, "There were in her at the moment two beings, one drawing deep breaths of freedom and exhilaration, the other gasping for air in a little black prison-house of fears. But gradually the captive's gasps grew fainter, or the other paid less heed to them: the horizon expanded, the air grew stronger, and the free spirit quivered for flight."

The notion that Lily's internal life contains two beings is crucial to her development throughout the rest of the novel. The troubled child who spoke with such honesty in Selden's apartment appears to be related to this sylvan being now drawing "deep breaths of freedom" in the open air. The captive self seems to be the Lily who is manacled to her fate by Mrs. Bart's training in fear and submission. Given Selden's example and encouragement, Lily's uncultivated potential as a free spirit grows stronger and quivers for flight. The image suggests her stationery's seal: the ship under full sail, with "Beyond!" beneath. Just as Lily was unconscious of the motives behind her walk, so "she could not herself have explained the buoyancy which seemed to lift and swing her above the sun-suffused world at her feet." Untutored and inarticulate, she cannot name her own feelings: "Was it love, she wondered, or a mere fortuitous combination of happy thoughts and sensations? How much of it was owing to the spell of the perfect afternoon, the scent of the fading woods, the thought of the dullness she had fled from?" Some kinds of desire she is well-acquainted with: "She had several times been in love with fortunes or careers, but only once with a man." And that "love," the narrator explains, was merely superficial, more a matter of blue eyes and wavy hair. Today's sense of freedom and "lightness" seems drawn from deeper springs: Lily and Selden's developing bonds of affinity and trust. Most people recognize love by comparing it to their experience of parental care and acceptance. Lily has no such model for these bonds, no prior experience by which to assess and name them.

The memory of this Sunday's conversation with Selden remains with Lily for the rest of her short life. Although it has no immediate consequences, their dialogue brings out new dimensions in their characters, new even to themselves. It will have a determining influence on Lily's final choices.[11] The dialogue begins with Selden's somewhat flippant response to Lily asking him, without a "tinge of coquetry," the reason for his being at Bellomont: "Because you're such a wonderful spectacle: I always like to see what you are doing" (53). For example, he continues, her walking with him "is only another way of making use of your material. You are an artist and I happen to be the bit of colour you are using today. It's part of your cleverness to be able to produce premeditated effects extemporaneously" (53). Lily cannot help smiling at Selden's acute ability to read her, but when she questions his imputation of premeditation, and asserts her ability to yield to impulse, he replies, "Have n't I told you that your genius lies in converting impulses into intentions?" At this Lily brings in a new note of "weariness." "My genius? . . . . Is there any final test of genius but success? And I certainly have n't succeeded" (54).

Now their dialogue probes a deeper subject. Selden asks Lily, given her sense of failure, for her definition of success. Hesitating, she answers, "Why, to get as much as one can out of life, I suppose. It's a relative quality, after all. Is n't that your idea of it?" (54). Selden's response is prompt and unqualified: "My idea of it? God forbid! . . . My idea of success . . . is personal freedom." Puzzled, Lily asks if he means freedom from "worries," the only kind of freedom she has hitherto imagined. Here again, his answer is prompt and unqualified: "From everything — from money, from poverty, from ease and anxiety, from all the material accidents. To keep a kind of republic of the spirit — that's what I call success." Surprisingly, Lily answers "with a responsive flash": "I know — I know — it's strange; but that's just what I've been feeling today." At this Selden looks into her eyes with a "latent sweetness" and asks: "Is the feeling so rare with you?" At this sudden intimacy, she blushes, "You think me horribly sordid, don't you. But perhaps it's rather that I never had any choice. There was no one, I mean, to tell me about the republic of the spirit." Implicit in her comment is awareness of her upbringing and her isolation, as well as the new feelings Selden is awakening in her. Selden, however, disavows responsibility. "There never is" anyone to tell you, he says. "It's a country one has to find the way to one's self." But Lily won't let him off so easily: "But I should never have found my way there if you had n't told me." His answer again attempts to minimize his role: "Ah, there are sign-posts — but one has to know how to read them." But "in a glow of eagerness" she again assigns him the responsibility of guiding her: "Well, I have known, I have known! . . . Whenever I see you, I find myself spelling out a letter of the sign — and yesterday — last evening at dinner — I suddenly saw a little way into your republic" (55).

Several important themes of the novel are laid out here. First there is Selden's idea of success as "freedom from all the material accidents." A very Emersonian philosophy, it implies that true self-realization is based on an extreme individualism, one in which the individual exists independent of all outer influences: financial, social, emotional. One thinks of Thoreau alone in his cabin fighting off loneliness, and discovering that a solitary walk in the woods dispels his mood and allows him to classify his need for human companionship as a kind of insanity.[12] Self-reliance is all, and even the well-intentioned help of others is suspect, as Selden suggests when he tells Lily that there never is anyone to tell you about the republic of the spirit. To be taught is to be dependent, and to be dependent is dangerous. Bronson Alcott's own version of this philosophy led to his disavowing of family ties and his experiment with celibacy at Fruitlands, an experiment that nearly led to his suicide and resulted in his revising his philosophy to base moral development not only on the individual but also on the family.[13] This is the debate that Lily, with her eager probing, is reviving. How can she become morally and spiritually literate without first being taught "how to read the signs"? Marmee gave her daughters careful instructions and a map to guide them on their pilgrimage. Lily is asking Selden for similar help.

While he makes no commitment to the task, Selden does respond by looking at Lily "with a changed eye." Hitherto, he has treated her as an "aesthetic amusement"; his attitude had been an "admiring spectatorship, and he would have been almost sorry to detect in her any emotional weakness which should interfere with the fulfillment of her aims" (54). Now her confession of weakness reveals a different Lily, one more vulnerable, more uncertain than the proud mannequin he had known. Moreover, he sees that her hesitations and her blushes represent a spontaneous response to him that could not possibly be part of her "scheme of life." In other words, she cannot control her attraction to him, and he cannot help but be flattered by it. And so, despite having "renounced sentimental experiments," he is drawn into the deepening conversation. Referring back to his republic of the spirit, he asks if she is "going to become one of us?" He draws out a cigarette and she eagerly reaches for the case, explaining that she has not smoked for days due to the requirements of her role as a *jeune fille*. Here Selden takes the opportunity to tease her: *jeune filles à marier* are not acceptable in the republic, not because it is a celibate order, though he is "bound to say that there are not many married people in it," but rather because she "will marry someone very rich and, and it's as hard for rich people to get into the kingdom of heaven" (56). Selden's comment both critiques Lily's role-playing as antithetical to his republic's insistence on personal integrity, and links its individualistic ethic back to the anti-materialist bias of the Protestant tradition.

Lily, however, questions the traditional association of material wealth with spiritual poverty. Such restrictions, she thinks are unjust, "because, as I understand it, one of the conditions of citizenship is not to think too much about money, and the only way not to think about money is to have a great deal of it." This, of course, is her faith that only money will free her from "worries." Selden is again unhesitating: "You might as well say that the only way not to think about air is to have enough to breathe. That is true enough in a sense; but your lungs are thinking about the air, if you are not. And so it is with your rich people — they may not be thinking of money, but they're breathing it all the while; take them into another element and see how they squirm and gasp!" (56). The imagery here recalls the description of Lily as a "hot-house flower," formed to live within an environment insulated by wealth. Within that hothouse she can live, she believes, serenely unconscious of the role money plays in her survival. Selden rightly points out that, deprived of that insulation, she will be made quickly aware of her dependence. Ignorance, in other words, is not independence.

Lily has no answer to this argument, so she responds *ad hominem*: "It seems to me . . . that you spend a good deal of your time in the element you disapprove of." Selden, however, turns her thrust aside easily: "Yes; but I have tried to remain amphibious: it's all right as long as one's lungs can work in another air. The real alchemy consists in being able to turn gold back again into something else; and that's the secret that most of your friends have lost." He is making at least two points important to the novel. First, there is his notion of being "amphibious." Because he believes that his identity is not dependent upon "material accidents," he also believes that he can enter the world of the wealthy with a kind of protective detachment. He can breathe their air, but he is not dependent upon it. Second, there is his notion of "alchemy." In alchemy, base elements were combined in the quest to transform them magically into gold: the all-desired symbol of happiness. Selden, however, challenges this goal. Aside from its role as decoration, gold's value is purely symbolic. Lily's friends have been content to identify themselves through their possession of this "sign of happiness," but happiness itself is not the same as the gold that symbolizes it. To create that happiness, gold must be exchanged for something that can be put to "use" in the real world.[14]

Lily answers by drawing upon the old Protestant notion of stewardship: that the amassing of wealth is morally acceptable so long as one uses it not for self-aggrandizement but for the greater good. Social position and wealth should be seen as opportunities, to be used for good or ill. At this Selden agrees with her, but counters that so few in society see their wealth as a means and not as an end: "The people who take society as an escape from work are putting it to its proper use; but when it becomes the thing worked for it distorts all the relations of life." Selden here appears to referring not just to society, but to the whole system of status so ably critiqued by Wharton's contemporary Thorstein Veblen.[15] Too often, the wealthy see their freedom from work as the source of their worth; the overriding goal of status substitutes for the more far-reaching goals of labor. "I don't underrate the decorative side of life," he continues. "It seems to me the sense of splendour has justified itself by what it has produced. The worst of it is that so much human nature is used up in the process. If we're all the raw stuff of the cosmic effects, one would rather be the fire that tempers a sword than the fish that dyes a purple cloak. And a society like ours wastes such good material in producing its little patch of purple!" Again, his complaint is that the status symbols that drive consumer culture have only decorative, not use, value. The purple cloak, like the purple silk an envious Meg March purchases (only to sacrifice later for her husband's sake) is the sign of the aristocrat, but if one's energy must be expended somewhere, how much better to devote it to making a functional object, a sword, that does real work in the world. Selden tactfully refrains from applying his lesson to Lily, but of course, she herself is her society's ultimate decorative object: designed as a wealthy husband's sign of prestige. Her "human nature" has been used up in making herself the equivalent of that purple cloak.[16]

The connection, however, is not lost on Lily, and she eventually protests, "Ah, you are as bad as the other sectarians . . . why do you call your republic a republic? It is a close corporation, and you create arbitrary objections in order to keep people out." To this Selden tries to play the gallant: "It is not *my* republic; if it were, I should have a *coup d'état* and seat you on the throne." Lily is not be deterred: "Whereas, in reality, you think I can never even get my foot across the threshold? Oh, I understand what you mean. You despise my ambitions — you think them unworthy of me!" Now she is at the heart of matter, and it leads Selden to smile without irony: "Well, is n't that a tribute? I think them quite worthy of most of the people who live by them." At this she again draws on the notion of stewardship to justify those ambitions. "But is n't it possible that, if I had the opportunities of these people, I might make better use of them? Money stands for all kinds of things — its purchasing quality is n't limited to diamonds and motor-cars." However, Selden knows Lily's appetite for luxury too well to believe that jewels and motor cars aren't her primary goals; in her case stewardship would be a rationalization, not a reality: "Not in the least: you might expiate your enjoyment of them by founding a hospital." Lily catches the implication and turns it back adroitly: "But if you think they are what I should really enjoy, you must think my ambitions are good enough for me." Selden laughs, and aims his barb straight at the faith that has guided her so long: "Ah, my dear Miss Bart, I am not divine Providence, to guarantee your enjoying the things you are trying to get!" At this she draws "a deep breath": "Then the best you can say for me is, that after struggling to get them I probably shan't like them? . . . What a miserable future you foresee for me!" And now Selden twists his barb and thrusts it deeper: "Well — have you never foreseen it for yourself?" Now he has hit home. In the process of this dialogue her fleeting and inarticulate emotions have been brought to full consciousness: "The slow colour rose to her cheek, not a blush of excitement but drawn from the deep wells of feeling; it was as if the effort of her spirit had produced it." Gently, Selden has brought her to the moment of confession: "Often and often . . . But it looks so much darker when you show it to me!" (56).

She has asked him for help reading the signs, and he has given it. She has begun to see the meaning of her own feelings. Now he has no answer to her exclamation of dismay. As they sit in silence "something throbbed between them in the wide quiet of the air," then Lily cries out with "a kind of vehemence": "Why do you do this to me? . . . Why do you make the things I have chosen seem hateful to me, if you have nothing to give me instead?" Selden is as surprised as she by the turn in their conversation, so far from his initial expectation of her, yet, "it was one of those moments when neither seemed to speak deliberately, when an indwelling voice in each called to the other across unsounded depths of feeling." And so he responds with similar gravity, "No, I have nothing to give you instead . . . If I had, it should be yours, you know." At this she hides her face in her hands and weeps. Selden, with a gesture "less passionate than grave," draws her hands away, all the way thinking to himself "somewhat cruelly, that even her weeping was an art." This flicker of detachment allows him to gain control of his voice as he asks, "between pity and irony": "Is n't it natural that I should try to belittle all the things I can't offer you?" At this she seems comforted, but then she withdraws her hands "not with a gesture of coquetry, but as though renouncing something to which she had no claim." Her counter is clear, if gentle: "But you belittle *me*, don't you . . . in being so sure they are the only things I care for?" Selden answers her straightaway: "But you do care for them, don't you. And no wishing of mine can alter that" (58).

Many words are said here, but one significantly is not. When Selden admits that he has "nothing" to replace the material wealth he has made hateful to Lily, he leaves unnamed the possibility of love. Here we see Selden's own fear of intimacy, of attachment. For Lily, love threatens her chance at wealth; for Selden, love threatens his right to freedom. Both have been drawn into unknown territory through their dialogue. Selden as much as Lily finds himself speaking from "unsounded depths of feeling," with the double meaning of "unsounded" referring to feelings unspoken as well as unexplored. Both act without premeditation, to return to the question that opened their conversation. Suddenly that conversation takes a new turn as Lily turns on him: "Ah . . . for all your fine phrases you're really as great a coward as I am, for you would n't have made one of them if you had n't been so sure of my answer." Now she is the one reading the signs, and the shock crystallizes Selden's "wavering intentions": "I am not so sure of your answer . . . And I do you the justice to believe that you are not either." They are engaged in a kind of poker, raising the stakes and calling each other's cards. Lily asks him point-blank: "Do you want to marry me?" He laughs and hedges his bet: "No, I don't want to—but perhaps I should if you did!" But when she accuses him of experimenting with her for his own amusement, he replies, "I am not making experiments . . . Or if I am, it is not on you but on myself. I don't know what effect they are going to have on me—but if marrying you is one of them, I will take the risk." Her challenge has loosened an inhibition long upheld in him; now she can afford to be more honest herself. "It would be a great risk, certainly—I have never concealed from you how great." And now he can afford to challenge her in turn: "Ah, it's you who are the coward!"

Wharton has brought them to the crisis of their dialogue. As they standing facing each other: "The soft isolation of the falling day enveloped them: they seemed lifted into a finer air. All the exquisite influences of the hour trembled in their veins, and drew them to each other as the loosened leaves were drawn to the earth." As Selden repeats his challenge, "She leaned on him for a moment, as if with a drop of tired wings: he felt as though her heart were beating rather with the stress of a long flight than the thrill of new distances." Then, "with a little smile of warning," Lily accepts his proposal in her own way: "I shall look hideous in dowdy clothes; but I can trim my own hats." The moment seems to bring them together in some private republic of the spirit. They stand in silence, "smiling at each other like adventurous children who have climbed to a forbidden height from which they discover a new world. The actual world at their feet was veiling itself in dimness, and across the valley a clear moon rose in the denser blue" (59).

In Louisa May Alcott's world, this moment would usher in a new phase of life for our heroine: married happiness and moral maturity. However, Wharton shadows this couple's mutual discovery with intimations of its fragility. Although Lily's inner spirit has managed its flight to freedom, she leans on Selden as if her strength is now gone, not renewed. While they seem to have found their way to the republic of the spirit, that "new world" is dangerously isolated and the "actual world" is hidden from their view. Most important, they come to this moment more like children than adults. They are unprepared for the consequences of their avowals. Significantly, although Lily believes that she can "trim her own hats," painful experience will teach her later that she cannot. She does not have the training, practical or moral, necessary to mitigate the deprivations of relative poverty. It is no wonder their intimacy is only momentary.

What breaks it is "a remote sound, like the hum of a giant insect, following the high-road, which wound whiter through the surrounding twilight." The automobile, one of the luxurious commodities they have just discussed, appears as a "black object" that cuts "across their vision." It seems to waken Lily from a dream. She moves instantly toward the downward path: "I had no idea it was so late! We shall not get back until after dark." Given what has just happened, she need not worry about their late return, but she seems to have instantly forgotten that she is no longer playing the role of the *jeune fille*. While for a moment it seemed that some authentic self had found its voice and accepted Selden's proposal of marriage, that self is now discarded as if it too were a role she were playing. "Selden was looking at her with surprise: it took him a moment to regain his usual view of her; then he said, with an uncontrollable note of dryness: 'That was not one of our party; the motor was going the other way.'" Although she reddens under his gaze, she persists, "But I told them I was not well — that I should not go out. Let us go down!" The Lily he had called forth is gone. She is no longer of his party. Perhaps her weeping *was* an art, merely a performance. "Selden continued to look at her; then he drew his cigarette-case from his pocket and slowly lit a cigarette. It seemed to him necessary, at that moment, to proclaim, by some habitual gesture of this sort, his recovered hold on the actual: he had an almost puerile wish to let his companion see that, their flight over, he had landed on his feet." As she takes a cigarette from him, she asks, as if a game had concluded, "Were you serious?" Her voice has "an odd thrill of gaiety which she might have caught up, in haste, from a heap of stock inflections, without having time to select the just note." With his own voice under better control, Selden retorts, "Why not? . . . You see I took no risks in being so" (60).

The Emersonian woods may be a place where the usual social conventions do not hold, and where one may safely drop the masks that society requires. But sooner or later, and here sooner rather than later, one must descend from the mountain and take one's place in society again. The key, Emerson himself believed, was to bring the detachment and equanimity of the woods back into town with you. However, this requires more strength than Lily has. Identity is shaped and reflected by its context, both natural and social. The latent identity hitherto uncultivated in Lily that begins to bloom in the relative safety of the autumn woods at Bellomont under the gentle encouragement of Lawrence Selden is too fragile, too lightly rooted to survive even the slightest intrusion of the world in which Lily normally sees herself. Alcott, as we have seen, also believed that identity needed more support than a trip into the woods could give it; hence her emphasis on the family and its conscious furthering of values. Lacking that support, Lily comes to this moment with Selden unprepared.

Later in the novel Selden recovers from this disappointment long enough to approach Lily again. This time he realizes the risk but is still willing to take it. He imagines the *Beyond!* on her stationery as "a cry for rescue," and sees himself as the mythic Perseus who comes to the aid of Andromeda, the beautiful maiden chained to a rock in the sea as a sacrifice to the gods. Given his experience at Bellomont, however, Selden now knows that "Perseus's task is not done when he has loosed Andromeda's chains, for her limbs are numb with bondage, and she cannot rise and walk, but clings to him with dragging arms as he beats back to land with his burden." And yet Selden believes that he has "strength for both — it was her weakness which had put the strength in him. It was not, alas, a clean rush of waves they had to win through, but a clogging mass of old associations and habits, and for the moment its vapours were in his throat. But he would see clearer, breathe freer in her presence: she was at once the dead weight at his breast, and the spar which should float them to safety" (125–26). What Selden does *not* see, however, is that Lily is so crippled by her bondage that she has come to love her chains.

Despite Lily's abrupt abandonment of Selden, and her disavowal of the free spirit he called forth, their dialogue reverberates through the novel. Its influence continues to shape her responses across a range of experiences. Given the scene's centrality to Lily's development and to Wharton's architectonic plot, it is worth taking a moment to explore its implications in more depth. As noted, Lawrence Selden, with his avowed membership in the republic of the spirit and freedom from all material accidents, seems a quintessential Protestant, if of the individualist Emersonian rather than the Edwardsian school. His influence on Lily reveals not only Wharton's view of her two main characters but also her core ideas about the power and limitations of Selden's approach to life's challenges. And here I would argue that while Wharton offers a compelling anti-materialistic ethos through Selden, she also subtly demonstrates its internal contradictions.

In this analysis I draw on the anthropologist Webb Keane's recent work on Protestantism's construction of the human subject as an individual separate from the material accidents of both conventional or customary language and symbolic goods.[17] Keane argues that the Protestant understanding of the self sees it as an abstract spirit, disembodied and set for contrast against a world of material objects. Similarly, the speech of the Protestant subject should be sincere, in the sense that it should be unmediated by tradition, custom, or social coercion. Language, like the self, should also be separated from its embeddedness in the material, social world and arise spontaneously from the interiority of the subject's soul. Keane thus sees a significant continuum between the Protestant suspicion of the supposedly materialistic practices of idolatrous Catholics — their enchanted objects and magical rituals — and their linguistic practices — their prescribed prayers and repeated litanies. Sincere speech, according to Protestant ideology, should be transparent, reflecting only the intentions of the individual subject and not carrying the burden of the external world. "Honest," "true," sincere speech has, as Lionel Trilling has noted, a moral implication.[18]

While Keane sees this link between attitudes toward material goods and toward individual speech as characteristically Protestant, he also sees these attitudes as characteristically modern. Moreover, he sees them as raising similar questions and problems as revealed in the ceremonial exchange of marriage gifts and the public performance of Protestant conversion narratives among the Sumbanese, the cultural group he studies. In the case of Sumbanese marriage gifts, Keane notes a shift from the traditional cultural view that such gifts are embodiments of the value and dignity of the participants to the more Protestant view that such gifts do not embody values but function as symbols of abstract virtues, an assessment that is of a piece with my earlier discussion of the attitudes toward consumer goods and the representation of individual identity. Similarly, Keane notes the anxiety in Sumbanese concern about the public performance of conversion where such performances are required to be spontaneous and sincere, an honest externalization in speech of internal states. Here, as in *Little Women*, authentic self-knowledge results in sincere speech.

However, Keane sees problems in these examples of gift exchange and conversion narratives. Those problems have, he argues, "two things in common": "One is that they both concern conflicting assumptions about the human subject that emerge in changes in its material mediations and objectifications. The second is that these conflicts ideologically align Protestant Christianity with the idea of modernity, referential language (as expressed in the values of transparency and truth) and the signifying practices that underlie abstract value (as expressed in money and commodities) in opposition to paganism, the past, performative and magical language, and ceremonial exchange." In what could be seen as a description of Lawrence Selden's comprehensive worldview, Keane writes, "In this highly simplified conceptual alignment, Protestantism and modernity (and, one might add, capitalism) *alike*, even *conjointly*, seek to abstract the subject from its material and social entanglements in the name of freedom and authenticity." These common problems reveal a "suppressed link between modernity's views of language and things and the more theological concerns expressed by Protestant and other religious reformers: the value of freedom and abstraction lies, at least in part, in their offer of transcendence. Gifts symbolic of intentions, words true to the heart and to the world of referents, actions taken without deference to other persons, and the abstract value represented by money are the quotidian forms of such transcendence."[19]

However, Keane argues that these efforts to disentangle people and things, individual speech and its social context, "suggest how, even in its most abstract and transcendent, the human subject *cannot* free itself from objectification. . . . It retains a material and social body, it continues to work on, transact, possess, and know itself through objects, and it is surrounded by social others. And it cannot even be sincere without publicly recognizable, socially indexical, materially embodied forms of speech." The crux of Keane's argument is that "agents continually constitute themselves through signifying practices that contain an irreducible material dimension. They are dynamically involved in a full-fledged representational economy in which the various ways that words and things circulate have not only logical implications but also causal consequences for one another." Thus, counter Lawrence Selden's rather self-aggrandizing pronouncement of his freedom from material accidents and social coercion, Keane believes that "people cannot free themselves from the practices by which they are embedded in the world of other persons: The tension between the project of transcendence and abstraction, on the one hand, and the inescapability of material and social mediations, on the other, will stubbornly persist."[20]

It is this stubborn persistence, even a stubborn need for these mediations, to which Lily calls attention. Selden's admonishment that the republic of the spirit is a place that one must discover for oneself is countered by Keane's observation that even the language by which that republic is named and through which one identifies with it circulates within a representational economy that is historical, shared, and learned. Lily, by her upbringing, has been shut out of this particular set of representations; these are signs she has not been taught and has not learned to read. Her request for help thus ironically questions the very foundations of the ideological community she wishes to join. However, I think it is worth adding an important qualification to Keane's valuable analysis, one that concerns the anti-foundational implications of this ideology as he describes it. In his account Protestantism and modernism are nearly conflated. Keane argues that their shared version of the subject, "to the extent it aspires to modernity . . . seeks to act as the source of its own authority. In many Protestant versions, at least, this source cannot be the physical body, material goods, or social standing, but rather the character and condition identified with its own interiority. And crucial to the concept of interiority, and the practices that promote it, is language."[21] Here, it seems to me, Keane is treating a Protestantism that no longer grounds the subject's authority and authenticity in divine, transforming grace. This modern, liberal Protestantism certainly informs Wharton's portrayal of turn-of-the-century New York, a society in which, as we have seen earlier, Protestant morality has lost much of its otherworldly reference.

Selden, for example, is a secularized Protestant subject who has lost his spiritual foundation, whether a belief in a God capable of granting him grace and a new heart, the Word of God as expressed in scripture, or even the vague "Over-Soul" on which Emerson's self-reliance ultimately depends. In *Little Women*, faith in crisis conversion and individual reliance on a divine source of grace was replaced by Christian nurture and the trustworthy responses of the family, in the authority of the parents and saving grace of affective bonds as activated through mourning and the consequent growth of moral awareness. Sentimentalism and Christian nurture, as numerous critics such as Jane Tompkins and Mary Louise Kete have shown, offer a critique of traditional Protestantism's emphasis on the individual, and hence represent one response to the contradictions inherent in Protestantism that Keane points out.[22] While *Little Women* certainly offers a classically Protestant emphasis on the separation of people from things and on the need for sincere speech, it also acknowledges that such practices must have a social foundation. In this sense, Alcott's emphasis on the crucial role of dialogue between parent and child, mentor and student, stresses the embeddedness of subject, for better or worse, in relationship with others. In true dialogical form, the subject's moral awareness is "called forth" through dialogue with a knowledgeable other, who, as we have seen, teaches her to reads the signs of the Protestant's representational economy.[23] However, by foregoing reliance on the miracle of crisis conversion and grounding moral development on its social context, sentimentalism and Christian nurture leave those who lack the appropriate guidance out in the cold, in the wilderness without a map.

My argument here is that while Lawrence Selden plays the role of mentor in a similar moral dialogue — he calls forth and then affirms Lily's sincere speech and thereby begins the process of her coming to self-awareness and the development of an authentic interiority — he then refuses the responsibility of guiding her. His allegiance to the individualism of his republic leads him to deny Lily's vulnerability and human need. Harriet Beecher Stowe famously wrote that orthodox Calvinists such as Jonathan Edwards and Samuel Hopkins showed congregants a ladder to heaven, then knocked out the intervening rungs and told them to get up thither.[24] There is something of this coldness and inflexibility in Selden. If he represents the "Protestant gaze" in this novel, it is a gaze that ultimately remains culpably detached from his object. It is poignant to see Lily's inner Protestant begin to develop and grow in response to Selden's influence only to be thwarted by her inner conflicts, her adherence to other ideologies and representational economies, and her inability to find a guide who will direct her on her own pilgrim's progress, or, perhaps most crucially, comfort her on that journey, thereby giving her the strength to acknowledge her frailty and mortality. And the reference to *Pilgrim's Progress* is not superficial, but crucial. For as we shall see in the crisis of book 1, Wharton's vision of Lily's development draws on that older Calvinist vision of human nature, particularly its emphasis on human mortality and moral frailty. Growth for Lily, as for Bunyan's Christian, requires painful self-scrutiny, a scrutiny that is hard to bear alone. Thus while Wharton disavows the orthodox Protestant vision of salvation, she also subtly critiques the individualism of Selden's secular version, as well as the optimism of Alcott's sentimental one.[25]

Finally, Keane's analysis of Protestantism presents it as a part of a representational economy that "involves relations among such things as language ideology, habits of interpreting material things, explicit religious doctrines, and tacit expectations of interaction." However, he adds that "there is no reason in principle to assume they all snuggle harmoniously together. And in circumstances of dramatic historical transformation, we should expect to find a clash between language ideology and religious doctrine, between the presuppositions of speech pragmatics and explicit, public concepts."[26] The point is that an individual subject may well find herself in a cultural environment which presupposes, elicits, and constructs very different conceptions of that subjectivity. As Keane explains, "if we want to talk about different kinds of selves, we cannot ignore the possibility that such clashes between the tacit and the explicit, among different speech genres, and among presupposable selves, or, for that matter, between workings of exchanges and the meanings of the objects that flow through them, are, in fact, commonplace, or at least an always lurking potential."[27] This discussion of the construction or production of different "presupposable selves" through the clashes of different representational economies offers a good description of Lily's situation and the different selves that begin to war within her. At first the "Protestant" self elicited through her dialogue with Selden gives her a sense of liberation, of going "beyond" the constraints of the social and the material. However, the demands for authenticity and anti-materialistic values that underpin this particular construction of selfhood not only make her conscious of her potential for transcendence but also of her failure to meet its demands. In other words, powered by emotions drawn from the "deep wells of feeling," the new discourse she has begun to appropriate creates what we might, for lack of a better term, call a conscience, one whose values and language are distinctly at odds with those she had been taught.

Lily's struggle with these completing constructions of her own selfhood forms the core of the novel's drama. The often-noted spiraling structure of its plot is driven by the recursive action of one construction temporarily dominating the other and then its consequent domination in turn. This spiraling motion might be described as one step forward for Protestant morality, two steps backward for materialistic success, then one step forward for materialistic comfort, two steps backward for Protestant authenticity. It is an agonizing process that I will not analyze in all its particulars. However, a close reading of the crisis which closes book 1 illuminates this dynamic's key elements and gives us a way to trace the significance of Lily's choices in book 2, especially in its final scenes.

The next time Lily encounters Selden, he meets her with a near-facsimile of their original friendship, a facsimile she cannot fully muster. He has attempted to recover his original view of her, and she has seemingly evaded the influence of his Protestant gaze. However, even a brief meeting with him triggers a recall of the values he articulated for her. They are at the wedding of her cousin, Jack Stepney, to Gwen Van Osburgh. Catching sight of Selden immediately throws Lily off-balance, a response made visible through her uncontrollable blush, a physical sign of emotion often aroused by his presence. However, the narrator notes that "the rise of her blood as their eyes met was succeeded by a contrary motion, a wave of resistance and withdrawal. She did not wish to see him again not because she feared his influence, but because his presence always had the effect of cheapening her aspirations, of throwing her whole world out of focus" (70).

Their conversation is subtly pertinent to their last encounter. Selden comments on Gerty Farish's innocent delight in the expensive gifts on display, a delight that evokes Webb Keane's description of the Sumbanese newly converted to Protestantism who believe that such gifts are transparent symbols of beneficent intentions. As Selden puts it, Gerty "appears to regard their number and value as evidence of the disinterested affection of the contracting parties" (75). Selden's irony here reflects both his allegiance to Protestant values and his critique of wealthy New York society's hypocritical performance of them, a performance that the more naïve Gerty takes as "sincere." And Lily cannot help but sense the reference to her own, more materialistic, attitude toward marriage and its rewards: "Ah, I envy Gerty that power she has of dressing up with romance all our ugly and prosaic arrangements! I have never recovered my self-respect since you showed me how poor and unimportant my ambitions were." If she had meant to keep the conversation on a less intimate plane, she has certainly failed, but his response keeps the tone light, although his meaning is sharp: "I thought, on the contrary . . . that I had been the means of proving to you that they were more important to you than anything else." The effect of this is painful and immediate: "It was as if the eager current of her being had been checked by a sudden obstacle which drove it back upon itself. She looked at him helplessly, like a hurt or frightened child: this real self of hers, which he had the faculty of drawing out of the depths, was so little accustomed to go alone!" Wharton is explicit here about Lily's divided nature. Selden has drawn out of the depths a subject that Wharton names Lily's "real self," but significantly this self is undeveloped, only a child in need of guidance. And not only is this real self a child, but a hurt or frightened child, whose appeal for help he has denied. Even so, "the appeal of her helplessness touched in him, as it always did, a latent chord of inclination. It would have meant nothing to him to discover that his nearness made her more brilliant, but this glimpse of a twilight mood to which he alone had the clue seemed once more to set him in a world apart with her" (75).

This twilight mood is soon broken by the approach of two very different men who lack that clue: Gus Trenor and Simon Rosedale. The male figures in this novel maintain radically different relationships to New York's history and culture. Although both Percy Gryce and Lawrence Selden represent the residual culture of old Protestant New York, Gryce's version of that culture is emptied of its true moral and spiritual content, a void to which he is oblivious. Selden, with his "amphibious" nature, both honors the old values and recognizes their contemporary eclipse. By contrast, Trenor and Rosedale represent the dominant and emergent faces of the new mercantile city. If Gryce and Selden are the past, Trenor is the present, and Rosedale the future. And here it is necessary to lay out this novel's complex plot, if we are to follow the tortuous path of Lily's development. One more critical element in this plot, in addition to Trenor and Rosedale, is Bertha Dorset. If Gerty Farish represents the values described in Louisa May Alcott's *Little Women*, Bertha represents the values analyzed in Veblen's *Theory of the Leisure Class*. Openly hypocritical and frankly materialistic, she is a successful example of the course Mrs. Bart advocated for Lily. Bertha has married for money and assuages the boredom consequent on being the wife of a dull, dyspeptic man by taking a series of clandestine lovers, including Lawrence Selden. When Selden appears at Bellomont where Bertha is also a guest, she assumes he is there to reopen an affair he had, we learn later, recently broken off. She was once the object of his amphibious social desire, as well as the reason for his current renunciation of "romantic experiments." When Lily temporarily abandons her hunt for Gryce in favor of her walk with Selden, Bertha takes revenge by informing Gryce about the "real" Lily, in this case the Lily who smokes, gambles, and runs up her dressmaker's bill. The enlightened Gryce quickly retreats into the safety of an engagement to one of the plainest and most conservative Van Osburgh daughters, leaving Lily once more contemplating her mounting bills and her knack for self-sabotage.

As a stop-gap, Lily turns to her Bellomont host, Gus Trenor, husband of her friend, Judy. Lily has heard rumors that Gus has lent money to another unmarried woman in their circle, Carry Fisher, a divorced mother with a young child who makes her living as a kind of social facilitator for the newly rich. Lily makes a point of meeting Gus Trenor at the train station, where he is returning from Wall Street. Sensing the tired man's vulnerability, she begins to flatter him for his hard work. Under the warmth of her attention, he becomes expansive and confiding. His wife and her friends don't understand what it takes to keep their show going. And yet he has just made a "very neat stroke of business" thanks to Simon Rosedale, a rising financial power on the Street. The problem, he explains, is that none of the women who wield social power in New York are willing to accept Rosedale in their homes. He appeals to Lily for help persuading his wife to be "decently civil" to him: "He's going to be rich enough to buy us all out one of these days, and if she'd only ask him to dine now and then I could get almost anything out of him. The man is mad to know the people who don't want to know him, and when a fellow's in that state there is nothing he won't do for the first woman who takes him up" (65). Lily brushes off the appeal impatiently; the man is "impossible." Trenor persists: "Oh, hang it — because he's fat and shiny, and has a shoppy manner! Well, all I can say is that the people who are clever enough to be civil to him now will make a mighty good thing of it. A few years from now he'll be in it whether we want him or not, and then he won't be giving away a half-a-million tip for dinner" (65).

Trenor's comment suggests the intricate networks of favors and influence that lace the city. Lily's cousin, Jack Stepney, has been Rosedale's main sponsor in his attempts to enter high society, and both Stepney and Trenor have been recipients of valuable "tips" from Rosedale, who expects social favors in return. Yet however appreciative these men may be, they have not been able to engineer the acceptance that Rosedale, a newly rich Jewish outsider, craves. Money alone is not enough. "Distinction," that cultivated combination of taste and manners, is the primary requirement, counting in a man even more than cash, as the social desirability of Lawrence Selden testifies.[28] Trenor's "neat stroke of business" suggests another aspect of Rosedale. Unlike Selden, who presents himself as a paragon of integrity, free of all material accidents, Rosedale is presented as a master of such material accidents. He trades in insider knowledge, exchanging valuable information for the social advantages his background has denied him. In book 1 of the novel, Rosedale's presence is persistent, yet muted. His quest for status is a counterpoint to Lily's equally materialistic quest, an ironic counterpoint since she is openly disdainful of his goal, so similar to her own. As we shall see when we turn to book 2 and examine Rosedale in more detail, he eventually becomes Lawrence Selden's true competitor for Lily's allegiance. For now, however, Lily still believes she can reject Rosedale with impunity, and yet the mention of his financial power leads her to think that perhaps she too can somehow profit from Wall Street's magic.

Like most women of her time, the narrator explains, Lily's knowledge of financial dealings is hazy at best. However, this very haziness seems to lessen the "indelicacy" of turning to someone like Trenor for help. While she could not "imagine herself, in any extremity, stooping to extract a 'tip' from Mr. Rosedale," Trenor, she theorizes, is the husband of her best friend, and therefore almost a brother to her. Although "in her inmost heart Lily knew it was not by appealing to the fraternal instinct that she was likely to move Gus Trenor," the narrator explains that "this way of explaining the situation helped to drape its crudity, and she was always scrupulous about keeping up appearances to herself" (65–66). Lily's veiling of her conscience is carefully presented: "Her personal fastidiousness had a moral equivalent, and when she made a tour of inspection in her own mind there were certain closed doors she did not open" (66).

As Trenor eagerly rises to her bait and provides the technical explanation of how the stock market can be manipulated in her favor, Lily is too genuinely ignorant to understand his presentation or to see where he has "slurred" key points. And yet, "through the general blur her hopes dilated like lamps in a fog," and she grasps at the main idea: "Her modest investments were to be mysteriously multiplied without risk to herself . . . within a short time." Any "lingering scruples" dissipate and worries melt away under his assurances. Armed with new financial expectations, she feels able to face any future demands, "even the immediate one of letting Trenor, as they drove homeward, lean a little nearer and rest his hand reassuringly on hers, costing her only a momentary shiver of reluctance." Trenor's sense of physical entitlement suggests the true nature of their transaction, one which Lily has shrouded behind her rationalizations. However, his move prompts Lily to reflect on the new role she has initiated: "It was part of the game to make him feel that her appeal had been an uncalculated impulse, provoked by the liking he inspired; and the renewed sense of power in handling men, while it consoled her wounded vanity, helped also to obscure the thought of the claim at which his manner hinted" (68). As she had done with Percy Gryce, Lily has created a persona designed to attract a man able to fund her expensive tastes and to control him by manipulation of his weakness: "He was a coarse dull man who, under all his show of authority, was a mere supernumerary in the costly show for which his money paid: surely, to a clever girl, it would be easy to hold him by his vanity, and so keep the obligation on his side" (68).[29]

At first Lily's strategy appears to succeed. Trenor supplies her with large checks, and Lily immediately blooms with new purchases: beautiful new gowns from her dressmaker, elegant hats and accessories. A check for $1,000 appears soon after her conversation with Trenor, and by the time of Jack Stepney's wedding, he has another for four thousand. At the same time, his tone towards Lily becomes increasingly proprietary. At the wedding, he familiarly touches her on the arm, and though she bristles, she cannot deny him the right. And yet, while he repeatedly asks her for more intimate meetings, she manages to hold him off with a show of friendly ignorance. In the meantime, two other elements of the plot are carefully put in place toward the end of book 1. Both are enabled by Lily's new funds, although they seem to represent warring principles.

The first is an act of charity. Delighting in her new powers of consumption, Lily is lingering over the purchase of an elegant dressing-case when she encounters Gerty Farish, repairing a watch at the same shop. Their conversation reveals the difficulties of sustaining the charitable organization in which Gerty is involved. Its aim is to better the lives of young working women, a goal in which Gerty finds few wealthy patrons are interested. Lily, the narrator explains, "had decided to defer the purchase of the dressing-case till she should receive the bill for her new opera-cloak, and the resolve made her feel much richer than when she had entered the shop. In this mood of self-approval she had a sympathetic eye for others and she was struck by her friend's air of dejection" (88). With Lily's encouragement, Gerty passionately describes her association's philanthropic aims: "The other-regarding sentiments had not been cultivated in Lily, and she was often bored by the relation of her friend's philanthropic efforts, but today her quick dramatizing fancy seized on the contrast between own situation and that represented by some of Gerty's 'cases.'" For once, Lily sees that the "dingy" working women, who so often seemed only the backdrop to her own beauty, might have affinities with herself—might also be pretty, and have a "trace of her finer sensibilities." As she pictures herself in their place, with only the most squalid of opportunities, she shudders sympathetically, and puts a liberal portion of the price of the deferred dressing-case in Gerty's hand: "The satisfaction derived from this act was all that the most ardent moralist could have desired. Lily felt a new interest in herself as a person of charitable instincts: she had never thought of doing good with the wealth she had so often dreamed of possessing, but now her horizon was enlarged by the vision of prodigal philanthropy" (88).

It seems as if Lily might learn the lesson the March sisters absorb when they sacrifice their Christmas pancakes to feed the starving Hummels. That is, she might learn how the pleasures of altruism outweigh those of consumption, and how her identity is enriched, not impoverished, by material sacrifice. However, Wharton is skeptical about Lily's possibilities for insight. In fact, Lily's charity, rather than curbing her materialistic tendencies, ironically seems to confirm them: "By some obscure process of logic, she felt that her momentary burst of generosity had justified all previous extravagances, and excused any in which she might subsequently indulge. Miss Farish's surprise and gratitude confirmed this feeling, and Lily parted from her with a sense of self-esteem which she naturally mistook for the fruits of altruism" (88). This assessment of Lily's mistaken interpretation echoes that of a much older moralist. In his classic text *The Nature of True Virtue*, Puritan theologian Jonathan Edwards rigorously judged apparent acts of virtue perpetrated out of hidden sinful motives, particularly the sins of pride and self-approval. Closer to home, Lawrence Selden had earlier deflated Lily's avowal of material stewardship by suggesting that she might "expiate" her pleasure in diamonds and motor cars by founding a hospital. Though this particular donation is on a much smaller scale, its motives appear to be those Selden so astutely critiqued.[30]

The second plot element takes us back to the novel's opening pages. As Lily leaves Selden's bachelor apartment, she carefully checks the landing to make sure she is unobserved. Although her visit involved no more than conversation and tea, she is well aware that even the appearance of indiscretion would be compromising. As she heads for the stairs, there is no one but a cleaning woman in sight. However, this woman occupies so much of the space that Lily is forced to pull her skirts aside and press to the wall. As she does, "the woman paused in her work and looked up curiously, resting her clenched red fists on the wet cloth she had just drawn from her pail. She had a broad sallow face, slightly pitted with small-pox, and thin straw-colored hair through which her scalp shone unpleasantly" (13). Lily attempts to put her in her place through a show of politeness, to which the woman is unresponsive. She merely pushes her pail to the side, and continues to stare as "Miss Bart swept by with a murmur of silken linings" (13). Flushing, Lily wonders,

What did the creature suppose? Could one never do the simplest, the most harmless thing, without subjecting one's self to some odious conjecture? Half way down the next flight, she smiled to think that a charwoman's stare should perturb her. The poor thing was probably dazzled by such an unwonted apparition. But *were* such apparitions unwonted on Selden's stairs? But she put aside that thought with a smile at her own fears, and hastened downward, wondering if she should find a cab short of Fifth Avenue. (13)

Lily's switch from assuming the cleaning woman's stare is critical to assuming it is admiring reveals her own mixed self-assessment. Her dismissal of the idea that the woman has seen other female visitors descending from Selden's flat suggests her ability to repress thoughts she finds disturbing. But this notion resurfaces when she returns home from Bellomont. With the bitter taste of her failure to capture Percy Gryce still with her, she finds her aunt's house especially distasteful. As she comes downstairs, she encounters a puddle of soapy water: "It seemed to her that she was again descending the staircase from Selden's rooms; and looking down to remonstrate with the dispenser of the soapy flood, she found herself met by a lifted stare which had once before confronted her under similar circumstances. It was the char-woman of the Benedick who, resting on crimson elbows, examined her with the same unflinching curiosity, the same apparent reluctance to let her pass" (78). This time, Lily is "on her own ground," and she orders the servant sharply to make way. However, "the woman at first seemed not to hear; then, without a word of excuse, she pushed back her pail and dragged a wet floor-cloth across the landing, keeping her eyes fixed on Lily as the latter swept by. It was insufferable that Mrs. Peniston should have such creatures about the house; and Lily entered her room resolved that the woman should be dismissed that evening" (78–79).

Before Lily has a chance, however, the cleaning woman, Mrs. Haffen, comes to Lily's room, asking for a word with her. After some preliminary remarks about her husband's bad luck and their subsequent poverty, she gets to the point and presents a dirty package which she unwraps carefully. Inside is a bundle of letters, torn in half, but still legible. They are letters Mrs. Haffen has retrieved from Lawrence Selden's wastebasket, letters that she assumes are Lily's. They are not, but Lily immediately recognizes the handwriting of their author: Bertha Dorset. She also recognizes their nature: pleas for the resumption of an illicit affair. Mrs. Haffen's assumption that Lily is their author doubtless stems from that first sighting of her leaving Selden's apartment, and she has figured on blackmailing the young lady. Although Lily feels repulsed by both the woman's appearance and motive, as well by the secret that has been revealed, she decides to buy the letters, if only to protect Selden: "If she weighed all these things it was unconsciously: she was aware only of feeling that Selden would wish the letters rescued, and that therefore she must obtain possession of them" (83). Again, her own fastidious nature keeps her from the probing their contents: "She had no idea of reading the letters; even to unfold Mrs. Haffen's dirty newspaper would have seemed degrading" (84). And at first, she believes she will destroy them, but then, recalling Bertha's belittling treatment following the Bellomont debacle, Lily suddenly resolves to keep them. As she does so, "it struck her with a flash of irony that she was indebted to Gus Trenor for the means of buying them" (87).

This incident lays the groundwork for the novel's crisis in its final pages. And it is worth taking a moment to look at the principal actor in it: the Benedick cleaning woman. In many ways, she appears the antithesis of Lily. With her heavy body, disfigured face, and thinning hair, she seems a kind of grotesque. In Mikhail Bakhtin's famous study *Rabelais and His World*, he describes the opposition between two figures such as Lily and Mrs. Haffen as signifying the opposition in Western culture between virgin and whore, spirit and body. The first figure is the classical body, as exemplified in the sculptured Greek nude: pure, smooth, perfectly clean, without bodily openings or orifices, its marble surface resistant to death or change. The second is the living grotesque body: distended, punctuated by orifices and smeared with dirty fluids, creased and marked with the signs of age and decay.[31] As Anne McClintock shows, in the Victorian period this opposition also structured the opposition between leisure-class lady and working-class servant.[32] Here, Mrs. Haffen is the degraded servant who is supposedly invisible in commodity culture: the laborer who creates the pristine settings for Lily's performances. In this case, however, Lily's seeming transgression has made her vulnerable to the other woman's judgment. The servant, no longer invisible, occupies the central spaces of this domestic setting and gazes upon her "better" with critical impunity. Their roles now threaten to reverse. Not only has Lily, with her dream of being a jewel impervious to organic life, met her worst fear, but the apparently grotesque servant implies that it is not she who is dirty, but Lily. Moreover, the servant has obtained leverage over the lady through her job of emptying the wastebasket and carting away discarded letters. She has gained power through uncovering the dirt a hypocritical society tries to hide. Lily may be repulsed by Mrs. Haffen's physical appearance, but Mrs. Haffen's blackmail is a threat to uncover an even more devastating moral ugliness. The opposition between these two figures — classical beauty and disfigured creature — subtly patterns the final, climatic scenes of book 1.

Wharton sets up that climax with the ancient device, taken from Greek tragedy, of raising her heroine high before bringing her crashing down. Lily's appearance on the heights is her performance at the Wellington Brys' *tableaux vivants*. This is a scene much studied by critics, and worth a close look for its complexity and implications. Lily's participation gives her a richer opportunity for artistic expression than she has ever had. Under the tutelage of Paul Morpeth, the society painter directing the event, Lily's "plastic sense, hitherto nurtured on no higher food than dress-making and upholstery, found eager expression in the disposal of draperies, the study of attitudes, the shifting of lights and shadows"

(103). Her theatrical ability is also turned to more legitimate uses than snaring wealthy bachelors: "Her dramatic instinct was roused by the choice of subjects, and the gorgeous reproductions of historic dress stirred an imagination which only visual impressions could reach" (103). And yet she retains the mixed motive of vanity, since "keenest of all was the exhilaration of displaying her own beauty under a new aspect: of showing that her loveliness was no mere fixed quality, but an element shaping all emotions to fresh forms of grace" (103). However, this description of Lily's desire to display herself also reveals complex underpinnings. On the one hand, there is vanity and the desire for approval. But on the other is a more honorable pride in aesthetic accomplishment. "Shaping all emotions to fresh forms of grace," Lily's art orders her emotions and gives her deepest feelings beautiful form.[33]

Lily's choice of subject is Sir Joshua Reynolds's painting, *Portrait of Mrs. Lloyd*.[34] She had considered Tiepolo's *Cleopatra* for its "splendid setting," but then rejected it. The decision is interesting, since it reveals Lily's mixed feelings about the material splendor that has often tempted her. This time she rejects that temptation and "yields to the truer instinct of trusting to her unassisted beauty, and . . . purposely chooses a picture without distracting accessories of dress or surroundings." Her "artistic intelligence" leads her to choose a style consonant with her own, so much so that the tableau seems more a "portrait of Miss Bart" than of Reynolds's Mrs. Lloyd: "Her pale draperies, and the background of foliage against which she stood, served only to relieve the long dryad-like curves that swept upward from her poised foot to her lifted arm." This is the sylvan Lily that Selden had glimpsed briefly during their walk at Bellomont. Seeing her from the audience now, he recognizes again "the noble buoyancy of her attitude, its suggestion of soaring grace, [which] revealed the touch of poetry in her beauty that Selden always felt in her presence, yet lost sense of when he was not with her." He is so moved "that for the first time he seemed to see before him the real Lily Bart, divested of the trivialities of her little world, and catching for a moment a note of that eternal harmony of which her beauty was a part" (106). Yet during this long moment, he also has "time to feel the whole tragedy of her life. It was as though her beauty, thus detached from all that cheapened and vulgarized it, had held out its suppliant hands to him from the world in which he and she had once met for a moment, and where he felt an overmastering longing to be with her again" (107). As the curtain falls, Gerty Farish, seated next to him, enthuses: "Wasn't she too beautiful, Lawrence? Don't you like her best in that simple dress? It makes her look like the real Lily — the Lily I know." He meets Gerty's eyes, which are brimming with tears, and corrects her: "The Lily *we* know" (107).

And is this the real Lily? The Lily they, and we, know? Critics range across a whole spectrum of opinion. For example, Carol Singley believes the answer is yes: the image of the sylvan nymph freed from all material accidents is Lily's essential self.[35] Sharon Kim says no: the frivolous gold-digger is Lily's authentic and immutable self, one whose inherited traits she cannot change no matter how she hard to tries.[36] Then there is Jill Kress, who says that Lily seems merely a proliferating collection of performative masks donned according to social necessity: "*The House of Mirth* presents its heroine, a lily in full bloom, in all the flush of her beauty and self-centeredness — a quality that indicates the ultimate irony of the text, for Lily Bart seems to have no 'center.' If she does, it is the artful cluster of relationships she has accumulated in the hopes of securing a social position for her 'self' as a wife."[37] However, Kress goes on to say that "even while the social arena appears to meticulously breed itself Lilies, Wharton alludes to a portion of the self that cannot be expressed in this light."[38] In fact Kress argues that the critical question raised by this scene is one with which Wharton herself, along with many philosophers and writers of her generation, struggled: "Consistently in her novels, Wharton refers to what she calls a 'real self,' an entity that appears to exist without reference or attachment to anything social, though she simultaneously establishes a network of connections between such selves and their environment" — hence the *tableau vivant* scene's critical importance, since "it anticipates debates between essentialism, which relies upon some natural, irreducible 'essence' for human identity, and the social construction of identity."[39] While I will return to this debate in later chapters, for now I would simply say that the answer to the question of whether this is the real Lily is: yes and no.

The vision of Lily in the *tableau vivant* is the *ideal* Lily, the image she wishes to present to the world. As we have seen, beauty for Lily is a vision of order, cleanliness, purity, and perfection. Its achievement requires disciplining and shaping the world, in all its dinginess and vulnerability to age and mortality, through style and taste. It is not conspicuous consumption or display simply for the sake of status, but also a dream of happiness, a classicism that for all the simplicity and purity of its forms can only be realized through material goods. Lily wants her life to be like a jewel, hard, crystallized, an "ineffable gorgeousness that has nothing to do with God," to borrow a phrase from F. Scott Fitzgerald.[40] It is a transcendence achieved not by escaping materiality but by working through it: a realization of the material world's potential to express human dreams. The *tableau vivant* allows Lily to become, for a single moment, the sculpture (and the sculptor) she aspires to be.[41] Significantly, when the painter Paul Morpeth is asked if he would like to paint Miss Bart, he declines on the grounds that her face is "too controlled for expression" (186). And yet, as we have seen, in Selden's presence she loses control of that face, which blushes and pales, signaling emotions she cannot name.

Both Selden and Gerty are especially appreciative of Lily's choice of costume and its unadorned, classical style — virtually a form of Greek drapery, as if Lily was costumed as the dryad to which Wharton compares her. The simple "Greek" style of Reynolds's Mrs. Lloyd is seen here as a mark of the authentic, as opposed to the "Oriental" gorgeousness of Tiepolo's Cleopatra, which Lily has rejected. This choice represents Lily's potential to forego splendid display and develop an art concerned only with beauty and self-expression, free from all material accidents. Eschewing the fashionable and the ornamental, it is the costume of the republic of the spirit. That both Gerty and Selden see this spectacle as the real Lily suggests their shared inability to accept Lily's mixed nature; their need to separate her beauty from its actual social and even human context. They say this is the Lily "we know," and yet they do know other versions of Lily. However, those are versions they cannot accept: the frightened child, the manipulative gold-digger, the status-hungry materialist. All those are ruled out as inauthentic. For Selden, this fastidiousness rejection of Lily's divided nature will ultimately make it impossible for him to help her escape her chains.

Lily's self-presentation in this scene is particularly interesting in relation to a similar scene in *Little Women*: Amy March's appearance at the ball in Europe. By this point in her story, Amy has become a kind of "dream artist." She has realized that what is important in the expression of identity is not the actual materials used to create an image, but the effect conveyed by them. In this scene Amy successfully expresses her intrinsic character through the skillful use of inexpensive tulle, adorned with green vines and fresh flowers. Unable to afford a fashionable dress or jewels, she uses her imagination to create a powerful sign for her own beauty and desirability. That this sign is classically Greek, adorned with living greens, is the common thread between the two scenes. Both Amy and Lily draw on the Enlightenment and Romantic traditions that associate the authentic, essential self — with its universal appeal and transcendence of material accidents — with the classical Greek style. In *Little Women*, Amy's adoption of this style makes visible her true inner nature, particularly her achievement of a developing maturity that will enable her to overcome a materialism similar to Lily Bart's. While Amy also wishes to marry for money and eagerly strives for social status among the newly rich, she has learned to make do, to live within her means and to express herself through her own imaginative and artistic power. Unlike her older sister, who was initially humiliated by her appearance in the white tarlatan at the Moffats' party (or Wharton's own mother who underwent a similar humiliation and never recovered), Amy has transcended her need for fashionable social approval. For Alcott, this classical vision in white *is* the real Amy, although her triumph over materialism and self-interest still needs to be tempered by grief, through the death of her sister Beth, before it is complete. Finally, although Laurie gazes admiringly on this vision of Amy as "Diana," he can also accept Amy's complexity and forgive the faults she has struggled to overcome.

Both *Little Women* and *The House of Mirth* explore the relationship between artistic expression and individual identity; however, *Little Women* asserts that there is no gap between them, no disjunction between one's true style and one's real self; anything else is a disguise, a show, or a counterfeit. Art, like language, should be a transparent window into the artist's soul. Moreover, Alcott assumes (at least in this text) that the confidence man or woman will always be unmasked; the false front will always give itself away. Romantics like Emerson or Alcott would have us believe that only good people can write good books: that true artistic expression depends upon sincerity. Only those who qualify to enter the republic of the spirit can wear its signs. Thus Amy can express her Diana-like style only when she has reached a corresponding level of moral integrity. Similarly, Jo can write the first book of *Little Women* only when she has gained the necessary self-awareness.[42] Things are more complicated in Wharton's world. Wharton suggests that Lily can project, sincerely, an idealized self, a manufactured image that has real imaginative power. However, that image's relation to its author is not one to one: it is not a window into the author's soul or a mirror of inner reality. The portrait of Miss Bart in the *tableau vivant* is an aspirational dream, an imaginative construction that soars "beyond" its author's own conflicted and needy life. This idealized image is "real" in so far as it offers sincere, reliable evidence of Lily's aspirations and artistic achievement. However, its truth is only partial, since it fails to represent her complete, deeply divided character. Just as Lily is unable to integrate her conflicting desires and impulses, her self-portrait does not reveal the whole of her innermost self.

Wharton subtly demonstrates this disjunction in the moments following Lily's triumph. Whereas Gerty and Selden now see Lily as having transcended corrupting influences, the narrator shows that Lily, on the contrary, is basking in the spotlight of the very society they believe she has escaped. For example, Selden overhears old Ned Van Alstyne comment, "Deuced bold thing to show herself in that get-up; but, gad, there isn't a break in the lines anywhere, and I suppose she wanted us to know it!" (106). Van Alstyne's implication is that Lily's presentation is a kind of advertisement, an interpretation shared by many Wharton critics, who point out that Mrs. Lloyd in Reynolds' portrait is busy carving her husband's initials on a nearby tree: a pose Lily doubtless selected with an eye to suggesting her own suitability for a similar role. Selden, newly under Lily's idealized spell, angrily rejects Van Alstyne's judgment: "It was not the first time that Selden had heard Lily's beauty lightly remarked on, and hitherto the tone of the comments had imperceptibly coloured his view of her. But now it woke only a motion of indignant contempt. This was the world she lived in, these were the standards by which she was fated to be measured! Does one go to Caliban for a judgment on Miranda?" (107).

And yet, as Selden makes his way to congratulate Lily on her success, she is ecstatically accepting the homage of men she would normally shun: "At such moments she lost something of her natural fastidiousness, and cared less for the quality of the admiration received than for its quantity. Differences of personality were merged in a warm atmosphere of praise, in which her beauty exploded like a flower in sunlight; and if Selden had approached a moment or two sooner he would have seen her turning on Ned Van Alstyne and George Dorset the look he had dreamed of capturing for himself" (108). However, Selden comes upon Lily after the others have left, and "finding the expected look in her eye, he had the satisfaction of supposing he had kindled it. The look did indeed deepen as it rested on him for even in that moment of self-intoxication Lily felt the quicker beat of life that his nearness always produced. She read too, in his answering gaze the delicious confirmation of her triumph and for the moment it seemed to her that it was for him only that she cared to be beautiful" (108). The ambiguity here is sharply drawn. Lily's motives are not pure and idealistic, but still profoundly mixed. Nevertheless, one of those motives is inspired by what the narrator will later call the "blind motions of her mating-instinct"(248),her deep, uncontrollable attraction to Selden, while his own need to believe in her potential for transformation rules out his recurring doubts, at least for the moment.

As it was during their Bellomont walk, the setting here is pastoral and isolated: the Wellington Brys' conservatory. Beneath the hothouse trees, the atmosphere is "dream-like," with a sense of "unreality." They have re-entered that twilight space where they seem to speak from deep wells of feeling. Again, Selden's presence calls forth the hidden, uncultivated self in Lily that is unaccustomed to going alone. She suddenly raises her eyes to Selden "with the beseeching earnestness of a child" and murmurs, "You never speak to me — you think hard things of me" (108). He answers honestly, "I think of you at any rate, God knows!" Speaking "as though the words were drawn from her unwillingly," Lily replies, "Then why do we never see each other? Why can't we be friends? You promised once to help me." Again, his answer is prompt and unconsidered, "The only way I can help you is by loving you." Now she has no answer.

Instead she turns her face "to him with the soft motion of a flower. His own met it slowly, and their lips touched." But, as at Bellomont, this is a moment Lily cannot sustain. She pulls away from him suddenly, catches his hand to her cheek, and sighs, "Ah, love me, love me — but don't tell me so!" Then she turns and slips "through the arc of boughs, disappearing into the brightness of the room beyond" (109).

With its dreamlike setting, the conservatory is once more too removed from the realities of Lily's life to transform her. The next day she receives a letter from Selden asking to call on her: "Her first movement was one of annoyance: this unforeseen act of Selden's added another complication to life. It was so unlike him to yield to such an irrational impulse! Did he really mean to ask her to marry him?" Lily evidently prefers to keep their love unspoken, unnamed, safe in a liminal, twilight world where it cannot threaten her chosen goals. And yet here again her feelings are mixed. While she admits that she had once shown him the impossibility of such a hope, his acceptance of her rejection was "somewhat mortifying to her vanity" (110). Now she feels the sweetness of her renewed power over him. She knows that "since she could not marry him, it would be kinder to him, as well as easier for herself, to write a line amicably evading his request to see her: he was not a man to mistake such a hint, and when next they met it would be on their usual friendly footing" (110). However, when she sees his handwriting again, she cannot resist tasting that sweetness once more. She wants to relive the "the moment when she had read in his eyes that no philosophy was proof against her power. It would be pleasant to have that sensation again"(110). Writing him an invitation to call the next day at four, Lily tells herself: "I can easily put him off when tomorrow comes" (110). It is hard to see Lily's behavior here as anything but manipulative and self-serving. She is toying with Selden, simply for the pleasure of satisfying her vanity and heightening her "self-intoxication." Her artistic triumph has not confirmed the moral qualities that would enable her to enter the republic of the spirit. Rather, it has ironically refreshed her materialistic ambitions; they are burning more brightly than ever. The troubled child is still with her, but Lily's renewed sense of power has silenced its cry for help.

From the summit of her triumph, Lily is quickly brought down. The agent is Gus Trenor, whose growing sense of frustration and entitlement Lily has managed to evade. Her increasingly luxurious appearances at New York's most splendid occasions have brought her new admiration and attention, capped by the spectacle of her beauty in the *tableau vivant*. And the money behind those appearances has come from him, an uncomfortable obligation Lily has shunted to the edges of consciousness while she has kept Trenor himself at bay. Unlike Amy March's enchanting white dress, fashioned from inexpensive tulle, Lily's equally enchanting dress was made of far more expensive materials, materials that she could not afford herself. In an irony central to the novel, and to the dynamics of consumer culture itself, Lily's classical costume signifies her identity as a free spirit, liberated from all "material accidents," but the means of its acquisition tighten the chains of her economic dependence, as she soon learns.[43] For if Lily has managed to repress her obligation to him, Trenor's awareness of it has been heightened by Lily's visibility and success. Soon after the Brys' event, he forges a note from his wife inviting Lily to make an evening visit at the Trenors' townhouse in New York. When she arrives, she finds only the servants and Trenor amongst the sheeted furniture. He has been drinking, and he is determined to get her attention at last. When they are alone, she confronts him about the fraudulent note and asks what he wants from her. He replies: "I'll tell you what I want: I want to know just where you and I stand. Hang it, the man who pays for the dinner is generally allowed to have seat at table" (114). Crude but clear, he rips aside the veil that has obscured their transaction. While Lily "flames with anger and abasement," she also feels "the sickening need of having to conciliate where she longed to humble" (114).

When Lily draws on her honor to defend herself, Trenor lays out his view of their relationship: "Don't talk stage rot. I don't want to insult you. But a man's got his feelings — and you've played with mine too long. I didn't begin this business — kept out of the way, and left the track clear for the other chaps, until you rummaged me out and set to work to make an ass of me — and an easy job you had of it, too. That's the trouble — it was too easy for you — you got reckless — thought you could turn me inside out, and chuck me in the gutter like an empty purse" (114). The language may be brutal, but the analysis is on target: "But, by gad, that ain't playing fair: that's dodging the rules of the game. Of course I know what you wanted — it wasn't my beautiful eyes you were after — but, I tell you what, Miss Lily, you've got pay up for making me think so — " (114). Lily had thought that "for a clever girl" it would be easy to hold Trenor by his vanity. However, she underestimated the strength of that vanity, and overestimated her own skill at manipulating it. Much more hypocritical than a Percy Gryce, Trenor is correspondingly more ruthless. Most importantly, Lily willfully misunderstood the nature of the game she was playing. Her own vanity led her to avert her eyes from her role in that game, and the price it would require her to pay.

As the truth begins to penetrate, she asks him falteringly, "Pay up? . . . Do you mean that I owe you money?" This draws a laugh from him: "Oh, I'm not asking for payment in kind. But there's such a thing as fair play—and interest on one's money—and hang me if I've had so much as a look from you—" (116). Now Lily begins to see the consequences of her willed ignorance: "Your money? What have I to do with your money? You advised me how to invest mine . . . you must have seen I knew nothing of business . . . you told me it was all right—" And Trenor follows up, "It *was* all right—it is, Lily: you're welcome to all of it, and ten times more. I'm only asking for a word of thanks from you." And yet Lily still hopes that her original rationalization will somehow make things right: "What more have you done than any friend might do, or any one accept from a friend?" (116). Trenor demolishes her argument with even greater crudity: "I don't doubt you've accepted as much before—and chucked the other chaps as you'd like to chuck me. I don't how you settled your score with them—if you fooled 'em I'm that much to the good. Don't stare at me like that—I know I'm not talking the way a man is supposed to talk to a girl—but, hang it, if you don't like it you can stop me quick enough—you know I'm mad about you" (116). Now there can be no doubt about his interpretation: Lily's game is to seduce men into giving her money for the promise of sexual favors. Moreover, Trenor argues that her game is a con: she takes their money and reneges on her side of the deal. While Trenor is wrong about Lily's past, he is right about her treatment of him.

As Trenor grows more insistent, he moves closer to her, and his hand seems to loom in her vision. Within, Lily again senses two selves: one that feels "weak and defenseless" while another "sharpens itself to vigilance." Confronted with her own complicity, she feels a "sea of humiliation" break: "wave crashing on wave so close that the moral shame was one with the physical dread. It seemed to her that self-esteem would have made her invulnerable—that it was her own dishonor which put a fearful solitude about her" (116). The frightened self within starts to drag her down, and she tries to escape Trenor's claim by saying that if she owes him money, she'll pay it back. He dismisses her offer scornfully; she'll just get the money from Selden or Rosedale and fool them as she fooled him, unless she's "settled other scores already—and I'm the only one left out in the cold!" (116). Repulsed, she pulls back, a response that brings out "the primitive man" in him while she stands "silent, frozen to her place. Her heart was beating all over her body—in her throat, her limbs, her helpless, useless hands. Her eyes traveled despairingly about the room—they lit on the bell, and she remembered that help was in call. Yes, but scandal with it—a hideous mustering of tongues. No, she must fight her way out alone" (116). Using her last shreds of self-esteem, Lily manages to draw herself up into a semblance of the proud, pure figure she presented in the *tableau vivant*. Controlling her terror, she faces him down: "I am here alone with you . . . What more have you to say?" This show of assurance staves off the threatened rape: "Old habits, old restraints, the hand of inherited order, plucked back the bewildered mind which passion had jolted from its ruts. Trenor's eye had the haggard look of the sleep-walker waked on a deathly ledge" (117). By violating the code of genteel womanly behavior, Lily has made herself vulnerable to Trenor's assault. Mustering the strength to recreate the image of her forfeited respectability, she forces Trenor back within the bounds of acceptable behavior. As he withdraws, she continues her performance for the servants, making her conventional farewell and sending best wishes to Trenor's wife, all the while moving rapidly toward her escape.

Once safely in a hired carriage outside, however, Lily breaks down: "She seemed a stranger to herself, or rather there were two selves in her, the one she had always known, and a new abhorrent being to which it found itself chained" (117). Clearly, this sensation of doubleness is different in kind from the sensation Lily felt at Bellomont. There the second, new self was a buoyant, freedom-loving spirit that challenged her more conventional and familiar self, crouching in a "prison-house" of fears. Now there seems to be another new self, not sylvan and free, but frightening and abhorrent, associated not with the pastoral woods of Greek poetry, but with the dark caves of Greek tragedy: "She had once picked up, in a house where she was staying, a translation of the Eumenides, and her imagination had been seized by the high terror of the scene where Orestes, in the cave of the oracle, finds his implacable huntresses asleep, and snatches an hour's repose. Yes, the Furies might sometimes sleep, but they were always there, always in the dark corners, and now they were awake and the iron clang of their wings was in her brain" (117).

Although this new self seems an abhorrent fury rather than a charming dryad, it may be that Lily's situation has simply turned one into the other. If the dryad represents Lily's potential for spontaneous action and authentic emotion, it might also represent Lily's capacity for self-awareness and moral judgment. To a troubled child who has not been taught how to live with her thoughts and has no compassionate heart to lean on, an internalized conscience might well seem an abhorrent, frightening voice she cannot hope to appease, but only long to escape.[44] Outside the carriage windows, Lily sees her world entirely changed: "There was a great gulf between today and yesterday. Everything in the past seemed simple, natural, and full of daylight — and she was alone in a place of darkness and pollution — Alone! It was the loneliness that frightened her" (117). With language recalling Bunyan's *Pilgrim's Progress*, Wharton writes that Lily must now "find some way out of slough into which she has stumbled." She has failed to read the signs on her moral journey, and having taken a decisively wrong turn, she now seems irretrievably lost, mired in a slough of overwhelming despond.

Her first thought is how to survive a night of sleepless agony: "She had a vision of herself lying on the black walnut bed — and the darkness would frighten her, and if she left the light burning the dreary details of the room would brand themselves forever on her brain." In this crisis her hatred of her room at Mrs. Peniston's intensifies. "Its ugliness, its impersonality, the fact that nothing in it was really hers," all these seem to magnify her isolation and leave her exposed to the furies who reproach her. "To a torn heart uncomforted by human nearness a room may open almost human arms, and the being to whom no four walls mean more than any others, is, at such hours, expatriate everywhere" (118). For all Lily's hunger for material comfort, she has no home of her own, no place to retreat for warmth and solace.[45] Given the superficiality of their relationship Mrs. Peniston has no help to offer, "but even had the two been in closer contact, it was impossible to think of Mrs. Peniston's mind as offering shelter or comprehension to such misery as Lily's." What Lily needs is understanding and forgiveness, the kind of unconditional care and absolution that Mrs. March gives a Meg, Jo, or Amy: "As the pain that can be told is but half a pain, so the pity that questions had little healing in its touch. What Lily craved was the darkness made by enfolding arms, the silence which is not solitude, but compassion holding its breath" (118). In the opening chapter of *Little Women*, Jo draws on Bunyan's parable to describe Mrs. March's emotional rescue of her daughters: "We were in the Slough of Despond to-night, and mother came and pulled us out like Help did in the book."[46] There is only one person in Lily's world who compares with Alcott's heroic maternal figure, and Lily turns to Gerty Farish almost blindly, instinctively seeking the care she must have to survive. Her carriage is "nearing Gerty's corner. If only she could reach there before this laboring anguish burst from her breast to her lips — if only she could feel the hold of Gerty's arms while she shook in the ague-fit of fear that coming upon her!" (118).

When Gerty hears the summons at her door, she opens it to see the "white ruin" of Lily's face (129). Having learned from prior experience attending to those suffering and needy, Gerty tactfully refrains from questioning her guest and offers her some warming tea. As she prepares it, "Lily sat quiet, leaning toward the fire: the clatter of cups behind her soothed her as familiar noises hush a child whom silence has kept wakeful." Now the child in Lily has come forward again, and as with Selden she begins to voice feelings never before articulated. With Gerty's gentle prompting, she suddenly breaks out: " 'Oh, Gerty, the furies . . . you know the noise of their wings alone at night, in the dark? But you don't know — there is nothing make the dark dreadful to you — '" (131).

When Gerty asks what has frightened her, Lily answers: "I'm not frightened: that's not the word. Can you imagine looking into your glass some morning and seeing a disfigurement—some hideous change than has come to you while you slept? Well, I seem to myself like that—I can't bear to see myself in my own thoughts—I hate ugliness, you know—I've always turned from it—but I can't explain to you—you wouldn't understand" (131). But Gerty's compassionate response encourages Lily to go on, to try to explain, although her thoughts are nearly incoherent: "How long the night is! And I know I shan't sleep tomorrow. Some one told me my father used to lie sleepless and think of horrors. And he was not wicked, only unfortunate—and I see now how he must have suffered, lying alone with his thoughts! But I am bad—a bad girl—all my thoughts are bad—I have always had bad people about me. Is that any excuse? I thought I could manage my own life—I was proud—proud! but now I'm on their level—" (131).

Lily's growing self-awareness, a process begun in Laurence Selden's flat, here reaches an overwhelming climax. The identity created for her by her mother and sustained over many years of materialistic striving has collapsed. Lily's image of herself has shattered. Her beautiful, controlled face is disfigured by painful emotions she cannot repress. Knowledge that she had always managed to veil has thrust itself upon her consciousness and will not be refused. Her voice, like her sense of self, is fragmented and confused. Now she thinks of those dingy working girls whose lives she had scorned: "There are bad girls in your slums. Tell me—do they ever pick themselves up? Ever forget, and feel as they did before? . . . Don't they always go from bad to worse? There's no turning back—your old self rejects you, and shuts you out." Gerty struggles to calm her, telling her first that she must be dreaming, and then that Selden had left the apartment earlier that evening meaning to find Lily elsewhere. At this "Lily's face melted from locked anguish to the open misery of a child. Her lips trembled and her gaze widened with tears." Now the links in the process of self-discovery are revealed: "He went to find me? And I missed him! Oh, Gerty, he tried to help me. He told me—he warned me long ago—he foresaw that I should grow hateful to myself!" (132). Lily's reserve and self-control are gone, and she cries openly for the first time.

But if Selden's name "had loosened the spring of self-pity" in Lily's breast, it also awakens new hope: "Gerty, you know him—you understand him—tell me; if I went to him, if I told him everything—if I said: "I am bad through and through—I want admiration, I want excitement, I want money—yes, *money!* That's my shame, Gerty—and it's known, it's said of me—it's what men think of me—If I said it all to him—told him the whole story—said plainly—Oh,

Gerty, you know him, you can speak for him: if I told him everything would he loathe me? Or would he pity me, and understand me, and save me from loathing myself?" (132). Lily's confession, though voiced to Gerty, is meant for Selden. It is Selden's compassion and forgiveness she craves; Gerty is just a stand-in. And yet the confession is passionately honest. Lily's description of herself—"I've sunk lower than the lowest, for I've taken what they take, and not paid as they pay"—makes explicit the implication of Trenor's accusation: Lily is not a prostitute, but a con-woman, a criminal, who has taken money on false pretenses. At least a prostitute can be trusted to pay her side of the exchange. The imagery Lily uses in her anguish aligns her with the "dirty" servants and street women she once shunned: the disfigured, pockmarked cleaning woman she once called a "creature," not a person. The mirror in which she now sees herself is an interior one that reflects her moral ugliness and emotional poverty.

However, this confession, however passionate, is no more a complete, integrated portrait of herself than the vision of the *tableau vivant*. Lily's attempt to narrate herself lurches from total self-condemnation to halting attempts at self-justification. In one moment she is "bad—a bad girl—all my thoughts are bad." But in the next, she reflects that "I have always had bad people about me." And yet she in turn refuses to pass responsibility onto her environment: "Is that any excuse?" Is her bad behavior the result of an intrinsically bad nature, a kind of innate depravity working itself out? Or is it the result of failed nurture, the influence of bad people? Is it the product of pride, a mortal sin? "I thought I could manage my own life—I was proud—proud! but now I'm on their level—" (131). As Lily struggles to understand aspects of her own behavior and motives that she always kept hidden, she cannot construct a narrative that makes sense of herself. Her words are a disconnected jumble, drawing on multiple discourses, none of them integrated.[47] Her struggles lead her to think of her father's death and his own sense of failure: "And he was not wicked, only unfortunate—and I see now how he must have suffered, lying alone with his thoughts!" Lily's greatest pain comes from the sense of isolation that her new awareness brings her. But, in this moment, it is also significant that she recalls her thwarted sympathy for her father on his deathbed. Her own pain now awakens new compassion for him and prompts a hope for such compassion from another for her own pain and loss—a compassion she asks Gerty whether Selden can provide.

Because of her own love for Selden, a love which she has learned will never be returned, Gerty is tempted to tell Lily that Selden is no better than other men, that he will judge her harshly and leave her to her fate. But also because she loves Selden, Gerty cannot bear to "blaspheme" her image of him, and so she answers, "Yes, I know him; he will help you" (133). With more tears and a new resolve to seek Selden's forgiveness, Lily believes she can at last sleep. Although her own disappointment at learning that Selden's love is for Lily and not herself is both sharp and bitter, Gerty takes her friend into her small bed. But she cannot bear to touch this woman, so much more beautiful than herself. Rather, Gerty holds herself rigidly apart, her hands at her sides. Only a deep sense of duty enabled her to give Lily the care she needed up until now; taking her rival into her own bed seems beyond that call. Then in the dark she hears sobs, and Lily reaches for her hand with the cry, "Hold me, Gerty, hold me, or I shall think of things" (133). Gerty cannot refuse, and "silently slipped an arm under her, pillowing her head in its hollow as a mother makes a nest for a tossing child. In the warm hollow Lily lay still and her breathing grew low and regular. Her hand still clung to Gerty's as if to ward off evil dreams, but the hold of her fingers relaxed, her head sank deeper into its shelter, and Gerty felt that she slept" (133).

The scene is powerfully emotional, maternal and yet subtly erotic: "As Lily turned, and settled to a completer rest, a strand of her hair swept Gerty's cheek with its fragrance. Everything about her was warm and soft and scented: even the stains of her grief became her as rain-drops do the beaten rose." Gerty is acutely aware of Lily's scent, her soft skin, her silken hair; her attempted withdrawal seems defensive, a self-protection at the sensuousness of Lily's presence: "every fibre in her body shrank from Lily's nearness: it was torture to listen to her breathing, and feel the sheet stir with it." And yet Lily's demand to be held is not that of an adult demanding erotic pleasure, but that of a child demanding comfort. Lily here repeats the pattern of regressive behavior we have seen in her dialogues with Selden. The needs of the troubled child supersede the desires of the adult woman. Lily needs mothering most of all.

Wharton's treatment of this scene is direct and unsparing. It might easily have become stereotypically sentimental, a return to the passionate same-sex, homosocial friendships seen in nineteenth-century novels by those women writers from whom she was trying to distance herself. In this case, Gerty herself is a kind of throwback to those sentimental novels, with her philanthropy and idealism, as well as her sense of feminine duty. And yet Wharton's handling of this friendship is far different from an Alcott's or even a Sarah Orne Jewett's. Gerty is seduced, almost against her will, into playing the maternal role. And the next morning the two women face each other like ill-acquainted people who have consummated a one-night stand whose passion they are reluctant to recall. When Lily wakens, she first feels only the physical discomfort of having slept in such a narrow bed. Then, as awareness returns, she looks about Gerty's apartment with renewed distaste. The air is stale and "the smell of cooking penetrated the crack of the door" (133-34). When Gerty herself enters the bedroom, hatted and ready for work, she hands over a cup of tea and "glanced shyly at Lily, asking in an embarrassed tone how she felt; Lily answered with the same constraint, and raised herself to drink the tea" (134). Having commandeered Gerty's compassion, Lily now relegates her to the world of the dingy. Her friend's "face looked sallow and swollen in the dreary light, and her dull hair shaded imperceptibly into the tones of her skin. . . . It was relief to her that Gerty was obliged to hasten away: the two kissed silently, but without a trace of the previous night's emotion" (134).

Gerty's way of life has been seen by critics such as Hermione Lee as an important and positive alternative to the values that guide Lily. On the other hand, Lawrence Buell believes Wharton treats Gerty as a social caricature and is critical of her naïveté.[48] I would argue that the negative caricature in initial descriptions of Gerty comes not from Wharton, but from Lily, who is anxious to disassociate herself from Gerty's choices. And while Gerty may start out as a stereotypical "do-gooder," overly optimistic about the world's potential for reform, her view darkens and gains complexity as the novel develops. Her selfless care for Lily is coupled with a deepening awareness that she cannot heal her friend's distress. In novels by women of Alcott's generation, loving care could restore almost any soul. Although sentimental writers depended on Christian nurture to effect changes of the heart, rather than the crisis conversions of more orthodox Protestantism, such miraculous transformations could still be achieved through compassion and forgiveness that raised consciousness and changed the subject's awareness of others. Ironically, the greatest popular example of such fiction was written not by a woman but by a man. Charles Dickens's *A Christmas Carol* shows us how Scrooge's cold heart is thawed and renewed by his return to the scenes of his painful, neglected childhood. He is healed by his own therapeutic tears and the related awakening of his compassion for others, beginning with his tentative feelings of paternal concern for the crippled child, Tiny Tim.[49] Of course, Scrooge himself harbors a crippled child within, one who is healed through his care of the one without. Wharton's assessment of Lily's potential for renewal, an assessment that Gerty will eventually and reluctantly come to share, is much more pessimistic. In this crisis, Gerty's heroic effort to give Lily the care she craves does not result in miraculous change, but only momentary solace. Moreover, unlike Marmee who offers her daughters absolution and reassuring interpretations of their behavior when they confess their failings, Gerty cannot help Lily construct a narrative that would make sense of her behavior and guide her future choices. The sobering message of this scene is one Wharton doubtless read in the work of her friend Henry James, a writer who often refused his characters the luxury of personal renewals and happy endings. For Lambert

Strether in *The Ambassadors*, for example, it is simply "too late" to realize the rich possibilities of life. For Lily Bart it may be too late to mend the crippling damage of childhood in a materialistic society.[50]

When she returns to Mrs. Peniston's, Lily adds up her debt to Trenor for the first time: $9,000. Aware now that none of the money was her own, she determines to pay it all back "to restore her self-respect." That she cannot do so adds to her new sense of insignificance: "She was realizing for the first time that a woman's dignity may cost more to keep up than her carriage; and that the maintenance of a moral attribute should be dependent upon dollars and cents, made the world appear a more sordid place than she had conceived it" (134–35). While she wants comfort from Selden, she does not want to ask him for money; for that she determines to go to her aunt. But her aunt's response is cool rejection. Mrs. Peniston is willing to pay for Lily's clothing, since keeping up appearances is, to her mind, a legitimate expense. However, the reason Lily offers for her debt—losses at bridge—shocks Mrs. Peniston's sense of propriety and she refuses her help: "When I offered you a home I didn't undertake to pay your gambling debts" (137). The amazed Lily can only plead that she will be disgraced, but her aunt is implacable: "I consider that you *are* disgraced, Lily: disgraced by your conduct far more than by its results. You say your friends have persuaded you to play cards with them; they may as well learn a lesson too. They can probably afford to lose a little money—and at any rate, I am not going to waste any of mine in paying them" (137). Given this judgment, the real source of Lily's debt is even less likely to move her.

A devastated Lily now turns more fervently to the image of Lawrence Selden. Wharton's description of Lily's thinking is especially revealing: "As she had lain at Gerty's side the night before, she had thought of his coming, and of the sweetness of weeping out her pain upon his breast. Of course she meant to clear herself of its consequences before she met him—she had never really doubted that Mrs. Peniston would come to her aid." With that confidence, Lily does not initially imagine Selden as her rescuer, for "she had felt, even in the full storm of her misery, that Selden's love could not be her ultimate refuge; only that it would be sweet to take a moment's shelter there, while she gathered fresh strength to go on" (138). In other words, even as Lily was imagining being comforted by Selden, she was not planning to marry him. She saw him, rather as she saw Gerty, only as a source of momentary solace, "not an ultimate refuge." Far from being the instrument for her moral transformation, he was to be the instrument for her renewed ambition.

With Mrs. Peniston's refusal to help her, Lily sees Selden in a new light, for "now his love was her only hope, and as she sat alone with her wretchedness the thought of confiding in him became as seductive as the river's flow to the suicide. The first plunge would be terrible—but afterward, what blessedness might come!" (138). For the first time she seems consciously to choose a different life; indeed she seems willing to perform a kind of suicide, a sacrifice of her past identity: "Oh, if he really understood—if he would help her to gather up her broken life, and put it together in some new semblance in which no trace of the past should remain!" (138). Although she dreads confessing to him, she clings to Gerty's reassurance that Selden will understand, and trusts that he will, as he once offered, help her by loving her, for "love was what she needed—it would take the glow of passion to weld together the shattered fragments of her self-esteem" (138).

However, the narrator wryly comments that Lily's dependence on Gerty's reassurance that Selden will help was misplaced, for "it had never dawned upon her blindness that Gerty's own judgment of him was coloured by emotions far more ardent than her own" (138). Loving Selden, Gerty imagines him as motivated by the same sentimental values as herself. But Selden, it turns out, is more skeptical, more fastidious in his judgments than Gerty. The night before, when Selden, full of renewed ardor for Lily, went to search for her, he happened to be standing outside the Trenors' townhouse just as Lily was leaving. Informed earlier that Judy Trenor was not in town, Selden draws the obvious conclusion. Appearances confirm the gossip he had previously rejected concerning Lily's relationship to Trenor. Disgusted, Selden resolves to escape his attachment; he discards his plan to see Lily the next day and goes abroad as soon as possible without informing her. Twice he was willing to rescue his Andromeda; this time he cannot muster the faith necessary for the task.

As Lily waits impatiently for Selden, the time for his arrival passes without him. Later, as she steps in the hall, "she felt herself once more the alert and competent moulder of energies, and the remembrance of her power over Selden flushed her with sudden confidence. But when the drawing-room door opened it was Rosedale who came in" (139). The substitution of Rosedale for Selden marks the climax of book 1, along with Lily's discovering through a newspaper notice that Selden has abandoned her and left the country. Plunged back into the slough of despond, bereft of any guide to help her find her way out, Lily is on the verge of accepting a marriage proposal from Rosedale when a telegram arrives from Bertha Dorset, inviting her to join them on a Mediterranean cruise. That Lily accepts this invitation eagerly as an escape from her moral perplexity shows that once again she has failed to read the signs on her moral journey.

Here it worth recalling Wharton's source for her novel's title, Ecclesiastes 7:4: "The heart of the wise is in the house of mourning; but the heart of fools is in the house of mirth." The surrounding verses elaborate on the theme: "Sorrow is better than laughter: for by the sadness of the countenance the heart is made better" (7:3) and "It is better to hear the rebuke of the wise, than for a man to hear the song of fools" (7:5). The emphasis on the wisdom to be gained from accepting the "rebuke of the wise" and undergoing the transforming power of sorrow are echoed in *Little Women*'s stress on the importance of grief in awakening awareness. The March sisters' confessions of their childish vanities, greed, ambition, aggression, and rage to their forgiving mother testify to Alcott's belief in the importance of acknowledging one's frailty, of accepting the "burden" of one's human nature and its faults, not to say sins. Here also Alcott, and I would argue Wharton as well, draws on the developmental model of Bunyan's *Pilgrim's Progress*. It is Christian's sudden awareness of his sinfulness and mortality that drives him to abandon his family and journey to find the Celestial City. Terror is the force that propels him, along with anguish at his fallen state. However, as Bunyan's narrator explains, after his pilgrim has won his battle with Apollyon and gone through the "Valley of Humiliation," this terror is one that every true Christian must face: "Now at the end of this valley was another, called the Valley of the Shadow of Death, and Christian must needs go through it, because the way to the Celestial City is through the midst of it. Now this valley is a very solitary place. The Prophet Jeremiah thus described it, 'A wilderness, a land of deserts and of pits, a land of drought and of the shadow of death, a land that no man (but a Christian) passeth through and where no man dwelt [Jeremiah 2:6].'"[51] This solitary confrontation with mortality and personal frailty is a necessary condition for salvation, for, as Christian's companion Faithful explains,

> A work of grace in the soul discovereth itself, either to him that hath it or to standers by.
>
> To him that hath it, thus: it gives him conviction of sin, especially of the defilement of his nature and the sin of unbelief (for the sake of which he is sure to be damned, if he findeth not mercy at God's hand by faith in Jesus Christ). The sight and sense of things worketh in him sorrow and shame for sin. . . .[52]

The anguish Lily experiences, her sense of inward shame and disfigurement, are, in this context, the beginnings of grace, as is her excruciating sense of personal exposure, an exposure that parallels Amy March's own journey through the "valley of humiliation," when she is publically chastised by her teacher and forced to stand before her schoolmates as an example of wrongdoing, wrongdoing that also involves financial debt and social display.[53] Facing these painful feelings and accepting them as true reflections of her inward state would, in this context, bring Lily closer to salvation. For, as Faithful explains, sorrow and shame can lead the sinner to long for Christ's mercy and to acknowledge "the absolute necessity of closing with him for life."[54] And yet, Faithful also acknowledges that this painful but necessary recognition of sinfulness is oftentimes more than a body can bear. Moreover, an accurate interpretation of these emotions, and their true implications, is difficult to achieve without guidance: "But though I say it discovereth itself thus unto him, yet it is but seldom that he is able to conclude that this is a work of grace, because his corruptions now and his abused reason makes his mind to misjudge in this matter; therefore in him that hath this work there is required a very sound judgment, before he can with steadiness conclude that this is a work of grace."[55]

Indeed, in Christian's dialogue with Ignorance, Ignorance refuses this recognition outright: "I will never believe that my heart is thus bad." Faithful counters by referring to scripture as a source of authority, "Why the Word of God saith that man's ways are crooked ways, not good, but perverse. It saith they are naturally out of the good way, that they have not known it. Now when a man thus thinketh of his ways, I say when he doth sensibly and with heart-humiliation thus think, then hath he good thoughts of his own ways, because his thoughts now agree with the judgement of the Word of God."[56] Later, in conversation with his other companion, Hopeful, Christian asks what he thinks of men such as Ignorance and Talkative who deny their sinfulness, "Have they at no time, think you, conviction of sin, and so consequently, fears that their state is dangerous?" Hopeful turns to the question back to Christian: "Nay, do you answer that question yourself, for you are the elder man." Christian replies, that sometimes "they may, but they, being naturally ignorant, understand not that such convictions tend to their good; and therefore do they desperately seek to stifle them, and presumptuously continue to flatter themselves in the way of their own hearts." Hopeful confirms Christian's analysis, "I believe as you say, that fear tends much to men's good, and to make them right at their beginning to go on pilgrimage." And Christian sums up the lesson this way: "Without doubt it doth, if it be right. For so says the Word, 'The fear of the Lord is the beginning of wisdom.'"[57]

In light of these passages, including the one from which Wharton originally drew the novel's title, we can see Lily's motivation more clearly: a desperate need to escape her own growing self-awareness, a self-awareness that might offer integrity and transcendence, but only after a passage through painful self-scrutiny and condemnation. Her heartfelt confession of internal disfigurement and fragmentation in Gerty's apartment might have been "the beginning of wisdom" for Lily; however, she has no true guide to instruct her on its larger meaning. There is no Faithful to interpret her suffering; no Hopeful to encourage her perseverance; no scripture to draw on, not even a small book about the best life ever lived to map her way through this terrifying valley. Her impulse to confess to Selden and to accept the death of her materialistic identity for the sake of his forgiveness and the renovation of her "shattered self-esteem" is similar to Christian's desire to fling himself on Christ's mercy and beg for a new heart, for saving grace from a higher power. However, Selden is no savior, let alone a wise Marmee capable of guiding a frightened and exposed Lily through a valley of humiliation. Thrown back upon her own resources, Lily attempts to stifle those convictions that would tend to her good. Rather than gain wisdom in the house of mourning, she is determined to reenter the house of mirth and console herself with the song of fools.

CHAPTER 4

Smart Jews and Failed Protestants

Book 2, like book 1, opens with Lawrence Selden turning his gaze on Lily Bart. Now the setting is the French Riviera, where Lily has traveled under the patronage of the Dorsets on their expensive steam yacht. While Selden sees that Lily's beauty is intact, he senses that the wayward impulses that had briefly opened her nature to his influence have been put rigidly "under the control of the state." From his point of view, her nascent authenticity, spontaneous speech, and eager reaching for a transcendent "beyond," have been repressed in the service of materialistic strivings. Her personality seems to have acquired a hard, protective glaze, whereas earlier it had a transparency that allowed for flashes of impulse and fresh perception, such as those that led to their moment of intimacy at Bellomont. He now senses that her whole personality has "crystallized" into a single substance. The implication is that her interiority and selfhood, prerequisites for membership in his republic of the spirit, have been sacrificed to her social ambition. However, those impulses and the new awareness that Selden himself elicited are not dead, but merely in abeyance, tightly but imperfectly repressed, and book 2 traces Lily's struggle with conflicting forces within her.

While book 1 is dominated by Lawrence Selden and his thwarted courtship of Lily, book 2 is dominated in many ways by Simon Rosedale. If Selden represented the possibility of a life free from the material accidents and a love based on intrinsic qualities rather than mere self-interest and financial greed, Rosedale appeals to less admirable aspects of Lily's character: her selfish narcissism and her materialistic desires. And if Selden typifies the old Protestant bohemian individualism, with its fastidious judgments and disdain for materialism, Rosedale represents a new materialistic "cleverness" that is defined here as specifically Jewish. Critics have often noted the apparent antisemitism of Wharton's portrayal of Rosedale, who is present from the very start of the novel and who is used throughout book 1 primarily as a counterpoint to Lawrence Selden.[1] However, his character and relationship to Lily also develop in ways that result in his coming into full, complex focus by the book's close. Selden awakens and encourages the growth of a new anti-materialistic awareness in Lily, but Rosedale appeals to the materialistic values and worldview she was initially taught by her ambitious mother. In him those values find powerful expression, one seductive enough to vie with Selden's idealism for Lily's allegiance. As we shall see, Wharton carefully balances the illuminated moment between Lily and Selden at Bellomont with an equally influential but starkly contrasting moment between Lily and Rosedale. If, as Webb Keane explains, a society in the midst of change can support disparate "representational economies" and individuals can even find themselves divided by contradictory constructions of selfhood, then Selden and Rosedale represent two such competing economies. In the deepening struggle that defines the novel, their appeals to Lily call her conflicting selves into play.

Before turning to Rosedale, however, it is worth attending to the dynamics of that struggle. Key episodes in its history include Lily's Mediterranean cruise with the Dorsets, her continued sojourn abroad under the auspices of the Duchess of Beltshire, her subsequent disinheritance by her aunt, Mrs. Peniston, her stay as a companion with the Gormers, and her employment as a social secretary for the social-climbing divorcée Norma Hatch. In each case, Lily attempts to escape from the painful psychological and physical consequences of her materialistic behavior by ensconcing herself in a new "house of mirth." While close textual explication of the entire book 2 would reveal Wharton's careful detailing of Lily's downward cycle from her initially high, if precarious, social position to the seedy boarding house in which she finishes her life, for the purposes of this study a quick overview of that process will have to do.

As we have seen, Lily distracts herself from the pain of Selden's abandonment and the shame of Gus Trenor's accusations by boarding the Dorset's yacht. However, the terms on which she is given access to the luxuries of this trip include her drawing George Dorset's attention away from his wife's developing adulterous relationship with young Ned Silverton. In a brief meeting on the Riviera with Selden, who has observed her situation, Lily refuses to listen to his anxiety about the danger she is in. Just as he warns, Bertha salvages her own reputation and marriage at the last moment by accusing Lily of having an affair with her husband, then ostracizing her publicly. Made a scapegoat, Lily, who is innocent of the adultery of which she is accused, again evades the consequences of her actions by remaining abroad with another morally equivocal character, the Duchess of Beltshire. However, while Lily is consoling herself under the duchess's wing, Bertha Dorset returns to the States and spreads the false rumor of Lily's supposed attempt to seduce her husband. By the time Lily returns home, her reputation has been tarnished to the point that her friends shun her and Mrs. Peniston has virtually disinherited her. On her aunt's death, Lily discovers she has been bequeathed only $10,000. After paying what she owes to Gus Trenor once the estate is settled, she will have only one thousand.

In this case, although the basest motivation ascribed to her is false, Lily's need for luxury and her willingness to play such a morally ambiguous part nevertheless renders her vulnerable to Bertha's charges. And ironically, her own moral scruples, weak and unnurtured as they are, are what render her unable to mount a successful defense against the more unprincipled Bertha. Advised by her friend Carry Fisher that she could reclaim her reputation by giving George Dorset the information he needs to charge his wife with adultery, Lily refuses. Bertha, unhampered by any similar sense of personal integrity, is thus better equipped for survival in the social jungle than Lily. Moreover, when Gerty Farish urges Lily to defend herself against Bertha's charges, not by responding tit for tat as Carry Fisher advised, but by telling the "whole truth" about what happened, Lily rejects that strategy out of hand: "'The whole truth?' Miss Bart laughed. 'What is truth? Where a woman is concerned, it's the story that's easiest to believe. In this case it's a great deal easier to believe Bertha Dorset's story than mine, because she has a big house and an opera box, and it's convenient to be on good terms with her'" (176).

Disturbed by the frank cynicism of Lily's answer, Gerty presses her further: "But what *is* your story, Lily? I don't believe anyone knows it right." Here again Lily rejects the underlying assumption of Gerty's question: "My story? — I don't believe I know it myself. You see I never thought of preparing a version in advance as Bertha did — and if I had, I don't think I should take the trouble to use it now." But Gerty persists, "with her quiet reasonableness," asking for the kind of "authentic" and "sincere" performance of self that one of the March sisters would have offered to their own Marmee: "I don't want a version prepared in advance — but I want you to tell me exactly what happened from the beginning." But Lily refuses to accept the underlying premises of the question: "'From the beginning?' Miss Bart gently mimicked her. 'Dear Gerty, how little imagination you good people have! Why, the beginning was in my cradle, I suppose — in the way I was brought up, and the things I was taught to care for. Or no — I won't blame anybody for my faults: I'll say it was in my blood, that I got it from some wicked pleasure-loving ancestress, who reacted against the homely virtues of New Amsterdam, and wanted to be back at the court of the Charles!'" But when a troubled Gerty continues to press for the "true story," Lily fends her off impatiently, "You asked me just now for the truth — well, the truth about any girl is that once she's talked about she's done for; and the more she explains her case the worse it looks. — My good Gerty, you don't happen to have cigarette about you?" (176–77)

With her defiant request for a cigarette, a request which rejects the innocent image of the *jeune fille* that Gerty's attitude assumes, Lily reveals her awareness of the conflicting views that might define her. There are at least three, and as in her earlier attempt to tell her story to Gerty after Gus Trenor's attempted rape, she cannot integrate these views into a coherent narrative. The first view of her motives is that she was raised with the "wrong" values: the problem is nurture. But then she suggests, somewhat playfully, the possibility that these bad values are actually a kind of genetic inheritance, a throwback to an anti-Puritan ancestress whose "wicked pleasure-loving" traits have contributed to a moral failing in her "blood," a trait intrinsic to her nature. Finally, there is the assertion that neither of these possibilities may be true, but that the "truth" about one's character is a social construction, defined not by one's intrinsic, essential nature, but by a marketplace of opinion in which social expediency determines which truth has the highest exchange value.

Given this ambivalence about her own motives and behavior, it is not surprising that, even if Lily had been able to return home to refute Bertha Dorset's "version" of the story, and even if she had had any faith in the efficacy of such "explanations and counter-charges," "some obscure disdain and reluctance would have restrained her." This reluctance stems, the narrator suggests, from that unaided sense of moral integrity that Lily still shelters. What holds her back from defending herself to Gerty, let alone to Bertha and the society of which she is part, is a "feeling that was half pride and half humiliation." Although she knows that she is innocent of what Bertha accuses her, "yet she had been perfectly aware from the outset that her part in the affair was, as Carry Fisher brutally put it, to distract Dorset's attention from his wife. That was what she was 'there for': it was the price she had chosen to pay for three months of luxury and freedom from care."

Lily's way of accepting the consequences of her own moral weaknesses also forces her to accept the consequences of the appearances those weaknesses create, even if the appearances are false: "Her habit of resolutely facing the facts, in her rare moments of introspection, did not now allow her to put any false gloss on the situation. She had suffered for the faithfulness with which she had carried out her part of the tacit compact, but the part was not a handsome one at best, and she saw it now in all the ugliness of failure" (177).[2] And yet, if Lily privately acknowledges her complicity, however limited, in the events on the

Dorsets' yacht, she is still unable to construct an integrated narrative about her own responsibility for them. Her ironic responses to Gerty's earnest questions are evasive and partial, humorously damning herself one moment, then lightly damning the society that dares to judge her the next. At the end of book 1, Lily's confession to Gerty was wrenching and heartfelt, but also conflicted and fragmented. Now Lily seems to have gained considerable insight into the workings of social judgment, enough to grant her a satirical detachment from its condemnation. However, the version of the story she is able to articulate is still deeply divided and incomplete.

This is a pattern that is repeated several times in book 2, as Lily's inner conflicts cause her to cycle socially downward in new variations on the struggle that shaped the first book. Lily's dependence on luxury for self-worth and comfort, a fault that she wryly notes might be in her blood, leads her to make choices that hurt her reputation and increase her vulnerability. In each case, her materialism puts her in a position where she takes on the appearance of corruption. Although she recoils just in time to escape the full, destructive force of that corruption, because of her fatally divided motives she is slow in reading the signs. And when she finally does read them, it is too late to save her social standing, even if she has saved the struggling tendrils of her moral idealism. Ironically, her place in New York society is thus destroyed as much by her noble impulses as by her ignoble ones. With the loss of her expected inheritance, the game turns harsher and her choices are more limited. Her lack of financial support makes her even more vulnerable and her choices have more devastating consequences. However, as the stakes grow higher and Lily's status falls lower, her awareness of social hypocrisy and of her own conflicted character expands and deepens, even if her control over these forces seems ever weaker.

While Lawrence Selden, representing the eyes and voice of Protestant idealism, presided over book 1 and Lily's abortive attempt to fly "beyond" her material conditions, Simon Rosedale, as noted earlier, presides over her cycling downward in book 2. His "stocktaking eyes" track her fluctuating value in the marketplace of marriageable women, and his voice articulates the values that truly govern New York's behavior. As this chapter will show, attending to that voice draws Lily deeper into the representational economy of modern materialism. In order to understand Rosedale's significance in book 2, it is well worth tracing his earlier development in book 1.

Lily first encounters Rosedale as she leaves Selden's apartment in the opening chapter. She has just passed the staring char-woman on the stairs, and as she

makes her way outside, she finds Rosedale, who "stood scanning her with interest and approval. He was a plump rosy man of the blond Jewish type, with
smart London clothes fitting him like upholstery, and small sidelong eyes which
gave him the air of appraising people as if they were bric-a-brac" (13). Discomfited at being seen in what could be a compromising situation, Lily responds
to Rosedale's question about why she is there with a lie; rather than admit she
was visiting Selden in his apartment, she says she was visiting her dressmaker.
Unfortunately, Rosedale is the owner of the building and well aware that its oc-
cupants include Lawrence Selden — and no dressmaker. After making her aware
of these facts, he offers to accompany Lily, who almost instinctively recoils and
snubs him, but then immediately senses a second mistake, "That stupid story
about her dress-maker was bad enough — it would have been so simple to tell
Rosedale that she had been taking tea with Selden! The mere statement of the
fact would have rendered it innocuous. But, after having let herself been surprised in a falsehood, it was doubly stupid to snub the witness of her discom-
fiture" (15). Having made herself vulnerable, she realizes that she should have
appeased Rosedale, who is eager for social approval: "If she had had the presence of mind to let Rosedale drive her to the station, the concession might have
purchased his silence. He had his race's accuracy in the appraisal of values, and
to be seen walking down the platform at the crowded afternoon hour in the
company of Miss Lily Bart would have been money in his pocket, as he might
himself have phrased it" (15).

The outlines of Rosedale as a stereotypical figure, "the Jew," are clearly established in this opening encounter at the Benedick. In its habit of "appraising
people as if they were bric-a-brac," his gaze is directly contrasted with Selden's
seemingly anti-materialistic outlook. Selden's gaze in the opening scene ap-
praises Lily as an aesthetic object, with a beautiful surface. With his amphibious
awareness, he appreciates Lily's skillful self-presentation within the materialistic
society she inhabits and that he occasionally visits. And yet, as discussed earlier,
he has disciplined himself to repress any desire for acquisition. Moreover, as
we have seen in their Bellomont dialogue, his vision of Lily shifts as he elicits and then discovers her nascent interiority. Rosedale's gaze is presented as
much more frankly commercial; he "scans" Lily as a merchant might examine
a piece of merchandise. He assesses relationships according to their power to
affect value, in particular his own value in the New York social marketplace. At
this point Lily's status is high: her acceptance of his presence would be a kind of
purchase on her part, indicating a rise in his own social desirability and hence
"money in his pocket." And perhaps most significantly, the narrator identifies
these qualities as those of Rosedale's "race."

While the novel's use of the term "race" is comparatively loose, as I shall discuss in more detail later, the narrator makes it clear the Rosedale is seen as a representative of Jews as a group and that he possesses the qualities, both undesirable and desirable, associated with them. And the antisemitism of New York society is vocal and unapologetic. When Lily's cousin Jack Stepney attempts to get Rosedale invited to Bellomont as a kind of return on Rosedale's financial advice, Judy Trenor refuses and "declared he was the same little Jew who had been served up and rejected at the social board a dozen times within her memory" (16). Later, when Gus Trenor urges Lily to help him over his wife's scruples, Lily protests that Rosedale "was impossible" (65). Trenor's reply reveals how much of the social rejection is due to Rosedale's style as much as to his pedigree: "Oh, hang it — because he's fat and shiny, and has a shoppy manner! Well, all I can say is that the people who are clever enough to be civil to him now will make a mighty good thing of it. A few years from now he'll be in it whether we want him or not, and then he won't be giving away a half-a-million tip for dinner" (65). Just as Lawrence Selden's anti-materialistic idealism is expressed in his elegant, Romantic bohemian style of self-presentation (with its feminine analogue in Lily's *tableau vivant* costume), so Simon Rosedale's values and characteristic world view result in his seeming "fat and shiny" with a "shoppy manner."

Numerous critics such as Irene Goldman-Price, Gary Levine, and Jennie Kassanoff, as well as Elizabeth Ammons, have examined the problem of Rosedale's Jewishness and Wharton's possible antisemitism in detail, but I think that it is worth going into the issue once more, in part to show that Wharton's treatment of Rosedale's Jewish identity is woven into the entire fabric of the novel and is intimately connected to her treatment of Lily's development as whole.[3] As argued earlier, Simon Rosedale and Lawrence Selden embody and express contrasting representational economies, opposing ideologies that vie for dominance in Lily's life. Through these men Wharton embodies the underlying forces competing for the allegiance of modern New York and even modern society as a whole: the worldly asceticism of a waning Protestantism and the emergent materialism of a new commercial class unfettered by lingering scruples about its worldly ambitions. Before returning to the text for a close reading of those scenes in which we can see Rosedale's influence and values at work, an overview of contemporary attitudes toward and common stereotypes about Jews in Wharton's immediate and more distant contexts can provide a helpful interpretive framework.

According to John Higham's classic study *Send These to Me: Immigrants in Early America*, Protestant attitudes toward Jews in eighteenth- and early nineteenth-century America were remarkably positive.[4] Although significant negative stereotypes existed, they stood alongside and conflicted with relatively benign images. Higham, in fact, urges historians to "guard against the categorizing tendency that distinguishes too sharply between anti-Semites and philo-Semites. . . . Stated positively, this premise simply means that most people waver between conflicting attitudes and seldom enjoy an undivided state of mind."[5] These diverse and even contradictory attitudes resulted in the stereotype of the Jew taking "two entirely different forms, one religious and the other economic; and in either case attractive elements mingled with the unlovely one."[6] From the Protestant religious viewpoint, "the Jew was a portentous figure, at once the glorious agent of divine purpose and the deserving victim of His vengeance." In their role as God's chosen people, the Jews were an exemplar for American Puritans' own version of the new Israel. However, in the Jews' rejection of Christ as their Savoir, "they were also an unfaithful people who suffered justly for their betrayal."[7] I would add that, with their adherence to dietary restrictions and other bodily disciplines such as circumcision, Jews also represented a disturbing form of materialism despite their historical rejection of idolatry. In the Protestant view, they worshipped the letter over the spirit of God's law.

Higham argues that "a similar duality complicated the economic stereotype of Jews: they represented both the capitalist virtues and the capitalist vices." In an emergent capitalist, urban, and industrial economy, "the Jew commonly symbolized an admirable keenness of resourcefulness in trade. In this sense his economic energy seemed very American." However, "in another mood . . . keenness might mean cunning; enterprise might shade into avarice." Thus Higham sees praise for Jewish enterprise — a vision of "the Jew as a progressive economic force — a model of commercial energy and integrity." However, this praise was uneasily accompanied by "frequent references to conniving Shylocks." In fact, Higham notes that the figure of the Jew first entered American theater as a type of Shylock and that the verb "to Jew," "meaning to cheat by sharp practice, was becoming a more or less common ingredient of American slang."[8]

Again, the more positive of these images predominated up until the end of the nineteenth-century. And even then, Protestant ministers and Jewish rabbis enjoyed each others' mutual respect and even "frequently exchanged pulpits."[9] As society became increasingly secularized, however, it was the economic version of the Jewish stereotype that came into sharper focus as the Jews' role as the chosen people of the "Old Testament" waned in importance. Moreover, the more negative appraisal of Jewish commercial enterprise began to predominate over an earlier positive view of the Jewish model as progressive — an example of American economic know-how and energetic hustle. An important factor in this shift was a change in the makeup of the Jewish population in the United States and rising anxiety among American Protestants about the influx of immigrants, not only Jews but also ethnic groups such as the Italians and Chinese.

As literary historian Irene Goldman-Price explains, Jews entered America in general and New York in particular in three waves, each from a distinctive cultural background. The first wave, which arrived in North America with the earliest Dutch settlers, was made up of Sephardic Jews of Spanish and Portuguese descent. They were very much assimilated into American culture and many rose to the heights of New York society, where they entered occupations similar to those of Wharton's own ancestors. In fact, "well into the 1890s Hendrickses, Lazaruses, and Nathans (all Jews) belonged to The Union Club, the most exclusive club in the city, to which Joneses, Stevenses, and Schemerhorns (all Wharton's relatives) also belonged."[10]

The second wave, to which Goldman-Price believes Rosedale would have belonged, was made up of German Jews who entered the country mainly between 1837 and the 1880s. Many of these immigrants also became highly assimilated and enjoyed the positive appraisal that Higham describes. One of the most successful was August Belmont, who was associated with the banking house of Rothschild. Belmont married into Old New York society, raised his children as Episcopalians (although he himself never converted), and enjoyed considerable respect and prestige. He is mentioned several times in Wharton's memoir *A Backward Glance*, and, according to Goldman-Price, the Belmonts "were among the families she visited both in New York and in Newport; a good friend of hers married one of Belmont's sons."[11] By all accounts a highly educated and cultivated man, noted for his good taste, Augustus Belmont does not seem to have suffered from antisemitic prejudice. For these reasons, Goldman-Price does not accept the thesis, put forward by some critics, that he was the model for Simon Rosedale. (He sounds more like the model for that mysterious and elegant financier in *The Age of Innocence*, Julius Beaufort).[12] Rosedale, with his initial vulgarity and social awkwardness, seems "much more of an outsider than Belmont. He seems to be drawn from the wealthy German Jewish businessmen making fortunes in retailing and investment banking at the end of the century (such now-familiar names as Seligman, Bamberger, Altman, Bloomingdale, Lehman, Goldman, Sachs, Bache, Schiff, Kuhn, Loeb)." Goldman-Price also explains that, unlike Yankee Protestant bankers, who loaned money for notes, these German-Jewish investment bankers would loan in return for stock, a practice that put them, like Rosedale, "in the position to give 'tips.'" While this group of German Jews tended to keep to itself, some members were eager, again like Rosedale, to enter New York high society. And some did slowly work their way into this elite world. For example, "Otto Kahn became the first Jew on the Board of Directors of the Metropolitan Opera in 1903, until then an all-society Board, and gradually other such Boards accepted Jewish members."[13]

The third wave of Jewish immigration arrived from Eastern Europe in the late nineteenth century and continued through the 1920s. Many in this group came from Russia, Poland, and Lithuania. Unlike the German Jews, who were often highly educated and relatively liberal in their religious practices, these new Americans, described powerfully by writers such as Abraham Cahan and Anzia Yszierska, were apt to be more orthodox in their Judaism and less educated (although, as Cahan shows in *The Rise of David Levinsky*, some had received sophisticated schooling at yeshivas and were skilled in Talmudic interpretation). Many of these new arrivals spoke Yiddish as their primary language, rather than the German that was more acceptable to ears accustomed to Western European culture. Even more significant, many were poor and were forced to live in the crowded tenements of the lower east side, a neighborhood that was an embarrassment to the well-situated German Jews in New York, as Yzeirska's stories about the interactions between the two groups testify.[14]

For many native-born Protestants, Eastern European immigrants merged with other "foreign" groups who tended to create their own homogenous urban neighborhoods such as Little Italy and Chinatown. As John Higham points out, the rise in antisemitism at the turn of the century was linked to the rise in anti-immigration agitation and anxiety about "foreigners" generally. Comparing Jews to other ethnics groups, Higham finds that "although rapid social advancement apparently exposed and sensitized many Jews to more social discrimination than other European groups felt, in other respects they fared somewhat better. They did not fall victim to as much violence as did the Italians, and there was no organized anti-Semitic movement comparable to the anti-Catholic American Protective Association."[15] Nevertheless, he concludes that "the Jews did constitute one of the prominent ethnic targets in the 1880's and the 1890's." Of those doing the targeting, Higham identified three groups whose antisemitism went "beyond mere social discrimination: some of the agrarian radicals caught up in the Populist movement; certain patrician intellectuals in the East, such as Henry and Brooks Adams and Henry Cabot Lodge; and many of the poorest classes in urban centers. Different as they were, each of these groups found itself at a special disadvantage in the turmoil of an industrial age — the poor because it exploited them, the patricians because it displaced them."[16]

Edith Wharton and many of her close associates and peers certainly fall into this patrician category. Higham uses Henry Adams as a representative sample: "Henry Adams, whose anti-Semitism lacked the democratic restraints that qualified the thinking of the Populists, agreed with them in identifying the Jew with the menace of plutocracy. To judge from his published letters, it was only the 1880's, after a sense of the powerlessness of his own aristocratic class had settled upon him, that Adams began to see the Jew as the supreme expression of a commercial, bourgeois society."[17] The economic panic and depression of the 1890s intensified these fears. For both Henry and his brother, Brooks Adams, "the economic collapse indicated to them the approach of a general social catastrophe, and the Jew loomed as both the symbol of a materialistic society and an agent of its destruction. 'In a society of Jews and brokers,' Henry Adams wrote in 1893, 'I have no place.'"[18]

In her valuable overview of ideas current among men such as Adams, Henry Cabot Lodge, and Theodore Roosevelt, all of whom Wharton admired and visited as she was writing *The House of Mirth*, Goldman-Price quotes Lodge's definition of race as one they would have shared: "The men of each race possess an indestructible stock of ideas, traditions, sentiments, modes of thought, an unconscious inheritance from their ancestors, upon which argument has no effect. What makes a race are their mental, and above all, their moral characteristics."[19] Men such as Lodge, Adams, and Roosevelt located the source of American democracy in the Anglo-Saxon, Teutonic peoples and believed that the Nordic race (also referred to as the Aryan race in Germany) was superior to all others in this evolving taxonomy. And just as Nordics were seen as superior, Jews were racialized and seen as problematic: "Though originally a linguistic differentiation, in the 19th century the terms 'Aryan' and 'Semitic' took on a physical, anthropological meaning, and despite research to the contrary . . . the Jews began to be considered a separate race. And to be a separate race meant more than just to have certain physical characteristics."[20]

According to Goldman-Price, another important source for Wharton's stereotype of the Jew was William Lecky, whose 1893 review of "Israel Among Nations" by Anatole Leroy-Beaulieu, acknowledges the persecution of Jews and the group achievements, but "characterizes the Jews as 'shrewd, thrifty, and sober,' with a 'rare power of judging, influencing, and managing men,' and asserts that 'the great Jewish capitalists largely control the money markets of Europe.'"[21] Although Lecky admits that Jews have been surprisingly successful at assimilating into a wide range of European cultures, he also writes that they are unable to modulate their ambitious and grasping ways, and have therefore been slow to acquire graceful and charming manners. Rather, as parvenus in "good" society, they tend to demonstrate a "love of the loud, the gaudy, the ostentatious, and the meretricious," and an inability to "master the happy mean between arrogance and obsequiousness."[22] Goldman-Price concludes that Wharton and her friends found certain Jews "quite presentable" — "when cleaned up, on an individual basis" (and Wharton would later in life include among her closest friends two nonpracticing Jews, the Comtesse Robert de Fitz-James and Bernard Berenson). Nevertheless, Goldman-Price believes, and Hermione Lee's assessment of antisemitic comments in Wharton's unpublished correspondence confirms, that Wharton and her contemporaries found Jews overall "distasteful." Their consensus was that "in the main, with their foreign ways, their natural bad taste, and their incorrect usage, their suspicious ability to make money quickly and to spend it quickly, Jews were at best avoided, at worst abhorred."[23]

Some cultural critics have seen deeper historical differences as shaping the antisemitic attitudes emerging at this time. Gary Martin Levine's fine study *The Merchant of Modernism: The Economic Jew in Anglo-American Literature, 1864–1939*, traces some of the conventional ideas about Jewish culture to the early modern and even medieval periods in European history. Drawing on Hillel Levine's *The Economic Origins of Anti-Semitism* (1994), Levine explains that commonplaces about Jewish people and their alleged special economic characteristics were influenced by key cultural factors.[24] He begins with the role of Jews as moneylenders in medieval Europe. Although currency was available in this period, "economic development was hindered by religious [Christian] traditions that prohibited all forms of lending upon interest, an attitude toward capital supported by the recovery of classical philosophy, with its emphasis on a 'real' that existed out of the human mind."[25] Hillel Levine argues that "this realist religious and philosophical viewpoint was challenged by a nominalist one that questioned the existence of an object's 'reality' and saw meaning as derived from human consensus. Nominalist economic thinking saw value as an issue of supply and demand, rather than as a measure of labor, and allowed for new methods of bookkeeping, new types of contracts, and new types of currency such as bills of exchange."[26] Jews were especially well-equipped to take advantage of these nominalist attitudes toward capital because, Hillel Levine believes, they had "a religious tradition of nominalism, especially in Talmudic modes of interpretation, and a relatively elaborate body of religious law that circumvented restrictions of usury."[27] In addition, I would suggest that strong family ties, coupled with an awareness of the relativity of custom and tradition prompted by their marginalized status in many of the cultures where they settled, may also have contributed to Jews' development of nominalist ideas about the social construction of value.

Hillel Levine's analysis thus locates the origins of modern capitalist thought, dependent upon nominalist economic thinking not only in the Protestant reformation, as Max Weber had argued, but also within Jewish culture and its particular tradition of textual interpretation. Gary Levine finds a precedent for this belief in Werner Sombart's *Die Juden und das Wirtschaftsleben (The Jews and Capitalism)* (1911). Sombart, writing explicitly in response to Weber's *The Protestant Ethic and the Spirit of Capitalism* (1905), asserts that it was actually the Jews who originated capitalism, not the Protestants.[28] Considered by Sander Gilman to be "the most important German sociologist of the turn of the century to comment on the nature of Jewish genius," Sombart accounted for the shift of the European economic center from South to North in this earlier historical period with the diasporic movement of Jews from Spain to Holland and England: "Sombart claimed that the Jews had invented impersonal credit instruments and transferable securities and that Jews had been the principal creators of Europe's stock markets and the first speculators."[29] And, like Hillel Levine, Sombart finds the roots of Jews' economic thinking in their tradition's religious and philosophical texts such as "the Bible, Talmud, Mishna, Gemara, Code of Maimonides, and Sulchan Aruch."[30] According to Gary Levine, Sombart also argues that "medieval Jews were not cheats, but merely went against the guild-like gentile commercial practices of fixed prices and fixed incomes. Jews were behind the growth of advertising, which scarcely existed in the seventeenth century because advertising prices meant undercutting competitors, and praising your goods above those of your neighbors was looked down upon as an un-Christian practice."[31]

In this particular reading of the differences between Protestants and Jews and their respective contributions to the rise of capitalism, Hillel Levine argues that both traditions played an important role: Weber and Sombart were both right. However, Weber would also attribute to Protestant thought an emphasis on internal restraint, the famous worldly asceticism that supposedly allowed them to accumulate wealth and goods not for their own aggrandizement but for the greater glory of God and the realization of the kingdom of heaven on earth. Not my will but thine. This idea of internal restraint led, as we have seen earlier, to an understanding of goods as "merely" symbols of internal moral and spiritual qualities, qualities that, though immaterial, rested on the foundation of divine order and personal redemption. From the Protestant perspective, Jewish nominalism contributed to a capitalistic practice of economic aggression and accumulation that was unrestrained by internal spiritual scruples. While the Protestant referred to the otherworldly lexicon of salvation for the meaning of goods, the Jew was seen as referring to the shifting marketplace of socially constructed values: to the fluctuating "arbitrary" lexicon of social status and worldly prestige. This marketplace is the true vanity fair, a foundationless world in which mastery goes to those who can best read and manipulate its shifting codes.

In the Protestant imagination, this figure of the Jew differs significantly from that of the Catholic. Whereas the Catholic idolatrously believes that material objects can confer spiritual qualities, the Jew is supposedly not interested in otherworldly redemption. The magic this figure seeks is a wholly human construction, a foundation built of human desire and imagination, whose aim is not moral salvation but worldly success. The Protestant says there is a gap between the material signifier and the immaterial signified, that the immaterial spirit has an essential reality that the signifier does not share. The Catholic says that under certain circumstances, such as the ritual of the mass and holy Eucharist, they do share an essence. The Jew, according to the stereotype we are examining here, says there is no essence, only the nominalist, socially constructed value in the signifier: existence precedes essence. Essence, like monetary value, is a social construction, created by exchange and the arbitration of supply and demand: human desire and perceived desire. There is no value outside of the social marketplace, or if there is, it does not count because it is ineffectual within that marketplace. Such value is, in a sense, sentimental, because it is wholly personal and cannot be circulated or traded in the open, public market. The value of a keepsake cannot be commodified for exchange; sentimental association has no surplus value for buyers who do not hold the same affective associations.

In this portrait we can again see the doubleness in the figure of the Jew as described by John Higham. We can also see how this figure can be easily conflated with that of the Protestant hypocrite, who pretends to accumulate his (or her) wealth for the glory of God, but who, without true grace, is in truth amassing worldly goods for his own self-aggrandizement. In other words, the Jew can be seen as a Protestant capitalist without grace, without the internal referent of divine purpose. However, while the Protestant hypocrite most likely takes pains to maintain at least the appearance of worldly asceticism, if only to maintain moral standing within the Protestant community, where the ostentatious display of wealth would be seen as a sign of the unregenerate state of one's soul, the Jew supposedly suffers from no such inhibition; he feels no need to camouflage his worldly ambitions, but can display them openly, sincerely, and can avow his belief in the power of the social market to confer meaning, personal as well as economic. This is perhaps the most scandalous aspect of the Jew: the rejection of even the pretense of worldly asceticism, of materialistic restraint, and the embrace of vanity fair and its power to confer both identity and worldly prestige, if not happiness.

In the Protestant imagination of the early twentieth century then, the figure of the Jew replaces the Catholic as the representative of materialism, but this materialism is "modern." Whereas Catholic materialism was perceived as idolatrous and regressive, a kind of fetishistic primitivism, modern materialism is not fetishistic in the same way—a difference that lies in the anti-foundationalism of the stereotypical Jew and his diasporic homelessness. This is a point made by Gary Levine. While Levine emphasizes the identification of the Jew with the practice of speculation and stock trading, practices that resulted in sudden changes in values and hence became associated with social instability, he also links the figure to issues of national as well as religious and ethnic identity. As Levine explains, "Here the problem of capitalist signification in stock markets reinforces those issues of identity examined by Hannah Arendt, Michael Ragussis, Bryan Cheyette, Zygmunt Bauman and others in which 'the Jew' became a problematic figure to the discourses of nineteenth-century nationalism and imperialism and the growing rhetoric of racial theory."[32] As national, as well as religious and ethnic identities became racialized, a crucial question arose: "Were converts to Christianity such as Disraeli authentic Englishmen or did they remain secret Jews? If one could assimilate into a society, then what did its national character consist of?"[33] Read against the idea of fixed, unchangeable racial identities, the diasporic, "homeless" Jew became a devious shape-shifting figure, wholly performative, chameleon-like, adapting its identity to the external demands of each new cultural environment: "Able to assimilate and thrive, so varied in physical appearance, 'the Jew' destabilized race-theory and epitomized social instability."[34] As Zygmunt Bauman writes: "In the mobile world, the Jews were the most mobile of all; in the world of boundary breaking, they broke most boundaries; in the world of melting solids, they made everything, including themselves, into a formless plasma in which any form could be born, only to dissolve again." And given the challenge that this paradoxically essential formlessness and plasticity posed, "Doing something about the Jews was not just an effort to make the world pleasingly uniform again, but an effort to fight the world's contingency, opacity, uncontrollability."[35]

While these anxieties were heightened by the rise of Eastern European (as well as Asian and Mediterranean) immigration into the United States and the subsequent destabilizing of the foundations of national and cultural identity, those foundations had already been weakening within Protestantism itself as, over the course of the nineteenth century, orthodox belief in scriptural authority and crisis conversion was challenged by scientific and historical inquiry and replaced by liberal theological innovations such as Friedrich Schleiermacher's Romantic Protestantism and Horace Bushnell's Christian nurture. This liberal theology substituted human agency for divine election in the development of moral awareness and individual salvation. As discussed earlier, Karen Halttunun explores the anxieties and contradictions produced by these shifts in her study *Confidence Men and Painted Women*, where she locates a moment in the ante-bellum period when the belief in a core, essential soul, answerable only to God, was transformed into a reliance on "character," an unstable coalition between an inner, supposed authentic identity and its sincere display in outward appearance.[36] When challenged by the increasing anonymity of the emergent urban industrialized society, this instability resulted as a matter of course in tremendous anxiety about the performance of self.

In the case of *Little Women*, as we have seen, the turn to Christian nurture assuaged this anxiety by providing a moral foundation through human mediation, specifically through the agency of the family, which is presented as the only reliable mirror of the sincere, and therefore true, self. The problem here is that the power of the family to transmit these discourses and guide the development of character depends upon its adherence to the Protestant representational economy and its ability to teach children to read its signs. If the family cannot provide this training, if the vessel of inherited tradition is broken, to use terms that would later become crucial to Wharton's vision, then the precious wine of these values is lost. Hence Lily Bart's situation: inwardly as malleable as wax, unguided and as vulnerable as a sea-plant to the flux of any cultural tide.

This dynamic explains why Gary Levine and Webb Keane see both the Jew and the Protestant as harbingers and exemplars of modernism, but also helps account for differences between these two stereotypical figures, and for the weakness of liberal Protestantism in the face of modernity's challenges. Sentimentalism, for example, substitutes the more "immanent," historical and material, bonds of human nurture for the miracle of conversion and ultimately turns to the wholly secular practices of the therapeutic ethos.[37] In this sense, sentimentalism is, curiously, part of the continuing disenchantment of Protestantism. However, this brand of Protestantism, despite its reliance on human instruction and institutions, still denies the dependence of spiritual identity upon the materiality and social mediation of language and human relationships. According to Webb Keane, a discussed earlier, modern Protestantism still asserted its faith in an essential self and its ultimate truth, separate from its material environment.[38] In Keane's analysis, as in Halttunen's, this internal contradiction produced an increased emphasis on sincerity. The material signifier of one's external appearance and behavior are separated from the immaterial reality of one's internal spiritual and moral state; however, the outward performance and display of that inward reality must match the inward reality. Social behavior is only a performance, but it must be a sincere performance, must be transparent in its display. If it is not, the result is hypocrisy or, worse, the criminal manipulation of appearance in the service of personal gain: hence the confidence man, a figure that Halttunen argues dominated the imagination of popular American literature in the mid-nineteenth century because it so perfectly exemplified the fears prompted by the eroding stability of identity. In Wharton's time, it will be, as Zygmunt Bauman argues, not the confidence man, but the Jew who represents these fears of the unordered, the purely performative, the shape-shifter.[39]

According to Halttunen, such internal contradictions and attendant anxieties were partially resolved by Protestantism's acceptance of a certain degree of performativity in self-presentation. This was particularly noticeable in shifting evaluations of "respectable" taste, which at the height of the demand for sincerity had been defined, as we have seen in *Little Women*, as the honest expression in material form of one's internal moral and spiritual character. By the century's end, however, taste had been accepted as a social construction, a material display signifying one's identification with a particular social group, but not necessarily one's moral character. Interestingly, as Halttunen points out, the preferences for a simple style and understated display persisted as the hallmarks of middle-class respectability, although the underlying belief in them as reliable indicators of morality had faded away.[40] However, this acceptance of a certain amount of social performativity still excluded those who could not master the material style of the Protestant elite, an elite that questioned the authenticity of those who imitated its style without possessing the prerequisite religious, racial, or ethnic background. The motivations of the poseur and the parvenu were still regarded with suspicion, as Wharton's work demonstrates so powerfully.

As many historians have noted, by the turn of the century these tensions over the social construction of identity produced a "crisis of representation," along with what historian Warren Susman notably described as a new concept of "personality," a notion of selfhood released from the demand for essential authenticity and open to endless permutations determined solely by continuous adaptation to social context.[41] Certainly, the figure of the Jew fits this definition of the modern "personality," as opposed to the earlier "character" described by Karen Halttunen. However, Andrew Heinze has criticized Susman's definition of personality as the quintessential modern form of the subject, drawing as Susman does primarily on consumer culture and late-stage capitalism for its source. Rather, Heinze argues, the influx of immigrants from other cultures created a core confusion about the foundation of American identity, a confusion that produced a *Schizophrenia Americana*, characterized by a sense of inner fragmentation and self-contradiction.[42]

It seems to me that these two interpretations of the modern subject, Susman's and Heinze's, are not mutually exclusive, but complementary. Certainly the American lexicon of identity had versions of the performative self available in the figure of the Protestant hypocrite, who hid his or her selfish drives under a mask of pious consumption. And de Tocqueville had early noticed Americans' unique social mobility and the persistent anxiety that such shape-shifting elicited.[43] However, Heinze seems correct in noticing that these concerns were heightened and given new force by waves of non-Protestant, even non-Christian immigrants. Moreover, Webb Keane's theory of representational economies provides a theoretical basis for Heinze's notion of this "schizophrenia," since it explains how competing and contradictory ways of defining the self can circulate within a given social setting and even within an individual subject. As we have seen, the figure of the performative Jew, supposedly able to assume the mask of any socially desirable identity, seemed particularly well-equipped to negotiate the complicated currents of America's newly turbulent social waters. Hence, as Bauman notes, the Jew became the focus of these anxieties about destabilization, particularly among the Protestant elite, those patricians who feared that their privileged position would be lost to a rising tide of commercial entrepreneurs.[44]

Here I should also note several key responses to these anxieties concerning the eroding foundations of spiritual identity, both Protestant and Catholic. Beginning in 1916, the German neo-orthodox theologian Karl Barth passionately rejected what he saw as liberal Protestantism's dependence on social relations for the communication and reproduction of its core values and the construction of its subjects (a dependence that Keane also argues liberal Protestantism denied and repressed). Instead, Barth radically reasserted the human necessity for crisis conversion and argued that culture could not perform the miracle of moral regeneration. That, only God could perform. Barth's rejection of "immanentism" was a direct disavowal of the theology espoused by German philosophers such as Friedrich Schleiermacher, a theology that had provided much of the foundation not only for the Christian nurture of Horace Bushnell but also for the transcendental spirituality of Concord, Massachusetts, and for the Romantic sentimentalism of the Alcott family itself.[45] Turning away from this dependence on the merely human, Barth and other neo-orthodox theologians reasserted the otherness of God and of God's will in the election of the soul to grace and salvation.

In a related move, Roman Catholicism in this period asserted the supreme authority of the Catholic church, introducing the doctrine of papal infallibility, a radical strike against any notion of historical relativity or of spiritual power outside the sacred vessel of its core institutions. In 1907, Pope Pious X issued the papal encyclical "Pascendi Dominici Gregis," which religion commentator Peter Seinfels describes as "a sweeping and vehement condemnation of a loose movement of Catholic biblical scholars, philosophers, and theologians who were labeled 'modernist.'" Influenced by secular philosophy and liberal Protestant theology, the Catholic leaders condemned by the pope were receptive to historical criticism of the Bible and "looked to intuition and interior yearning as the basis for religious belief." Pious X followed up his encyclical in 1910 with the requirement that "all current and future Catholic clergymen swear a lengthy oath against modernism, ratifying in detail the condemnations of 'Pascendi.'"[46]

For the Protestants of Wharton's class, however, neither of these moves held much appeal as a way to shore up the eroding foundations of their identity. As discussed earlier, what did appeal to many, including Theodore Roosevelt and other members of the Old New York elite, was the Darwin-influenced scientific racism of writers like Henry Cabot Lodge and Madison Grant, who stabilized patrician identity by racializing it. Bringing to sinister realization the growing speculation about racial essences, Grant's enormously influential *Passing of the Great Race* posited that racial traits included, as in the Lodge quotation above, "unchangeable" beliefs that produced traditions, attitudes, and moral behaviors. These beliefs were both "unconscious" and "impervious to argument."[47] Thus the core of the Protestant subject, a core that had earlier been seen as formed through: 1) spiritual conversion, 2) universal Reason, or 3) the beloved community of the regenerate (including the Protestant family itself), was now seen as an inherited racial type, resting on a specifically racial foundation. White Anglo-Saxon Protestants behave as they do not because of God's grace, a universal moral sense, or Christian nurture, but because of inherited traits. The salient feature of their identity is no longer religious, but genetic. It is not their Protestantism that matters, but their Nordicism.

Within the new framework of scientific racism, the Jew became a significantly contradictory, even paradoxical figure whose identity was "fixed" in its formlessness. According to Grant (and the later Nazi theorists who adapted Grant's ideas), the Jew's adaptation to different cultural contexts is always an imitation, a shape-shifting in service of a hidden agenda, which is a secretive, parasitical quest for dominance over the host culture. In this view the Jew's behavior is always wholly performative; there is no authentic Jewish self or even the possibility of sincere moral behavior. In answer to the question of whether Benjamin Disraeli could become a Briton, a scientific racist like Grant would say no, because national identity was now racialized as unchanging and impervious to argument. As for the question of whether a Jew could be converted to Christianity, the answer would also be no, because the essence of Christian belief, its authentic spirit, was also now racialized, even Nordicized (one scientific racist even suggested that Jesus Christ was essentially Aryan) and therefore inaccessible to Jews, who could only hypocritically imitate its outward form in the quest for cultural acceptance and ultimate domination.[48]

Wharton, like many of her elite New York peers, moved in the opposite direction from Karl Barth's neo-orthodox Protestantism and Roman Catholic traditionalism. Like many of her educated peers, she also rejected liberal Protestantism because it still rested on a foundation of otherworldly faith and still advocated Christianity's "cursed assumption of a separation between body & soul." However, while Wharton's interest in evolutionary theory and her reading of writers like Lodge and Lecky is well-documented, her opinions on racial identity seem more complex than those readings might initially suggest. Take the critical instance of the Dreyfus case. The charges of treason brought against Alfred Dreyfus, a French military officer accused of spying, deeply divided public opinion and set off a contentious debate among French intellectuals over whether Dreyfus could overcome his Jewish background to be a "true" — that is, authentically patriotic — Frenchman, as he claimed he was. Wharton took the side of Dreyfus, which put her in opposition to her close friend, the conservative Paul Bourget, who passionately denounced him.[49] Critic Sharon Kim provides, I believe, some important insights into Wharton's complex approach to these issues.

Kim describes Wharton's philosophy in the years when she was writing *The House of Mirth* as a "material monism" whose interpretive, shaping discourse was largely Darwinian theory.[50] However, Wharton, as Kim persuasively argues, modified her use of the Darwinian theory of human development with Larmarckian ideas about the transmission of acquired traits over time and generations: a modification that was very popular and widespread among writers of Wharton's generation. According to Kim, "by the late nineteenth century Lamarckism evolved beyond its original claims. It was taken to explain not only physical diversity and basic instinct but even traits like religious disposition, the artistic faculty, monogamy, Catholicism, conscience, taste in foods, paying taxes, and democratic government."[51] Historian L. J. Jordova explains the theory's popularity this way: "Lamarck offered psychologists and social theorists ways of linking the physiological, mental, and cultural aspects of evolution, as he had done for Spencer. The notion of habit Lamarck employed could provide a biological account of the processes the nascent social sciences were seeking to explain, such as the progress of civilisation or the development of the human races."[52] As a result, Kim writes, Lamarck's followers could "take a spiritual or cultural trait, or even a political ideology, and render it material, biological, and heritable. This form of Lamarckism pervaded the late nineteenth century."[53]

For Wharton, Kim argues, the medium of this transmission was "blood," through which the acquired traits, the results of a "slowly-accumulated history," passed from one generation to the next. (Hence Lily Bart half-seriously argues that her materialistic behavior stems from traits inherited in her "blood" from that wicked, anti-Puritan ancestress.) Kim also argues, however, that only those who have a "continuity" of cultural tradition can truly acquire traits in this fashion. They cannot be simply learned by someone who is outside the culture in which the traits are preserved and accumulated. Time is an important dimension of this process. Thus, Kim writes that Wharton held to ideas about identity that were similar to those of scientific racists like Madison Grant. That is, because these traits can only be transmitted over long periods of time, someone like Rosedale can never change his essential nature; his identity is still fixed. As Kim explains, "Rosedale may learn certain things, and buy certain things, but he himself, the substance of who he is in his blood, remains an outsider, so his social culture seems vulgar, annoying, prosthetic."[54] And Kim argues something similar about Lily. Because Lily is the product of a frivolous society, she is, Kim believes, essentially frivolous herself and, although she may superficially learn the values of a deeper, more moral culture through her interactions with Lawrence Selden, because she is not truly embedded in his culture, these perceptions only serve to alienate her further. They bring her not transcendence but despair. The blood of the Lily's frivolous ancestress must ultimately prevail over more recently acquired values.

Kim's work is an important addition to our understanding of Wharton's thinking. However, I would make some key revisions to her assessment. Most importantly, I see Wharton's turn to Larmarckian thought as an extension of nineteenth-century liberal Protestant immanentism, now purged of its otherworldly elements and linked to a more "modern" evolutionary viewpoint. Yes, Wharton rejects a dualistic view that pits the material against the spiritual. "Blood" is crucial to her understanding of the transmission of values and cultural traits. However, these traits are not impervious to the influence of current environmental forces. Rather, "blood" in her writing seems to signify the flow of feelings and desires, particularly those that are below the threshold of consciousness. Moreover, in "Life & I" Wharton describes her blood as responding to the affective "messages" she encounters in the present moment.[55] In this sense blood is the medium through which emotional responses are registered and individual potential is shaped and cultivated, "nurtured."[56] As we have seen in *Little Women*, the preferred mode for this kind of nurture is the Socratic dialogue in which the potential for certain behaviors and attitudes is encouraged and the potential for less desirable behaviors, such as aggression and materialism, is discouraged. As we have also seen, the emotional attachment between parent and child, mentor and mentee, is crucial to the effectiveness of this nurture, since it is through such attachments that blood is enlisted and feelings and desires are bent toward specific goals.

In this sense, we can see Wharton's use of terms like "blood" and "race" as referring not to fixed and unchangeable biological entities, predetermined by their genetic inheritance, but rather to the mix of developed potentialities and inclinations that have been fostered through training and history, an impress of values so deep as to direct the flow of feeling and desire and to link people who have been similarly affected by their history and culture.[57] For Wharton, I would argue, "the continuity of life" includes not only the reproductive transmission of genetic information, but also the impress of cultural nurture that shapes natural potential into its various mature forms. The taste for altruism that Mrs. March nurtures in her daughters is thus an acquired trait, with a strong affective component that powers its expression and a familial legacy that ensures its transmission to future generations.

This is an education of the sentiments, and, again, dialogue occurring within a context of emotional attachment is the royal road to teaching such tastes. As Pierre Bourdieu has pointed out, "taste" itself implies that a particular preference is natural, and therefore biologically determined; however, his sociological research also shows that taste is socially acquired and reflects the influence of class and other affiliations over time.[58] For example, certain tastes seem to mark Wharton's characters as members by blood of specific "races," and yet on examination these groups are not what anyone would technically refer to as races at all; they are rather groups comprising people with affinities of acquired tastes and traits, and since these tastes and traits are acquired, inherited through time and affiliation, I would argue, unlike Kim, that people can learn them, as Simon Rosedale and Lily Bart do. However, I would also argue that this acquisition brings the pain of conflict with tastes and traits acquired earlier in other cultural contexts. That is, Rosedale's and Lily's new ways of seeing must eventually compete with other "representational economies," the discourses that their characters previously internalized and activated in their responses to life: their earlier goals and values, their ideas of happiness, identity, and fulfillment.

It is now worth turning to the one of the core questions in *The House of*

Mirth. Is the book governed by the emerging discourse of scientific racism? Is Rosedale capable of conversion to the Protestantism that Selden represents? Is he eligible for membership in the republic of the spirit, or does his racial inheritance make it impossible for him to even comprehend its core principles? And, if Rosedale's racial difference is ineradicable, would Lily's mating with him result in her miscegenation?[59]

Critics assessing the novel's antisemitism tend to focus on either the racial essentialism — Rosedale is unacceptable because he is racially Jewish (Elizabeth Ammons, Jennie Kassanoff) — or the cultural/religious critique — Rosedale is unacceptable because he is unapologetically materialistic and nominalist (Gary Levine, Irene Goldman-Price). Nature or nurture? Walter Benn Michaels says that Wharton is not interested in race, although Ammons and Kassanoff argue to the contrary that the novel exhibits a recoiling from miscegenation, represented by the marriage of Lily, a "lily-white Anglo-Saxon," to a Jew.[60] The question often debated is what Wharton means by "inherited tendencies," a term that critics such as Kassanoff have taken to refer to the unchanging traits of scientific racism. However, the narrator's statements about the motivation of various characters range from the seemingly biological to the explicitly learned. For example, Rosedale's attitude and behavior are attributed to "race," but also to his "race's" history. In another example, Wharton refers to the workers in the hat shop where Lily briefly works as a "race," grouped by the behaviors they have learned from growing up in a particular economic and social position. Her use of the term in this case appears more metaphorical than literal: "like a race."

A similar usage appears early in the novel when Lily is musing on the parallels between her pursuit of Percy Gryce and her cousin Jack Stepney's equally opportunist courtship of Gwen Van Osburgh. She sees the two wealthy targets as alike in their complacency and banality and reflects that they would never turn to each for a mate (a reflection that will be proven incorrect by Gryce's subsequent marriage another equally banal Van Osburgh): "Yet they wouldn't look at each other . . . they never do. Each of them wants a creature of a different race, of Jack's race and mine, with all sorts of intuitions, sensations, and perceptions that they don't even guess the existence of" (40). Race here clearly has little or nothing to with Anglo-Saxon or Nordic extraction, but rather refers to a style of being, a set of cultivated perceptions and tastes dependent on the acquisition of specific forms of cultural capital. Teasing out firm boundaries between nature and nurture in this text, between "race" and "culture," is extremely difficult because, I would argue, Wharton is exploring how they are merged and interpenetrated. For example, Gus Trenor, with his impeccable Nordic and Protestant credentials, is not only described in exactly the same terms as Rosedale — as "predatory" and as a "brute"—but in the end he is less sympathetic than the Jewish businessman his wife snubs. And in the novel's conclusion the narrator describes Lily's adult character as a resulting from "inherited tendencies . . . combined with early training" (234). The phrase clearly indicates that inheritance is not fixed and predetermined, but driven only by "tendencies" whose ultimate expression is open to "training," and therefore open to change. The horticultural metaphors Wharton, the passionate and sophisticated gardener, uses throughout the novel suggest that people, like plants, can be pruned and shaped, their natural potentialities stunted or cultivated by nurture.[61]

Moreover, Wharton also omits from her portrait of Rosedale many of what scientific racists believed to be the bodily markers of the Jew. Rosedale is carefully described as blonde and "glossy." He has no elongated or arched nose, no hairy protuberances, as does F. Scott Fitzgerald's character Meyer Wolfsheim, whom Wharton later famously praised as Fitzgerald's "perfect Jew."[62] There is significantly nothing to distinguish Rosedale physically from the Anglo-Saxon Protestants in the novel except his heightened glossiness, his plumpness, and his "shoppy" manner: his strutting and fawning, his slangy, overly familiar language, discussed by Goldman-Price as a marker of Jewish outsider status and unacceptability. Although he is not represented as a member of the well-assimilated Sephardic and German Jewish groups, there are no traces of Yiddish in his speech, markers that would link him to the more recently arrived Eastern European Jews. My point is that Rosedale is not presented as a Jew through his racial traits or his ethnic markers, let alone in his religious practices, which appear to be nonexistent, but rather through his materialistic values and his unabashed expression of them: his "tasteless" performances of self.[63]

For example, while Trenor and the others in Lily's social set behave, in Irene Goldman-Price's phrase, "no better than Jews," they also display lingering inhibitions about openly articulating the values that truly guide them. As we have seen, they attempt, somewhat weakly, to maintain the façades of Protestant respectability. Rosedale has none of these inhibitions. His Jewishness lies in the purity of his economic motivation. Rosedale is the *Homo economicus* in his worship and mastery of the nominal world: the world of custom and socially constructed meaning, the marketplace of human exchange in which meaning is not intrinsic or essential, but always fluctuating, always relational. In this he is disturbingly similar to the quintessential American self-made man, the capitalist democrat, but without the moral restraint of Puritan worldly asceticism. He is the shape-shifter, ever aspiring, rising upward. With his lack of family antecedents, Rosedale is a later version of Halttunen's liminal urban man on the make; like R. W. B. Lewis's American Adam, he is "a man in space."[64] Moreover, Rosedale's ability to read the signs of this fragmented almost postmodern world also promises to make him its new panopticon, constantly scanning the social scene for profitable opportunities. Moving among all levels of society, he knows what the cleaning woman found in Selden's wastebasket and can assess its value on the social market; before Lily's death he alone of her friends and acquaintances enters the boarding house where fate abandons her. As the following close readings of the novel will show, Rosedale is double, ambivalent in his character: at once more democratic and yet less principled than the fastidious, "specialized" Selden, less integrated than Selden, but more fluid in his constant social adaptation. The combination, as Wharton displays it, fuels a seemingly single-minded dynamism, an engine designed for social and economic dominance. One thinks of Fitzgerald's description of Wolfsheim, the Jewish gangster, eating his hash with "ferocious delicacy." However, with his potential for refinement, Rosedale could also be a version of Fitzgerald's Jay Gatsby, a man born of his own imagination.[65]

Nonetheless, although Wharton's portrayal of Rosedale certainly draws on these stereotypes of the Jew, Rosedale himself is not simply a stereotype. Wharton shows him instead as complex and developing. Just like Lily, Rosedale is learning to "read the signs" throughout the novel, whether these are the signs of elite taste necessary for his acceptance into old New York society, or the signs of Lily's moral "distinction," which he begins to dimly recognize and value toward the novel's end. His dialogue with her is affecting his vision, just as her dialogue with Selden altered hers. The problem with Rosedale may be that, given his diasporic, assimilated identity, he also has no culture to help him read the signs. This representation is, of course, written purely from a Protestant-Christian view in which the core morality and values of actual Judaism are completely unrecognized. As the novel opens, Rosedale is very much as Sombart and Lecky described the stereotypical Jew: a figure without tradition, without cultural foundation, without moral instruction, totally oriented to the marketplace and nominalism.[66] However, we can see the developing tendrils of a new awareness begin to grow in Rosedale in response to his dialogues with Lily, as sympathy struggles to break through "the hard surface of his material ambitions." And just as Marmee in *Little Women* cultivates a taste for sincerity and honor in her daughters, so Rosedale first learns to refine his material tastes, then ultimately progresses to an appreciation, a cultivated taste, for Lily's moral scruples by the novel's end. Thus, although Wharton uses the language of race, she does not, I argue, present characters that are racial in essence, whose behavior is wholly determined by race. Rather "Protestants" can be interpellated into a "Jewish" materialism, and "Jews" can be taught how to read and value the signs of a "Protestant" anti-materialistic discourse. In the complex vanity fair of modern, urban New York, individuals such as Lily Bart and Simon Rosedale can internalize competing, even contradictory discourses. And, as we shall see, not Lily alone, but all three of this novel's major characters shift like sea-plants in the currents of cultural exchange.

Finally, before moving to close readings of key passages in which Rosedale appears, I would like to argue that Simon Rosedale is in many ways not only not a portrait of a "real" Jew but a disguised portrait of Wharton's worst fears about materialistic Protestants. Like the Africanist presence that Toni Morrison analyzed so persuasively in her study *Playing in the Dark*, the Jewish presence in this novel is actually a figure from the Protestant imagination, a projection of its repressed anxieties and desires. As Morrison says so eloquently, the "dream is about the dreamer."[67] In the later novel *The Custom of the Country* Wharton no longer felt the need to mask this figure under the cloak of "the Jew," but let him step out into the open as a Midwestern Baptist businessman on the make: Elmer Moffatt, the epitome of American enterprise and social mobility. Moffatt, whose name seems to reference the materialistic, newly rich Moffat family of *Little Women*, is described in virtually identical terms to Rosedale: he is "glossy," "fat," "shoppy," slangy, unapologetically materialistic and ambitious. He also manipulates inside information to make his way upward and does not hesitate to advise others to use pressures verging on blackmail to gain personal advantage. Ralph Marvell, Wharton's representative of old New York in this novel, even sees Moffatt and his kind as alien "invaders" taking over the territory of patrician "aborigines." The new commercial capitalists here appear "like a race," although it is clear that they come from the same native "stock" as the "aborigines" whose social and economic power they are usurping.

As Moffatt makes his inexorable way to worldly success, we also see him, like Rosedale, refining his social skills and material tastes, until, by the novel's end, he has become not only fabulously rich but also a discriminating collector, ruthlessly acquiring the cherished heirlooms of owners less rapacious and more morally worthy than himself. Moffatt's materialistic pilgrimage is paralleled in this case not by the descending spiral of Lily Bart, destroyed by her own conflicted motives, but by the ascending spiral of Undine Spragg, magnificently unified in her materialistic drives and disturbingly lacking in interior life. At the novel's close, Elmer and Undine, who began their careers married in the Protestant heartland, the Midwestern city of Apex, are reunited at another apex, a transatlantic victory over their economic and social rivals. Still striving, never satisfied, the ultimate realization of capitalistic self-invention without moral restraint, this quintessentially modern couple dominates their vanity fair like a plaster bride and groom atop a gigantic, wealth-engorged wedding cake.

Turning now to closer readings of the novel, Rosedale in book 1 seems comparatively stereotypical and two-dimensional, as manifested most obviously in his flashy taste and overly familiar manners. At the Van Osburgh wedding, the irreproachable Protestant Gerty Farish stops to ask who could have given a particularly ostentatious wedding gift, a diamond pendant as "big as a dinner-plate." When she learns the donor was Rosedale, she exclaims, "What, that horrid man? Oh, yes—I remember he's a friend of Jack's, and I suppose cousin Grace had to ask him today; but she must rather hate having to let Gwen accept such a present from him'" (72). As the narrator explains, Rosedale "was a man who made it his business to know everything about everyone" and whose "idea of showing himself to be at home in society was to display an inconvenient familiarity with the habits of those with whom he wished to be thought intimate." However, old New York's initial distaste at Simon Rosedale fails to take account of the man's adaptability. Lily, for example, "though usually adroit enough where her own interests were concerned . . . made the mistake, not uncommon to persons in whom the social habits are instinctive, of supposing that the inability to acquire them quickly implies a general dullness." And yet the narrator sees what Lily's prejudice leads her to overlook: "Because a blue-bottle bangs irrationally against a window-pane, the drawing-room naturalist may forget that under less artificial conditions it is capable of measuring distances and drawing conclusions with all the accuracy needful to its welfare" (90).

Indeed Rosedale can size up situations with remarkable speed: "He was sensitive to shades of difference which Miss Bart would never have credited him with perceiving because he had no corresponding variations of manner; and it was becoming more and more clear to him that Miss Bart herself possessed precisely the complementary qualities needed to round off his social personality" (96). Thus, although Lily rejects him instantly, he recognizes the particular advantage proximity to her confers:

Rosedale, with that mixture of artistic sensibility and business astuteness which characterizes his race, had instantly gravitated toward Miss Bart. She understood his motives, for her own course was guided by as nice calculations. Training and experience had taught her to be hospitable to newcomers, since the unpromising might be useful later on, and there were plenty of available *oubliettes* to swallow them if they were not. But some intuitive repugnance, getting the better of years of social discipline, had made her push Mr. Rosedale into his *oubliette* without a trial. (16)[68]

Significantly, the narrator suggests here that Lily's "instinctive repugnance" might actually be result of her unconscious recognition of her similarity with Rosedale. Lily may be trying to cling to her slippery perch at the top of the social hierarchy and Rosedale may be trying to climb toward it, but their motives and "nice calculations" are, at heart, much the same.

The first full exposure of Rosedale's character and motives comes at the very end of book 1. Until this point he has been a kind of shadowy counterpoint to the socially established men in Lily's orbit. We get glimpses of his slow and patient social ascent. With his preternatural business skills he manages to prosper during an economic downturn. Acquiring an elegant mansion (abandoned by another, less skilled, businessman) and providing entertainment during a lusterless season, he begins, with the patience of "his race," to gain access to a social setting previously closed to him. Following the *tableaux vivants*, Rosedale feels that the moment is right to make his move. He comes forward with a marriage proposal to Lily and a kind of personal apologia. His singling out of this moment and Lily's particular self-presentation demonstrate how well he has observed the "shades of difference" in the culture he wishes to enter. Indeed, he begins his proposal by critiquing the Brys' entertainment: "I would have spent more money on the music. But that's my character: if I want a thing I'm willing to pay: I don't go up to the counter, and then wonder if the article's worth the price. I wouldn't be satisfied to entertain like the Welly Brys; I'd want something that would look more easy and natural, more as if I took it in my stride." Rosedale has begun to recognize the cultural distinction expressed through the "easy and natural." He is trying to divest himself of the social markers of the parvenu. He wants to looks as if he took his new prestige "in his stride." Moreover, "it takes two things to do that, Miss Bart: money, and the right woman to spend it . . . I've got the money . . . . 'and what I want is the woman—and I mean to have her too'" (139).

Rosedale' assessment of his need for a wife like Lily Bart, and his need for Lily Bart specifically, is characteristically penetrating: "I generally *have* got what I wanted in life, Miss Bart. I wanted money, and I've got more than I know how to invest; and now the money doesn't seem to be of any account unless I can spend it on the right woman. That's what I want to do with it; I want my wife to make all the other women feel small. I'd never grudge a dollar that was spent on that. But it isn't every woman can do it, no matter how much you spend on her" (139–40). Without a wife to display his economic power in the Veblenesque contests for prestige, Rosedale is at a terrible disadvantage. And he needs not just any wife, but a wife who can display the requisite hauteur, the required distinction and superior taste necessary to humble her competitors in the fashionable arena. And here is where the image of Lily at the *tableaux vivants* comes into play: "When I looked at you the other night at the Brys', in that plain white dress, looking as if you had a crown on, I said to myself: 'By gad, if she had one she'd wear it as if it grew on her.'" As he explains, "There was a girl in some history book who wanted gold shields, or something, and the fellows threw 'em at her, and she was crushed under 'em: they killed her. Well, that's true enough: some women look buried under their jewelry. What I want is a woman who'll hold her head higher the more diamonds I put on it."

And yet, this is hardly a woman who does not care about money: "Tell you what it is, though, that kind of woman costs more than all the rest of 'em put together. If a woman's going to ignore her pearls, they want to be better than anybody else's — and so it is with everything. You know what I mean — you know it's only the showy things that are cheap" (140). As he winds up his proposal, Rosedale closes with a kind of testament of materialistic faith: "'Well, I should want my wife to be able to take the earth for granted if she wanted to. I know there's one thing vulgar about money, and that's the thinking about it; and my wife would never have to demean herself in that.' He paused, and then added, with an unfortunate lapse to an earlier manner: 'I guess you know the lady I've got in view, Miss Bart'" (140).

If Rosedale's speech makes it clear that he now knows that the style of patrician, Protestant New York is to act as if money did not matter, it also makes clear that he does not recognize the worldly asceticism on which this style was once founded. What's more he does not recognize the need to pretend to recognize it. As we have seen, Lily's self-presentation as Mrs. Lloyd, clothed in diaphanous neoclassical drapes, is susceptible to multiple readings, no one of which can claim precedence. Selden and Gerty, for example, see this image as the "real" Lily, an idealized nymph, symbol of the republic of spirit, freed from all material accidents. Rosedale interprets her quite differently, as a socially superior figure whose dominance is founded on material wealth. His comment that "there's one thing vulgar about money, and that's the thinking about it," echoes Lily's own comment to Selden at Bellomont that the only way not to think about money was to have enough of it: an idea that Selden rejected vehemently. In Rosedale's proposal, Lily is seeing her own deeply held beliefs reflected back at her, naked and unabashed. Similarly, Rosedale's vision of Lily's potential for triumphant self-realization is one of worldly self-aggrandizement; he wants her to "make all the other women feel small." This is his idea of success, a far cry from Selden and Gerty's vision of Lily's expressing the human aspiration for beauty, but uncomfortably close to Lily's earlier thoughts about using Percy Gryce's vanity to her own advantage. Rosedale's comment that "there's one thing vulgar about money and that's the thinking about it," is also a maxim with which old New Yorkers like Edith Wharton's parents might have agreed, although their rule had to do more with the talking about it. This, again, was a vestige of the Protestant ethic, in which one's personal desire for money was subordinate to one's stewardship of God-given wealth. That is, one shouldn't talk about money because one shouldn't think about money, at least not as an end in itself. Unlike them, Rosedale is perfectly willing to talk about money, and aims to stop thinking about it, too, though not by directing his thoughts to the spiritual good he can do with it, but by accumulating so much that he can satisfy every worldly desire.

Lily's response to this proposal is at first polite dismissal, but Rosedale interrupts her abruptly and cuts to the chase with "a plain business statement of the consequences." Although he is "confoundedly gone on her," he knows that she is "not very fond of me—*yet*." However, he also knows what she *is* fond of: "luxury, and style, and amusement, and of not having to worry about cash. You like to have a good time, and not have to settle for it; and what I propose to do is to provide for the good time and do the settling." Seeing the worst aspects of her character described so baldly, Lily immediately defends herself: "You are mistaken in one point, Mr. Rosedale: whatever I enjoy I am prepared to settle for." However, Lily has not counted on Rosedale's willingness to dispense with politeness. He presses on,

> I didn't mean to give offence; excuse me if I've spoken too plainly. But why ain't you straight with me—why do you put up that kind of bluff? You know there've been times when you were bothered—damned bothered—and as a girl gets older, and things keep moving along, why, before she knows it, the things she wants are liable to move past her and not come back. I don't say it's anywhere near that with you yet; but you've had a taste of bothers that a girl like yourself ought never to have known about, and what I'm offering you is the chance to turn your back on them once for all. (140–41)

The reference to Lily's transactions with Trenor, transactions to which Rosedale himself was a party, is all too clear. Rosedale's vision of marriage as a business deal accepts its likeness to prostitution without apology.

Lily blushes furiously. Indignant, she verges on the brink of an angry repudiation. However, she also sees how she has left herself open to this kind of proposition. Given Rosedale's knowledge of her secret and his possible use of it should he turn against her, she must appease him. Like "a breathless fugitive . . . at the cross-roads," Lily pauses and tries "to decide coolly which turn to take." Mustering the necessary self-restraint, she manages to put him off while at the same time admitting at least part of the truth he has insinuated:

> You are quite right, Mr. Rosedale. I *have* had bothers; and I am grateful to you for wanting to relieve me of them. It is not always easy to be quite independent and self-respecting when one is poor and lives among rich people; I have been careless about money, and I have worried about my bills. But I should be selfish and ungrateful if I made that the reason for accepting all you offer, with no better return to make than the desire to be free from my anxiety. You must give me time — time to think of your kindness — and of what I could give you in return for it — . (141)

Lily's response masterfully manages to acknowledge her vulnerability while at the same time asserting her honorable freedom from purely materialistic motives. She will not marry simply for money, at least not without love to offer in return. And, what she leaves unsaid, she will not offer simple sex in return either. For his part, Rosedale, "disciplined by the tradition of his blood to accept what was conceded, without undue haste to press for more," accepts this dismissal, "with its hint of future leniency." Yet Lily is still disturbed by the encounter: "Something in his prompt acquiescence frightened her; she felt behind it the stored force of a patience that might subdue the strongest will" (141).

Lily's next encounter with that stored force comes after her disastrous trip to the Mediterranean with the Dorsets and consequent loss of the major part of her aunt's inheritance. Snubbed by the elite women who once invited her to their homes, Lily is adrift, burdened by her debt to Gus Trenor, which will take virtually all the $10,000 she stands to gain once her aunt's will is settled. In this situation only one of her friends stands by her, that is, only one besides the stalwart Gerty Farish, and that is Carry Fisher, who makes her living as a kind of social guide for nouveau riche aspirants to elite circles. Carry's advice is sharp and uncompromising: Lily must marry and marry quickly. She offers two candidates, Simon Rosedale and George Dorset. Dorset, still married to Bertha, could be released from that bond if Lily was willing to testify to witnessing his wife's adultery. He would then presumably be free to marry Lily. The drawback to the plan is not only that Lily has no affinity with Dorset but also that the plan would confirm Bertha's original story that Lily was out to get her husband. Faced with Dorset's personal appeal, Lily easily rejects him. However, the second candidate is Rosedale, and his appeal is stronger than it once was, given Lily's diminished social and economic resources. Moreover, if Lily has tumbled downward on the social hierarchy, Rosedale has patiently worked his way upward. And for that, although she still dislikes him, "she no longer absolutely despised him. For he was gradually attaining his object in life, and that, to Lily, was always less despicable than to miss it" (188). Rosedale has begun to be accepted in some circles, being named to charitable boards and even being nominated to an exclusive club (although he has not yet won membership): "All he needed now was a wife whose affiliations would shorten the last tedious steps of his ascent." Although she is aware she has lost those precious affiliations, Lily is reassured by the sense of Rosedale's "personal inclination" toward her beneath his avowed "utilitarian motives." Now is the time to exercise her powerful attraction: "What if she made him marry her for love, now that he had no other reason for marrying her?" (188–89).

As in her earlier pursuit of Percy Gryce, Lily does not allow herself to think beyond the point of marriage to her prey. Everything after that "faded into a haze of material wellbeing, in which the personality of her benefactor remained mercifully vague. . . . there were certain things not good to think of, certain midnight images that must at any cost be exorcised — and one of these was the image of herself as Rosedale's wife" (194). In this mood, Lily meets Rosedale once more at Carry Fisher's, where she first finds him on his knees attending to her friend's little daughter in the drawing room. Without an adult audience to witness his action, this Rosedale seems to have a "quality of homely goodness"; he appears "a simple and kindly being." And Lily, watching unobserved," has time to feel that "yes he would be kind . . . kind in his gross, unscrupulous, rapacious way, the way of the predatory creature with his mate" (195). Her response is mixed, unsure "whether this glimpse of the fireside man mitigated her repugnance, or gave it, rather, a more concrete and intimate form" (195).

The next afternoon, she sets out with Rosedale for a walk that Wharton, with her architectural skill, poses as a negative reflection of Lily's walk with Selden in book 1. The contrast is so strong it is apparent to Lily herself: "Something in the lines of the landscape, and in the golden haze which bathed them, recalled to Miss Bart the September afternoon when she had climbed the slopes of Bellomont with Selden. The importunate memory was kept before her by its ironic contrast to her present situation, since her walk with Selden had represented an irresistible flight from just such a climax as the present excursion was designed to bring about" (197). She muses on her previous failures and their source in her own possible "unsteadiness of purpose." Now, however, she is determined not only to win her ultimate social and economic security, but also to triumph over

Berth Dorset: "As the wife of Rosedale — the Rosedale she felt it in her power to create — she would at least present an invulnerable front to her enemy" (197–98).

However, only by dwelling on this desired consequence, like "a fiery stimulant," can she even bear Rosedale's presence: "As she walked beside him, shrinking in every nerve from the way in which his look and tone made free of her, yet telling herself that this momentary endurance of his mood was the price she must pay for her ultimate power over him, she tried to calculate the exact point at which concession must turn to resistance, and the price *he* would have to pay be made equally clear to him." As with Gryce and even Gus Trenor, Lily is convinced that her power to capture and subdue her male admirer will allow her to manage and control him. However, Rosedale seems strangely impervious to her manipulation, and Lily senses "something hard and self-contained behind the superficial warmth of his manner" (198). And so it is that when Lily reintroduces his original marriage proposal and gravely announces that she is now willing to accept it, that Rosedale, rather shockingly, laughs and "with plump, jeweled fingers," takes a gold-tipped cigarette, contemplates it for a moment, as if contemplating his future options, and simply states, "My dear Miss Lily, I'm sorry if there's been any misapprehension between us — but you made me feel my suit was so hopeless that I had really no intention of renewing it." Rosedale is a more formidable, single-minded opponent than Lily had anticipated or previously encountered. While she tries to retreat with as much dignity as she can muster, Rosedale, grasping her hand, urges her, "Why do you talk of saying goodbye? Ain't we going to good friends all the same?" Drawing that hand away, she comes to the point, "What's your idea of being good friends? . . . Making love to me without asking me to marry you?" But Rosedale is not embarrassed by her accusation; instead he merely laughs again, "Well, that's about the size of it, I suppose. I can't help making love to you — I don't see how any man could; but I don't mean to ask you to marry me as long as I can keep out of it." Lily gives him a quiet smile, and tries again to withdraw, "I like your frankness; but I am afraid our friendship can hardly continue on those terms."

However, Rosedale is not only a cunning opponent; he is also a determined one. He stops her once again: "You're beastly hard on a fellow; but if you don't mind speaking the truth I don't see why you shouldn't allow me to do the same." As he further explains, "We're neither of us such new hands that a little plain speaking is going to hurt us. I'm all broken up on you: there's nothing new in that. I'm more in love with you than I was this time last year; but I've got to face the fact that the situation is changed." When she responds that she supposes that he no longer finds her as desirable a match as he once did, he admits the fact readily and goes on to address the core issue: "I won't go into what's happened. I don't believe the stories about you — I don't *want* to believe them. But they're there, and my not believing them ain't going to alter the situation." At this point Lily plays the role of the idealist in their dialogue: "If they are not true ... doesn't *that* alter the situation?" (199). But the idealist position is not one Rosedale will take; indeed he turns the tables on her, unveiling her own less than noble motives in the afternoon's negotiations:

> He met this with a steady gaze of his small stocktaking eyes, which made her feel herself no more than some superfine human merchandise. "I believe it does in novels; but I'm certain it don't in real life. You know that as well as I do: if we're speaking the truth, let's speak the whole truth. Last year I was wild to marry you, and you wouldn't look at me: this year — well, you appear to be willing. Now, what has changed in the interval? Your situation, that's all. Then you thought you could do better; now — ." (200)

Rosedale reads her so well because he recognizes himself in her. Since he does not disguise his own motives from himself, as she so often disguises her own, he can announce those motives openly:

> It's this way, you see: I've had a pretty steady grind of it these last years, working up my social position. Think it's funny I should say that? Why should I mind saying I want to get into society? A man ain't ashamed to say he wants to own a racing stable or a picture gallery. Well, a taste for society's just another kind of hobby. Perhaps I want to get even with some of the people who cold-shouldered me last year — put it that way if it sounds better. Anyhow, I want to have the run of the best houses; and I'm getting it too, little by little. But I know the quickest way to queer yourself with the right people is to be seen with the wrong ones; and that's the reason I want to avoid mistakes. (200)

While Rosedale acknowledges the taboo against social climbing, he refuses to defer to it: to be ashamed of that ambition or of his willingness to sacrifice Lily should she get in its way. Most significantly, he is quite willing to acknowledge that the stories about Lily are false. However, in the marketplace of public opinion Lily has only the value her agreed-upon appearance there gives her. She has no essential value apart from that arena, at least none for which Rosedale would sacrifice his own ambitions.

Lily's quiet acceptance of these hard facts is a kind of surrender: "She received this with a look from which all tinge of resentment had faded. After the tissue of social falsehood in which she had so long moved it was refreshing to step into the open daylight of an avowed expediency." When Lily earlier tried to break through this tissue of social falsehood in her conversation with Gerty about how the "truth" of a social reputation was actually constructed, the idealistic Gerty resisted. Now, without rancor, Lily recognizes in Rosedale a kind of comrade in arms and says simply, "I understand you . . . A year ago I should have been of use to you, and now I should be an encumbrance; and I like you for telling me so quite honestly." As she puts out her hand for a conciliatory handshake, Rosedale seems to lose his self-control, "By George, you're a dead game sport, you are!" As she begins to leave, he offers a new proposition: "Miss Lily — stop. You know I don't believe those stories — I believe they were all got up by a woman who didn't hesitate to sacrifice you to her own convenience — ." Lily at first is repelled by this show of sympathy for the injustice done her, especially from a man who has just refused to help rectify that injustice. However, Rosedale now wants to put "a plain case" before her (200).

In almost legalistic fashion he sets out a plan for her social rehabilitation, a rehabilitation that would allow him to marry her without jeopardizing the social status he craves. The plan depends upon her possession of Bertha Dorset's love letters to Laurence Selden. When Rosedale demands why Lily has not used the letters to subdue her enemy, Lily is at first simply shocked and bewildered that he knows she possesses them, but here is where Rosedale's panopticon-like power comes into play: "You're wondering how I found out about 'em? . . . . Perhaps you've forgotten that I'm the owner of the Benedick — but never mind about that now. Getting on to things is a mighty useful accomplishment in business, and I've simply extended it to my private affairs. For this *is* partly my affair, you see — at least, it depends on you to make it so." For Rosedale, nothing is sacred; everything is grist for the commercial mill, including the most personal information.

And his plan is superbly engineered for the New York market. Lily is to approach Bertha privately and make her aware of the consequences should Lily decide to make the letters public; the price for Lily not doing so would be Bertha's social acceptance of Lily and the furthering of her status. Once Lily's rehabilitation is complete, Rosedale will marry her. As Rosedale, like a businessman selling a proposal or a lawyer defending a case, explains the intricacies and advantages of the deal, Lily is at first horrified, but after the first moment she is held spellbound, "subdued to his will," by the plan's "subtle affinity to her own inmost cravings." Lily, as we have seen, has managed her career by making as "nice calculations" as Rosedale has. That analytical skill comes immediately to her aid as she sees "in a flash the advantage of this course over that which poor Dorset had pressed upon her. The other plan depended for its success on the infliction of an open injury, while this reduced the transaction to a private understanding, of which no third person need have the remotest hint." With all its ethical implications discreetly veiled, "put by Rosedale in terms of business-like give-and-take, this understanding took on the harmless air of a mutual accommodation, like a transfer of property or a revision of boundary lines. It certainly simplified life to view it as a perpetual adjustment, a play of party politics, in which every concession had its recognized equivalent." Answering to her "inmost craving," the plan also offers Lily respite from her own conscience, her confused wavering between moral idealism and materialistic desire: "Lily's tired mind was fascinating by this escape from fluctuating ethical estimates into a region of concrete weights and measures" (202).

Rosedale picks up on Lily's silent submission and reads into it not only acceptance of his plan but also "a dangerously far-reaching perception of the chances it offered." Assuming the worst about her, he quickly breaks her trance: "You see how simple it is, don't you? Well, don't be carried by the idea that it's *too* simple. It isn't exactly as if you'd started in with a clean bill of health. Now we're talking let's call things by their right names, and clear the whole business up." Bertha, he explains, would never have gained this ascendancy over Lily if questions about Lily's behavior hadn't already been raised. Those questions "prepared the ground" for the stories that cost Lily her social place. Rosedale sympathetically notes that these little questions are bound to arise for a "good-looking girl with stingy relatives," but Lily needs to prevent them from cropping up again: "It's one thing to get Bertha Dorset into line — but what you want is to keep her there. You can frighten her fast enough — but how are you going to keep her frightened? By showing her that you're as powerful as she is. All the letters in the world won't do that for you as you are now; but with a big backing behind you, you'll keep her just where you want her to be. That's *my* share in the business — that's what I'm offering you." In other words, reputation alone is not enough; Lily needs to put some muscle, some money, behind it. Speaking directly to his fears about Lily, Rosedale continues: "'You can't put the thing through without me — don't run away with any idea that you can. In six months you'd be back among your old worries, or worse ones; and here I am, ready to lift you out of 'em tomorrow if you say so. *Do* you say so, Miss Lily?' he added, moving suddenly nearer" (202).

With this last appeal, Lily is released from her spell: "Light comes in devious ways to the groping consciousness, and it came to her now through the disgusted perception that her would-be accomplice assumed, as a matter of course, the likelihood of her distrusting him and perhaps trying to cheat him of his share of the spoils. This glimpse of his inner mind seemed to present the whole transaction in a new aspect, and she saw the essential baseness of the act lay in its freedom from risk" (203).[69] Almost instinctively she recoils, and replies "in a voice that was a surprise to her own ears, 'You are mistaken — quite mistaken — both in the facts and in what you infer from them.'" Rosedale, confident just a moment before, now stares, "puzzled by her sudden dash in a direction so different from that toward which she had appeared to be letting him guide her." The subtle reference to Lily's earlier plea to Laurence Selden for guidance, for help reading the signs, is unmistakable. This guide is pointing her in quite a different direction, indeed in the very opposite direction from the one Selden showed her at Bellomont. Her sudden reversal indicates a revival of the momentarily stunned moral perceptions Selden helped awaken. And Rosedale is smart enough, and well-informed enough, to ascertain the reason for her sudden balkiness: "'Now what on earth does that mean? I thought we understand each other!' he exclaimed; and to her murmur of 'Ah, we do *now*,' he retorted with a sudden burst of violence: 'I suppose it's because the letters are to *him*, then? Well, I'll be damned if I see what thanks you've got from him!'" (203).

While Lily appears to reject Rosedale's proposal decisively, the consequences of this dialogue are more far-reaching. At Bellomont, her dialogue with Selden also resulted in her seeming to reject both a way of seeing the world and an offer of marriage, and yet the effects of that dialogue on her consciousness were long-lasting, as we have seen. Here, as well, Rosedale's open articulation of motives and desires that Lily had always partially veiled gives them new power. As the narrator explains, "She had rejected Rosedale's suggestion with a promptness of scorn almost surprising to herself: she had not lost her capacity for high flashes of indignation. But she could not breathe long on the heights; there had been nothing in her training to develop any continuity of moral strength" (204). Without that training, without that guidance, "what she craved, and really felt herself entitled to, was a situation in which the noblest attitudes should also be the easiest." As a result she has managed to retain her self-respect only through "intermittent impulses of resistance." Unable to compose a consistent self from the contradictory pieces available to her, Lily's course is a recursive one: "If she slipped she recovered her footing, and it was only afterward that she was aware of having recovered it each time on a slightly lower level. She had rejected Rosedale's offer without conscious effort; her whole being had risen against it; and she did not yet perceive that, by the mere act of listening to him, she had learned to live with ideas which would once have been intolerable to her" (204).

This particular passage clearly displays the representational economy latent in Lily's upbringing. As such, it is a crucial piece in Wharton's thematic design. Balancing the dialogue at Bellomont, the dialogue here expresses values that explicitly compete with those expressed by Lawrence Selden. The resulting conflict will end by destroying the young woman who has internalized those opposing values without the ability to resolve their contradictions. Looking at Rosedale's proposal more closely with this in mind, it is clear that its foundation is the nominalist definition of value described earlier. However, it is also worth noting that Rosedale is fully aware that this socially constructed value is just that: a construction. In fact, he acknowledges the "truth" of Lily's actual history, and even sympathizes with her inability to counter the more "convenient" beliefs that circulate about her. However, he is not about to challenge the judgment of the marketplace: he lives by those judgments, since his only definition of personal success depends on them, either through monetary profit or social prestige. In this Rosedale differs from the Protestant's stereotype of the consumer idolater or fetishist. Rosedale does not believe that money and status confer any kind of otherworldly or spiritual salvation or that they possess any magically transformative power; he is not persuaded that wealthy or socially elite people are somehow better than he is. If anything, he is secretly contemptuous of their hypocrisy and proud of his ability to manipulate their desires in service of ambitions he is unashamed to acknowledge.

Lily's disgusted sense that "the essential baseness of the act lay in its freedom from risk" also sheds an important light on Rosedale's thinking. With his "stocktaking eyes" assessing her like "a piece of superfine human merchandise," Rosedale is interpreting the situation along market principles. Marriage would be an investment in Lily, but as a commodity her value has been lowered. But blackmailing Bertha would force Bertha to "invest" in Lily, thereby raising Lily's stock in the social marketplace. Until that rise is accomplished, Rosedale will not risk his own social capital by investing in, that is, marrying, her; however, in a kind of insider trading scheme, he knows in advance that this secret transaction with Bertha will take place. His implicit threat to expose the blackmail should Lily back out on him once her stock has risen means that he has, in a sense, secured a first option on her purchase at that later time, but done so at the lower price her market value before the exchange with Bertha. At the same time, he has taken no risk in doing so. Should the trade with Bertha not go through, for whatever reason, he has risked, and lost, nothing. He has not dirtied his hands with actual blackmail. And he has not committed himself to a woman who could not further his ambitions or who might even render them impossible. The contrast with Selden could not be greater, for it was Selden who was willing to "take the risk" of marrying Lily, knowing her weakness. But Rosedale, valuing material success over sentiment, rejects that risk and disowns his love for the "real" Lily, a Lily whose innocence and whose vulnerability he knows even better than Selden.

The deep initial appeal of Rosedale's proposal to Lily also deserves a closer look. As noted, the system of values Rosedale represents is labeled as specifically Jewish. And, as the earlier scenes demonstrate, Rosedale does seem to fulfill many of the Protestant expectations about stereotypically Jewish behavior. This is particularly apparent when we turn to the orthodox Protestant vision of the Jew presented in Bunyan's *Pilgrim's Progress*.[70] Earlier we have seen how Christian entered into conversation with Ignorance and Talkative, who refused to accept their own sinfulness and attempted to evade the fear of God that Faith explained would have been the beginning of their salvation. Rosedale offers another way to escape these fears and lift Lily's burden: her "bothers" and "worries."[71] In this case, his advice mirrors that of Mr. Worldly Wiseman and his friend, Legality. In fact, Legality, who lives at the base of Mount Sinai, is described explicitly by Bunyan as a representative of Judaism.

When Christian first encounters Mr. Worldly Wiseman, he speaks of the difficult journey on the path which the Evangelist has set for him. Mr. Worldly Wiseman responds with ready sympathy: "there is not a more dangerous and troublesome way in the world than is that unto which he hath directed thee; and that thou shalt find, if thou wilt be ruled by his counsel." Mr. Worldly Wiseman not only knows the Evangelist and the path to which he directs his followers, but he also knows the trials of that path well: "Thou hast met with something (as I perceive) already; for I see the dirt of the Slough of Despond is upon thee; but that slough is the beginning of the sorrows that do attend those that go on in that way." Like Rosedale outlining the continuing difficulties Lily will face if she stubbornly persists in maintaining her moral integrity, Mr. Worldly Wiseman goes on: "Hear me, I am older than thou! Thou art like to meet with in the way which thou goest wearisomeness, painfulness, hunger, perils, nakedness, sword, lions, dragons, darkness, and in a word, death, and what not? These things are certainly true, having been confirmed by many testimonies. And why should a man so carelessly cast away himself by giving heed to a stranger?"[72]

When Christian replies that his fear of God's judgment is more than all these more material dangers, Mr. Worldly Wiseman waves his objection away: "How camest thou by thy burden at first?" When Christian replies that it was by reading "this book in my hand," Mr. Worldly Wiseman dismisses its authority: "I thought so; and it so happened unto thee as to other weak men, who, meddling with things too high for them, do suddenly fall into distractions; which distractions do not only unman men, as thine, I perceive, has done thee, but they run them upon desperate ventures, to obtain they know not what."[73] When Christian reminds him that he does know what he seeks to obtain, which is "ease for my heavy burden," Mr. Worldly Wiseman has another ready answer: "But why wilt thou seek for ease this way, seeing so many dangers attend it, especially since, hadst thou but patience to hear me, I could direct thee to the obtaining of what thou desirest, without the dangers that thou in this way wilt run thyself into; yea, and the remedy is at hand. Besides, I will add, that instead of those dangers thou shalt meet with much safety, friendship, and content."[74]

The new path to which Mr. Worldly Wiseman directs Christian leads to a nearby village, named Morality: "There dwells a gentleman whose name is Legality, a very judicious man (and a man of very good name) that has skill to help men off with such burdens as thine are from their shoulders; yea, to my knowledge he hath done great deal of good this way. Ay, and besides, he hath skill to cure those that somewhat crazed in their wits with their burdens. To him, as I said, thou mayest go, and be helped presently." In addition to Legality, Christian might also find at home Legality's "pretty" young son, Civility, who can lift Christian's burden "as well as the old gentleman himself."[75] The houses in the town of Morality, Mr. Worldly Wiseman goes on, are easily available and well-provisioned. In other words, life in Morality, guided by Legalism and his son Civility, at the base of Mount Sinai, is good.

And so Christian sets out in this new direction, seeking Mount Sinai. However, "when he got now hard by the hill, it seemed so high, and also that side of it that was next the wayside did hang so much over that Christian was afraid to venture further, lest the hill should fall on his head. Wherefore he stood still, and wotted not what to do. Also his burden, now, seemed heavier to him than while he was in his way. There came flashes of fire out of the hill that made Christian afraid that he should be burned."[76] At this critical juncture, with Christian full of fear and perplexity, the Evangelist reappears, asking why Christian has turned out of the straight path he had advised him to take. When Christian confesses to his conversation with Mr. Worldly Wiseman, the Evangelist replies, "I will now show thee who it was that deluded thee, and who 'twas also to whom he sent thee. The man that met thee is one Worldly Wiseman, and rightly is he so called; partly, because he favoureth only the doctrine of this world (therefore he always goes to the town of Morality to church) and partly because he loveth that doctrine the best, for it saveth him from the cross; and because he is of a carnal temper, therefore he seeketh to prevent my ways, though right."[77]

Then he explains there are three things in Mr. Worldly Wiseman's counsel that Christian must "abhor": "1. His turning thee out of the way. 2. His labouring to render the cross odious to thee. 3. And his setting thy feet in that way that leadeth unto the administration of death."[78] The parallel of the first of these with Rosedale's dialogue with Lily is simple enough, but the second also applies, since Rosedale's offers explicitly offers to lift the "burden" of moral anxieties from her conscience, along with the burden of her financial worries. And Lily is temporarily seduced by this offer of rescue from "the cross." As she listens "spellbound," her "tired mind" is fascinated by this potential escape from her moral struggle. She is saved from acquiescence only by her sudden flash of revulsion at Rosedale's refusal to risk his reputation for her sake, a flash that recalls her earlier dialogue with Selden, who plays the equivalent in this moral drama of the Evangelist himself. As for the third thing in Mr. Worldly Wise's counsel, Lily's sporadic, but desperate attempts to escape the furies of her conscience will ultimately set her feet in the way that leads to her death. However, the moral of her story is more ambiguous than this parallel might suggest.

Now the Evangelist unmasks to Christian the true identity of Legality: "the son of the bondwoman [Galatians 4:21-31] which now is, and is in bondage with her children, and is in a mystery, this Mount Sinai, which thou hast feared would fall on thy head. Now if she with her children are in bondage, how canst thou expect by them to be made free? This Legality therefore is not able to set thee free from thy burden. No man was as yet ever rid of his burden by him, no, nor ever is like to be; ye cannot be justified by the works of the law, for by the deeds of the law no man living can be rid of his burden."[79] This, of course, is the orthodox Protestant interpretation and critique of Jewish legalism. Since it follows the letter of the law and not its spirit, since it depends upon worldly works and not divine grace as the source of happiness and salvation, "therefore Mr. Worldly Wiseman is an alien, and Mr. Legality a cheat; and for his son Civility, notwithstanding his simpering looks, he is but an hypocrite, and cannot help thee."[80] If Rosedale's proposition can offer her material comfort and acceptance of a hypocritical society, those remedies in the end come at a cost: the loss of whatever sense of moral integrity and inner worthiness Lily still possesses. If anything, Rosedale's solution will only render her burden of conscience that much heavier.

This view of Rosedale's role in Lily's inner ethical drama is darker than that of even those critics who have probed the antisemitic aspects of his characterization. For example, Gary Levine argues that "Rosedale, though he values Lily primarily as a means to greater social status, is willing to marry her even after that value has evaporated."[81] This appraisal is wrong on both counts. First of all, Rosedale never indicates in the novel that he will marry Lily without her having recovered her social value; blackmailing Bertha is always his precondition for commitment. Secondly, Rosedale comes to appreciate Lily's intrinsic value, not just her social value, and yet he will not marry her despite that appreciation, because of his greater respect for outer appearance than internal reality and his overwhelming desire for social acceptance. Irene Goldman-Price openly acknowledges that much of Wharton's characterization of Rosedale is based on Jewish stereotypes, and yet she also asserts that Wharton's portrait goes beyond those stereotypes: "Instead of simply making Rosedale rich and vulgar, she makes him a real person to us, and she has him change over time. His sins are primarily against taste rather than morality; we never actually see him perform an immoral act. Though he does suggest that Lily commit black-mail, he doesn't carry it out without her. Thus we cannot easily judge or dismiss him."[82] However, Rosedale's failure to perform an immoral act "on stage," so to speak, is not evidence of his innocence. In fact, his proposition to Lily re-veals his cunning ability to get around the appearance of immorality. He will make Lily perform the blackmail while he sits back and reaps the social bene-fits. Again, if Lily were an actual stock, this would qualify as insider trading, a very skillful manipulation of the market. If anything, his proposition underlines Rosedale's lack of moral scruples. His skill at hiding his manipulations and his disciplined avoidance of any sentimental restraints on his ambition make him all the more dangerous. However, if Levine and Goldman-Price are, I think, too easy on Rosedale in this respect, their assessment of his complexity seems to me correct. Although he does certainly fulfill the darkest Protestant fears about Jews, Rosedale also is presented as a character who does, as Goldman-Price says, "change over time." Although Gary Levine sees Rosedale as more racial-ized than Goldman-Price does, and therefore as more "fixed" and unable to develop beyond his racial traits, nevertheless Levine also sees Rosedale as "a figure who ultimately emerges as surprisingly complex and sympathetic."[83] As Goldman-Price concludes, we cannot easily dismiss him.

These sympathetic qualities can be seen in the next two encounters between Rosedale and Lily, encounters in which a new complexity emerges in his re-sponses to her. The first comes at a time when Lily has reached a new low in her fortunes. She has taken a position as social secretary to Norma Hatch, a Western divorcée eager to make her way into the New York elite. Lulled into complacency by the luxury of Mrs. Hatch's gaudy but expensive hotel suite, Lily manages to overlook the dubious maneuvers of Mrs. Hatch's new friends, maneuvers that include using Lily as a front to cover up their effort to marry Mrs. Hatch off to young Freddy Van Osburgh, heir to the Van Osburgh for-tunes. Alarmed at Lily's situation, Gerty urges Selden to warn Lily away, but

Lily, in her pride, refuses to listen. Only at the last minute, disgusted by one of the conspirators promise of future financial benefit if she "sees them through," does Lily quit her position, just in time to avoid actual complicity, but too late, as usual, to protect her reputation, which suffers fresh damage.

Still waiting for her aunt's legacy, her funds and resources nearly exhausted, Lily next takes a job as a worker in a millinery shop. Refusing to display herself as a model in the showroom, she accepts a place at the worktable where she initially expects to rise rapidly through the ranks due to her superior taste. However, she soon learns that the actual skills of construction are hard-learned and that she comes to them too late. Untrained, weak, she cannot compete and is soon let go. Reduced to living in a boarding house defined by the dinginess she has always abhorred, Lily can longer find solace in the material comfort and luxury now denied to her. Instead, she attempts to revitalize herself during the days with ever more cups of strong tea, lulling herself to sleep at night with chloral acquired through a prescription made out to her former employer, Mrs. Hatch. In this state, so weak she is about to faint, she encounters Rosedale on the street and actually asks him to stay with her for a moment. He takes her promptly to a shop for a cup of tea, which he encourages her to take strong. Temporarily fortified, she answers his inquiries about her situation and explains that she left Mrs. Hatch's, "lest people say I was helping Mrs. Hatch to marry Freddy Van Osburgh—who is not in the least too good for her—and as they still continue to say it, I see that I might as well have stayed where I was." At this, Rosedale shows his appreciation of her innocence, despite the nasty gossip that circulates about her: " 'Oh, Freddy—' Rosedale brushed aside the topic with an air of its unimportance which gave a sense of the immense perspective he had acquired. 'Freddy don't count—but I knew *you* weren't missed up in that. It ain't your style'" (227). Rosedale's faith in Lily and appreciation of her "style" signal his awareness of those ethical scruples he earlier recognized in his admission that he knew the stories Bertha Dorset spread about her were not true. The idea of this being a style is also significant, since it connects her moral sensibility to her aesthetic taste. And yet it is this very taste for morality that allowed Lily to resist Rosedale's earlier proposed blackmail.

Now, however, in response to this comment, "Lily coloured slightly: she could not conceal from herself that the words gave her pleasure" (227). When Rosedale continues to probe, asking her why she felt the need to work in a millinery shop when she was expecting a legacy, Lily is anxious to explain that she owes nearly every penny of that legacy. Her eyes on Rosedale's face, Lily puts her case to him: "I think Gus Trenor spoke to you once about having made some money for me in stocks." This time she is the one speaking plainly and it is

Rosedale who, "congested with embarrassment, muttered that he remembered something of that kind." In fact, he had used this insider information as a means to pressure her into marriage, as an example of the "bothers," of which he would relieve her once she met his conditions. Now Lily has the opportunity to present her own version of the story:

> "He made about nine thousand dollars," Lily pursued, in the same tone of eager communicativeness. "At the time, I understood that he was spec-ulating with my own money: it was incredibly stupid of me, but I knew nothing of business. Afterward I found out that he had *not* used my money — that what he said he made for me he had really given me. It was meant in kindness, of course; but it was not the sort of obligation one could remain under. Unfortunately I had spent the money before I discov-ered my mistake; and so my legacy will have to go to pay it back. That is the reason why I am trying to learn a trade." (228)

Given Rosedale's earlier honesty with her, along with his sympathy and re-spect, Lily suddenly finds herself willing to speak: "She made the statement clearly and deliberately, with pauses between the sentences, so that each should have time to sink deeply into her hearer's mind. She had a passionate desire that some one should know the truth about this transaction, and also that the rumour of her intention to repay the money should reach Judy Trenor's ears." Perhaps Rosedale, who has Trenor's confidence, would be the right person to tell her side of the story: "She even felt a momentary exhilaration at thus re-lieving herself of her detested secret; but the sensation gradually faded in the telling, and as she ended her pallour was suffused with a deep blush of misery" (228). Ironically, it is Rosedale with whom Lily is able to be most sincere at this point. Sharing in the same representational economy — the materialistic values of New York's vanity fair — she and Rosedale can interpret its signs together. For once, her self-narration seems clear and unambiguous. That she is drawing on "deep wells of feeling" is indicated by the "deep blush of misery" that suddenly animates her face.

Rosedale then asks if repaying Trenor "cleans you out altogether" and when Lily "calmly" says it does, he exclaims abruptly, "See here — that's fine." But now Lily retreats from his praise and rises from her seat "with a deprecating laugh. 'Oh, no — it's merely a bore'" (228). When Rosedale offers to help with "backing," she refuses, thanking him instead for the cup of tea, which has "given me tremendous backing. I feel equal to anything now" (229). Nevertheless, he is not dismissed, but walks her back through garbage-strewn streets to her bleak boarding house. He "scans" its "blistered brown stone front, the windows draped with discoloured lace, and the Pompeian decoration of the muddy vestibule; then he looked back at her face and said with a visible effort: 'You'll let me come and see you some day?'" At this Lily, sharing his aesthetic distaste, "smiled, recognizing the heroism of the offer to the point of being frankly touched by it. 'Thank you—I shall be very glad,' she made answer, in the first sincere words she had ever spoken to him" (229). This new sincerity in her response to Rosedale arises from his own sincerity in appreciating her ethical struggle and its heroism: "See here—that's fine." More than Selden, more than Gerty, Rosedale knows what that heroism costs her and believes in its reality. Unlike them he does not look for an idealized version of the "real" Lily; he knows her "secret craving" and what it has cost her to resist it. He knows how painful that ugly boarding house would be to someone whose aesthetic sensibilities are a sensitive as his own.

And he makes good on his offer to visit her at that boarding house, although its shabbiness shocks him into making a new proposal to rescue her: "Look here, Miss Lily, I'm going to Europe next week; going over to Paris and London for a couple of months—and I can't leave you like this. I can't do it. I know it's none of my business—you've let me understand that often enough; but things are worse with you now than they have been before, and you must see that you've got to accept help from somebody." He then brings up her debt: "You spoke to me the other day about some debt to Trenor. I know what you mean—and I respect you for feeling as you do about it." Lily blushes with surprise as he rushes on, "Well, I'll lend you the money to pay Trenor; and I won't—I—see here, don't take me up till I've finished. What I mean is, it'll be a plain business arrangement, such as one man would make with another. Now, what have you got to say against that?" (233). Without openly referring to his earlier proposal, in which marriage and sexual exchange were part of the deal, Rosedale makes it clear that he respects Lily's unwillingness to sell her own body as a commodity. It would be a deal "as one man would make with another." At this "Lily's blush deepened to a glow in which humiliation and gratitude were mingled; and both sentiments revealed themselves in the unexpected gentleness of her reply." That reply indicates how much she has learned on her tortuous journey downward: "'That . . . is exactly what Gus Trenor proposed; and . . . I can never again be sure of understanding the plainest business arrangement.' Then, realizing that this answer contained a germ of injustice, she added, even more kindly: 'Not that I don't appreciate your kindness—that I'm not grateful for it. But a business arrangement between us would in any case be impossible, because I shall have no security to give when my debt to Trenor has been paid.'" Business is business, Lily indicates, and should be kept separate from sentiment, because once tangled up together, business will always triumph. And, as she well knows, given her lack of other marketable assets, her body will inevitably again become her only security. She wishes to keep clear of such confusions. "Rosedale received this statement in silence: he seemed to feel the note of finality in her voice, yet to be unable to accept it as closing the question between them" (233).

Rosedale's silence and his wavering resolution signal a change in his attitude. "Lily had a clear perception of what was passing through his mind. Whatever perplexity he felt as to the inexorableness of her course — however little he penetrated its motive — she saw that it unmistakably tended to strengthen her hold over him" (233–34). Just as her dialogue with Selden had awakened new ways of seeing, new kinds of values, so Rosedale's dialogue with her is rousing a new awareness in him: "It was as though the sense in her of unexplained scruples and resistances had the same attraction as the delicacy of feature, the fastidiousness of manner, which gave her an external rarity, an air of being impossible to match. As he advanced in social experience this uniqueness had acquired a greater value for him, as though he were a collector who had learned to distinguish minor differences of design and quality in some long-coveted object" (234). Now he is beginning to see that her air of external rarity may actually be the manifestation of an internal, moral quality that is more rare and unmatched in his social experience than the finest surface polish: "Lily, perceiving all this, understood that he would marry her at once, on the sole condition of a reconciliation with Mrs. Dorset; and the temptation was the less easy to put aside because, little by little, circumstances were breaking down her dislike for Rosedale. The dislike, indeed, still subsisted; but it was penetrated here and there by the perception of mitigating qualities in him: of a certain gross kindliness, a rather helpless fidelity of sentiment, which seemed to be struggling through the hard surface of his material ambitions." While this "helpless fidelity of sentiment" has not yet broken through — Lily senses that the condition of reconciliation with Bertha Dorset still stands — Rosedale is no longer the single-minded figure he first appeared. Sentiment and an appreciation of qualities outside the materialistic realm now compete with his former ambitions: "Reading his dismissal in her eyes, he held out his hand with a gesture which conveyed something of this inarticulate conflict" (234).

Scientific racists like Madison Grant argued not only that racial types were impervious to argument and proof against conversion but that mating between a member of a "higher" type, such as the Nordic, with a "lower" one, such as the Jew or Negro, would inevitably produce offspring of the lower type. Miscegenation always brought the higher species down and never raised the lower one. However, these dialogues between Lily and Rosedale result in a kind of mutual discursive miscegenation. Neither is impervious to argument — far from it. While their conversations pull Lily toward a franker, more unapologetic materialism, this influence works both ways. Lily is also drawing Rosedale toward the representational economy of Protestantism, with its respect for mysterious interior scruples and its rejection of material appearances. Moreover, Rosedale's values are not, I would argue, totally rejected, but rather subtly worked into the final pattern Wharton weaves of these competing discourses. Rosedale is the one who fully acknowledges the ultimate materiality of Lily's existence: the reality of the financial pressures that hound her daytime struggles like the furies who haunt her dreams. For Rosedale, as for Wharton, death is not some peaceful transition to an afterlife where one is now alive and well once more, but a true ending, just as poverty is not a genteel opportunity for the exercise of transcendental imagination, but a very real constraint on the possibilities of life. And while Wharton might not approve of Rosedale's failure to live by values other than those of the society he strives to impress, her novel does acknowledge the honesty and tough-mindedness of his assessment of that society and its power. Rosedale may be a materialist, but he is not hypocrite. And yet, as seen in these final scenes, he also is incomplete. Pursuing happiness through materialistic means leaves him wealthy but still striving, insatiable, much like Carrie in Dreiser's *Sister Carrie* or Undine in *The Custom of the Country*. Although Bunyan represents the Jew as a type of Satanic figure, a tempter directing Christian to the wrong path, Wharton represents Rosedale as another confused pilgrim. Far from being "fixed," Rosedale, like Lily, has become conflicted, fragmented. He may begin the novel as a Jewish stereotype, a single-minded *Homo economicus*, but he ends it as a quintessential modern American, yet another case of *Schizophrenia Americana*.

CHAPTER 5

Lily in the Valley of the Shadow

This chapter turns to an analysis of the final scenes of *The House of Mirth* where we see a growing self-awareness and interiority in Lily — an awareness of her weaknesses as well as her failed aspirations. However, the novel also unsparingly portrays Lily's continuing inability to "live with her thoughts." As a result of this inability, her self-awareness, rather than prompting a clearer sense of moral direction, actually increases her anxiety, making the temptation to escape her worries more insistent. In a typical sentimental or orthodox Protestant narrative of development, awakened moral vision would recenter a character, either through revised affiliations leading to a transformed sense of self, as in Christian nurture, or through crisis conversion, leading to a spiritual rebirth and moral renewal. However, Lily is incapable, as even the affectionate Gerty Farish reluctantly admits, of such a complete re-centering, at least not without help, which she does not receive (in the case of Selden) or which she cannot accept (in the case of Gerty). Rather, she is split and torn apart by opposing forces: financial needs and moral judgments, materialistic logic and spiritual requirements, the competing visions of different representational economies. Growing in self-awareness and yet struggling to escape the painful emotions provoked by that awareness, Lily repeatedly chooses the wrong road. Tempted by seductive offers to remove the burden of her anxiety, she habitually turns to temporary and superficial sources of renewal, sources that inevitably fail. The addictive nature of these escapes into the "house of mirth" becomes increasingly obvious, and dangerous, as Lily's economic security diminishes and her psychological distress increases.

And then there is another factor: Lily's pride. As these tensions build in book 2, the narrator refers more and more to Lily's pride as a motivation. In fact, her felt need to repay Gus Trenor, the need that drives the novel's plot, is attributed to her pride. However, given that pride is hardly a virtue in traditional Christian theology, the narrator's attention to it raises questions about the moral status of this motive. While readers may see Lily's final decision to sacrifice her legacy to the repayment of her debt as a kind of moral vindication that ushers her into an enduring republic of the spirit, the narrator suggests that this sacrifice may be enough to save her pride, but not Lily herself. Finally, I would argue that Wharton's novel depicts not a conflict between realism and sentimentalism, nor a rejection of one and descent into the other, but an attempt to forge a realism that incorporates the insights of sentimentalism into a painstaking depiction of a failed or conflicted attempt at the formation of identity and moral awareness.[1] What happens to those who lack the secure foundation required for a moral life? To those who were never taught how to "read the signs"? Wharton's answer is not a hopeful one.

To begin with the question of Lily's attempts to escape anxiety. Lily already displays this pattern as the novel opens. Her response to the studied luxury of her Bellomont bedroom is a "dilation" of her whole being, a dilation that enables her to forget her minimal funds long enough to gamble most of them away. Later, when Trenor says he has his first check in his pocket for her, "The news filled her with the glow produced by a sudden cessation of physical pain" (73). Along with the pressure to escape it, her anxiety is immeasurably heightened in the climatic scenes of book 1 with the trauma of Gus Trenor's accusations and near-rape. The resultant shock of self-recognition and accusation begins the cycle that shapes rest of the novel, one in which shame and "hurt pride" alternate with further attempts at denial and escape. Significantly, these escapes do temporarily block the distress caused by her debt and the behavior that led to it. As the narrator points out, "Moral complications existed for her only in the environment that had produced them; she did not mean to slight or ignore them, but they lost their reality when they changed their background" (153). Lily's "faculty for renewing herself in new scenes, and casting off problems of conduct as easily as the surroundings in which they had arisen, made the mere change from one place to another seem not only a postponement but a solution of her troubles" (153). And yet the cost of this renewal — whether her Mediterranean cruise on the Dorsets' yacht, her socializing with the Gormers' riotous friends, or her morally ambiguous tenure as social secretary to the social-climbing Mrs. Hatch — is in every case another eventual blow to her pride, which has been temporarily sacrificed for a respite from the furies of conscience and the fear of poverty. In this sense, Lily's escapist behavior becomes increasingly addictive, a quality the narrator at first subtly and then not-so subtly underscores.

Lily's cravings for luxury and comfort, for example, become increasingly insistent as her troubles grow. In the passage quoted above, the narrator describes how Lily is able to forget her debt to Trenor while on the Dorsets' yacht. However, her denial also extends to the role she must play in return for this luxurious respite, a price she is ultimately forced to pay in a scene of public humiliation. Upon her return to America, having lost her expected fortune from Mrs. Peniston, Lily accepts responsibility, in the conversation with Gerty Farish discussed earlier, for damaging her reputation and losing her legacy; however, when she is offered a chance to spend the summer with the Gormers, a couple whose behavior she disparages, she cannot resist: "To be taken in on such terms — and into such a world! — was hard enough to the lingering pride in her; but she realized, with a pang of self-contempt, that to be excluded from it would, after all, be harder still. For, almost at once, she had felt the insidious charm of slipping back into a life where every material difficulty was smoothed away" (184). This "insidious charm" produces "a state of moral lassitude agreeable enough after the nervous tension and physical discomfort of the past weeks." Lily feels she "must yield to the refreshment her senses craved — after that she would reconsider her situation, and take counsel with her dignity" (184). Later, after a similar negotiation with her bruised pride and dignity, Lily takes the position with Mrs. Hatch: "When Lily woke on the morning after her translation to the Emporium Hotel, her first feeling was one of purely physical satisfaction. . . . Analysis and introspection might come later; but for the moment she was not even troubled by the excesses of the upholstery or the restless convolutions of the furniture. The sense of being once more lapped and folded in ease, as in some dense mild medium impenetrable to discomfort, effectually stilled the faintest note of criticism" (212). Unfortunately, analysis and introspection again arrive too late to save Lily's reputation.

Wharton's description of "the insidious charm" that Lily finds in the Emporium Hotel's "dense mild medium," echoes a description found in Theodore Dreiser's 1900 novel *Sister Carrie*, which Wharton admired.[2] In a scene that comes late in the novel, George Hurstwood has fallen far below his initial, secure place in Chicago's upper-middle-class society. Now living in New York, he has lost his social reputation (by attempting to steal his former employer's money in a moment of weakness), and he is unemployed and out of funds. Depressed, unable to find work, and too discouraged to look any further, Hurstwood begins to spend his days in hotel lobbies: "Accordingly he ascended into the fine parlor of the Morton House, then one of the best New York hotels, and finding a cushioned seat, began to read. It did not trouble him much that his decreasing sum of money did not allow of such extravagance. Like the morphine fiend, he was becoming addicted to his ease."[3] Dreiser's connection between morphine addiction and Hurstwood's retreat to the hotel's cushioned chairs is telling, as is the parallel with Lily. As Dreiser explains, Hurstwood's need for escape is so intense that he would try "anything to relieve his mental distress, to satisfy his craving for comfort. He must do it. No thoughts for the morrow — he could not stand to think of it, any more than he could of any other calamity. Like the certainty of death, he tried to shut the certainty of soon being without a dollar completely out of his mind, and he came very near doing it."[4]

Lily's stay at the Emporium Hotel, like Hurstwood's time at the Morton House, is her last experience of being "lapped and folded in ease." The next station on her path is a job as a millinery worker, and her home surroundings are now those of a boarding house, representing the poverty and dinginess she has fought so hard to escape. With the narcotic effects of luxury no longer available to her, Lily cannot so easily evade the humiliating awareness that haunts her. Tormented by that hurt pride, she turns to two other sources of false renewal: tea and chloral. With her usual paths of escape blocked and her resources, economic and social, rapidly dwindling, Lily's understanding of her own complicity in her situation deepens. However, that deepening awareness only heightens her distress and craving for relief.

We can see this awareness clearly in the crucial moments when Lily does manage to resist the temptations that face her. Approached by George Dorset, Lily, despite the recent loss of her legacy and social standing, rejects his plea for help in establishing his wife's adultery and obtaining a divorce. Drawing once more on the imagery of *Pilgrim's Progress*, the narrator describes Lily at a moral crossroads, "She stood silent, gazing away from him down the autumnal stretch of the deserted lane. And suddenly fear possessed her — fear of herself, and the terrible force of the temptation. All her past weaknesses were like so many eager accomplices drawing her toward the path their feet had already smoothed"(191). Lily has a similar moment of near-seduction when Rosedale proposes that she blackmail Bertha Dorset, a proposal that speaks to an "inmost craving" in her, but which she is able to reject out of hand, once she is able to recall the moral direction provided by her dialogue with Selden. By the novel's final scenes, Lily has come to a clear-eyed, if intermittent, understanding of her own weakness, her own susceptibility to temptation. As she considers her future receipt of the $10,000 legacy from her aunt, she weighs the option of not repaying the $9,000 debt to Trenor immediately, but rather using the full amount to set herself up in the millinery business, thereby slowly accumulating a large clientele and enough savings to clear her debt and restore her now blighted self-esteem. However, while assessing the years of discipline and even privation it will require, she sees that these considerations are only "superficial," for "under them lurked the secret dream that the obligation might not always remain intolerable." Significantly, Lily is now able to recognize her inner conflicts: "She knew she could not count on her continuity of purpose, and what really frightened her was the thought that she might gradually accommodate herself to remaining indefinitely in Trenor's debt, as she had accommodated herself to the part allotted her on the *Sabrina*, and as she had so nearly drifted into acquiescing with Stancy's scheme for the advancement of Mrs. Hatch" (230–31). Not only is Lily now able to name her weakness and its past consequences, but she knows its source: "Her danger lay, as she knew, in her old incurable dream of discomfort and poverty; in the fear of that mounting tide of dinginess against which her mother had so passionately warned her" (231). And what is most disturbing, Lily also knows how little strength she has left to control her weakness or the fears that drive it.

These dynamics are revealed in a key scene between Lily and Gerty just before Lily decides to join Mrs. Hatch at the Emporium Hotel. The conversation begins with Lily expressing her fears that her worries are beginning to mark her face, leaving it pale and lined. She complains of her sleepless nights, each one leaving a new line, yet laments that with "such dreadful things to think about," she simply cannot sleep. When Gerty ask what things she means, Lily first replies simply, "Well, poverty, for one — and I don't know anything that's more dreadful" (208). But then she turns suddenly to the cost she must pay for the privilege of living with the rich. Referring to Ned Silverton, who has dissipated the savings of his sisters, she exclaims:

> You think we live *on* the rich, rather than with them: and so we do, in a sense — but it's a privilege we have to pay for! We eat their dinners, and drink their wine, and smoke their cigarettes, and use their carriages and their opera-boxes and their private cars — yet, there's a tax to pay on every one of those luxuries. The man pays it by big tips to the servants, by playing cards beyond his means, by flowers and presents — and — and — lots of other things than that; the girl pays it by tips and cards too — oh, yes, I've had to take up bridge again — and by going to the best dress-makers, and having just the right dress for every occasion, and always keeping herself fresh and exquisite and amusing! (207–8)

Listening to Lily, Gerty has "a startled perception of the change in her face — of the way in which an ashen daylight seemed suddenly to extinguish its artificial brightness. She looked up, and the vision vanished." Lily's sincerity has briefly eclipsed the artificiality of her normal manner, but although this sincerity is natural as daylight, it is also ashen, drained of vitality. And so Lily continues: "It doesn't sound very amusing, does it? And it isn't — I'm sick to death of it! And yet the thought of giving it up nearly kills me — it's what keeps me awake at night, and makes me so crazy for your strong tea. For I can't go on this way much longer, you know — I'm nearly at the end of my tether." And then she turns to the crux of the matter: her inability to forge, or imagine, another way of life: "And then what can I do — how on earth can I keep myself alive. I see myself reduced to the fate of that poor Silverton woman — slinking about to employment agencies, and trying to sell painted blotting-pads to Women's Exchanges! And there are thousands and thousands of women trying to do the same thing already, and not one of the number has less idea how to earn a dollar than I have!" (208).

Lily's description of her desperate need to maintain her social position and access to luxury is surprisingly perceptive, as is her admission that the financial and psychological cost to her well-being is greater than any benefit she receives. It is the fantasized promise of happiness, not the reality, which draws her. Life with the rich provides only a temporary respite from the fear of poverty that threatens to engulf her. However, the price of this respite is Lily's purchase of expensive goods signifying her membership in this privileged group, a display that ironically eats away at her chances for real economic security. The poignancy of her comment lies in her admission that she is unable to resolve this conflict, unable to control or perhaps even fully understand the needs that are destroying her. Later Gerty reflects on Lily's confession and its implication of addiction: she "could see no hope for her friend but in a life completely re-organized and detached from its old associations: whereas all Lily's energies were centred in the determined effort to hold fast to those associations, to keep herself visibly identified with them, as long as the illusion could be maintained. Pitiable as such an attitude seemed to Gerty, she could not judge it as harshly as Selden, for instance, might have done" (209). Whereas once, along with Selden, she had believed that the vision of the *tableau vivant*, an idealized beauty soaring free from all material accidents, was the real Lily, "Gerty could smile now at her own early dream of her friend's renovation through adversity: she understood clearly enough that Lily was not one of those to whom privation teaches the unimportance of what they have lost. But this very fact, to Gerty, made her friend the more piteously in want of aid, the more exposed to the claims of a tenderness she was so little conscious of needing" (205).

It is this last insight that is the most telling: Gerty's recognition that Lily is deeply in need of compassion and tenderness, but also unable to accept it. Lily does not wish from Gerty "the kind of help she could give" (209). Only once, out of real anguish, did Lily accept that help. The night of the near rape by

Gus Trenor, Lily had begged, "Hold me, Gerty, hold me, or I shall think of things" (133). Even then, however, Gerty was well aware that "Lily disliked to be caressed"; she had therefore "long ago learned to check her demonstrative impulses toward her friend" (133). When Gerty now turns to Selden to beg him to help Lily, she admits, "I don't like to go to her, because I am afraid of forcing myself on her when I'm not wanted." However, she asks Selden to go "because she once told me that you had been a help to her, and because she needs help now as she has never needed it before. You know how dependent she has always been on ease and luxury—how she has hated what was shabby and ugly and uncomfortable. She can't help it—she was brought up on those ideas, and has never been able to find her way out of them." Gerty's insights are, again, both astute and compassionate, as is her assessment of Lily's desperate state: "But now all the things she cared for have been taken from her, and the people who taught her to care for them have abandoned her too; and it seems to me if some one could reach out a hand and show her the other side—show her how much is left in life and in herself" (211–12).

In Gerty, we see a descendant of Alcott's Marmee. Marmee herself is portrayed as a social worker whose childrearing strategies have a quasi-professional ring to them, a sense of theoretical underpinnings well-suited to a character created by Bronson Alcott's daughter. In Gerty Farish, these skills, while not yet those of the modern, certified family therapist or social worker, continue to extend the insights of Christian nurture to the healing of damaged souls beyond the middle-class family circle. And yet Wharton's depiction of Gerty's social gospel service and therapeutic practice reveals their limitations. Despite her empathy, insight and care; despite having even, in one powerful image, "seemed to feel her very heart's blood passing into her friend" during the night she held Lily in her distress, Gerty finally cannot reach her friend (209). Some damage cannot be healed, even by the most skilled and well-intentioned members of the helping profession. Gerty's admission of failure is coupled with another key insight into Lily's character, "'I can't help her myself: she's passed out of my reach . . . I think she's afraid of being a burden to me" (211–12). Although Gerty initially feels unable to speak of Lily to Selden because of her own loss and disappointment, her concern for Lily now "breaks the bounds of self" and turns her "wasted personal emotion into the general current of human understanding" (209). However, Gerty's ability to transcend personal boundaries is not shared by her friend. While Lily's reserve may be founded most obviously on a fear of both intimacy and loss of emotional control, it is also premised on a stubborn pride, an unwillingness to admit her need or weakness and an inability to accept the human vulnerability that any admission of dependency would bring.

This pride is most often associated in the novel with the image of Lily's "surface." As Selden first trains his gaze on Lily in the opening scene, he wonders if her polished and exquisite surface is one with the substance that lies beneath it. Later, in their dialogue at Bellomont, he senses a new and different Lily whose spontaneity temporarily disrupts her carefully controlled performance. And later, after he has attempted to disengage his feelings from her, he aims his gaze on Lily once more at Nice: "A subtle change had passed over the quality of her beauty. Then it had a transparency through which the fluctuations of her the spirit were sometimes tragically visible; now its impenetrable surface suggested a process of crystallization which had fused her whole being into one hard brilliant substance" (149). Although to Carry Fisher this hard brilliancy, fostered by Lily's access to the Dorsets' luxury, seems "a rejuvenation," to Selden it seems the result of a chilling repression: "He felt she had at last arrived at an understanding with herself: had made a pact with her rebellious impulses, and achieved a uniform system of self-government, under which vagrant tendencies were either held captive or forced into the service of the state" (150). Now, after his conversation with Gerty, Selden reflects that "every step she took seemed in fact to carry her farther from the region where, once or twice, he and she had met for an illumined moment; and the recognition of this fact, when its first pang had been surmounted, produced in him a sense of negative relief" (212). It is easier for Selden simply to accept Lily Bart according to the "conventional view of her," according to the surface she presents to the elite society whose approval she covets. In this, his judgment of her is indeed less compassionate than Gerty's. Nevertheless, in response to Gerty's appeal, he does approach Lily once she is ensconced at the Hotel Emporium and in danger of being compromised by her apparent complicity with the conspiracy to marry off Mrs. Hatch. He warns her of the danger to her reputation and he urges her to leave in language that is direct and even harsh. The result is the opposite of Gerty's hopes.

First, Lily in her despair had "in truth felt his long absence as one of the chief bitternesses of the last months: his desertion had hurt sensibilities far below the surface of her pride." Yet these hurt sensibilities cannot breach that surface so easily. Lily's dependence on Selden now appears more a threat rather than a reassurance: "In his presence a sudden stillness came upon her, and the turmoil of her spirit ceased; but an impulse of resistance to this stealing influence now prompted her" (216). As the narrator explains, "The situation between them was one which could have been cleared only by a sudden explosion of feeling; and their whole training and habit of mind were against the chances of such an explosion. Selden's calmness seemed rather to harden into resistance, and Miss Bart's into a surface of glittering irony" (216). As Selden tells Lily abruptly that she should leave her present situation immediately, she asks him equally abruptly where he thinks she could find shelter. And when he replies that she could find it with Gerty, her feelings are "in a flame of revolt": "To neglect her, perhaps even to avoid her, at a time when she had most need of her friends, and then suddenly and unwarrantably to break into her life with this strange assumption of authority, was to rouse in her every instinct of pride and self-defense" (217). So resistant is she that "however doubtful she might feel her situation to be, she would rather persist in darkness than owe her enlightenment to Selden" (219).

Rather than opening themselves to the vulnerability and risks of sincerity, their dialogue soon leads them into sharp, ironic blows: "I don't know . . . why you imagine me situated as you describe; but as you have always told me that the sole object of a bringing-up like mine was to teach a girl to get what she wants, why not assume that that is precisely what I am doing?" The imagery here is not one of depths and underlying wells of feeling, but of surfaces turned into defenses: "The smile with which she summed up her case was like a clear barrier raised against further consequences: its brightness held him at such a distance that he had a sense of being almost out of hearing as he rejoined: 'I'm not sure that I have ever called you a successful example of that kind of bringing-up.'" Selden's ironic reply might actually be read as a recognition that her failure at gold-digging is to her credit. However, Lily, steeling herself "with a light laugh," sharply refuses the implication, "'Ah, wait a little longer — give me a little more time before you decide!' And as he wavered before her, still watching for a break in the impenetrable front she presented: 'Don't give me up; I may still do credit to my training!' she affirmed" (219). The irony here is even more pointed. Virtually parodying his earlier risk in trusting her, she now challenges him to watch her realize the materialistic ambitions he once criticized and she briefly attempted to escape. It is a magnificent show of bravado, but also a deep denial of her innermost feelings.

Shortly after this scene, as we know, Lily, in one of her spasmodic assertions of moral will, leaves Mrs. Hatch and the comforts of the hotel. However, her social standing is now so damaged that she must turn to the job as a millinery worker to survive. Exhausted by a labor at which she finds herself, to her surprise and despair, only minimally competent, Lily withdraws further into her isolation and pride. Walking back to her bleak boarding after a hard day ending in criticism from her supervisor, Lily rejects the sympathy and friendship of a fellow worker, just as she still resists Gerty's offer of shelter: "Something of her mother's fierce shrinking from observation and sympathy was beginning to develop in her, and the promiscuity of small quarters and close intimacy seemed on the whole, less endurable than the solitude of a hall bedroom in a house where she could come and go unremarked among the other workers" (225). And yet the hall bedroom's privacy can no longer compensate for the ugliness and discomfort of the boarding house. She can only return to her room with dread. It is now, having rejected human sources of solace and deprived of material ones, that Lily turns to more overtly addictive means of renewal.

Lily's tendency toward addiction is suggested right from the opening of the novel, when she begs Selden for some tea and then a cigarette (taking a few extra and pocketing them for later). Tea drinking becomes a motif throughout the pages that follow. There is her preparation of tea on the train to Bellomont, a performance designed to impress Percy Gryce with her womanly skills. There is Simon Rosedale's assertion of his improved taste when he assures her, after sipping tea at Mrs. Peniston's at the end of book 1, that he will ask his "man" to send her something really worth drinking. By the time Lily confesses her despair to Gerty in book 2, her need for the stimulant has gone beyond social performance. Finishing off her first cup, she says, "Another, and stronger, please; if I don't keep awake now I shall see horrors tonight—perfect horrors!" When Gerty protests, "But they'll be worse if you drink too much tea," Lily replies "imperiously": " 'No, no—give it to me; and don't preach, please.' Her voice had a dangerous edge, and Gerty noticed that her hand shook as she held it out to receive the second cup" (206-7).[5]

With Lily's descent into the lonely boarding house, her need grows even sharper and she turns to chloral, using a prescription she had once filled for Mrs. Hatch. Now Lily fluctuates daily between the stimulant and the opiate: the tea to keep her awake during the day, the choral to send her into a sleep deep enough to escape the furies, "perfect horrors," that pursue her even into her dreams. When Rosedale takes her to a tea shop after meeting her nearly fainting in the street, "Lily smiled faintly at the injunction to take her tea strong. It was the temptation she was always struggling to resist. Her craving for the keen stimulant was forever conflicting with that other craving for sleep—the midnight craving which only the little phial in her hand could still. But today, at any rate, the tea could hardly be too strong; she counted on it to pour warmth and resolution into her empty veins" (226).

As for the chloral, her turn to its power comes not only from her loss of material comforts, but also from the failure of her last meeting with Selden. One of the reasons she avoids Gerty is to avoid Selden: "To meet him now was pure pain. It was pain enough even to think of him, whether she considered him in the distinctness of her waking thoughts, or felt the obsession of his presence through the blur of her tormented nights. That was one of the reasons why she had turned again to Mrs. Hatch's prescription" (230). In Lily's "natural dreams," Selden sometimes appears as he had at Bellomont, "in the old guise of fellowship and tenderness; and she would rise from the sweet delusion mocked and emptied of her courage. But in the sleep which the phial procured she sank far below such half-waking visitations, sank into depths of dreamless annihilation from which she woke each morning with an obliterated past" (230). And yet this obliterated past and the "stress of old thoughts," like the memory of Trenor's debt which she had hoped the Dorsets' yacht would leave behind, "would return; but at least they did not importune her waking hour. The drug gave her a momentary illusion of complete renewal, from which she drew strength to take up her daily work" (230).

The narrator's description of Lily's procuring her last vial of chloral makes obvious her lack of control over her addiction: "But what she dreaded most of all was having to pass the chemist's at the corner of Sixth Avenue. She had meant to take another street: she had usually done so of late. But today her steps were irresistibly drawn toward the flaring plate-glass corner" (225). Inside the shop, "she caught the eye of the clerk who had waited on her before, and slipped the prescription into his hand. There could be no questions about the prescription: it was a copy of one of Mrs. Hatch's, obligingly furnished by that lady's chemist. Lily was confident that the clerk would fill it without hesitation; yet the nervous dream of a refusal, or even of an expression of doubt, communicated itself to her restless hands as she affected to examine the bottles of perfume stacked on the glass case before her" (225). While the clerk quickly fills the prescription, he pauses before handing it over to warn her against increasing the dose: "It's a queer-acting drug. A drop or two more, and off you go — the doctors don't know why." Lily hardly listens; she is so afraid he will withhold the drug that her "heart contracted. What did he mean by looking at her in that way? . . . . The dread lest he should question her, or keep the bottle back choked the murmur of acquiescence in her throat; and when at length she emerged safely from the shop she was almost dizzy with the intensity of her relief" (225). Her response to receiving the choral is strikingly similar to her earlier response to the news of Gus Trenor's check, news that, like a narcotic, "filled her with the glow produced by a sudden cessation of physical pain"(73). Now "the mere touch of the packet thrilled her tired nerves with the delicious promise of a night of sleep, and in the reaction from her momentary fear she felt as if the first fumes of drowsiness were already stealing over her" (225). The link between this kind of comfort and monetary solace is one Lily ironically makes herself. Rising from the tea-table where Rosedale has offered not only his sympathy but also a loan, Lily gently rejects his offer of financial "backing," but then says his tea has "given me tremendous backing. I feel equal to anything now" (229). But, of course, she is not.

That night Lily makes her searching assessment of her ability to resist the temptation to keep the full amount of her legacy. Acknowledging her past lapses and their sources in her fear of discomfort and poverty, she sees "a new vista of peril [open] before her" (231). While she recognizes that she cannot in good conscience accept a loan from Rosedale, the offer "began to haunt her insidiously." Moreover, she feels sure that he will come to see her at her boarding house and that she can then get him to marry her, if she accepts his conditions. "Would she still reject them if they were offered? More and more, with every fresh mischance befalling her, did the pursuing furies seem to take the shape of Bertha Dorset; and close at hand, safely locked among her papers, lay the means of ending their pursuit. The temptation, which her scorn of Rosedale had once enabled her to reject, now insistently returned upon her; and how much strength was left her to oppose it?" (231). Her answer to this question is: very little. Believing that she cannot sustain another night marred by disturbing dreams or by a wakefulness in which "the dark spirit of fatigue and loneliness crouched upon her breast," she sees the chloral as her only alternative to Rosedale's financial support and its conditions: "The only hope of renewal lay in the little bottle at her bed-side; and how much longer that hope would last she dared not conjecture" (231).

When Rosedale does come to see her at the boarding house, although his offer of marriage, with its conditions, is not openly discussed, Lily sees clearly that he would repeat it if she made the slightest sign. And her resistance to him has slowly broken down as she has felt his sympathy for her plight and admired his honesty in explaining his motives. Although gross and unscrupulous, he would also be, as she saw in his interaction with Carry Fisher's daughter, kind. In fact, his sympathy and understanding now stand in marked contrast to Selden's judgmental harshness during their last conversation. Moreover, Lily's strength to resist Rosedale's offer has grown even weaker since her assessment of the options provided by her legacy. Then she might have had a future in the millinery business; by this point, she has lost her position at the shop and even that future has dimmed.

Rosedale leaves with Lily still resisting her temptation to meet his conditions, but that night she does not take her chloral. Foregoing her drugged sleep, she confronts the possibilities before her once more. Now that her situation is even more desperate, the legalistic arguments Rosedale had once presented in favor of his scheme begin to seem more salient. In refusing his terms, "had she not sacrificed to one of those abstract notions of honour that might called the conventionalities of the moral life? What debt did she owe to a social order which had condemned and banished her without trial? She had never been heard in her own defense; she was innocent of the charge on which she had been found guilty; and the irregularity of her conviction might seem to justify the use of methods as irregular in recovering her lost rights" (234). Recalling that Bertha, her nemesis, had lied openly to destroy her reputation, Lily wonders, "Why should she hesitate to make private use of the facts that chance had put in her way? After all, half the opprobrium of such an act lies in the name attached to it. Call it blackmail and it becomes unthinkable; but explain that it injures no one, and that the rights regained by it were unjustly forfeited, and he must be a formalist indeed who can find no pleas in its defence." Lily here draws on the nominalist philosophy that Rosedale represents: the belief that morality is only a social construction after all, and that context trumps any notion of essential right or wrong: "The arguments pleading for it with Lily were the old unanswerable ones of the personal situation: the sense of injury, the sense of failure, the passionate craving for a fair chance against the selfish despotism of society" (234).

Added to these arguments is Lily's recognition of her own weakness, both psychological and economic: "She had learned by experience that she had neither the aptitude nor the moral constancy to remake her life on new lines; to become a worker among workers, and let the world of luxury and pleasure sweep by her unregarded. She could not hold herself much to blame for this ineffectiveness, and she was perhaps less to blame than she believed" (234). Here the narrator steps in to analyze Lily's failure: "Inherited tendencies had combined with early training to make her the highly specialized product she was: an organism as helpless out of its narrow range as the sea-anemone torn from the rock. She had been fashioned to adorn and delight; to what other end does nature round the rose-leaf and paint the humming-bird's breast? And was it her fault that the purely decorative mission is less easily and harmoniously fulfilled among social beings than in the world of nature? That it is apt to be hampered by material necessities or complicated by moral scruples?" (234–35). This, the narrator suggests, is the heart of the matter. Raised to be a beautiful object, a commodity, the purple cloak of an elite patron, Lily cannot fulfill her purely decorative mission without material support, support that comes into direct conflict with moral scruples: "These last were the two antagonistic forces which fought out their battle in her breast during the long watches of the night; and when she rose the next morning she hardly knew where the victory lay" (235).

As Lily enters this day, her last, "she was exhausted by the reaction of a night without sleep, coming after nights of rest artificially obtained; and in the distorting light of fatigue the future stretched out before her grey, interminable and desolate" (235). She is so revolted by the boarding house with its promiscuous smells and sounds that she cannot eat, but wanders out alone to a busy restaurant filled with women all occupied with socializing or preparing their work for the day: "A hum of shrill voices reverberated against the low ceiling, leaving Lily shut out in a little circle of silence. She felt a sudden pang of profound loneliness." Her sense of time has becomes distorted and "it seemed to her as though she had not spoken to anyone for days. Her eyes sought the faces about her, craving a responsive glance, some sign of an intuition of her trouble. But the sallow preoccupied women, with their bags and note-books and rolls of music, were all engrossed in their own affairs." Only Lily, it seems, is isolated in "a great waste of disoccupation." She drinks several cups of tea, which provides its habitual sense of temporary renewal. Once more on the street, with her brain feeling "clearer and livelier," she suddenly realizes that "as she sat in the restaurant, she had unconsciously arrived at a final decision. The discovery gave her an immediate illusion of activity; it was exhilarating to think that she had actually a reason for hurrying home" (235-36). This simple passage conveys the way that Lily's isolation, weaknesses, and dependency finally converge to produce her "unconscious" decision. She has decided to meet Rosedale's conditions, a decision that appears to promise her a "reason for hurrying home," an occupation, a future, even if it is founded on morally ambiguous grounds. In the conflict between material necessities and moral scruples, the material necessities seem to have won. As Lily retrieves the letters from her trunk, "even the contact with the packet did not shake her nerves as she had half-expected it would. She seemed encased in a strong armour of indifference, as though the vigorous exertion of her will had finally benumbed her finer sensibilities" (236).

With her feelings frozen, her proud surface hardened into an "armour of indifference," Lily makes her way uptown to negotiate the terms of her social reinstatement with Bertha Dorset. However, by chance or unconscious direction, she suddenly finds herself on the street near Selden's apartment. The memory of the September day when she entered the Benedick with him returns: "The recollection loosened a throng of benumbed sensations — longings, regrets, imaginings, the throbbing brood of the only spring her heart had ever known." As the armor of her indifference melts and allows repressed emotions to surface, Lily feels it "strange to find herself passing his house on such an errand. She seemed suddenly to see her action as he would see it — and the fact of his own connection with it, the fact that, to attain her end, she must trade on his name, and profit by a secret of his past, chilled her blood with shame" (237). The unconscious decision shaped in the isolation of the restaurant drew on the discourses of materialism, the moral direction provided by Rosedale; now her emotions awaken the memory of values Selden had affirmed. Just as Selden's arrival at Bellomont once transformed her vision of her situation, her memory of him transforms her vision once more, and it becomes clear that Lily has internalized his way of seeing. Selden's gaze has become hers as she scrutinizes her own behavior: "What a long way she had traveled since the day of their first talk together! Even then her feet had been set in the path she was now following — even then she had resisted the hand he had held out" (236). With this recognition of her responsibility for her fate, "All of her resentment of his fancied coldness was swept away in this overwhelming rush of recollection. Twice he had been ready to help her — to help her by loving her, as he had said — and if, the third time, he had seemed to fail her, whom but herself could she accuse?" The measure of her despair can be read in her resigned acceptance of failure: "Well, that part of her life was over; she did not know why her thoughts still clung to it. But the sudden longing to see him remained; it grew to hunger as she paused on the pavement opposite his door. The street was dark and empty, swept by rain. She had a vision of his quiet room, of the bookshelves, and the fire on the hearth. She looked up and saw a light in his window; then she crossed the street and entered the house" (237). Lily has changed her path once more.

Lily's return to Selden's apartment on the last day of her life creates an architectural symmetry with the novel's opening, just as her walk and dialogue with Rosedale in book 2 provided a similar ironic counterpoint to her illuminated moment with Selden at Bellomont in book 1. She has reentered the apartment where she first began to come to self-awareness. Although she was then at the top of her game, now she is exhausted and defeated. Yet her self-awareness is deep and penetrating. She understands what this setting means to her and the significance of the dialogue that began here. The strange lucidity and heightened sensitivity caused in part by her sleepless night, and perhaps from the withdrawal of the chloral, continue. In the restaurant earlier, she had felt bounded in a kind of personal isolation, alienated from the busy working women around her. The setting of Selden's apartment presents a strong contrast to that reverberating hollow space, where she sat in her "waste of disoccupation": "The library looked as she had pictured it. The green-shaded lamps made tranquil circles of light in the gathering dusk, a little fire flickered on the hearth, and Selden's easy-chair, which stood near it, had been pushed aside when he rose to admit her." The familiarity of the setting only heightens the memory of their earlier meetings: "The scene was unchanged. She recognized the row of shelves from which he had taken down his La Bruyère, and the worn arm of the chair he had leaned against while she had examined the precious volume. But then the wide September light had filled the room, making it seem a part of the outer world: now the shaded lamps and the warm hearth, detaching it from the gathering darkness of the street, gave it a sweeter touch of intimacy" (237).

This sharp contrast between the isolation in which she reached her decision to meet Rosedale's conditions and the intimacy of Selden's library brings to a head the full consciousness of her state and the consequences of her choices. Overwhelmed by this rush of feeling and memory, she hesitates on the threshold, while Selden, surprised by her appearance, stands silent, waiting for a sign from her. As his silence continues, Lily realizes the motivation of her visit: "Even on the way up the stairs, she had not thought of preparing a pretext for her visit, but now she felt an intense longing to dispel the cloud of misunderstanding that hung between them" (237). The words that rise to the surface come "spontaneously": "I came to tell you that I was sorry for the way we parted — for what I said to you that day at Mrs. Hatch's." Selden's reply is polite and measured: "I was sorry too that we should have parted in that way; but I am not sure that I did n't bring it on myself. Luckily I had foreseen the risk I was taking — ." Lily cannot help probing for a show of real feeling, "So that you really did n't care — ?" Selden, however, keeps his surface unruffled, "'So that I was prepared for the consequences,' he corrected good-humouredly." Through all this Lily is still standing at the threshold and, as the lamplight strikes her face, Selden sees how tired she looks, along with the "the pallour of her delicately-hollowed face." He invites her in and offers a seat and a comfortable cushion in the armchair by the fire. However, Lily ignores these conventional offers of hospitality; she is driven by a deeper need than physical comfort. Still standing, she struggles to make herself clear to him: "'I wanted you to know that I left Mrs. Hatch immediately after I saw you,' she said, as though continuing her confession." The narrator's use of the term "confession" is crucial here: Lily is no longer protecting her pride; her controlled surface is no longer intact.

Selden's initial response to this emotional exposure is telling, "'Yes — yes, I know,' he assented, with a rising tinge of embarrassment." He is discomfited by Lily's unaccustomed self-revelation, which continues, despite his lack of an equally emotional response, "And that I did so because you told me to. Before you came I had already begun to see that it would be impossible to remain with her — for the reasons you gave me; but I wouldn't admit it — I would n't let you see that I understood what you meant." Selden's response to Lily's confession is a polite rejection of her appeal for understanding and forgiveness: "Ah, I might have trusted you to find your own way out — don't overwhelm me with the sense of my officiousness!" As always, Selden refuses responsibility for guiding Lily, whether or not that guidance is heeded. He demands that she sees herself as standing alone, that she "find her own way out." As for Lily, literally still standing alone on his threshold, his "light tone," which "had her nerves been steadier, she would have recognized as the mere effort to bridge over an awkward moment, jarred on her passionate desire to be understood." This description again highlights Lily's peculiar state of mind, a "strange state of extra-lucidity, which gave her the sense of being already at the heart of the situation." In this state, "it seemed incredible that any one should think it necessary to linger in the conventional outskirts of word-play and evasion." I would argue that Lily's psychic state is in fact a kind of death-bed awareness prompted by the quasi-suicidal situation in which she finds herself. Feeling that the aspirational "real self" Selden glimpsed at Bellomont and to which she had given material form in her *tableau vivant* must be sacrificed, believing that that part of her life is now over, she enters Selden's rooms with a split persona, in the throes of saying goodbye to the idealized self-image she has decided to sacrifice. As I shall explore below, Wharton's depiction of this psychic state and Lily's consequent behavior draws deeply on sentimental depictions of deathbed scenes and their effects, both on the dying and those whose mourn them. But first, it is important to attend to the remaining details of this particular scene.

Lily is still standing, trying to make herself clear to him: " 'It was not that — I was not ungrateful,' she insisted. But the power of expression failed her suddenly; she felt a tremor in her throat, and two tears gathered and fell slowly from her eyes." Selden, taking her hand, again offers to seat her and make her comfortable, but she again refuses: "She shook her head and two more tears ran over. But she did not weep easily, and the long habit of self-control reasserted itself, though she was still too tremulous to speak." Selden now guides her to the armchair and puts a cushion behind her head. "Speaking as though to a troubled child," he offers to boil the water for tea, an offer that recalls even more strongly "the vision of that other afternoon when they had sat together over his tea-table and talked jestingly of her future. There were moments when that day seemed more remote than any other event in her life; and yet she could relive it in its minutest detail"(239).

But even this offer Lily refuses, " 'No: I drink too much tea. I would rather sit quiet — I must go in a moment,' she added confusedly" (239). While the tea in the restaurant had provided a temporary sense of renewal, in this psychologically charged moment Lily prefers her perceptions unadulterated. And those perceptions now sense the detachment beneath Selden's polite manner: "Her self-absorption had not allowed her to perceive it at first; but now that her consciousness was once more putting forth its eager feelers, she saw her presence was becoming an embarrassment to him. Such a situation could only be saved by an immediate outrush of feeling; and on Selden's side the determining impulse was still lacking." If Lily, caught up in her personal crisis, has dropped her mask of self-control and self-sufficiency, Selden has not. However, "the discovery did not disturb Lily as it might have once have done. She had passed beyond the phase of well-bred reciprocity, in which every demonstration must be scrupulously proportioned to the emotion it elicits, and generosity of feeling is the only ostentation condemned." And yet his reserve, which so belies the promise of intimacy held out by the setting and its memories, revives the terrible isolation she had felt earlier in the restaurant: "The sense of loneliness returned with redoubled force as she saw herself forever shut out from Selden's inmost self. She had come to him with no definite purpose; the mere longing to see him had directed her; but the secret hope she had carried with her suddenly revealed itself in its death-pang" (239).

This death-pang leads her to struggle with a final confession, a final exposure of her inner life: "'I must go,' she repeated, making a motion to rise from her chair. 'But I may not see you again for a long time, and I wanted to tell you that I have never forgotten the things you said to me at Bellomont, and that sometimes — sometimes when I seemed farthest from remembering them — they have helped me, and kept me from mistakes; kept me from really becoming what many people have thought me.'" For Lily this confession, halting as it is, is a personal triumph, the fruit of her struggle to learn how to read the signs of her own life: "Strive as she would to put some order in her thoughts, the words would not come more clearly; yet she felt that could not leave him without trying to make him understand that she had saved herself whole from the seeming ruin of her life."

As he listens, Selden starts to glimpse the intensity of her effort and its meaning: "A change had come over Selden's face as she spoke. Its guarded look had yielded to an expression still untinged by personal emotion, but full of a gentle understanding." And yet he still refuses to accept the responsibility she has attributed to him: "I am glad to have you tell me that; but nothing I have said has really made the difference. The difference is in yourself—it will always be there. And since it *is* there, it can't really matter to you what people think: you are so sure that your friends will always understand you." And, as always, Lily is quick to criticize this rejection, this detached individualism that denies the transformative bond between them, "'Ah, don't say that—don't say that what you have told me has made no difference. It seems to shut me out—to leave me all alone with the other people.' She had risen and stood before him, once more completely mastered by the inner urgency of the moment. The consciousness of his half-divined reluctance had vanished. Whether he wished it or not, he must see her wholly for once before they parted" (239).

This image of Lily standing again before Selden, as she began the scene standing at his threshold, recalls another moment when she stood alone, on stage and on display. That scene at the *tableaux vivants* seemed to Selden to reveal the "real Lily," but this moment reveals another Lily standing with dignity before him, the Lily who has struggled alone and unseen. Now it is not a spectacular image of aspiration that commands admiration, but a sincere speech of confession that seeks understanding, that demands he see her "wholly." The passage is worth quoting in full:

> Her voice had gathered strength, and she looked him gravely in the eyes as she continued. "Once — twice — you gave me the chance to escape from my life, and I refused it: refused it because I was a coward. Afterward I saw my mistake — I saw that I could never be happy with what had contented me before. But it was too late: you had judged me — I understood. It was too late for happiness — but not too late to be helped by the thought of what I had missed. That is all I have lived on — don't take it from me now! Even in my worst moments it has been like a little light in the darkness. Some women are strong enough to be good by themselves, but I needed the help of your belief in me. Perhaps I might have resisted a great temptation, but the little ones would have pulled me down. And then I remembered — I remembered your saying that such a life could never satisfy me; and I was ashamed to admit to myself that it could. That is what you did for me — that is what I wanted to thank you for. I wanted to tell you that I have always remembered; and that I have tried — tried hard . . ."
>
> She broke off suddenly. Her tears had risen again, and in drawing out her handkerchief her fingers touched the packet in the folds of her dress. A wave of colour suffused her, and the words died on her lips. Then she lifted her eyes to his and went on in an altered voice.
>
> "I have tried hard — but life is difficult, and I am a very useless person. I can hardly be said to have an independent existence. I was just a screw or a cog in the great machine I called life, and when I dropped out of it I found I was of no use anywhere else. What can one do when one finds that one only fits into one mold? One must get back into it or be thrown out into the rubbish heap — and you don't know what it's like in the rubbish heap!" (239–40)[6]

In this remarkable passage Wharton shows us that Lily is now capable of narrating her own life. We have seen her gaining this power slowly as the novel develops: in her ironic refusal to tell the "true story" to Gerty, in her partial recounting to Rosedale of her struggle to repay her debt to Trenor, in her revelation to Gerty of her inability to resist the seductions of luxury. But each of these narratives had a fragmented quality, a mixture of truth and irony, exposure and disavowal. This passionate confession, halting though it is it at points, gathers power as it proceeds, as if hearing her own voice articulate her experience and its meaning gives Lily new strength. Most important, the narrative has a coherence, a thread, a plot, the story of her conflict and struggle and of Selden's role in that struggle. Lily's urgent desire is that Selden, who initially gave her the language to author that narrative, should hear her tell it. But, significantly, the student has now surpassed her teacher. The story Lily now tells is much more psychologically and socially sophisticated than any that Selden could have told. Her anguished acceptance of her own weaknesses and dependency reveal an awareness of human complexity that his simplistic assertions of individualism could never encompass. Moreover, her need to be seen wholly, for once, has broken the surface of her pride. Toward the close of book 1, as she felt the furies gather around her for the first time, Lily imagined going to Selden for salvation: "But now his love was her only hope, and as she sat alone with her wretchedness the thought of confiding in him became as seductive as the river's flow to suicide. The first plunge would be terrible—but after, what blessedness might come!" (138). In that past crisis, she had hoped that his response would be "to help her to gather up her broken life, and put it together in some new semblance in which no trace of the past should remain!" Yet "she shrank at the thought of imperiling his love by her confession: for love was what she needed—it would take the glow of passion to weld together the shattered fragments of her self-esteem." Now, rather than welding together those fragments to reconstitute her self-esteem, she has found another path to wholeness: the confession of her broken life in itself. Now, it is not pride she seeks to recover, but sincerity, a sincerity that acknowledges her own divided character.

Selden, still uncertain and reserved, asks if she is planning to marry, to which Lily replies, "I shall have to come to it—presently. But there is something else I must come to first." She then pauses and tries to steady her voice and recover her smile, matching her self-presentation to Selden's more conventional manner: "There is some one I must say goodbye to. Oh, not *you*—we are sure to see each other again—but the Lily Bart you knew. I have kept her with me all this time, but now we are going to part, and I have brought her back to you—I am going to leave her here. When I go out presently she will not go with me—and she'll be no trouble, she'll take up no room." Then, still keeping her smile intact, she moves toward him and puts out her hand, as if to seal an agreement between them: "Will you let her stay with you?" (240). With this touch, the emotion that has not yet risen to the surface in Selden makes itself felt, "Lily — can't I help you?" With a gentle look, as if she is now the one teaching him how to read the signs, she replies, "Do you remember what you said to me once? That you could help me only by loving me? Well — you did love me for a moment; and it has helped. It has always helped me. But the moment is gone — it was I who let it go. And one must go on living. Goodbye" (241).

The Lily she wishes to leave with him is, of course, that "real Lily," free of material accidents, that Selden thought he saw for moment at Bellomont and again at the *tableaux vivants*. It was, however, not the whole Lily, but an aspiration, a possibility, made visible only momentarily, but nonetheless a part of her. Once she completes her transaction with Bertha Dorset, that idealized self can never be realized. She has found a way to resolve the conflict between her two selves by sacrificing one for the sake of the other: "She laid her other hand on his, and they looked at each other with a kind of solemnity, as though they stood in the presence of death. Something in truth lay dead between them — the love she had killed in him and could no longer call to life. But something lived between them also, and leaped up in her like an imperishable flame: it was the love his love had kindled, the passion of her soul for his." In this strange moment of death and rebirth, we see a portrayal of renewal through love. The ideals that Lily thought she must kill come back to life as she realizes her love for Selden. Although his love is not there to sustain her, her own love for him is powerful enough to bring those hopes back to life. In the light of this love, "everything else dwindled and fell away from her. She understood now that she could not go forth and leave her old self with him: that self must indeed live on in his presence, but it must still continue to be hers." A sense of crisis pervades this moment. As Selden holds her hand, he continues "to scrutinize her with a strange sense of foreboding. The external aspect of the situation had vanished for him as completely as for her: he felt it only as one of those rare moments which lift the veil from their faces as they pass." Significantly, it is the moment only that lifts the veil from its face and it is a moment that is passing. Selden himself has not exposed his inmost feelings as Lily has. Although moved, he remains veiled.

" 'Lily,' he said in a low voice, 'you must n't speak in this way. I can't let you go without knowing what you mean to do. Things may change — but they don't pass. You can't ever go out of my life.' " Hearing this, she "met his eyes with an illumined look" and replies, "No . . . . I see that now. Let us always be friends. Then I shall feel safe, whatever happens." The reference to friendship links this final dialogue to their conversation in his apartment that September, when she had confided to him that what she most needed was a friend. She has now accepted the impossibility of having him as a lover and returned to her original wish: it will have to suffice. But Selden, hearing an ominous tone in her voice, asks, "Whatever happens? What do you mean? What is going to happen?" Lily replies, "'Nothing at present—except that I am very cold, and that before I go you must make up the fire for me'" (241). She then walks toward the hearth and when Selden is not looking, slips the packet of letters into the fire. Of the two selves, she has chosen to sacrifice the one chained to material necessity. Without hope for rescue from Selden, she has nevertheless destroyed her means of material and social renewal for the sake of the idealized self he once loved. She then kisses him on the forehead and walks back out into the night alone.

Wharton's treatment of this transitional moment is powerful and subtle: "The street-lamps were lit, but the rain had ceased, and there was a momentary revival of light in the upper sky." This "revival of light in the upper sky" is, pointedly, only "momentary" (242). And true to that suggestion, Lily, at first unconscious of her surroundings, is "still treading the buoyant ether which emanates from the high moments of life. But gradually it shrank away from her and she felt the dull pavement beneath her feet." Her sacrifice, while deeply significant, is not enough to save her. She must come back to earth. As she enters Bryant Park, seeking a place to rest, "The melancholy pleasure-ground was almost deserted . . . . and she sank down on an empty bench in the glare of an electric street-lamp. The warmth of the fire had passed out of her veins, and she told herself that she must not sit long in the penetrating dampness which struck up from the wet asphalt." Now Lily has returned to the world "outside," like the reverberating, hollow restaurant where she sat earlier in her isolation. Whereas there it was tea that brought a sense of renewal to her veins, in Selden's apartment it was the warmth of the fire, and even more, the moral exhilaration of her sacrifice and the love that enabled it. But now even that warmth has left her veins. The image of the "melancholy pleasure-ground" suggests the failure of the house of mirth itself. Recalling the "inutility of self-sacrifice" in other Wharton texts such as *The Bunner Sisters* and *Ethan Frome*, Lily's moral heroism is not rewarded, but rather produces an even greater sense of loneliness and destitution: "Her willpower seemed to have spent itself in a last great effort, and she was lost in the blank reaction which follows on an unwonted expenditure of energy. And besides, what was there to go home to? Nothing but the silence of her cheerless room—that silence of the night which may be more racking to tired nerves than the most discordant noises: that, and the bottle of chloral by her bed." The appearance of the chloral signals that her sacrifice has in fact not resolved the core conflicts with which Lily struggles. Ironically, they seem to have become even more insistent, for where once the thought of Selden's past love for her was the light she held onto in the darkness, now "the thought of the chloral was the only spot of light in the dark prospect: she could feel its lulling influence stealing over her already."

And yet Lily is also disturbed by the chloral's diminishing ability to pull her down to unconsciousness. She worries that the narcotic's power will eventually fail, while she also remembers the chemist's warning about the drug's dangers. Although she fears increasing the dose, she fears the furies just as much. Torn, "her dread of returning to a sleepless night was so great that she lingered on, hoping that excessive weariness would reinforce the waning power of the chloral." And then, as the darkness and her isolation deepen, a figure comes out of the shadows, a woman who bends over her to ask if she is ill and suddenly recognizes her: "The speaker was a poorly-dressed young woman with a bundle under her arm. Her face had the air of unwholesome refinement which ill-health and overwork may produce, but its common prettiness was redeemed by the strong and generous curve of the lips" (242–43). This figure will prove to be Nettie Struther, associated with Gerty Farish's social club: a young working woman whose health had been restored by Lily's sporadic charity. Now Nettie returns the help, offering to bring Lily back to her own spare apartment where, after a hard day's work, her baby awaits. This encounter ushers in a scene that many critics see as Wharton's turn to sentimentalism and her abandonment of the realism and social criticism they believe characterized the novel's earlier sections. However, as I have attempted to demonstrate, the entire novel is in fact informed by the cultural discourse of sentimentalism, as that discourse is rooted in the core beliefs of liberal Protestantism and Christian nurture. It is in these last scenes that those core beliefs come most fully to the surface of Wharton's narration. A look at her sentimental precursors can help us see them more clearly.

In her effort to recover sentimentalism as a distinct literary genre, Joanne Dobson defined it as one that makes affective bonds between people as its primary concern and that centers its plots on the threat to those bonds.[7] Similarly, Mary Louise Kete explains that "recent work on the problem of sentiment has begun to erode the perception that sentimentality is characterized by a saccharine or false celebration of home and family. Instead, these two topics have come to be seen as crucial and savvy devices in a rhetoric of significant cultural import." While she agrees that home and family are "among the signal topoi of the sentimental mode," she argues that "it is more precise to say that two of the three fundamental subjects of sentiment are homes and families under the condition of loss."[8] Given the centrality of such loss, it makes sense that "the third subject concerns the bonds between those who grieve." These bonds are crucial to the "sentimental collaboration" Kete sees at the heart of this cultural discourse. Thus it is not only grief, but "successful communication — successful telling of sorrow — [that] yields the transformation of that sorrow into a permanent joy."[9] This transformation of sorrow into joy depends upon an achieved faith in continued existence after death, an achievement that represents what old-time Puritans referred to as the "victory" over mortal fears concerning loss of earthly attachments: "Heaven is a place where one will be in close community with one's friends, where one will participate in the shared project of worship and in the shared project of continued existence."[10]

Grief and loss in classic sentimental texts, as we have seen in *Little Women*, also serve an important pedagogical function. Just as Christian in *Pilgrim's Progress* is prompted to his pilgrimage through his apprehension of his own sinfulness and mortality, a cross that he is repeatedly tempted to avoid and yet whose embrace is the gate to his redemption, so the sentimental character is morally transformed, not only through his or her connection to others, but also through the awakening of spiritual awareness that comes with their loss. In this discourse, mourning becomes the immanent substitute for crisis conversion, the ground of moral development. As Wharton's title suggests to those who recall the full scriptural passage from which it is taken, "the heart of the wise is in the house of mourning." It is in sentimental deathbed scenes that we can see most clearly the particular dynamics of moral education and human development as these writers understood them. Since Harriet Beecher Stowe is one of the most complex and subtle of these writers, I have chosen passages concerning the death of Mara Lincoln in *The Pearl of Orr's Island* to serve as a literary template for the sentimental treatment of grief and loss.[11] (This novel's central character, a young woman engaged in be married in a small New England community, offers a clearer comparison with Lily Bart than Little Eva, the child heroine of Stowe's more famous, but equally sentimental, novel *Uncle Tom's Cabin*.) I then turn to parallel passages portraying the death of Beth March in *Little Women* to widen our understanding of its significance for Wharton and perhaps other realist writers as well. For example, before returning to Selden's apartment, I will examine the lingering influence of such deathbed scenes on a more immediate Wharton precursor: Henry James and his portrayal of Isabel Archer Osmond at Ralph Touchett's deathbed in *The Portrait of a Lady* (1881).[12]

To begin with Stowe: *The Pearl of Orr's Island* was published in 1862 and was one of the pioneer texts of local-color literature and regional realism. The pearl of the title is Mara Lincoln, a saintly young woman living with her old-fashioned Calvinist family on Orr's Island off the coast of Maine. Orphaned by the shipwreck drowning of her parents when she was an infant, saintly Mara is raised by her grandparents alongside an adopted brother, Moses Pennel, another child orphaned by the drowning of his mother and rescued by the Pennel family. The scenes relevant to our discussion concern Mara's lingering illness and death just as she enters womanhood and becomes affianced to the tempestuous Moses, whose name suggests his unregenerate nature. Selfless and beloved by all, Mara feels herself inexplicably weakening and losing her hold on life. At first she struggles and rebels against her fate, but then one day she seeks comfort at the home of Roxy and Ruey Toothacre, famous nurses and healers among these rural families. The elderly sisters offer Mara a bedroom in which to rest, and there Mara has a revelation that changes her understanding of her imminent death.

As Mara lies "in the passive calm of fatigue and exhaustion . . . she dropped into that kind of kind of half-waking doze, when the outer sense are at rest, and the mind is all the more calm and clear for their repose" (382). Unlike Lily, whose attempts at sleep are restless and tortured, Mara achieves a state of calm receptivity, one that Stowe's narrator defines as a kind of transitional psychic awareness: "In such hours a spiritual clairvoyance often seems to lift for a while the whole stifling cloud that lies like a confusing mist over the problem of life, and the soul has sudden glimpses of things unutterable which lie beyond." If a central goal of Protestantism, as Webb Keane describes it, is a kind of spiritual transparency, a lifting of the veil of the material, we see that goal achieved here. The narrator links this awareness directly to Bunyan's *Pilgrim's Progress*: "As the burden of Christian fell off at the cross and was lost in sepulcher, so in these hours of celestial vision the whole weight of life's anguish is lifted, and passes away like a dream; and the soul, seeing the boundless ocean of Divine love . . . comes and casts the one little drop of its personal will and personal existence with gladness into that Fatherly depth" (382–83).

As Mara falls into the deep, untroubled sleep of the righteous, the Toothacre sisters confer. "'Had n't you better wake her?' said Miss Ruey, 'a cup of hot tea would do her much good.'" (383). The reference to the renewing powers of tea has a odd parallel here with tea's role in *The House of Mirth*, for "Miss Ruey could conceive of few sorrows or ailments which would not be materially better for a cup of hot tea. If not the very elixir of life, it was indeed the next thing to it." But Miss Roxy, the wiser of the two sisters, thinks differently: "'Well,' said Miss Roxy, after laying her hand for a moment with great gentleness on that of the sleeping girl, 'she don't wake easy, and she's tired; and she seems to be enjoying it so. The Bible says, 'He giveth his beloved sleep,' and I won't interfere. I've seen more good come of sleep than most things in my nursin' experience' . . . and she shut the door gentle gently, and the two sisters sat down to their noontide meal" (383).

When Mara does wake from her sleep, she seems transformed, even transfigured: "Both sisters were struck with a change that had passed over her. It was more than the result of mere physical repose. Not only had every sign of weariness and bodily languor vanished, but there was about her an air of solemn serenity and high repose that made her seem, as Ruey afterward said, 'like an angel jest walked out of the Bible'" (384). She has "passed beyond sorrow — yes, forever." In orthodox Puritan terms, she has been weaned from material life and its burden of mortality; she has achieved, in the old-fashioned religious term, the victory.

Now that Mara has been liberated from the expectations of worldly life, Stowe's narrator goes about weaning her readers from similar expectations: "There are no doubt many, who have followed this history so long as it danced like a gay little boat over sunny waters, and who would have followed it gaily to the end, had it closed with the ringing of marriage-bells, who turn from it indignantly, when they see that its course runs through the dark valley. This, they say, is an imposition — a trick upon our feelings. We want to read only stories which end in joy and prosperity" (396). This passage anticipates Wharton's own experience with American audiences. When playgoers bitterly complained that the stage version of *The House of Mirth* denied them the pleasure of Lily's happy marriage to Lawrence Selden, William Dean Howells, who had accompanied Wharton to the play's first night in New York, comforted her by remarking ruefully, "Yes — what the American public always wants is a tragedy with a happy ending."[13] In this case, Stowe's narrator sternly questions her readers, "But have we then settled it in our own mind that there is no such thing as a fortunate issue in a history which does not terminate in the way of earthly success and good fortune? Are we Christians or heathen?" There is a different understanding of ultimate happiness and success in Christianity: "*Was* Mary the highly-favored among women, and was Jesus indeed the blessed, — or was the angel mistaken? If they were these, if we are Christians, it ought to be a settled and established habit of our souls to regard something else as prosperity than worldly success and happy marriages" (396).

Nevertheless, Stowe's narrator acknowledges that, as embodied creatures, "God has given to us, and inwoven in our nature a desire for a perfection and completeness made manifest to our senses in this mortal life . . . such is the ideal of happiness which he has interwoven with our nerves, and for which our heart and our flesh crieth out; to which every stroke of a knell is a violence, and every thought of an early death is an abhorrence" (396–97). Yet while the terror evoked by the threat of death is "inwoven in our nature" and "interwoven with our nerves," this terror can be overcome, as Mara has overcome it. And it is this victory that Christ represents: "Of his own, he had nothing, neither houses, nor lands, nor family ties, nor human hopes, nor earthly sphere of success; and as a human life, it was all sacrifice and defeat" (397). Indeed, the narrator concludes, this worldly happiness for which the flesh cries out, must finally be rejected if salvation is to be achieved: "But the life of Christ and his mother sets the foot on this lower ideal of happiness and teaches us that there is something higher. His ministry began with declaring, 'Blessed are they that mourn.' It has been well said that prosperity was the blessing of the Old Testament, and adversity of the New."

Defiantly Protestant in its rejection of the material as an ultimate good or even ultimate reality, Stowe's narrator continues to explain the purpose of such suffering and early death as Mara Lincoln's: "This, then, is the great and perfect ideal of what God honors. Christ speaks of himself as *bread* to be eaten, — bread, simple, humble, unpretending, vitally necessary to human life, made by the bruising and grinding of the grain, unostentatiously having no life or worth of its own except as it is absorbed into the life of others and lives in them" (397–98). Mara will leave no marker behind of her worldly success and yet Stowe wishes to favor her as the story's heroine. Characters like her, marked for early death, serve a higher purpose in this life, as homely versions of Christ Himself: "If we could look with the eye of faith, we should see that their living and dying has been bread of life to those they left behind" (398). Central to this notion of the dying becoming bread for those who survive is, of course, the sacramental nature of grief. In this Stowe draws on the traditional Protestant notion of the Eucharist as an outward and visible sign of an invisible and inward grace, but it is not a miraculous agent in itself. These dying young people are not miracle workers, but they enable a remembrance of their lives that transforms those who mourn them. Thus Stowe writes, "It is expedient for us that they go away. Like their Lord, they come to suffer, and to die; they take part in his sacrifice; their life is incomplete without their death, and not till they are gone away does the Comforter fully come to us" (398–99).[14]

As Mara's Christ-like acceptance of her death and sacrifice deepens, those around her are subtly transformed by her influence. The most obvious example is her fiancé, Moses. As he watches by her deathbed, "unconsciously, even to himself, sorrow was doing her ennobling ministry within him, melting off in her fierce fires trivial ambitions and low desires, and making him feel the sole worth and value of love" (414). Thus Moses, whose very name recalls the supposed materialism and pride of the Old Testament, is converted to Christian humility and otherworldliness, and converted by Mara, whose name signifies, Stowe tells us, "bitterness"—in this case the wholesome bitterness of grief. However, this bitterness is one that human beings, with a desire for the sweetness of life "interwoven in their nerves," initially reject: it is a taste that must be acquired.

The importance of memory in this process is especially clear in Moses's case. As he confronts Mara's loss, his remembrance of her begins to change the narrative of his life: "He saw a thousand actions, he heard a thousand words, whose beauty and significance never came to him till now. And alas! He saw so many when, on his part, the responsive word that should have been spoken, and the deed should have been done, was forever wanting." Grief is bringing repressed and inarticulate perceptions to the surface, breaking the hard shell of his worldly pride. His understanding of their shared past suddenly shifts, and a new interpretation of its meaning emerges: "Something he had never felt before struck him as appalling in the awful fixedness of all past deeds and words,—the unkind words once said, which no tears could unsay,—the kind ones suppressed, to which no agony of wishfulness could give a past reality" (415). This deathbed encounter sparks a kind of miniature, individualized apocalypse, in which the inner life is finally transparent and one is accountable for all that is revealed there: "True, all had been a thousand times forgiven and forgotten between them, but it is the ministry of these great vital hours of sorrow to teach us that nothing in the soul's history ever dies or is forgotten, and when the beloved one lies stricken and ready to pass away, comes the judgment-day of love, and the dead moments of the past arise and live again" (415). Deathbed dialogue has a kind of ultimate significance, a sincerity enabled by its finality. Mara, hitherto reserved and submissive before Moses' domineering ways, now claims the authority to define both herself and him: "Moses . . . for all I know you *have* loved me dearly, yet I have felt that in all that was deepest and dearest to me, I was alone. . . . There is something sacred and beautiful in death; and I may have more power over you, when I seem to be gone, than I should have had living" (424).[15] In the final scenes, the community gathers around Mara's dead "form," which is described as "shrouded and coffined, but with such a fairness and tender purity, such a mysterious fullness of joy in its expression, that it seemed more natural to speak of that rest as some higher form of life than of death." Here death, its terror vanquished, is strangely conflated with sleep and the mourners themselves seem to share in Mara's victory: "The room was full of sweet memories, of words of cheers, words of assurance, words of triumph, and the mysterious brightness of that young face forbade them to weep" (430).

The death of Beth March in *Little Women* is portrayed in terms very similar to Mara Lincoln's, although the language is, for the most part, less explicitly Protestant or even Christian in its references. As Beth begins to feel her life ebbing away, Jo, with her literary earnings, takes Beth away to the seaside in hopes of restoring her health. When her sister continues to fail, Jo passionately rebels against her sister's fate: "God won't be so cruel as to take you from me" (459). However, Beth has come to accept the inevitability of her early death. In that submissiveness Beth reveals herself as one of the Christ-like emissaries Stowe describes. However, Alcott departs from Stowe's more orthodox approach to the "victory." Rather than stressing rejection of worldly bonds, Alcott writes that Beth did "not rebuke Jo with saintly speeches, only loved her better for her passionate affection, and clung more closely to the dear human love, from which our Father never means us to be weaned, but through which He draws us closer to Himself. She could not say, 'I'm glad to go,' for life was very sweet to her; she could only sob out, 'I'll try to be willing,' while she held fast to Jo, as the first bitter wave of this great sorrow broke over them together" (459–60).

In Stowe's depiction, acceptance of death comes only through an almost violent weaning from materiality and embodiment. These bonds are, of course, to be superseded by more purely spiritual ones, but in Alcott, bodily and spiritual bonds merge almost imperceptibly one into the other. Although Beth seems to have some foreknowledge of her early death, she also has some resistance to that "bitter wave of sorrow." And far from seeing herself as a Christ-like heroine, Beth feels a sense of worldly failure at first. It is Jo who rescues Beth from this sense of failure, by writing a poem in which she expresses all that her selfless sister has meant to her and what she is painfully learning from that impeding loss. Like the equally tempestuous and rebellious Moses, Jo is slowly being chastened through grief. Moreover, when Beth reads Jo's poem, she becomes aware that her life, like Mara's, has had its hidden, pedagogical purpose. Assuming the role of mentor, she explains to her sister, "love is the only thing that we can carry with us when we go, and it makes the end so easy" (513). If Jo is not to be weaned from earthly love, she is to be weaned from ambition and any earthly desires other than love itself, which remains supreme. In this dialogue, as in the deathbed dialogue between Mara and Moses, it is the submissive but saintly dying character who has the last word and pronounces the last judgment.

When it comes time for Beth's actual death, Alcott discreetly obscures the final moments: "Those who have sped many parting souls know, that to most the end comes as naturally and simply as sleep. As Beth had hoped, the 'tide went out easily'; and in the dark hour before the dawn, on the bosom where she had drawn her first breath, she quietly drew her last, with no farewell but one loving look and a little sigh" (514). Here, as in Stowe's treatment, the death of the righteous is paralleled to "natural sleep." In this case, the naturalness is underlined by a final, framing portrait of Beth drawing her last breath on her mother's breast, another indication that Alcott does not see as firm a boundary between body and spirit as Stowe does, or as strong a need to be weaned from earthly attachments, for it was Marmee who taught Beth how to read the signs of the moral life, a language meant to be as nurturing as mother's milk.

Signaling this victory over death's terror, the members of the March family, like Mara's mourners, find their grief transformed into a confirmation of faith. The final image of Beth's dead body is also much like Mara's, an image marked more by renewal than loss: "When morning came, for the first time in many months the fire was out, Jo's place was empty, and the room was very still. But a bird sang blithely on a budding bough, close by, the snow-drops blossomed freshly at the window, and the spring sunshine streamed in like benediction over the placid face upon the pillow — a face so full of painless peace, that those who loved it best smiled through their tears and thanked God that Beth was well at last" (514). Finally, as we saw in chapter 1, Beth's death and its transformative effect enable Jo to find her true literary style, a sincere expressiveness that results in the first book of *Little Women* itself. As Alcott's narrator explains, Jo's outer self had been like the bristling, forbidding covering of the chestnut-burr; it took the hard frost of grief to split that surface and reveal the interior heart within. In Jo's case, as in that of Moses, this miniature judgment-day recenters her identity and allows her to create a new narrative of her life and its meaning

Turning to such a consummate realist, secular psychologist, and understated stylist as Henry James following such scenes of classic sentimental "excess" may seem incongruous. However, James's depiction of Isabel's reconciliation with her cousin, Ralph Touchett, toward the close of *The Portrait of a Lady*, shares, I believe, certain key features with these other scenes and provides an important link between them and Wharton's treatment of Lily on her dying day. These features include a developmental process that moves from grief and loss to a breakdown of pride and its defensive surface. The result is a passionate disinhibition of speech and the emergence of a "sincere" life narrative that incorporates new insights. However, in James's and especially Wharton's texts, the outcome of this process is significantly more ambiguous and troubled than in Stowe's or Alcott's.

Like *The House of Mirth*, which opens with Lily's dialogue with Selden in his New York apartment and returns to that apartment for one of its climatic scenes, James's novel begins with the young Isabel Archer's introduction to her cousin at Gardencourt, the English country estate owned by the Touchett family. Its closing scenes return the older Isabel, emotionally and morally bruised, to Gardencourt and her cousin's deathbed. Ralph, like the sentimental heroines Mara and Beth, is fated to die young. Although not virginal like these young women, he is well enough aware of the progress of his consumption to refrain from marriage. In love with his spirited but relatively impoverished cousin, he has secretly arranged for his dying father to leave half of his inheritance to Isabel, thereby providing her the financial freedom to realize her life's ambitions, whatever they may be. Rather than giving Isabel the freedom to soar "Beyond!" as the seal on Lily Bart's letters proclaims, however, the new fortune ironically makes Isabel vulnerable to fortune-hunters. When Ralph tries to warn her that the man she is about to marry is a petty, materialistic conformist, incapable of love or freedom of thought, Isabel rejects Ralph indignantly and passionately describes Gilbert Osmond as she mistakenly imagines him: as a sensitive idealist who needs her help. When Ralph's diagnosis proves all too accurate, Isabel, out of pride, hides the truth from her cousin, disguising her pain under a mask of wifely contentment. It is only when Osmond's manipulation and betrayal, his moral "malignancy," are finally revealed and when Isabel learns that Ralph is dying that she flees her husband in Rome and returns, shocked and heartbroken, to Gardencourt.

Isabel's state of mind as she meets her friend, Henrietta Stackpole, and her fiancé, Robert Bantling, at the London train station is revealing. She first asks Bantling if he looks sad because he has been at Gardencourt with Ralph, but then: " 'I don't believe you ever look sad. You look kind,' said Isabel, with a frankness that cost her no effort. It seemed to her that she should never again feel a superficial embarrassment." Like Lily as she enters Selden's apartment, Isabel is beyond the conventionalities of polite reserve; however, "Poor Mr. Bantling . . . was still in this inferior stage. He blushed a good deal, and laughed, and assured her that he was often very blue, and that when he was blue he was awfully fierce" (476). Like Selden, who keeps his suave surface intact and seems discomfited by Lily's unwonted self-revelation, Bantling is uncertain how to handle this unusual display of emotion. However, there is no such uncertainty when Isabel is finally allowed access to Ralph Touchett's sickroom at Gardencourt.

Overwhelmed, Isabel "had lost all her shame, all wish to hide things. Now he might know; she wished him to know, for it brought them supremely together, and he was beyond the reach of pain" (486). She asks Ralph if it was he who had made her rich, and he confesses that it was, but also that he fears it had ruined her by making her prey to Osmond and his cohort, Madame Merle. This death-bed dialogue, with its strong confessional quality, evokes the sense of ultimate sincerity so central to earlier sentimental texts. The approach of death enables an honesty previously unthinkable: "She was full of the sense that he was beyond the reach of pain; he seemed already so little of this world. But even if she had not had it she would still have spoken, for nothing mattered now but the only knowledge that was not pure anguish — the knowledge that they were looking at the truth together" (487). Isabel now confesses to Ralph what she had hidden out of pride: Osmond's cruelty, the fact that he had married for her money, that she had been used. As she explains, "I don't hurt you in saying that. How can I? I only want you to understand. I always tried to keep you from understanding; but that's all over." When Ralph replies that he had always understood, Isabel says, "I thought you did, and I didn't like it. But now I like it." Ralph then says simply, " 'You don't hurt me — you make me very happy.' And as Ralph said this there was an extraordinary gladness in his voice. She bent her head again, and pressed her lips to the back of his hand. 'I always understood,' he continued" (487). Admitting her mistake, foregoing her pride, allows the transparency of understanding, the shared narrative that is so crucial to these scenes of deathbed reconciliation and transformed memory — miniature judgment days.

When Ralph asks if Isabel if she is going back to her husband to fulfill her wifely vows, she says she doesn't know: "I don't care for anything but you, and that is enough for the present. It will last a little yet. Here on my knees, with you dying in my arms, I am happier than I have been in a long time. And I want you to be happy — not to think of anything sad; only to feel that I am near you and love you. Why should there be pain? In such hours as this what have we to do with pain? That is not the deepest thing; there is something deeper" (487–88). But Ralph is weakening: "I am very tired. You said just now that pain is not the deepest thing. No — no. But it is very deep. If I could stay . . . ." Isabel easily interrupts his faltering voice, "For me you will always be here," and he replies after a moment, "It passes, after all; it's passing now. But love remains. I don't know why we should suffer so much. Perhaps I shall find out. There are many things in life; you are very young" (488). And then, in his last words to her, he offers Isabel absolution for her mistake and for her pride in hiding it from him. He predicts that she will continue to live, to grow young again, despite her suffering, "I don't believe that such a generous mistake as yours — can hurt you more than a little. . . . And remember this . . . . that if you have been hated, you have also been loved" (488). With this, Isabel throws herself down upon the deathbed to embrace Ralph in a final surrender.

In sum, the deathbed scene in sentimental fiction has a special function: the revelation of perfect Protestant sincerity. Rather than the sacrament of extreme unction, mediated by a Roman Catholic priest who hears the final confession, there is instead a secularized, psychological moment of self-revelation, a baring of soul to soul, a reciprocal understanding and farewell that "clears the air" and paves the way for human forgiveness and final understanding. Now the interior soul becomes fully visible as pride gives way to love and as humility renders worldly, material identity transparent. In all three of these scenes, love is the re-demptive force that counters suffering and death and points to a spiritual, rather than a purely materialistic, source of identity. In James's version, however, this love has no divine referent; it seems purely human. There is no suggestion of an otherworldly realm where Ralph will be well once more, although Isabel does glimpse what may be his departing spirit in the dawn hour after his death. There is no victorious escape from death's terror into an assurance of an afterlife nor is there is any reassurance that such suffering and premature death are meaningful in themselves. Ralph asks gently, "perhaps we shall know why we suffer," but it is only a suggestion, slight as a watercolor stroke, that death may reveal the answer to his questions. Rather than the illuminated faces of mourners whose faith has been renewed or even awakened, James offers only the possibility of "illuminated moments" in this world, after which there is no other. However, love, which gives these moments transforming power, is deeper than suffering and the remembrance of that love is what gives Ralph's life meaning for those who mourn him — and perhaps what guides Isabel in her final decision, when she sees a "very straight path" before her, one that leads her back to Rome, per-haps to confront her husband, but also perhaps to save her step-daughter, Pansy, from his domination. And yet, if love is deeper than pain, Ralph confesses that pain also goes very deep. As we will see with Lily, pain is also very powerful.

In light of these earlier models, the scene in Selden's apartment may also be viewed as a kind of deathbed scene, but one in which the final reconciliation is never reached. Earlier sentimental texts such as Stowe's show the dying figures becoming almost physically transparent. Similarly, Lily's physical wasting ren-ders her beauty almost supernatural; it seems to spiritualize it. However, the text is clear that Lily's body isn't becoming angelic. Rather, it's anorexic, starv-ing. She's still very much embodied.[16] And yet the seeming transparency of her body is related to the image of a transparent surface through which Selden had earlier believed he glimpsed her true spirit. The angularity and "hollowed out" quality of Lily's body still fits the sentimental pattern, as does her disinhibition: she has nothing more to lose. Like Isabel confronted with Ralph's death, Lily embraces the cross with abandonment, discarding her pride and confessing herself to Selden. In this abandonment she achieves the voice of Protestant sincerity, narrating her story with confidence in its truth, a passionate outpouring motivated by a desire to understood, to be seen as she is, flawed and even broken, yet emotionally alive and morally aware. Equally important, she is confident that this is *her* version of her story, not society's. However, the crucial moment of shared empathy and final understanding does not occur. Selden cannot read the signs of Lily's distress. He cannot give her help or absolution. He insists, once more, that she stand alone, unsupported. Although the narrator offers the image of the moment that removes the veil from its face, Selden cannot interpret what he sees there until the next morning, when it is too late. The love that transfigures and transforms the grieving characters in Stowe, Alcott, and James remains unspoken on Lily's part and dormant, perhaps dead, on Selden's.

The failure of this potentially redemptive dialogue can be attributed to Selden as much, perhaps even more, than to Lily. Although Selden is Lily's moral exemplar, his gaze is not stable, but divided. Amphibious, he can adjust his eye to assess Lily's elegant surface, just as Rosedale does when he "scans" her. Modern in its flexibility and its irony, Selden's gaze is morally weakened as a result.[17] This is quite unlike his counterpart in *Little Women*, Laurie, who is shocked by Meg's behavior at vanity fair and condemns her fashionable, highly sexualized appearance. Selden's affair with Bertha Dorset is especially revealing. He confesses to Gerty that "he had never wanted to marry a 'nice' girl: the adjective connoting, in his cousin's vocabulary, certain utilitarian qualities which are apt to preclude the luxury of charm" (120). Selden espouses a belief in moral integrity and freedom from material accidents, but has not been able to hold himself to these ideals, as if Alcott's Laurie were having a secret, adulterous affair with the unhappy Sallie Moffat and confessed that, against his own better judgment, he preferred stylish, pretty society women like her to frumpy, sincere do-gooders like the March sisters. Another case of *Schizophrenia Americana*, Selden will find his life ruined by this division. He initially found Lily's sexual manipulation of men like Percy Gryce "amusing." Later, despite his developing love for her, he could not overcome the fastidious individualism that foreclosed compassion for her weakness. In this last crisis, he fails to respond to her appeal. Moreover, however proud he might be of his freedom from convention, Selden is still influenced by the very people he disdains: "It was pitiable that he, who knew the mixed motives on which social judgments depends, should still feel himself so swayed by them. How could he lift Lily to a freer vision of life, if his own vision of her was to be coloured by any mind in which he saw her reflected?" (126). One of the novel's many ironies is that the devastated, frightened Lily Selden abandoned at the end of book 1 was the Lily closest to the truth of her heart, the one most open to his love, the most susceptible to change.

The Lily he then preferred, the frozen ideal beauty of the *tableau vivant*, would never have married him. Now, as Lily sits in the gathering dark of Bryant Park's "melancholy ground," she is bereft of hope for either the material security that Selden's adulterous letters might have purchased or the renewal that Selden's love and forgiveness would have brought.

And so we return to the appearance of Nettie Struther, the young working woman who offers Lily her help. Wharton's use of narrative symmetry shows again in her construction of this scene. In this case, Nettie Struther's entrance is contrasted with Lily's first appearance in the novel: framed against a crowd of undifferentiated working women, who seem to Lawrence Selden's discerning eye "a different species" in comparison to Lily's polished surface. Now one of these working women detaches herself from the faceless crowd and reveals herself as strong and generous: not a different species, but a fellow human being, capable of offering sympathy and aid. Lily recognizes her as the former Nettie Crane, a young woman whom Lily, in one of the spasmodic acts of charity prompted by Gerty, had helped back to health by funding her trip to a sanatorium. Lily also recalls, with some irony, that it was Gus Trenor's money that had made Nettie's recovery possible. On the way home to care for her child, Nettie offers to bring Lily with her to her apartment, an offer the weak and disheartened Lily accepts. Once there, Nettie brings Lily into the warm kitchen, which "revealed itself to Lily as extraordinarily small and almost miraculously clean" (244). As the fire shines in the stove, the baby sits upright in her crib, "with incipient anxiety struggling for expression on a countenance still placid with sleep." Nettie, "having passionately celebrated her reunion with her offspring, and excused herself in cryptic language for the lateness of her return . . . restored the baby to the crib and shyly invited Miss Bart to the rocking-chair near the stove." Explaining "with pardonable pride" that although she does have a parlor she supposes that it is warmer in the kitchen for Lily and that she needs to feed the baby, a priority that trumps even the visit of the fabled Miss Bart. Lily, who usually shuns kitchens, with their smells of cooking and associations with the dinginess she so fears, now accepts the invitation gratefully. Somehow this space, like Selden's apartment, seems a kind of haven, its "miraculous" cleanliness compensating for its humble role in the production of food, a production usually veiled from Lily's sight.

As Nettie prepares a bottle of milk for her baby and proceeds to feed her, she can't help expressing wonder that the Miss Bart should be in her apartment. "Beaming," she offers Lily a cup of coffee, warmed up with some of the baby's leftover milk: "It's too lovely having you here. I've thought of it so often that I can't believe it's really come true. I've said to George again and again: 'I just wish Miss Bart could come see me *now*—.'" Unbeknownst to Lily, this hidden fan had eagerly followed Lily's success in the newspaper and worried when her name began to disappear. Nettie says she almost made her self sick with such worry, but then explains, 'Well, I can't afford to be sick again, that's a fact: the last spell nearly finished me. When you sent me off that time I never thought I'd come back alive, and I did n't much care if I did. You see I did n't know about George and the baby then" (244). Then the full story of Nettie's illness and recovery comes out: "I never thought I'd get married, you know, and I'd never have had the heart to go on working just for myself." As the baby struggles impatiently to satisfy her hunger, Nettie simultaneously soothes her and recalls her story for Lily, whose eyes encourage her. With a "flush under her anaemic skin," Nettie explains,

> You see I wasn't only just *sick* that time you sent me off—I was dreadfully unhappy too. I'd known a gentleman where I was employed—I don't know as you remember I did type-writing in a big importing firm—and—well—I thought we were to be married: he'd gone steady with me six months and given me his mother's wedding ring. But I presume he was too stylish for me—he traveled for the firm, and had seen a great deal of society. Work girls are n't looked after the way you are, and they don't always know how to look after themselves. I did not . . . and it pretty near killed me when he went away and left off writing . . . it was then I came down sick. (245)

While it is not clear whether Nettie had become pregnant by her betrayer, it is clear that she felt her reputation had been ruined. She hadn't been "looked after" the way she, ironically, imagines Lily has been, and her involuntary blush suggests that she had become sexually involved with the man who left her. When Lily's charity rescued her, she was suicidal. Despite Nettie's fond imagining of Lily's insulation from such troubles, the parallels with Lily's own case—the ruined reputation, the suicidal impulses—are clear. And so is Nettie's triumph over them, initiated by Lily's generosity: "I thought it was the end of everything. I guess it would have been if you had n't sent me off. But when I found I was getting well I began to take heart in spite of myself." When Nettie, her strength renewed, goes home, "George came round and asked me to marry him. At first I thought I could n't, because we'd been brought up together, and I knew he knew about me. After a while I began to see that that made it easier. I never could have told another man, and I'd never have married without telling, but if George cared for me enough to have me as I was, I did n't see why I should n't begin over again — and I did" (245). Here the difference from Lily's case is highlighted; George, unlike Selden, has responded to Nettie's ruined reputation and consequent confession with forgiveness and compassion, caring for her enough "to have me as I was." "'The strength of the victory shone forth from her as she lifted her irradiated face from the child on her knees."[18]

Rich in the love that Lily has missed, with her baby now "blissfully replete," Nettie suddenly recalls Lily's exhausted state: "'But, mercy, I did n't mean to go on like this about myself, with you sitting there looking so fagged out. Only it's so lovely having you here, and letting you see just how you've helped me. . . . I only wish I could help *you* — but I suppose there's nothing on earth I could do' she murmured wistfully." Lily, rather than answer, replies with a significantly uncharacteristic gesture; she "rose with a smile and held out her arms; and the mother, understanding the gesture, laid her child in them" (245). This subtle exchange recalls the earlier moment in the Brys' conservatory following the *tableaux vivants*. There Selden had told Lily that the only way he could help her was by loving her. Triumphant in her white dress, she had replied, "Love me, love me, but don't tell me so." Rejecting his words of love, she was left bereft of what he offered. Now Lily's mute appeal to Nettie asks to share in the love that has renewed the working girl's life. As Lily takes Nettie's child into her arms, "The baby, feeling herself detached from her habitual anchorage, made an instinctive motion of resistance; but the soothing influences of digestion prevailed, and Lily felt the soft weight sink trustfully against her breast." Somehow the power of Nettie's attachment to her child, an attachment that has comforted the little girl in her hunger and distress, does transfer itself to Lily, for the "child's confidence in its safety thrilled her with a sense of warmth and returning life, and she bent over, wondering at the rosy blur of the little face, the empty clearness of the eyes, the vague tendrilly motions of the folding and unfolding fingers."

Nettie has made Lily her surrogate for moment, allowing her guest to participate in her motherhood. The experience is surprisingly complex: "At first the burden in her arms seemed as light as a pink cloud or a heap of down, but as she continued to hold it the weight increased, sinking deeper, and penetrating her with a strange sense of weakness, as though the child entered into her and became a part of herself" (245–46). As numerous psychological theorists have pointed out, the emotional dynamic between mother and child draws on deep reserves of identification in the mother.[19] For a mother to respond appropriately to a child's needs, she must recall, even if unconsciously, her own experience of infancy. As for the child, the mother's sensitivity in responding to her needs and interpreting her inarticulate cries generates trust and encourages those tendrils to attach themselves to a safe anchorage. This merging of identities, the pre-oedipal moment before speech, expressed in that "cryptic language" with which Nettie first greets her child, provides comfort for both body and spirit, material food that cannot be separated from emotional nourishment. Although the communication is preverbal, Nettie's ability to read her daughter's signs is still crucial to their dialogue's success. Satiated, the now sleepy baby accepts Lily as a maternal substitute and surrenders herself to Lily's care. When Lily looks up, she sees, "Nettie's eyes resting on her with tenderness and exultation." Still idolizing and emulating her guest, Nettie exclaims, "Would n't be too lovely for anything if she could grow up to be just like you? Of course I know she never *could*—but mothers are always dreaming the craziest things for their children." Lily's response, however, is as complex as her response to the child's surrender: "Lily clasped the child close for a moment and laid her back in her mother's arms" and then says, with a smile, "Oh, she must not do that—I should be afraid to come and see her too often!" Recognizing the sweetness and depth of this temporary attachment, Lily also poignantly denies her suitability for such responsibility. Making polite excuses to leave and promises to return, Lily finds her way out of the kitchen and onto the street, alone once more.[20]

Lori Merish, in one of the most discerning and persuasive discussions of this scene, notes that "beginning with James many critics have argued that the novel falters in the second book and especially in the final scenes, slipping from astute social criticism to banal sentimentality. That sentimentality is especially evident in Wharton's depiction of Nettie Struther's sentimental maternity and family life, and in the scenes preceding and immediately following Lily's death."[21] Other critics tend to agree. For example, Gary Levine writes that "naturalism falters and retreats to sentimentalism in *The House of Mirth*."[22] Even so sympathetic a critic as Hermione Lee calls the scene with Nettie Struther, "the novel's most piously moralistic moment" and Nancy Topping Bazin finds this ending "a defect in Wharton's vision."[23] However, Carol Singley sees these passages as expressing a tension between the notion of salvation portrayed in sentimental women's literature and a more modern despair about the possibility of its realization. The result is a thematic disjunction. As she explains, "Wharton draws on the elements of spiritual allegory to criticize Lily, her vain society, and popular views of social and moral evolution. The goal of a Christian spiritual narrative is to chart the pilgrim's 'progress' toward moral perfection, achievable finally only in heaven." However, "spiritual allegory implies absolute values, but 'the fluctuating ethical estimates' . . . that regulate Lily's relativistic society make the use of such allegorical structures disjunctive and ironic."[24] This argument goes straight to the conflicts at the heart of the novel, and I would agree that there is much about the novel's conclusion that is deeply ironic, and yet I do not believe that that these scenes represent a disjunctive break within the novel's structure. The moment in Nettie Struther's kitchen is not an abandonment of Wharton's preceding themes, but an unveiling and culmination of them.

In *Wharton's Dialogue with Realism and Sentimentalism*, Hildegard Hoeller argues that a close examination of Wharton's career reveals that "throughout her fiction she . . . negotiated the limitations of the realist method and explored the possibilities of the sentimental tradition."[25] However, Hoeller also sees Wharton as revising "sentimental voices to condemn rather than to celebrate marriage as an 'economic' institution. In that sense, she never fully embraces the traditional ideology of sentimental domestic fiction as it was prevalent in the mid-nineteenth-century American fiction."[26] Lori Merish's far-reaching discussion of these issues as they appear in *The House of Mirth* differs on this point from Hoeller: "In Nettie Struther's warm kitchen, Wharton delineates an alternative to the realm of publicity in *home life* . . . Indeed *The House of Mirth* appeals nostalgically to the vision of uncommodified value represented in domestic fiction."[27] Citing an important essay by Jeanne Boydson, Merish argues that the novel represents Lily's quest for a home, a central theme of nineteenth-century domestic fiction; moreover, the home she seeks is "the primary sphere of private and uncommodified value."[28] Merish persuasively links this haven from commodity culture and market values to the Christian discourse of self-sacrifice and sincerity, the discourse we have seen shaping those deathbed scenes in Stowe's and Alcott's fiction. While Merish argues that "in the final pages of *The House of Mirth*, Wharton mobilizes the twinned, nineteenth-century discourses of domesticity and Christianity to define an 'alternative' to the specular logic of the consumer public sphere," she also concludes that "Wharton's 'solution' to the commodification of women within the consumer public sphere is to (re)confine them within the heterosexual economy of nineteenth-century domesticity."[29]

While I generally agree with Hoeller's assessment of Wharton's close relationship to both realism and sentimentalism, in the case of *The House of Mirth* at least, I believe that Wharton was attempting to synthesize these two traditions, not just negotiate their differences. As for Merish, while her argument is a powerful one, with much in common with my own, it seems to share with Gary Levine a perception that the novel is a "nest of contradictions" marked by ambivalence and a retreat into sentimentalism and domesticity, a retreat signified by the title of this section of Merish's essay: "Domestic Nostalgia; or, The House of Mourning."[30] Merish's conclusion about the novel's "nostalgic" turn to the domestic seems to me too narrow; it does not take into account how Wharton might be revising that discourse as even she mobilizes it. For example, to argue that Wharton reconfines women "within the heterosexual economy of nineteenth-century domesticity" does not take into account the working-class status of Nettie, who is hurrying home from a job outside the home to attend to her child. Nor does it take into account the homosocial bonds that have supported Nettie's recuperation: Gerty Farish's intervention, Lily's financial support, or even the childcare provided by the unnamed female friend who makes Nettie's labor in support of her family possible. While there is no doubt that Wharton's portrait of the tenement kitchen and its domestic harmony is an idealized one, it is significantly not an idealization celebrating a female leisure class protected from the public economic sphere. Quite the opposite. Indeed, one of the things that Nettie possesses that Lily does not, in addition to a husband and a child, is a place in the world's "machinery," a place that Lily has lost. Wharton also lightly underscores the irony of Lily's transgressive use of Gus Trenor's funds to salvage Nettie. The original intention of those funds had been a sexual exchange: access to Lily's body in exchange for Trenor's financial support. Trenor wants to buy and essentially consume Lily: to have "a seat at the table" where he presumes other men have eaten their fill. Instead, the funds have been diverted to the rescue of a working-class woman whose reputation had been ruined by another male predator.

Perhaps most importantly, while Nettie's kitchen has provided Lily a shelter from the wasteland outside and revived the currents of life in Lily's veins, this moment is only temporary. It is not enough to rescue her; if anything, it seems ultimately to make Lily's losses all the more apparent, all the more painful. Wharton's depiction of Nettie's happiness may be idealization, but it is not presented, in itself, as a cure-all for Lily's situation. And to argue that this is somehow a retreat from the previous thematic patterns also seems to miss an important mark. This is a not a turn to some "easier" solution to the social conflicts Wharton has depicted earlier; rather, it is fully of a piece with those thematic patterns, the figure in the novel's carpet. A close look at the following scenes will show why.

Out on the street, Lily initially feels strengthened: "It was the first time she had ever come across the results of her spasmodic benevolence, and the surprised sense of human fellowship took the mortal chill from her heart." Although her first response was that the "little episode had done her good," a swift reaction sets in, leaving her with a "deeper loneliness." Rather than becoming more acceptable, the boarding house with its cooking smells seems even more disturbing and, although she realizes that she needs to eat, Lily is relieved to find she has missed the mealtime. Once in her room, she is seized by a need to organize her meager remaining possessions. She turns to the chest containing her dresses and begins examine them. Overwhelmed by the associations they recall, "she was startled to find how the atmosphere of her own life enveloped her. But, after all, it was the life she had been made for: every dawning tendency in her had been carefully directed toward it, all her interests and activities had been taught to centre around it. She was like some rare flower grown for exhibition, a flower from which every bud had been nipped except the crowning blossom of her beauty" (246–47). The metaphor here is emphatically one of nurture, rather than nature. As Lily had earlier observed Nettie's infant with its tendrilling hands, reaching out to form new attachments, she now sees how her own attempts at attachment had been clipped and repressed, how that energy had been carefully redirected to one goal: the objectification of her beauty. The solitary blossom atop its precarious, denuded stem is the result.

At last Lily retrieves the Reynolds dress she wore at the Brys' *tableaux vivants*. Disembodied, it now hangs "shapelessly," a "heap of white drapery." While the scent of violets still clings to it, it is not the scent of Lily's own body that inhabits it, but her perfume. The dress represents Lily's carefully constructed self, the externalization of her aspiration for beauty and transcendence, so inextricably and contradictorily mixed with her desire for wealth and social status. The dress, like the image of Lily it projected, was indeed a "specialized product," one that in its marshalling of material resources, including Gus Trenor's money, attempted to transcend those very forces. Its neoclassicism proclaimed a freedom from temporal restraints and material accidents, a transcendence of fashion and the marketplace. Yet it was still, ironically, deeply enmeshed in those material conditions, a dependency Lily now recognizes. Although she had been unable to give the dress away, she had also been unable to look at it until this point. The materialization both of the idealized self Selden had once loved and of the ambition that had led her to reject him, its odor of violets "came to her like a breath from the flower-edged fountain where she had stood with Lawrence Selden and disowned her fate." As she replaces the dresses in their trunk, her nerves are overwrought and impressionable; she feels herself "laying away with each some gleam of light, some note of laughter, some stray waft from the rosy shores of pleasure." Again, the undertone is of mourning, of death; she is laying to rest the hopes these dresses represented and, along with them, the versions of herself they once displayed.

At this sensitive moment, the mail arrives with her legacy check, the $10,000 for which she has been waiting. At first, the amount seems full of glittering promise, especially in relation to her recent poverty. However, Lily resolutely puts the check away to dampen her fantasies of replenished wealth and turns instead to her checkbook. A disciplined survey of her finances reveals that over the past months her need for material comfort, especially her brief succumbing to luxury at the Emporium Hotel, has led her into deeper debt, despite her good intentions. If she pays all her current bills, along with the one outstanding debt to Trenor, her financial conscience will be clear, but "she would have barely enough to live on for the next three or four months; and even after that, if she were to continue her present way of living, without earning any additional money, all incidental expenses must be reduced to the vanishing point" (247–48). However, while Lily has a sharp sense of the encroaching tide of dinginess just about to flood her, "It was no longer . . . from the vision of material poverty that she turned with the greatest shrinking. She had a sense of deeper empoverishment—of an inner destitution compared to which outward conditions dwindled into insignificance." Her frustrated bid for forgiveness and love from Selden and her glimpse of Nettie's domestic happiness have given her another standard of wealth: "It was indeed miserable to be poor—to look forward to a shabby, anxious middle-age, leading by dreary degrees of economy and self-denial to gradual absorption in the dingy communal existence of the boarding-house. But there was something more miserable still—it was the clutch of solitude at her heart, the sense of being swept away like a stray uprooted growth down the heedless current of the years." Now the imagery has shifted from the crowning bloom on its insecure, bare stem to a plant torn from its ground: "That was the feeling which possessed her now—the feeling of being something rootless and ephemeral, mere spin-drift of the whirling surface of existence, without anything to which the poor little tentacles of self could cling before the awful flood submerged them." The crowning blossom of her beauty has lost its use and Lily finds herself helpless and, what is more disturbing, she is fully aware of her helplessness and its source:

> And as she looked back she saw that there had never been a time when she had had any real relation to life. Her parents too had been rootless, blown hither and thither on every wind of fashion, without any personal existence to shelter them from its shifting gusts. She herself had grown up without any one spot of earth being dearer to her than another: there was no centre of early pieties, of grave endearing traditions, to which her heart could revert and from which it could draw strength for itself and tenderness for others. In whatever form a slowly-accumulated past lives in the blood—whether in the concrete image of the old house stored with visual memories, or in the conception of the house not built with hands—it has

the same power of broadening and deepening the individual existence, of attaching it by mysterious links of kinship to all the mighty sum of human striving. (248)

This complex passage, much cited by Wharton's critics, seems virtually a thesis statement, a kind of unveiling of Wharton's own thematic concerns. With its heightened language and emotional excess it recalls, as those critics have noted, the sentimental passages we have seen earlier in Stowe and Alcott.[31] Moreover, despite the reference to "blood," the full passage also refers to a "slowly-accumulated past," again a reference to history and nurture rather than nature alone. The narrator significantly does not designate only one way that an individual's life can be broadened and deepened. Rather, while an other-worldly faith, the "conception of the house not made by hands," might provide shelter from the awful flood of death and mortality, so too might attachment to a material home, stored with "visual memories," a foundation for familial and personal associations. The place that Nettie has found is not the only source of such security; there is also Gerty Farish's sense of mission, based on solidarity of feeling with those poorer and more disadvantaged than herself. The point is that a realized, fulfilled life must be founded on some faith, some hope, and that it is must be supported by affiliation with others, by a connection to "the continuity of life." As pride is a barrier to this affiliation, so humility, compassion, and forgiveness are the path. The core conception is connection to others and through them to the "mighty sum of human striving" as a shelter from the terror of death and a way of giving a larger meaning to individual existence.

Taught from an early age to resist such attachments and the self-transcending values they enable, Lily finds this conception entirely new: "Such a vision of the solidarity of life had never before come to Lily. She had had a premonition of it in the blind motions of her mating-instinct; but they had been checked by the disintegrating influences of the life about it. All the men and women she knew were like atoms whirling away from each other in some wild centrifugal dance: her first glimpse of the continuity of life had come to her that evening in Nettie Struther's kitchen."[32] The continuity of life that Lily glimpses encompasses, perhaps even originates in moments like Nettie's cryptic dialogue with her daughter, in the bonds between parent and child — the emotional rhythms of attachment and loss, connection and separation — that propel human development.[33] In the "blind motions of her mating-instinct," the narrator recalls Lily's almost involuntary attraction to Selden, her "putting forth of eager feelers" toward him, much like the tendrilling hands of Nettie's infant. However, these motions were "blind" in that Lily was never taught to understand their meaning; hence she "disowns her fate." She was not taught the read the signs of her own emotions; the word "love" was alien to her. Now, "the poor little working-girl who had found strength to gather up the fragments of her life, and build herself a shelter with them, seemed to Lily to have reached the central truth of existence. It was a meager enough life, on the grim edge of poverty, with scant margin for possibilities of sickness or mischance, but it had the frail audacious permanence of a bird's nest built on the edge of a cliff—a mere wisp of leaves and straw, yet so put together that the lives entrusted to it may hang safely over the abyss." However, Lily also sees now that "it had taken two to build the nest; the man's faith as well as the woman's courage. Lily remembered Nettie's words: *I knew he knew about me.* Her husband's faith in her had made her renewal possible—it is so easy for a woman to become what the man she loves believes her to be!" (248–49).

Even though Lily, in her confession to Selden earlier that evening, had revealed her own need for his faith and forgiveness, she now acknowledges his apparent inability to recognize or respond to that need:

> Selden had twice been ready to stake his faith on Lily Bart; but the third trial had been too severe for his endurance. The very quality of his love had made it the more impossible to recall to life. If it had been a simple instinct of the blood, the power of her beauty might have revived it. But the fact that it struck deeper, that it was inextricably bound up with inherited habits of thought and feeling, made it as impossible to restore to growth as a deep-rooted plant torn from its bed. Selden had given her of his best; but he was as incapable as herself of an uncritical return to former states of feeling. (249)

Selden's own training, his own reliance on ideals of independence and honor, undergirded his admiration for Lily's idealized image and potential for transcendence. However, her understanding of him now leads Lily to believe that this inheritance would also render him unable to forgive her when that image and potential were compromised. Just as he had despaired of her ability to move beyond her materialistic training, and so retreated to the conventional view of her character, so she now despairs of his ability to see her whole:

> There remained to her, as she had told, the uplifting memory of his faith in her; but she had not reached the age when a woman can live on her memories. As she held Nettie Struther's child in her arms the frozen currents of youth had loosed themselves and run warm in her veins: the old life-hunger possessed her, and all her being clamoured for its share of personal happiness. Yes—it was happiness she still wanted, and the glimpse

she had caught of it made everything else of no account. One by one she had detached herself from the baser possibilities, and she saw that nothing now remained to her but the emptiness of renunciation. (249)

Early in the novel Lily had reflected that, unlike Gerty Farish, who wished to be good, she wished to be happy. By "happy" Lily had meant being admired, wealthy, and lapped in luxury. By the novel's conclusion, like the surviving March sisters of *Little Women*, she has revised her definition of happiness. Now she wishes to love and be loved. And the model for her happiness is no longer the fashionable rich wives whose comfortable lives she had envied, but the working girl whose tiny kitchen has sheltered her. And, yes, this image of happiness is, as critics have said, banal. That, I would argue, is Wharton's point, as it was Tolstoy's in the famous opening lines of *Anna Karenina*: "Happy families are all alike; every unhappy family is unhappy in its own way."[34] The simplicity, the everydayness, the commonness of this scene makes its inaccessibility to Lily all the more poignant and disturbing. Moreover, while Wharton's narrator stresses the simplicity and efficacy of the Struthers' love and trust, which has woven the fragments of Nettie's once-ruined life back together, she also stresses the fragility and audacity of this nest situated, pointedly, on the edge of an abyss. Domestic love and happiness may seem or even be banal, but they are also hard-won, fragile, and endangered on every side. However much Lily may wish to emulate this seemingly artless model, its realization lies far beyond her reach.

And so, while her hunger for life is reawakened by this vision, so is Lily's sense of isolation and despair: "It was growing late, and an immense weariness once more possessed her. It was not the stealing sense of sleep, but a vivid wakeful fatigue, a wan lucidity of mind against which all the possibilities of the future were shadowed forth gigantically. She was appalled by the intense clearness of the vision; she seemed to have broken through the merciful veil which intervenes between intention and action, and to see exactly what she would do in all the long days to come" (249). This strange lucidity seems a distorted version of the deathbed vision granted to Stowe's and Alcott's characters: a removal of the veil between intention and action, another kind of personal apocalypse and judgment day. And in this moment Lily sees magnified her own fragmented character with its divided motives and vacillating will: "There was the cheque in her desk, for instance — she meant to use it in paying her debt to Trenor; but she foresaw that when the morning came she would put off doing so, would slip into the gradual tolerance of the debt. The thought terrified her — she dreaded to fall from the height of her last moment with Lawrence Selden. But how could she trust herself to keep her footing? She knew the strength of the opposing impulses — she could feel the countless hands of habit dragging her back into some fresh compromise with fate" (249). An addict who knows her addiction all too well, who acknowledges her lack of control over her desire, Lily agonizes over what the future will bring, her inability to sustain the moral height she had attained when, unseen, she burned the letters in Selden's fire: "She felt an intense longing to prolong, to perpetuate, the momentary exaltation of her spirit. If only life could end now — end on this tragic yet sweet vision of lost possibilities, which gave her a sense of kinship with all the loving and foregoing in the world!" Lily's impulsive wish raises again the specter of suicide. Just as the burning of the letters was an immolation of her main access to material well-being, she turns once more to the idea of sacrificing her financial survival as an affirmation of the anti-materialistic ideals Selden has taught her: "She reached out suddenly and, drawing the cheque from her writing-desk, enclosed it in an envelope which she addressed to her bank. She then wrote out a cheque for Trenor, and placing it, without an accompanying word, in an envelope inscribed with his name, laid the two letters side by side on her desk. After that she continued to sit at the table, sorting her papers and writing, till the intense silence of the house reminded her of the lateness of the hour" (249).

Wharton's treatment of Lily's attempt to meet the demands of her conscience is complex and deeply ironic. Although, according to Selden's severe standards, she has done the right thing by reconciling her debts, the result is surprisingly and emphatically not the peace of a satisfied conscience. When Mara Lincoln fights for the "victory" over her longing for life and its material satisfactions, she is granted a blessed sleep from which she awakens spiritually renewed and accepting of her death; she sees her individuality merged and lost in the immensity of God's love. Lily's attempt to achieve a similar victory over her material needs results not in peace but near-psychosis. As she sits at her boarding-house desk, she hears the vague noises of the city through a "deep unnatural hush" (249). If Lily's goal was to attach her self to the mighty sum of human striving, the effort has misfired, with unintended consequences: "In the mysterious nocturnal separation from all outward signs of life, she felt herself more strangely confronted with her fate. The sensation made her brain reel, and she tried to shut out consciousness by pressing her hands against her eyes. But the terrible silence and emptiness seemed to symbolize her future — she felt as though the house, the street, the world were all empty, and she alone left sentient in a lifeless universe" (250).

Her sacrifice has left her even more isolated, more bereft, not merged with the ocean of divine love, but alone in "a lifeless universe." The imagery recalls the prophet Jeremiah's Valley of the Shadow of Death, the valley through which

Bunyan's Christian made his solitary way, and also anticipates the landscape of T. S. Eliot's classic 1922 poem "The Waste Land." It is a vast merciless space, devoid of hope or love: "But this was the verge of delirium . . . she had never hung so near the dizzy brink of the unreal. . . . It was as though a blaze of electric light had been turned on in her head, and her poor little anguished self shrank and cowered in it, without knowing where to take refuge." The acts of burning the letters and paying her bills are like the image of herself at the *tableaux vivants* — self-constructions designed to project an image of moral responsibility and purification — but they are not the whole Lily any more than the vision in the white dress was. If anything, Lily's sacrifices have left her more isolated, more in need, more humanly alone. Most importantly, there is no one to witness her sacrifices, no one to forgive her weakness, no one to confer the love that would allow her to live with her thoughts and bring body and soul together. Render unto Caesar the things that are Caesar's: she has done that, but it is not enough to sustain her. She has performed the works of morality, but the solace of grace still eludes her.

The anguish and disappointment of this moment recalls an earlier Wharton story, *The Bunner Sisters*. There, Anna Eliza's relinquishing of a possible suitor in favor of her sister results not in her sister's happiness or her own, but the sister's disastrous marriage to an opium addict. Faced with these unintended consequences, Anna Eliza senses the "inutility of self-sacrifice" and loses her faith in a God that could permit such an outcome. Where once there had once been a promise of divine justice, now there is only "a black abyss above the roof of Bunner Sisters."[35] In Wharton's world, as in James's, there is no providential system to reward moral sacrifice in this life or in the hereafter. In signing away her legacy, Lily made her bid to join the republic of the spirit, but the severing of her ties to material survival results not in the peace of the righteous but an emerging terror of her own mortality. Nettie had renewed her will to live through her husband's love and faith. While the Struthers' fragile nest hangs precariously over the edge of the abyss, Lily looks over the edge of that abyss alone and unsupported, without shelter or refuge. She seems to inhabit a psychic immensity, an infinite space that exposes her to a blinding glare of unforgiving scrutiny. Lily has gained self-awareness; but without love or mercy, her awareness is frightening and destructive.

At the climax of book 1, Lily turned to Gerty in her desperate need to escape the gaze of the imagined furies who stood in judgment around her bed, a fearsome substitute for the admiring audience who had applauded her performance at the *tableaux vivants*. And Gerty, responding to her friend's guilt and distress, comforted Lily until she could finally sleep, taking Lily into her own bed and holding her as a mother makes a "nest for a tossing child." That scene is then paralleled by Nettie's solacing of her distraught daughter, lonely and hungry in her crib. Here also the mother makes a shelter for her child, a shelter in which the child's greed and rage — "Was it angry with Mommer?" Nettie asks — are forgiven and assuaged. The child's emotions, however negative, are named and accepted in a primal moment of maternal dialogue. Now, alone in her room, Lily cannot find the means to comfort herself. Never truly mothered, she cannot sooth the troubled child within her. And once more she turns to the chloral: "Sleep was what she wanted — she remembered that she had not closed her eyes for two nights. The little bottle was at her bedside, waiting to lay its spell upon her" (250).

Surprisingly, Lily's reasoning as she measures what will prove to be a fatal dose is not as overtly suicidal as when she determined to drain her checking account. In fact, her thinking, confused though it is, seems based on her desire to withstand the pain and turmoil she feels: "She had not imagined that such a multiplication of wakefulness was possible: her whole past was reenacting itself at a hundred different points of consciousness. Where was the drug that could still this legion of insurgent nerves? The sense of exhaustion would have been sweet compared to this shrill beat of activities; but weariness had dropped from her as though some cruel stimulant had been forced into her veins" (250). As when she had turned to the chloral before, she sees the drug as a means of renewal, a way to sleep to regain her strength: "She could bear it — yes, she could bear it; but what strength would be left her the next day? Perspective had disappeared — the next day pressed close upon her like a shrieking mob. She must shut them out for a few hours; she must take a brief bath of oblivion." Lily knows the dosage the chemist recommended, and yet "tonight she felt she must increase it. She knew she took a slight risk in doing so — she remembered the chemist's warning. If sleep came at all, it might be a sleep without waking. . . . She did not, in truth, consider the question very closely — the physical craving for sleep was her only sustained sensation. Her mind shrank from the glare of thought as instinctively as eyes contract in a blaze of light — darkness, darkness was what she must have at any cost" (250).

After swallowing the dose and blowing out her candle, Lily "lay very still, waiting with sensuous pleasure for the first effects of the soporific." Wharton's description of the drug's action subtly mimics the earlier soothing of Nettie's baby: "The gradual cessation of the inner throb, the soft approach of passiveness, as though an invisible hand made magic passes over her in the darkness" (250). Now her frightening sense of precarious suspension over an abyss is transformed: "The very slowness and hesitancy of the effect increased its fascination: it was delicious to lean over and look down into the dim abysses of unconsciousness." And, given her heightened tension,

> tonight the drug seemed to work more slowly than usual: each passionate pulse had to be stilled in turn, and it was a long while before she felt them dropping down into abeyance, like sentinels falling asleep at their posts. But gradually the sense of complete subjugation came over her, and she wondered languidly what had made her feel so uneasy and excited. She saw now there was nothing to be excited about — she had returned to her normal view of life. Tomorrow would not be so difficult after all: she felt sure that she would have the strength to meet it. She did not quite remember what it was that she had been afraid to meet, but now the uncertainty no longer troubled her. (251)

Like the infant whose hunger has been satiated and anxiety assuaged, Lily relaxes into a sleepy sense of well-being and renewed security: "She had been unhappy, and now she was happy — she had felt herself alone, and now the sense of loneliness had vanished" (251).

Wharton underlines the parallel by making it explicit: "She stirred once, and turned on her side, and as she did so, she suddenly understood why she did not feel herself alone. It was odd — but Nettie Struther's child was lying on her arm: she felt the pressure of its little head against her shoulder. She did not know how it had come there, but she felt no great surprise at the fact, only a gentle penetrating thrill of warmth and pleasure." With a movement mimicking the way Gerty had once "made a nest" to soothe her own distress, Lily now "settled herself into an easier position, hollowing her arm to pillow the round downy head, and holding her breath lest a sound disturb the sleeping child." The hallucinated child makes visible the psychological effect of the drug itself; it has provided the solace Lily was unable to muster alone. She is both child and mother, shelter and sheltered. And with this comes an emergent awareness, just on the edge of her drowsy consciousness: "As she lay there she said to herself that there was something she must tell Selden, some word she had found that should make life clear between them. She tried to repeat the word, which lingered vague and luminous on the far edge of thought — she was afraid of not remembering it when she woke; and if she could only remember it and say it to him, she felt that everything would be well." And yet this word, expressive of the well-being she now feels, slowly fades as she is overcome by sleep: "She struggled faintly against it, feeling that she ought to keep awake on account of the baby; but even this feeling was gradually lost in an indistinct sense of drowsy peace, through which, of a sudden, a dark flash of loneliness and terror tore its way." This dark flash is the loneliness and anxiety she is trying to escape, as well as the death toward which the drug is slowly, seductively leading her, masking its ultimate destination in the simulacrum of love and well-being. For a moment that drugged veil lifts and the glare of the terror she is desperately trying to evade breaks through: "She started up again, cold and trembling with the shock: for a moment she seemed to have lost her hold of the child. But no — she was mistaken — the tender pressure of its body was still close to hers: the recovered warmth flowed through her once more, she yielded to it, sank into it, and slept" (250–51).

In James Baldwin's classic story of addiction, "Sonny's Blues" (1957), the narrator, who has learned that his younger brother, Sonny, has been jailed for heroin possession, asks Sonny's friend, a fellow junkie, why his brother wants to kills himself. The friend replies, surprised, "Don't anybody want to kill himself. Sonny wants to live."[36] Much later, when the brothers have reunited and are attempting to reconcile, the narrator asks the same question directly of Sonny. His brother replies, simply, that heroin helped him survive, kept his life from shaking apart. Just as there is a curious ambiguity, a self-destructive component in Lily's morally sacrificial acts, there is a seeking of renewal in her use of chloral. It is the "life-hunger" in her, what Stowe called the desire for life "inwoven in our nature," that leads to her taking the fatal dose.[37] In this, the drug becomes yet another duplicitous path on her quest, one promising salvation and relief from the terror of mortality, but leading, in this case directly and literally, to death.

Seen from this perspective, by burning the letters and sacrificing her legacy, Lily effectively severs her access to the means of her material, bodily survival. Her confession to Selden thus becomes a kind of retrospective suicide note. In this final scene, writing out her checks, there is no speech, no confession, only a lonely act. She has become independent of her mentor, reading the signs alone, a true Protestant individualist. However, her final turn to the chloral and her dying dream of the comforted child reveal the emotional poverty of this conception of the self: its incompleteness and its tragic limitation. Selden has taught her to read the signs, but she, like her teacher, is missing a crucial word. Missing this word, his vision cannot sustain her; she cannot live on virtue alone. In her last dialogue with him, she confessed, "I have tried hard — but life is difficult, and I am a very useless person. I can hardly be said to have an independent existence. I was just a screw or a cog in the great machine I called life, and when I dropped out of it I found I was of no use anywhere else." Lily adopted Selden's vision of the need to be "free of material accidents." Judging herself by that high standard, she concluded, harshly, that she "can hardly be said to have an independent existence." And yet no one truly has an independent existence; no one is free from material accidents. All are caught in the dialectical, dialogical relationship of self and other, individual and society, material needs and idealistic hopes. Lily does what she believes Selden would require, but she cannot endure the human consequences alone.

Just as Wharton uses dramatic irony to turn the blessed rest of the righteous, conflated with the sleep of a beloved child, into the horror of a drug overdose, she uses the imagery of renewal to deepen the poignancy of Lily's death and the shock of Selden's loss. Lily's nearly seamless transition from sleep to death evokes those earlier sentimental deathbed scenes, with their victorious deaths seeming as natural as sleep. More specifically, it evokes Beth March's own death, cradled on her mother's breast. In those scenes, as we have seen, the survivors also achieve a victory over their attachment to life: accepting the translation of the dead into spiritual life through their affirmation of faith in an immortal love, the only thing, Beth tells Jo, that we can take with us. Later, as they view the tranquil face of the beloved dead, the mourners are surrounded by the imagery of renewal, of morning and springtime. And so Wharton's last chapter begins the morning following Lily's final sleep. The day is "mild and bright, with a promise of summer in the air" (251). A joyous burst of sunshine "gilds" Lily's dingy boardinghouse and tries to enter the window of her window. Selden, "intoxicated" with this new promise, wakes with a "youthful sense of adventure. He had cut loose from the familiar shores of habit, and launched himself on uncharted seas of emotion" (252). Although it is only 9 o'clock in the morning, too early for a polite visit, Selden suddenly feels himself past "all such conventional observances." As Lily had done only the evening before, suddenly Selden has shed his reserve: "He only knew that he must see Lily Bart at once — he had found the word he meant to say to her, and it could not wait another moment to be said. It was strange that it had not come to his lips sooner — that he had let it pass from him the evening before without being able to speak it. But what did that matter, now that a new day had come? It was not a word for twilight, but for the morning" (252).[38] Although Lily had despaired of Selden's ability to change — to accept and forgive her, despite her divided nature and frailty — Selden himself has "launched himself onto uncharted seas of emotion." Lily's confession has slowly done its work: awakening his compassion, transforming his vision, and opening him to the renewal of love.

And yet, when he arrives at the boarding house, where Lily's window with its pot of pansies provides the "one touch of beauty in the dingy scene," a surprised Selden is met by Gerty Farish and led to Lily's room: "Though the blind was drawn the irresistible sunlight poured a tempered golden flood into the room, and in its light Selden saw a narrow bed along the wall, and on the bed, with motionless hands, and calm unrecognizing face, the semblance of Lily Bart." Confronted with this still life, Selden resists naming what he sees: "That it was her real self, every pulse in him ardently denied. Her real self had lain warm on his heart but a few hours earlier — what had he to do with this estranged and tranquil face which, for the first time, neither paled nor brightened at his coming?" (252–53). Now he associates the real Lily not with some idealized, sculptural image but with the paling and brightening of her blood, the fluctuations of her spirit, visible beneath the surface. Although Gerty warns that, because the doctor has found the bottle of chloral, the authorities will be arriving soon to investigate the scene, he is still transfixed: "Selden was hardly conscious of what she said. He stood looking down on the sleeping face which seemed to lie like a delicate impalpable mask over the living lineaments he had known. He felt that the real Lily was still there, close to him, yet invisible and inaccessible; and the tenuity of the barrier between them mocked him with a sense of helplessness. There had never been more than a little impalpable barrier between them — and yet he had suffered it to keep them apart! And now, though it seemed slighter and frailer than ever, it had suddenly hardened to adamant, and he might beat his life out against it in vain" (253). The conflict between surface and depth has reached its crisis. The pride and reserve that separated them have hardened into an unbridgeable barrier. Closed the night before to the love Lily might have offered, Selden now brings the word that might have saved her, but too late. She has become as cold and impervious as the jewel she once wished to become.[39]

The revelation that you have missed your chance, that the window of opportunity has closed forever, is a persistent theme in Wharton's fiction, as well as that of her mentor and friend Henry James. In James's "The Beast in the Jungle" (1903), John Marcher remembers only after May Bartram's death how she, dangerously ill but still possibly "all recoverable," had stood before him offering her love wordlessly, an offer that, had he reciprocated, might have turned the tide of her life. So, Newland Archer in Wharton's *The Age of Innocence* (1920) fails to recognize his growing passion for the exotic Ellen Olenska, rushing instead into the safety of a proposal of marriage to the conventional May Welland. Then, just as he manages to declare his love for Ellen, a telegram from May arrives announcing their wedding arrangements. Looking back from a distance of decades, Newland muses that in failing to seize the moment with Ellen, he missed "the flower of life," but also that gaining that flower would have been as rare an achievement as winning the lottery, as much a matter of chance as character. Selden's missed opportunity is certainly of a piece with these other literary moments, as is his belated awareness of his failure and its source.[40]

Left alone by Gerty, who tells Selden in her wisdom that this is what Lily would have wished, Selden begins to search the room before the medical examiner comes. Avoiding the blank mirror that once reflected Lily's face, he finds the unsealed envelop addressed to Gus Trenor and, tempted to open it, refrains. Nevertheless, the doubts he had dispelled now return and he cannot help but wonder if his willingness to risk himself in that gilded morning light was justified. He then finds the note he had written Lily after the *tableaux vivants*, asking when he could come to her. He had reneged on his offer to come, but she had saved the note in spite of his abandonment: "His words overwhelmed him with a realization of the cowardice which had driven him from her at the very moment of attainment. Yes — he had always feared his fate, and he was too honest to disown his cowardice now; for had not all his old doubts started to life again at the mere sight of Trenor's name." Next, Selden opens the check-book, the most telling body of evidence in the room. There he finds the record of the legacy, its deposit, the payment of all the bills, including the large check made out to Trenor, and the final balance, drawn down to near-zero.

As Selden struggles to read these last signs of Lily's life, he finally pieces together the fragments of a narrative: "It was true then that she had taken money from Trenor; but true also, as the contents of the little desk declared, that the obligation had become intolerable to her, and that at the first opportunity she had freed herself from it, though the act left her face to face with unmitigated poverty" (255). Selden admits that this is "all he could hope to unravel of the story." He will never learn more from "the mute lips on the pillow . . . unless indeed they had told him the rest in the kiss they had left upon his forehead." However, he "could now read into that farewell all that his heart craved to find there; he could even find the courage not to accuse himself for having failed to reach the height of his opportunity" (255). As if resuming an interrupted dialogue with the dead woman before him, Selden confesses his complicity in their mutual failure: "He saw that the all the conditions of life conspired to keep them apart; since his very detachment from the external influences which swayed her had increased his spiritual fastidiousness, and made it made difficult for him to live and love uncritically." And yet, despite Lily's own loss of faith him as she turned to the bottle of chloral for solace, he tells himself, "at least he *had* loved her — had been willing to stake his future on his faith in her — and if the moment had been fated to pass from them before they could seize it, he saw now that, for both, it had been saved whole out of the ruin of their lives."

Selden now understands what Lily had meant in that last confession, how the memory of his faith in her had helped her: "It was this moment of love, this fleeting victory over themselves, which had kept them from atrophy and extinction;

which, in her, had reached out to him in every struggle against the influence of her surroundings, and in him, had kept alive that faith that now drew him penitent and reconciled to her side" (255–56). Yet it is not their lives that have been saved, nor even themselves. Only that one illuminated moment has been rescued from the ruin. Although this scene is one of perfect sincerity, confession, and reconciliation, it cannot save anyone, not even the survivor. While the veil between remembered intention and action has been rendered transparent, the veil between Lily and Selden will always remain. The love that might have lifted it can no longer be shared: "He knelt by the bed and bent over her, draining their last moment to its lees; and in the silence there passed between them the word which made all clear" (255–56). With that word passing in silence, since the moment in which it could truly live has passed, Selden is left with only the consolation of understanding. While much has been made of the "word unsaid" as the last word of the novel, the novel's actual last word is "clear." For Selden, it will have to suffice.

Notes

Because source material relating to this study,
including *Little Women* and *The House of Mirth*, is so
voluminous, making it impractical to include all such material
in the print edition of the book, extended notes prepared by the
author are being made available online. These electronic notes,
available on the *Sacramental Shopping* book detail page at
www.upne.com, supplement the notes printed here.

INTRODUCTION

EPIGRAPHS: *The Random House College Dictionary*, ed. Laurence Urdang (New York: Random House, 1972), 1159; Jean Baudrillard, *The Consumer Society, Myths and Structures* (1970; rpt. London: Sage, 1998), 3.

1. H. Barbara Weinberg, "Hassam in New York, 1889–1896," in *Childe Hassam, American Impressionist*, ed. H. Barbara Weinberg (New York: Yale University Press, 2004), 87–117. For more on Hassam and Tiffany's, see e-note.

2. For the history of the Tiffany box see www.tiffany.com/about/thetiffanystory/tiffany bluebox. For more details about the box, including a reference to it in Wharton's fiction, see e-note.

3. For research on the modern Christmas celebration, see e-note.

4. Louisa May Alcott, *Little Women*, ed. with an intro. by Madelon Bedell (1868–69; rpt. New York: Modern Library, 1983); Edith Wharton, *The House of Mirth*, ed. with an intro. by Elizabeth Ammons (1905; rpt. New York: Norton, 1990). Further references to these texts will be noted parenthetically. For scholarship on the rise of modern consumer culture, see e-note.

5. Thorstein Veblen, *The Theory of the Leisure Class*, ed. with an intro. by Martha Banta (1899; rpt. New York: Oxford University Press, 2007).

6. Edith Wharton, *A Backward Glance: An Autobiography* (1933, 1934; rpt. New York: Touchstone, 1998), 51.

7. Amazon.com currently lists well over fifty editions of *Little Women* in various formats including audiobooks and e-books. For more on the sales and popularity of *Little Women* and *The House of Mirth*, see e-note.

8. Max Weber, *The Protestant Ethic and the Spirit of Capitalism*, trans. Talcott Parsons (1904–5; rpt. New York: Scribner, 1958).

9. Colin Campbell, *The Romantic Ethic and the Spirit of Modern Consumerism* (Oxford: Blackwell, 1987).

10. John Bunyan, *The Pilgrim's Progress*, ed. by Catherine Stimson (1678; rpt. New York:

New American Library, 1964), 61. For the purpose of readability, I have quoted from an edition prepared by Catherine Stimson and based on the authoritative Oxford University Press version edited by James Blanton Wharey in 1928 and revised by Roger Sharrock in 1960. According to Stimson's "Note on the Text," this edition "modifies the seventeenth-century text, but the changes are as limited as possible, and those changes that do occur have been made only for the sake of lucidity, simplicity, and consistency." See also John Bunyan, *Grace Abounding to the Chief of Sinners and The Pilgrim's Progress from This World to That Which Is to Come*, ed. Roger Sharrock (1678; rpt. London: Oxford University Press, 1960, 1966).

11. Howard Mumford Jones, *American and French Culture, 1750–1848* (Chapel Hill: University of North Carolina Press, 1927), 290. See also Rosalind H. Williams, *Dream Worlds: Mass Consumption in Late Nineteenth-Century France* (Berkeley: University of California Press, 1982); Valerie Steel, *Paris Fashion: A Cultural History* (New York: Oxford University Press, 1988).

12. Henry David Thoreau, *Walden* (1854); rpt. in *The Portable Thoreau*, ed. Carl Bode (New York: Penguin, 1975), 280, 278.

13. *The Oxford English Dictionary's* definition of "materialism" addresses the historical link between materialism and sacramentalism directly: "2. Transferred uses. a. Applied in reproach to theological views (e.g., on the operation of the sacraments or the nature of the future life) that are supposed to imply a defective sense of the reality of things purely spiritual" (230–31). For examples of usage, the *OED* offers: "*1850* ROBERTSON *Serm.* III: vii (1863) 103 The miserable materialism of the mass. *1898* J.R. ILLINGWORTH *Div Immanence* vi 143 The growth of the sacramental system was an historical necessity; which, despite of the religious materialism into which it too frequently lapsed [etc.]" (231). *The Compact Edition of the Oxford English Dictionary* (New York: Oxford University Press, 1971). For a thorough discussion of these associations see David Hawkes, *Idols of the Marketplace: Idolatry and Commodity Fetishism in English Literature, 1580–1680* (New York: Palgrave, 2001).

14. Charles J. Rzepka's *Sacramental Commodities: Gift, Text, and the Sublime in De Quincy* (Amherst: University of Massachusetts Press, 1995) examines the life and work of British Romantic writer Thomas de Quincy, who, in contrast to the American writers discussed here, turned to a re-visioned Catholic sacramentalism as a response to the rise of the modern market economy. For more on De Quincy, see e-note.

15. There is an extensive scholarship on the gendering of consumption as female. See, for example, the theoretically sophisticated and complex analyses of middle-class women's consumption in Elizabeth Kowaleski-Wallace, *Consuming Subjects: Women, Shopping, and Business in the Eighteenth-Century* (New York: Columbia University Press, 1997); and Lori Merish, *Sentimental Materialism: Gender, Commodity Culture, and Nineteenth-Century American Literature* (Durham, NC: Duke University Press, 2000). For more on gender and consumption, including passages from both Kowaleski-Wallace and Merish, see e-note.

16. As Thorstein Veblen explained, upper-class women were both leisured and a symbol of the leisure class: "It is still felt that woman's life, in its civil, economic, and social bearing, is essentially and normally a vicarious life, the merit or demerit of which is . . . to be imputed to some other individual who stands in some relation of ownership or tutelage to the woman" (229–30).

17. The scholarship on the Transcendentalist movement and the Alcott family is too extensive to do it justice here. However, recent important studies of that relationship include

the following: John Matteson, *Eden's Outcasts: The Story of Louisa May Alcott and Her Father* (New York: W. W. Norton, 2007) and Philip F. Gura, *American Transcendentalism: A History* (New York: Hill and Wang, 2007). Other key texts are cited in chap. 1.

18. For a thorough discussion of the importance of "sincere" self-presentation to Victorian moralists, see Karen Halttunen's *Confidence Men and Painted Women: A Study of Middle-Class Culture in America, 1820–1870* (New Haven, CT: Yale University Press, 1982).

19. Webb Keane, "Sincerity, 'Modernity,' and the Protestants," *Cultural Anthropology* 17, no. 1 (2002): 65–92. Keane's analysis of the Protestant emphasis on "sincerity" has clear affinities with Karen Halttunen's earlier analysis. In *Roads to Rome: The Antebellum Encounter with Catholicism* (Berkeley: University of California Press, 1994), Jenny Franchot argues that Catholicism served as an oppositional "other," unifying Protestants against a common enemy (xvii). See also: Susan M. Griffin, *Anti-Catholicism and Nineteenth-Century American Fiction* (New York: Cambridge University Press, 2004). For more on Franchot's discussion of anti-Catholic sentiment in the period, see e-note.

20. One of the most important mid-nineteenth-century texts on child-rearing and moral development was by Horace Bushnell, a leading liberal theologian: "Discourses on Christian Nurture" (1847), in *Views on Christian Nurture and of Subjects Adjacent Thereto* (1847; rpt. Delmar, NY: Scholar's Facsimiles and Reprints, 1975), 1–121. Bushnell rejected the orthodox Calvinist belief in the child's original sin and natural depravity and instead argued for the individual's childhood openness to human influence, particularly the influence of the family. Moral development proceeded through human attachment and emotional interaction, not through crisis conversion. For more on Bushnell's ideas, their affinities with modern psychology, and their influence on writers such as Harriet Beecher Stowe, see e-note.

21. These dialogues reflect Bronson Alcott's educational theories as practiced both within his family and at his experimental Temple School in Boston. The Socratic method was the heart of Bronson Alcott's pedagogy, and a five-volume edition of Plato's dialogues was one of his most treasured possessions, alongside *The Pilgrim's Progress*. See Matteson, *Eden's Outcasts*, 55–85. Elizabeth Palmer Peabody, who taught at the Temple School, offers an important contemporary description in *The Record of a School: Exemplifying the General Principles of Spiritual Culture* (Boston: James Monroe, 1835).

22. The groundbreaking work on this shift came from Ann Douglas's *The Feminization of American Culture* (New York: Knopf, 1977), which generated vigorous rebuttal from other feminist scholars, most notably Jane Tompkins, in *Sensational Designs: The Cultural Work of American Fiction* (New York: Oxford University Press, 1985). For a more detailed discussion of these debates, as well as later critiques of their underlying assumptions, see e-note.

23. Overall, my own approach to sentimentalism is closest to Mary Louise Kete's in *Sentimental Collaborations: Mourning and Middle-Class Identity in Nineteenth-Century America* (Durham, NC: Duke University Press, 2000). For more on Kete's approach, see e-note.

24. While Alcott sidesteps these larger social structural questions in *Little Women*, she does address them more directly in her later novel *Work*, which is more socially progressive and even radical, but also substantially less popular, perhaps for that reason (*Work: A Story of Experience*, ed. with an introduction by Joy S. Kasson [New York: Penguin, 1994]). See also Matteson, *Eden's Outcasts*, 377–82; Carolyn R. Maibar, *Labor Pains: Emerson, Hawthorne, and Alcott on Work and the Woman Question* (New York: Routledge, 2004).

25. Louisa May Alcott, *Jo's Boys, and How They Turned Out* (1886; rpt. Boston: Little,

Brown, 1925), 357; Edith Wharton, *The Gods Arrive* (New York: Charles Scribner's Sons, 1932), 418–19.

26. Wharton's title and epigraph are taken from Ecclesiastes 7:4: "The heart of the wise is in the house of mourning, but the heart of fools is in the house of mirth."

27. Carol Singley, *Edith Wharton: Matters of Mind and Spirit* (New York: Oxford University Press, 1995); Katherine Joslin, *Edith Wharton and the Making of Fashion* (Durham: University of New Hampshire Press, 2009); Maureen Montgomery, *Displaying Women: Spectacles of Leisure in Edith Wharton's New York* (New York: Routledge, 1998).

28. Irene Goldman-Price, "The 'Perfect Jew' and *The House of Mirth*: A Study in Point of View," in *The House of Mirth: A Casebook*, ed. Carol J. Singley (New York: Oxford University Press, 2003), 163–79; Gary Levine, *The Merchant of Modernism: The Economic Jew in Anglo-American Literature, 1864–1939* (New York: Routledge, 2003); Hildegard Hoeller, *Edith Wharton's Dialogue with Realism and Sentimental Fiction* (Gainesville: University of Florida Press, 2000); Lori Merish, "Engendering Naturalism: Narrative Form and Commodity Spectacle in U. S. Naturalist Fiction," in *House of Mirth: A Casebook*, 229–70.

29. See: T. J. Jackson Lears, "From Salvation to Self-Realization: Advertising and the Therapeutic Roots of the Consumer Society, 1880–1930," in *The Culture of Consumption: Critical Essays in American History, 1880–1990*, ed. Richard Wrightman Fox and T. J. Jackson Lears (New York: Pantheon, 1983), 1–38. Ann Douglas also argues for closes link between liberal Protestantism, consumer culture, and the "therapeutic ethos." See also Philip Rieff, *The Triumph of the Therapeutic: The Uses of Faith After Freud* (New York: Harper and Row, 1966).

30. For therapeutic approaches to the treatment of destructive materialistic behavior, including compulsive consumption, see Tim Kasser and Allen D. Kanner, eds., *Psychology and Consumer Culture: The Struggle for a Good Life in a Materialistic World* (Washington, D.C.: American Psychological Association, 2003). An extensive literature has developed on the therapeutic uses of personal narrative. One of the most important, using a Foucaldian approach, is Michael White and David Epston's *Narrative Means to Therapeutic Ends* (New York: W. W. Norton, 1990). For more details, see e-note.

31. Merish, "Engendering Naturalism," 339–40; Levine, *The Merchant of Modernism*, 64.

32. Mary Douglas and Baron Isherwood, *The World of Goods: Toward an Anthropology of Consumption* (New York: Basic Books. 1979; rpt. with new intro. London: Routledge, 1996); Jackson Lears, *Fables of Abundance: A Cultural History of Advertising in America* (New York: Basic Books, 1994); Jay Mechling, "The Collecting Self and American Youth Movements," in *Consuming Visions: Accumulation and Display of Goods in America: 1880–1920*, ed. Simon Bronner (New York: W. W. Norton, 1989) 255–85.

33. Campbell, *Romantic Ethic*, 37; and Grant McCracken, "The Evocative Power of Things: Consumer Goods and the Preservation of Hopes and Ideals," in *Culture and Consumption: New Approaches to the Symbolic Character of Consumer Goods and Activities* (Bloomington: University of Indiana Press, 1988), 104–17.

34. Pierre Bourdieu, *Distinction: A Social Critique of the Judgment of Taste*, trans. Richard Nice (Cambridge, MA: Harvard University Press, 1984).

35. Warren Susman, " 'Personality' and the Making of Twentieth-Century Culture," in *Culture As History: The Transformation of American Society in the Twentieth Century* (New York: Pantheon, 1984), 271–86; Halttunen, *Confidence Men and Painted Women*, 33–55. For

a critique of Susman's influential theory see: Andrew R. Heinze, "*Schizophrenia Americana*: Aliens, Alienists, and the 'Personality Shift' of Twentieth-Century Culture," *American Quarterly* 55: no. 2 (2003): 227–56.

36. Ian Burkitt, *Social Selves: Theories of Self and Society*, 2nd ed. (Los Angeles: Sage, 2008); White and Epston, *Narrative Means to Therapeutic Ends*, 1–37.

37. As Daniel Gilbert, author of *Stumbling on Happiness* (New York: Alfred A. Knopf, 2006), which won the 2007 Royal Society Prize for Science, explains: "We know that the best predictor of human happiness is human relationships and the amount of time that people spend with family and friends. We know that it's significantly more important than money and somewhat more important than health. That's what the data shows. The interesting thing is that people will sacrifice social relationships to get other things that won't make them happy — money. That's what I mean when I say people should do 'wise shopping' for happiness'" ("A Conversation with Daniel Gilbert," *The New York Times* [22 April 2008], D2). For more on "happiness studies," see e-note.

38. Anne McClintock, *Imperial Leather: Race, Gender, and Sexuality in the Colonial Contest* (New York: Routledge, 1995).

39. Karl Marx, *Capital: A Critique of Political Economy*, vol. 1, ed. Frederick Engels, trans. Samuel Moore and Edward Aveling (1867; rpt. New York: International Publishers, 1967). For a key quotation from Marx on commodity fetishism, see e-note.

40. Keane, "Sincerity," 65–92.

41. Sander Gilman, *Smart Jews: The Construction of the Image of a Jewish Superior Intelligence* (Lincoln: University of Nebraska Press, 1996). See also Goldman-Price, "The 'Perfect Jew' and *The House of Mirth*"; Levine, *The Merchant of Modernism*; John Higham, *Send These to Me: Immigrants in Urban America*, 2nd ed. (Baltimore, MD: Johns Hopkins University Press, 1984); Zygmunt Bauman, "Allosemitism: Premodern, Modern, and Postmodern," in *Modernity, Culture and the Jew*, ed. Bryan Cheyette and Laura Marcus (Stanford, CA: Stanford University Press, 1998), 143–56.

42. Burkitt, 190–91.

43. Merish, "Engendering Naturalism," 339–40.

44. I should add that, although these last four chapters are primarily focused on *The House of Mirth*, comparisons to *Little Women* are threaded throughout the discussions. For example, the analysis of Lily's death by drug overdose is placed within a detailed reading of Beth March's death and comparable sentimental deathbed scenes in Harriet Beecher Stowe's *The Pearl of Orr's Island* (1862) and Henry James's *Portrait of a Lady* (1881).

CHAPTER 1. *Raising Virtuous Shoppers*

1. Louisa May Alcott, *Little Women*, ed. with an intro. by Madelon Bedell (1868–69; rpt. New York: Modern Library, 1983). Further references to this text will be noted parenthetically. For important critical studies of this novel, see e-note.

2. I take the term "the spirit of modern consumerism" from Colin Campbell's *The Romantic Ethic and the Spirit of Modern Consumerism*, a valuable study that has helped me to frame my analysis. Campbell's work builds upon Max Weber's classic *The Protestant Ethic and the Spirit of Capitalism*, as does my own.

3. See also Ruth K. MacDonald, *Christian's Children: The Influence of John Bunyan's*

The Pilgrim's Progress on American Children's Literature (New York: Lang, 1989), 68–78; Karla Walters, "Seeking Home: Secularizing the Quest for the Celestial City in *Little Women* and *The Wonderful Wizard of Oz*," in *Reform and Counterreform: Dialectics of the Word in Western Christianity Since Luther*, ed. John C. Hawley (Berlin: Mouton de Gruyter, 1994), 153–71.

4. See Grant McCracken, "The Evocative Power of Things: Consumer Goods and the Preservation of Hopes and Ideals," in *Culture and Consumption: New Approaches to the Symbolic Character of Consumer Goods and Activities* (Bloomington: University of Indiana Press, 1988), 104–17.

5. Jean Baudrillard, *The Consumer Society, Myths and Structures* (1970; rpt. London: Sage, 1998), 3.

6. On gift exchange and the psychological symbolism of gifts, see Lewis Hyde, *The Gift: Imagination and the Erotic Life of Property* (New York: Random House, 1979), 56–73. See also Marcel Mauss, *The Gift: The Form and Reason for Exchange in Archaic Societies*, trans. W. D. Halls, with a foreword by Mary Douglas (1954; rpt. New York: W. W. Norton 1990).

7. Bunyan's *Pilgrim's Progress* played a particularly intense role in Alcott family life. As Bronson recalled: "That book was incorporated into the very substance of my youthful being. I thought and spoke through it" (A. Bronson Alcott, *Journals*, Odell Shepherd, ed., 111; quoted in Madelon Bedell, *The Alcotts: Biography of a Family* [New York: Potter, 1980], 11). In *A Hunger for Home: Louisa May Alcott's Place in American Culture* (New Brunswick, NJ: Rutgers University Press, 1987), Sarah Elbert describes how Bronson and Abby, like the fictional March parents, had their daughters diagram Bunyan's plot and act out their own dramatizations as a form of moral instruction (34). See also John Matteson, *Eden's Outcasts: The Story of Louisa May Alcott and Her Father* (New York: W. W. Norton, 2007), 18–19, 25, 157.

8. Bedell, introduction to *Little Women* (1868–69; rpt. New York: Modern Library, 1983), xvi; hereafter cited as "Introduction." Although Bedell does not explore her insight in depth, she does note that "this is a book about *things* and the potent sense of life and individuality they impart to their possessors" (Bedell's emphasis). Of this opening Christmas scene she also writes, "there is nothing religious, nothing spiritual about all this. We are at the beginning of the age of consumption. The secular Christmas has arrived" (xvi). For more on Alcott and the "family of fashion," see e-note. For more on the modern Christmas, see introduction, e-note 3.

9. For more on the importance of color in the development of sophisticated marketing techniques, see William Leach, "Strategists of Display and the Production of Desire," in *Consuming Visions: Accumulation and Display of Goods in America, 1880–1920*, ed. Simon Bronner (New York: W. W. Norton, 1989), 99–132; and William Leach, *Land of Desire: Merchants, Power, and the Rise of a New American Culture* (New York: Vintage, 1993), esp. chap. 2, "Facades of Color, Glass, and Light," 39–70.

10. Richard Brodhead, "Sparing the Rod: Discipline and Fiction in Antebellum America," in *Cultures of Letters: Scenes of Reading and Writing in Nineteenth-Century America* (Chicago: University of Chicago Press, 1993), 13–47. Brodhead also addresses the influence of Horace Bushnell on religious and moral education: 18–19, 21, 47. See also, in the same volume, "Starting Out in the 1860s: Alcott, Authorship, and the Postbellum Literary Field," 69–106.

11. For discussions of the Alcott's childrearing and pedagogical theories, see Charles Strickland, *Victorian Domesticity: Families in the Life and Art of Louisa May Alcott* (Tuscaloosa: University of Alabama press, 1985); Bedell, *The Alcotts*, 52–109; Elbert, *Hunger for Home*, 21–39; and Matteson, *Eden's Outcasts*, 26–29, 38–54 ("A Birthday in Germantown"), 55–85 ("The Temple School"). For a contemporary record of his teaching practices at the Temple School, see Elizabeth Palmer Peabody, *The Record of a School: Exemplifying the General Principles of Spiritual Culture* (Boston: James Monroe, 1835).

12. William Ellery Channing, "Likeness to God" (1828), in *The Works of William Ellery Channing*, vol. 3 (Boston: 1848).

13. Friedrich Schleiermacher is considered by many religious historians to be the central architect of liberal Protestant theology, especially through his massive mature works such as *The Christian Faith* (2nd ed., trans. H. R. MacKintosh, ed. J. S. Stroud [1830–31; rpt. Edinburgh: T and T Clark, 1999]). For more on Schleiermacher's importance and his influence on the American Transcendentalists, see e-note.

14. For more on the liberal theology of Schleiermacher and the American Transcendentalists, see e-note.

15. See Jonathan Edwards, *A Treatise on the Religious Affections* (1746), excerpted in *Jonathan Edwards: Representative Selections*, ed. with an intro. by Clarence H. Faust and Thomas H. Johnson, rev. ed. (New York: Hill and Wang, 1935, 1962). His discussion of grace as "Consent to Being in General" may be found in *The Nature of True Virtue*, with a foreword by William K. Frankena (1765; rpt. Ann Arbor: University of Michigan, 1960). For more on the links between Edwards, Schleiermacher, and Transcendentalism, see e-note.

16. For a discussion of sentimentalism and its emphasis on deathbed scenes, emotional attachments and loss, see Ann Douglas, *The Feminization of American Culture* (New York: Knopf, 1977), 200–226; Jane Tompkins, *Sensational Designs: The Cultural Work of American Fiction 1790–1860* (New York: Oxford University Press, 1985), 122–46; Karen Halttunen's *Confidence Men and Painted Women: A Study of Middle-Class Culture in America, 1820–1870* (New Haven, CT: Yale University Press, 1982), 124–52; and Mary Louise Kete, *Sentimental Collaborations: Mourning and Middle-Class Identity in Nineteenth-Century America* (Durham, NC: Duke University Press, 2000). There is a great deal of feminist scholarship on the association of the "feminine" with the body and with nature. See, for example, Susan Bordo's *Unbearable Weight: Feminism, Western Culture, and the Body* (Berkeley: University of California Press, 1993), 1–42.

17. Kete, *Sentimental Collaborations*, xiv. On the centrality of sentimentalism to nineteenth-century American culture, see Shirley Samuels, "Introduction," in *The Culture of Sentiment: Race, Gender, and Sentimentality in Nineteenth-Century America*, ed. Shirley Samuels (New York: Oxford University Press, 1992), 3–8. For more on the difference between sentimentalism as a cultural discourse and sentimentality as a literary mode, sentimentalism's "written trace," see Kete, *Sentimental Collaborations*, 89, and chap. 5, e-note 31. See also June Howard, "What Is Sentimentality," *American Literary History* 11, no. 1 (Spring 1999): 431–59.

18. Louisa May Alcott, "Transcendental Wild Oats," first published in *The Independent* (1873). This text is now widely available in anthologies, including *Nineteenth-Century American Women Writers*, ed. Karen Kilcup (Oxford, UK: Blackwell, 1997), 247–56. For the history of the Fruitlands experiment, see Elbert, *Hunger for Home*, 56–77; Bedell, *The Alcotts*,

206–31; Matteson, *Eden's Outcasts*, 116–33, 134–49, 150–64; and Philip F. Gura, *American Transcendentalism: A History* (New York: Hill and Wang, 2007), 174–79. See also Clara Endicott Sears, *Bronson Alcott's Fruitlands* (Boston: Houghton Mifflin, 1915); and Sandra Harbert Petrulionis, "By the Light of Her Mother's Lamp: Woman's Work versus Man's Philosophy in Louisa May Alcott's "Transcendental Wild Oats," *Studies in the American Renaissance* (1995): 69–81.

19. This incident is described in fictionalized form in "Transcendentalist Wild Oats," and discussed in Bedell, *The Alcotts*, 217–31. The near breakup of the family is also mentioned in the journals Louisa kept during her time at Fruitlands and reprinted in *The Journals of Louisa May Alcott*, ed. Joel Myerson and Daniel Shealy, assoc. ed. Madeleine B. Stern (Athens: University of Georgia Press, 1997), 43–53. Bronson Alcott's ideas on the family as the unit of moral and social development may be found in Amos Bronson Alcott, manuscript journal, 1 August 1857, Houghton Library; quoted in Bedell, "Introduction," xxix–xxx. See also Matteson, *Eden's Outcasts*, 160–64.

20. The Alcott family was involved at various times, not only with dress reform, but also with dietary reform. The family was staunchly vegetarian and followed various other dietary regimens designed to purify the body and align it with the spirit. See Bedell's discussion of the reform ideas behind Fruitlands (*The Alcotts*, 206–31), as well as Matteson, *Eden's Outcasts*, 125–27. See also *L. M. Alcott: Signature of Reform*, ed. Madeleine B. Stern (Boston: Northeastern University Press, 2002).

21. Pierre Bourdieu, *Distinction: A Social Critique of the Judgment of Taste*, trans. Richard Nice (Cambridge, MA: Harvard University Press, 1984).

22. Nina Auerbach, *Communities of Women: An Idea in Fiction* (Cambridge, MA: Harvard University Press, 1978), 55. See also Auerbach, afterword to *Little Women*, by Louisa May Alcott (Toronto: Bantam, 1983).

23. The notion that moral order is created by individuals making virtuous selections in a marketplace of possible choices is posited in Adam Smith's *The Theory of Moral Sentiments*, ed. D. D. Raphael and A. L. Raphael (1759; rpt. Oxford: Oxford University Press, 1976). For more on Smith's ideas, see e-note.

24. Campbell, *Romantic Ethic*, chap. 4, "Traditional and Modern Hedonism" (58–76), and chap. 5, "Modern Autonomous Imaginative Hedonism" (77–95).

25. Campbell develops this argument throughout his intricate study, but these key points are summarized in pages 173–201 and 202–27. See pages 175–77 for his discussion of the gothic novel's contribution to the development of modern consumerism.

26. Halttunen, *Confidence Men and Painted Women*, 33–55.

27. John Cotton, "Swine and Goats" and "Hypocrites and Saints," in *The New Covenant* (London: 1654), excerpted in *The Puritans: A Sourcebook of Their Writing*, ed. Perry Miller and Thomas H. Johnson, vol. 1, rev. ed. (New York: Harper and Row, 1938, 1963): 314–18.

28. Weber, *The Protestant Ethic*, 155–83. For more on the "Protestant ethic" in the United States, see David E. Shi, *The Simple Life: Plain Living and High Thinking in American Culture* (New York: Oxford University Press, 1985); and Daniel Horowitz, *The Morality of Spending: Attitudes Toward the Consumer Society in America, 1875–1940* (Baltimore, MD: Johns Hopkins University Press, 1985; rpt: Chicago: Ivan R. Doe, 1992), esp. 1–12.

29. See e-note for more on Protestant denunciations of sacramentalism. See also David

Hawkes, *Idols of the Marketplace: Idolatry and Commodity Fetishism in English Literature, 1580–1680* (New York: Palgrave, 2001), 68–75.

30. Jay Mechling, "The Collecting Self and American Youth Movements," in *Consuming Visions: Accumulation and Display of Goods in America: 1880–1920*, ed. Simon Bronner (New York: W. W. Norton, 1989), 255–85; Mary Douglas and Baron Isherwood, *The World of Goods: Toward an Anthropology of Consumption* (New York: Basic Books. 1979; rpt. with new intro. London: Routledge, 1996). For further discussion of this approach to materialistic behavior, see e-note.

31. See introduction in this volume, note 11 for sources on this issue.

32. For thorough discussions of materialistic values and their effect on "subjective well-being," see the essays in Tim Kasser and Allen D. Kanner, eds., *Psychology and Consumer Culture: The Struggle for a Good Life in a Materialistic World* (Washington, D.C.: American Psychological Association, 2003); and Tim Kasser, *The High Price of Materialism* (Cambridge, MA: MIT Press, 2002). For more titles in the field of "happiness studies" see introduction in this volume, note 37 and e-note 37.

33. Thoreau's fullest critique of consumer culture is "Economy," the opening chapter of *Walden* ([1854]; rpt. in *The Portable Thoreau*, ed. Carl Bode [New York: Penguin, 1975]), 258–333. For background on Thoreau's friendship with Bronson Alcott and his considerable influence on Louisa, see Bedell, *The Alcotts*, 262–66; Elbert, *Hunger for Home*, 88–89, 124, 150–51; Matteson, *Eden's Outcasts*, 88–89.

34. Ralph Waldo Emerson, "The Poet" (1844), in *Selections from Ralph Waldo Emerson*, ed. Stephen E. Whicher (Boston: Houghton Mifflin, 1957), 223. For an important discussion of the connections between style, self-expression, and middle-class women's consumption in this period, see Lori Merish, *Sentimental Materialism: Gender, Commodity Culture, and Nineteenth-Century American Literature* (Durham, NC: Duke University Press, 2000), esp. 1–27.

35. Thoreau, *Walden*, 279.

36. Mrs. March here seems, as Thoreau had advised, to take account only of the umbrella's functionality, and to have disregarded its socially constructed signifying powers. To use terms from Marxist analysis, she refuses to treat the umbrella as a commodity fetish or to recognize its "supplemental" value, but views it solely in its term of its use-value.

37. There is a large literature on the "fashion system" and its operations. Some key works can be found in the e-note.

38. McCracken, "Diderot Unities and the Diderot Effect," in *Culture and Consumption*, 118–29. See e-note for more on consumer objects and cultural codes.

39. For a discussion of anxieties about changes in fashion during this period, see Christopher Breward, "Nineteenth Century: Fashion and Modernity," in *The Culture of Fashion: A New History of Fashionable Dress* (Manchester, UK: Manchester University Press, 1995), 145–79. For more on this topic, see e-note.

40. For more on the Alcott family's opinions on dress reform, see e-note.

41. See Jenny Franchot, "'The Moral Map of the World': American Tourists and Underground Rome," in *Roads to Rome: The Antebellum Encounter with Catholicism* (Berkeley: University of California Press, 1994), 16–34.

42. Marmee's comment about money is reflected in a line from Alcott's later novel, *Lit-*

tle Men: Life at Plumfield with Jo's Boys (1873; rpt. New York: Children's Classics, 1991): "Money is the root of all evil, and yet it is such a useful root that we cannot get on without it any more than we can without potatoes" (124).

43. Erving Goffman, *The Presentation of Self in Everyday Life* (Garden City, NY: Doubleday Anchor, 1959). For an overview and discussion of Michel Foucault's theories of the socially constructed self, see Ian Burkitt, *Social Selves: Theories of Self and Society*, 2nd ed. (Los Angeles Sage, 2008), 85–110.

44. The association of the Quaker plain style with resistance to fashionable consumer culture and anti-materialism is another cultural commonplace. See E. Digby Baltzell, *Puritan Boston and Quaker Philadelphia: Two Protestant Ethics and the Spirit of Class Authority and Leadership* (New York: Macmillan, 1979). However, Meg March's expressive dress, while seemingly unfashionable, is fully consonant with the Romantic bohemian style described by Colin Campbell. For more on "bohemian" style, see e-note.

45. The title of this chapter again draws from Bunyan's *The Pilgrim's Progress*.

46. See Douglas and Isherwood, *World of Goods*, on the use of goods to "map" social territory.

47. Although Alcott's narrator is respectful toward the German immigrants, the Hummels, the narrative tone taken toward these Irish children is dismissive. This attitude is even more apparent in Alcott's *Work: A Story of Experience* (1873). For more on anti-Irish sentiment, especially among the Transcendentalists, see e-note.

48. Alcott's emphasis on the color "violet" is not random. For its historical significance as a mark of prestige, its mass market manufacture (through the discovery of a new violet pigment in 1856), and its consequent popularity in this period, see e-note.

49. In this achievement, Amy fits Colin Campbell's description of hedonistic bohemians in search of pleasure and self-expression not only through actual consumption, but also through day-dreaming and imaginative control of their experience and its meaning (*Romantic Ethic*, 76).

50. Alcott's description of Amy's "polish" is consistent with her father's ideas on the relationship between "cultivation" and the individual's intrinsic nature. For more on this issue, see e-note.

51. Laurie's description of Amy as "Diana" references a long tradition in the representation of women, with neoclassical and mythological imagery being especially prevalent after Sir Joshua Reynolds promoted it for female portraiture in the 1760s. See Joshua Reynolds, *Discourses on Art*, ed. R. Wark (New Haven, CT: Yale University Press, 1975); and see e-note for more information.

52. Bedell, "Introduction," xiv.

53. See Campbell, *Romantic Ethic*, 202–3 for a discussion of the relationship between modern conceptions of romantic love and consumer culture.

54. As Jenny Franchot explains, these symbolic oppositions were common to nineteenth-century Protestant thought: "The uncultivated nature of the New World that existed prior to advent of a spiritualizing Protestantism belonged, according to this symbolic logic, to Catholicism: and it was this New World nature — flesh-bound, violent, superstitious — that called for annihilation. Catholicism, then, represented the extremes of barbaric nature and overrefined civilization, while Protestantism existed in between, quarantined from the twinned corruptions of the wild and the artificial" (*Roads to Rome*, 67).

55. In "Economy," Thoreau writes: "Let him who has work to do recall that the object of clothing is, first, to retain the vital heat, and secondly, in this state of society, to cover nakedness, and he may judge how much of any necessary or important work may be accomplished without adding to his wardrobe" (276).

56. See e-note for related essays.

57. See Burkitt, *Social Selves*, esp. "Dialogue and the Social Self" (31–57) and "Ethics, Self, and Performativity" (58–84); and Michael White and David Epston, *Narrative Means to Therapeutic Ends* (New York: W. W. Norton, 1990), 1–37. For additional sources on narrative and identity, see introduction in this volume, note 30 and e-note 30, and note 36.

58. In *Hidden Hands: An Anthology of American Women Writers, 1790–1870* (New Brunswick, NJ: Rutgers University Press, 1985), the editors Lucy M. Freibert and Barbara A. White write that "in terms of overall sales, E. D. E. N. Southworth may have been the most popular novelist of nineteenth-century America" (68). She produced "from fifty to sixty novels, the exact number being difficult to fix because of the many title changes from serial to book. Her work remained popular into the twentieth century; in 1936 over half of her novels were still in print" (68). See e-note for more on Southworth.

59. The autobiographical source for this incident was Alcott's own story, "Pauline's Passion and Punishment," which initiated her career as a writer of popular sensation stories by winning a $100 prize and anonymous publication in *Frank Leslie's Illustrated Newspaper* (3 and 10 January 1863).

60. The discovery of Alcott's thrillers, published between 1863 and 1870, was made by Leona Rostenberg, who announced it in "Some Anonymous and Pseudonymous Thrillers of Louisa M. Alcott," *Papers of the Bibliographical Society of America* (October 1943). For more on Alcott's thrillers, see e-note.

61. The model for Jo's novel in this chapter is Alcott's *Moods*, first published in 1864 by Boston's A. K. Loring and then, in a revised edition 1882 by Roberts Brothers, as *Moods, A Novel*. Sarah Elbert's edition of the 1864 *Moods* (New Brunswick, NJ: Rutgers University Press, 1991) includes an appendix of the 1882 revisions plus an excellent introduction. For more on Elbert's analysis, see e-note.

62. Thomas Carlyle, *Sartor Resartus*, ed. Kerry McSweeney and Peter Sabor (Oxford, UK: Oxford University Press, 1987).

63. According to Madeleine Stern, "In all the Alcott thrillers the themes are shocking indeed to readers who know Louisa Alcott only as the 'Children's Friend.' To enumerate them briefly, we find . . . manipulative heroines and mind control, madness, child-brides and a hint at incest, hashish experimentation and opium addiction. Especially we find the manipulating heroine whose feminist fury is launched, usually with success, against an antifeminist world" ("Five Letters that Changed an Image," in *Louisa May Alcott: From Blood & Thunder to Hearth & Home* [Boston: Northeastern University Press, 1998], 88). See Campbell on contemporary anxieties concerning the moral effects of gothic thrillers (*Romantic Ethic*, 174–77). Leona Rostenberg's groundbreaking article, plus other pieces on Alcott's career are collected in Stern's *Louisa May Alcott: From Blood & Thunder*.

64. Louisa also seemed to believe that German men were more domestic and emotional, more "feminine" than American men. In *Little Men*, she describes how "the good Professor opened his arms and embraced the boys like a true German, not ashamed to express by gesture or by word the fatherly emotions an American would have compressed into a slap on the

shoulder and a brief 'All right'" (142). See Anne Dalke, "The House-Band: The Education of Men in *Little Women*," *College English* 47 (1985): 571–78.

65. Campbell, *Romantic Ethic*, 174–77.

66. Alcott's depiction of Beth's death and its effect on Jo draws on her experience of her sister Lizzie's death in 1858. See Matteson, *Eden's Outcasts*, 235–44, 277–78. Not all critics see the developmental changes initiated by Beth's death as positive. For examples, see e-note.

67. Part 1 of *Little Women*, which ends with Meg's engagement to John Pratt in the chapter "Aunt March Settles the Question," was published by Roberts Brothers of Boston in late 1868. Part 2, titled *Good Wives*, was published in the spring of 1869, also by Roberts Brothers. A decade later, the two halves, which had continued to be published separately, were combined into one, a format that still prevails in the United States.

68. White and Epston, *Narrative Means*, 1–37. Jo's development of a narrated self clearly draws on the Alcott family's history of journal-writing and communal storytelling. As John Matteson explains, during the "destitute" years the Alcott family spent in Boston after the Fruitlands debacle, "One of the strongest adhesives holding the family together was narrative; the tales they shared of their daily lives formed a bridge of sympathy and shared effort. They were Louisa's only consolation amid the dirty pots and unmade beds" (*Eden's Outcasts*, 199).

69. Abraham Maslow, *Religions, Values, and Peak-Experiences* (New York: Penguin, 1976, c. 1964).

70. See Campbell, *Romantic Ethic*, 36–57, 77–95. Chapter 5 opens with this epigraph (which Campbell attributes to George Bernard Shaw, although I have also heard it attributed to Oscar Wilde): "There are two tragedies in life. One is not to get your heart's desire. The other is to gain it" (77).

71. Theodore Dreiser, *Sister Carrie*, ed. John C. Berkey et. al., unexpurgated ed. (1900; rpt. New York: Penguin, 1981), 145.

72. Ibid., 116.

73. Ibid., 487. This passage ends the first 1900 Doubleday edition. However, the unexpurgated edition, from which this quotation is taken, ends with the character Hurstwood's suicide.

74. F. Scott Fitzgerald, *The Great Gatsby: The Authorized Text*, ed. Matthew J. Bruccoli (1925; rpt. New York: Scribner's, 1995), 169.

75. Ibid., 189.

76. Arthur Miller, *Death of a Salesman: Certain Private Conversations in Two Acts and a Requiem* (1949; rpt. New York: Penguin 1987), 138.

77. Alcott's novel arguably belongs within the framework of the "therapeutic ethos" described by T. J. Jackson Lears's "From Salvation to Self-Realization: Advertising and the Therapeutic Roots of the Consumer Society, 1880–1930," in *The Culture of Consumption: Critical Essays in American History, 1880–1990*, ed. Richard Wrightman Fox and T. J. Jackson Lears (New York: Pantheon, 1983), 3–38. Her overt resistance to modernity also aligns her with writers described in Lear's study *No Place of Grace: Antimodernism and the Transformation of American Culture, 1880–1920* (Chicago: University of Chicago Press, 1981, 1983). For more detail, see introduction in this volume, note 29. For a discussion of Baudrillard's argument that modern consumer society no longer offers authenticity or substance, but merely the signs or the *simulacra* of them, see Jean Baudrillard, *Simulations*

(New York: Semiotext(e), 1983/1990). For a related argument on the centrality of spectacle, see Guy Debord, *The Society of the Spectacle*, trans. Donald Nicholson-Smith (1967; English language translation, New York: Zone Books, 1994).

78. Charles Dickens, *A Christmas Carol. In Prose. Being a Ghost Story of Christmas*, with illustrations by John Leech (London: Chapman and Hall, 1843). For a discussion of Dickens and the "Carol Philosophy" of moral and social reform, see Paul Davis, *The Lives and Times of Ebenezer Scrooge* (New Haven, CT: Yale University Press, 1990), esp. chap. 3, "The Founder of the Feast: *A Christmas Carol* as Secular Scripture," 51–87.

79. For more on Alcott's attitude toward economic disparity, philanthropy, and social reform, see e-note.

80. Bourdieu, *Distinction*, 11–96. Lori Merish is particularly insightful about the way that consumer taste consolidates class identity: "The (middle-class) feminine consumer . . . marks her distance from material 'need' through the display of 'taste,' signified by fashionable clothing and consumer durables: taste constitutes both an expression of her 'subjectivity' and symbolizes her class position and that of her family" (*Sentimental Materialism*, 9). While the members of the March family may reject fashionable tastes in consumer goods, they do see personal style as expressing both subjectivity and class position (figured by them as moral status).

81. According to Madelon Bedell, "There was just a touch of imperiousness in [Abby Alcott's] bearing, for she was not only a Boston May, but also a descendant of the great Sewall and Quincy families of Massachusetts and Maine, who had provided New England with judges, scholars, and social reformers since colonial times. In all these things, she was the direct opposite of Bronson" (*The Alcotts*, 3). Bronson came from a much more plebeian Connecticut farming family.

82. In *The Christian Home in Victorian America, 1840–1900* (Bloomington: Indiana University Press, 1986), Colleen McDannell points out that, "at the same time that anti-Catholic sentiments raged, a new appreciation of ritual drama appeared among Protestants" (15). For more on the popular acceptance of "Catholic" practices in Protestant homes during this period, see e-note.

83. "The Carnival of Authors," *The Boston Daily Advertiser* (3 January 1879), 1; quoted in Alcott, *Journals*, ed. Myerson and Shealy, 220n3.

84. Louisa May Alcott, entry for May 1868, *Journals*, ed. Myerson and Shealy, 165.

85. Louisa May Alcott, letter to Thomas Niles, 15 July 1884, quoted in Stern, *From Blood and Thunder*, 232.

86. Louisa May Alcott, *Jo's Boys, and How They Turned Out* (1886; rpt. Boston: Little, Brown, 1925), 357.

87. From an interview in LaSalle Corbell Pickett, *Across My Path: Memories of People I Have Known* (New York: Brentano's, 1916), 107–8; quoted in Stern, *From Blood and Thunder*, 192–93.

88. Virtually all Alcott's biographers discuss these struggles, as well as Bronson Alcott's perception of his daughter as "other." Madelon Bedell, for example, discusses Bronson Alcott's belief that the Anglo-Saxon race produced a superior, "angelic" type of human being for whom "blood is history." According to his journals: "Intermarriage may modify but cannot blot out quite the fixed family type. In our case, it leaves to us the fair complexion, prominent features and slender form; while the intellectual disposition, though qualified

by intermarriage perhaps, and social position, run still visibly in the family, especially the Puritanism and Protestantism of our ancestors" (Amos Bronson Alcott, manuscript journal, 21 January 1853, Houghton Library; quoted in Bedell, *The Alcotts*, 316). Louisa, with her brunette coloring and dark eyes, sometimes violent temper and volatile moods, impressed her father as a distinctly different type from his own "fair" and "angelic" Anglo-Saxon. He took this perception to an extreme in an 1846 journal entry describing Louisa May and Mrs. Alcott: "Two devils, as yet, I am not quite divine enough to vanquish — the mother fiend and her daughter" (manuscript journal, 16 March 1846, Houghton Library; quoted in Strickland, 29). See also Matteson, *Eden's Outcasts*, 189–91.

89. Baudrillard, *The Consumer Society*, 196.

CHAPTER 2. *Lily Bart and the Pursuit of Happiness*

1. In her biography *Edith Wharton* (New York: Alfred A. Knopf, 2007), Hermione Lee writes that Wharton might best called a "sympathetic realist" who struggled to disassociate her self from "sentimentality," a term she used often pejoratively, while still attuned to "sympathy," which she used positively. As Lee comments, "This was the challenge . . . to try and write a novel that would fulfill the obligations of the American novelist toward the social material that lay all around, *and* create sympathy for her characters, *and* avoid being branded as a sentimental, over-emotional woman novelist" (211). For more on Wharton's distancing from her "sentimental" predecessors, see e-note.

2. Edith Wharton, *The House of Mirth*, ed. with an intro. by Elizabeth Ammons (1905; rpt. New York: W. W. Norton, 1990). For some important studies of this novel, including monographs and collections, see e-note.

3. Bunyan, *Pilgrim's Progress*; Nathaniel Hawthorne, "The Celestial Railroad," in *The Complete Novels and Selected Tales of Nathaniel Hawthorne*, ed. with an intro. by Norman Pearson (1843; rpt. New York: The Modern Library, 1937), 1076–1082. As Singley notes, Wharton "certainly read Nathaniel Hawthorne, who plays a larger part in her fiction than her disparaging comments about him lead us to be believe." Moreover, she writes, "The similarities between 'The Celestial Railroad' and *The House of Mirth* are striking. Both emphasize modern conveyances and selfish pleasures and both draw on Ecclesiastes to depict vanity and materialism" (*Edith Wharton: Matters of Mind and Spirit* [New York: Oxford University Press, 1995], 74; hereafter cited as *Matters*). Singley also cites Paul Pickrel's comparison of *The House of Mirth* and Thackeray's *Vanity Fair*, another novel making satirical use of Bunyan's parable: "*Vanity Fair* in America: *The House of Mirth* and *Gone with the Wind*," *American Literature* 59 (1987): 37–57.

4. Wharton, *A Backward Glance*, 207.

5. For key biographical and critical studies of Wharton, in addition to those already cited, see e-note.

6. Wharton, *A Backward Glance*, 9–10.

7. Ibid.

8. Edith Wharton, "Life & I," *Novellas and Other Writings*, ed. Cynthia Griffin Wolff (New York: Library of America, 1990), 1073.

9. Wharton, *A Backward Glance*, 57.

10. Edith Wharton, *The Age of Innocence*, ed. with an intro. by Carol J. Singley (1920; rpt. Boston: Houghton Mifflin, 2000). See also Singley, *Matters*, 8.

11. Singley, *Matters*, 91–92.

12. Wharton, *The Age of Innocence*, 157. For sources on these cultural changes, see e-note.

13. All quotations are from "Life & I," 1074.

14. Ibid., 1074.

15. Edith Wharton and Ogden Codman, Jr., *The Decoration of Houses* (New York: Scribner's, 1897). See also Edith Wharton, *Italian Villas and Their Gardens* (New York: Century, 1904) and Edith Wharton, *Italian Backgrounds* (New York: Scribner's, 1905). According to Hermione Lee, "Wharton was equally interested in the ethics of style, whether in the production values of her books, in her house and garden designs, in her appreciation of Europe or in her theorizing of interior decoration" (*Edith Wharton*, 125). For more sources, see e-note.

16. Wharton, "Life & I," 1083.

17. Ibid.

18. Ibid., 1084.

19. Ibid., 1087.

20. Ibid., 1089–90.

21. According to Lee, "the most interesting — and morbid of these early works came out under a pseudonym in a magazine called *The New York World* in 1879." The poem's subject is especially revealing and anticipates some of Wharton's later themes. It was "written in response to a newspaper account of a twelve-year-old boy in a Philadelphia reformatory who was put in solitary confinement and killed himself. The poem imagines the child's loneliness and vulnerability and the vanishing of 'his mother's face,' criticizes extreme punishment meted out for 'some little childish sin,' and ends with a stern Blakean note of reprimand ('In a Christian town it happened/In a home for children built') and a dutiful hope that God will have room for all unwanted children" (*Edith Wharton*, 44). See also "'Eagdyth' Wharton in the *New York World* 1879," *Yale University Gazette* 30, no. 2 (October 1955): 64–69.

22. Edith Wharton, "A Little Girl's New York," *Harper's Monthly Magazine* 176 (December 1937–May 1938): 362.

23. R. W. B. Lewis, *Edith Wharton: A Biography* (New York: Harper, 1975), 510. See also Maggs Brothers, "The Library of Edith Wharton," Edith Wharton Collection, Beinecke Rare Book and Manuscript Library, Yale University, New Haven, CT; and George Ramsden, comp., *Edith Wharton's Library: A Catalogue* (Settrington, UK: Stone Trough Books, 1999).

24. Wharton, A Backward Glance, 51.

25. Ibid., 51.

26. Ibid., 16–17 (all quotations in paragraph).

27. Ibid., 17.

28. See the discussion of these incidents in chap. 1.

29. Wharton, *A Backward Glance,* 18.

30. Wharton, "A Little Girl's New York," 362.

31. Wharton, *A Backward Glance*, 18–19.

32. Wharton, "A Little Girl's New York," 361.

33. Wharton, *A Backward Glance*, 18–19.

34. Ibid., 19–20.

35. Wharton, "Life & I," 1071.

36. Lee, *Edith Wharton,* 34.

37. Wharton, *A Backward Glance,* 39.

38. Lee, *Edith Wharton*, 35. Reverend Washburn, with whom Wharton had been infatuated as a child and who was a major influence on her early thinking about morality and religion, died shortly after her father did.

39. Edith Wharton, Letter to Anna Robinson, 2 November 1905, quoted in Lee, *Edith Wharton*, 63.

40. Wharton, "Life & I," 1086–87.

41. Ibid., 1087.

42. Ibid.

43. Gloria Erlich, *The Sexual Education of Edith Wharton* (Berkeley: University of California Press, 1992), 16–49.

44. Wharton, "Life & I," 1088.

45. Ibid.

46. Lee, *Edith Wharton*, 35. On Wharton's early relationship with her mother, see Erlich, *Sexual Education*, 16–49; Lee, *Edith Wharton*, 10–45; Cynthia Griffin Wolff, *A Feast of Words: The Triumph of Edith Wharton* (New York: Scribner's, 1977), 9–48; Susan Goodman, *Edith Wharton's Women: Friends and Rivals* (Hanover, NH: University Press of New England, 1990), 13–28.

47. Wharton, *The Age of Innocence*, 79. On the affair with Morton Fullerton, see Wolff, *Feast of Words*, 145–51; Lee, *Edith Wharton*, 309–60; Lewis, *Edith Wharton*, 198–264; Shari Benstock, *No Gifts from Chance: A Biography of Edith Wharton* (New York: Scribner's, 1994), 175–229. For primary sources, see Alan Gribben, ed., " 'The Heart is Insatiable': A Selection from Edith Wharton's Letters to Morton Fullerton, 1907–1915," Special Wharton issue of *The Library Chronicle of the University of Texas at Austin*, n.s. 31 (1985): 7–71; and Edith Wharton, "The Life Apart (L'âme close)," in " 'The Life Apart': Text and Contexts of Edith Wharton's Love Diary," by Kenneth M Price and Phyllis Mc Bride, *American Literature* 66 (1994): 663–88.

48. In "Language and Convention in Wharton's Hieroglyphic World," *Language and Gender in American Fiction* (Charlottesville: University Press of Virginia, 1997), Elsa Nettels writes: "The refusal to speak certain words may lead one to deny the realities they signify. Repression of feeling may atrophy emotion. For Edith Wharton, the crippling vice of old New York society was the code which forbade talk of the unpleasant and the scandalous and elevated equivocation to a moral duty" (89).

49. See Katherine Joslin, *Edith Wharton and the Making of Fashion* (Durham, NH: University of New Hampshire Press, 2009) and related texts cited in note 15 above.

50. Susan Goodman, *Edith Wharton's Women*; Susan Goodman, *Edith Wharton's Inner Circle* (Austin: University of Texas Press, 1994); Millicent Bell, *Edith Wharton and Henry James: The Story of Their Friendship* (New York: George Braziller, 1965).

51. Wharton, *A Backward Glance*, 119.

52. Wendy Gimbel, *Edith Wharton: Orphancy and Survival* (New York: Praeger, 1984). See also Erlich, *Sexual Education*, 16–49, 50–74; Jeanne Boydston, " 'Grave Endearing

Traditions': Edith Wharton and the Domestic Novel," in *Faith of a (Woman) Writer*, ed. Alice Kessler Harris and William McBrien (New York: Greenwood Press, 1988), 31–40; Joan Lidoff, "Another Sleeping Beauty: Narcissism in *The House of Mirth*," *American Quarterly* 32 (1980): 519–32.

53. Lee, *Edith Wharton*, 36. For Carol Singley's assessment of Wharton's "true nature," see e-note.

54. For studies of interior spaces in Wharton's work and in this novel in particular, see e-note.

55. Lee, *Edith Wharton*, 68. As Lee writes, "The surviving letters between them, and everything Wharton said about Berry, make clear what interested her in him: his rational skepticism, his cultural range, and his discriminating and fervent interest in literature" (68).

56. Lee, *Edith Wharton*, 23. Claire Preston, *Edith Wharton's Social Register* (New York: Palgrave Macmillan, 2000); Nancy Bentley, *The Ethnography of Manners: Hawthorne, James, Wharton* (New York: Cambridge University Press, 1995); Sharon Kim, "Lamarckism and the Construction of Transcendence in *The House of Mirth*," *Studies in the Novel* 38 (2006): 187–210; Singley, *Matters*, 57–64. For more on Wharton's interest in Darwinian and anthropological theory, see e-note.

57. See e-note for Sharon Kim on Lamarck's influence.

58. Singley, *Matters*, 8.

59. Singley, *Matters*, 151; Edith Wharton, letter to Sara Norton, The Mount, July 7 [1908], quoted in Edith Wharton, *The Letters of Edith Wharton*, ed. R. W. B. Lewis and Nancy Lewis (New York: Charles Scribner's Sons, 1988), 159. Wharton's comment was prefaced by a response to her reading of Nietzsche's *Jenseits von Gut und Böse*, trans. *Beyond Good and Evil* (1887): "I think it salutary, now & then, to be made to realize what he calls 'die Unwerthung aller Werthe' [The re-evaluation of all values], & really get back to a wholesome basis of naked instinct" (159).

60. Singley, *Matters*, 151; quoting from Wolff, *Feast of Words*, 90. Wharton kept her commonplace book, in which she copied favorite quotations, from 1896 until 1933, with most of the entries between 1901 and 1910.

61. Wharton, "A Little Girl's New York," 361; Lewis, *Edith Wharton*, 86.

62. On Wharton's love of Whitman, see also Singley, *Matters*, 147–55; and Susan Goodman, "Edith Wharton's 'Sketch of an Essay on Walt Whitman,'" *The Walt Whitman Review*, 10, no. 1 (Summer 1992): 3–9. Edith Wharton, "Sketch of an Essay on Walt Whitman," Beinecke Rare Book and Manuscript Library, Yale University.

63. Jill Kress, "Designing Our Interiors: Self-Consciousness and Social Awareness in Edith Wharton's *The House of Mirth*," in *The Figure of Consciousness: William James, Henry James, and Edith Wharton* (New York: Routledge, 2002), 131–59.

64. Singley, *Matters*, 168. See also Maggs Brothers, "The Library of Edith Wharton"; and Ramsden, comp., *Edith Wharton's Library*.

65. Edith Wharton, letter to Sara Norton, Biltmore House [Asheville, North Carolina], December 26 [1905], rpt. in Edith Wharton, *Letters*, 100–101. In this letter Wharton also writes of reading Walter Pater's *Plato and Platonism* (1893). On the influence of Plato, see Singley, *Matters*, 164–67; and Julia A Galbus, "Edith Wharton's Material Republic: *The House of Mirth*," *Edith Wharton Review* 20, no. 2 (2004): 1, 3–7. On Wharton's use of Greek

mythology in *The House of Mirth*, see Candace Waid, *Edith Wharton's Letters from the Underworld: Fictions of Women and Writing* (Chapel Hill: University of North Carolina Press, 1991), 15–49.

66. Lee, *Edith Wharton*, 676.

67. Edith Wharton, *The Cruise of the Vanadis*, ed. Claudine Lesage (Amiens: Sterne/ Presses de L'LUFR Clerc Université Picardie, 1992); Edith Wharton, *The Valley of Decision*, 2 vols. (New York: Scribner's, 1902); William L. Vance, "*The Valley of Decision*: Edith Wharton's Italian Mask," in *The Cambridge Companion to Edith Wharton*, ed. Millicent Bell (Cambridge, UK: Cambridge University Press, 1995), 169–98.

68. Thorstein Veblen, *The Theory of the Leisure Class*, ed. with an intro. by Martha Banta (1899; rpt. New York: Oxford University Press, 2007); Maureen Montgomery, *Displaying Women: Spectacles of Leisure in Edith Wharton's New York* (New York: Routledge, 1998); Amy Kaplan, "Crowded Spaces in *The House of Mirth*," in *The Social Construction of American Realism* (Chicago: University of Chicago Press, 1988), 88–103. For more sources on social display and conspicuous consumption in this novel, see e-note.

69. Donna Campbell, "Edith Wharton and the 'Authoresses,'" in *Resisting Regionalism: Gender and Naturalism in American Fiction, 1885–1915*, 146–73; Deborah Lindsay Williams, *Not in Sisterhood: Edith Wharton, Willa Cather, Zona Gale, and the Politics of Female Authorship* (New York: Palgrave, 2001). See also notes 2 and 53 above.

70. On the issue of Wharton's sentimentalism, Hildegard Hoeller, *Edith Wharton's Dialogue with Realism and Sentimental Fiction* (Gainesville: University of Florida Press, 2000); Boydston, "'Grave Endearing Traditions'"; and Merish, "Engendering Naturalism." See also Robin Beaty, "'Lilies That Fester': Sentimentality in *The House of Mirth*," *College Literature* 14 (1987): 97–108. For a discussion of this issue as it concerns a male naturalist writer, see Francesca Sawaya, "Sentimental Tentacles: Frank Norris's *The Octopus*," in *Sentimental Men: Masculinity and the Politics of Affect in American Culture*, ed. Mary Chapman and Glenn Hendler (Berkeley: University of California Press, 1999), 259–71.

71. Kete, *Sentimental Collaborations*, 89. For a discussion of the difference between sentimentalism and sentimentality, along with an analysis of how sentimentality, as a literary mode, shapes a crucial scene in *The House of Mirth*, see chap. 5 in this volume, e-note 31.

72. For an insightful study of the relationship between Wenzell's illustrations and Wharton's text, see Jason Williams, "Competing Visions: Edith Wharton and A. B. Wenzel in *The House of Mirth*," *The Edith Wharton Review*, 26, no. 1 (Spring 2010): 1–9.

73. Lee, *Edith Wharton*, 159.

74. Halttunen, *Confidence Men and Painted Women*, 33–55, 198–210.

75. Amy L. Blair, "Misreading *The House of Mirth*," *American Literature* 76 (2004): 149–75.

76. Horatio Alger, Jr., *Ragged Dick or, Street Life in New York with Boot Blacks*, ed. Hildegard Hoeller (1868; rpt. New York and London: W. W. Norton, 2008); Warren Susman, "'Personality' and the Making of Twentieth-Century American Culture," in *Culture as History: The Transformation of American Society in the Twentieth Century* (New York: Pantheon, 1984), 271–86; Halttunen, *Confidence Men and Painted Women*, 198–210.

77. Blair, "Misreading *The House of Mirth*," 160–65. See also Melanie Dawson, "Lily Bart's Fractured Alliances and Wharton's Appeal to the Middlebrow Reader," *Essays in Reader-Oriented Theory, Criticism, and Pedagogy* 41 (1991): 1–30.

78. Stephanie Harzewski, *Chick Lit and Postfeminism* (Charlottesville: University of Virginia Press, 2011), 108–9. Lois Tyson, "Beyond Morality: Lily Bart, Laurence Selden, and the Commodity Aesthetic in *The House of Mirth*," *Edith Wharton Review* 9, no. 2 (Fall 1992): 3–10.

79. Edith Wharton, *The Custom of the Country*, ed. with an intro. by Stephen Orgel (1913; rpt. New York: Oxford University Press, 1995).

80. For critics on Lily, self-commodification, and the marriage market, see e-note.

81. Studies that address Lily Bart's psychological development include Lidoff, "Another Sleeping Beauty"; Carol J. Wershoven, "*The Awakening* and *The House of Mirth*: Studies of Arrested Development," *American Literary Realism 1870–1910* 19, no. 3 (Spring 1987): 27–41; and Ellie Ragland Sullivan, "The Daughter's Dilemma: Psychoanalytic Interpretation and Edith Wharton's *The House of Mirth*," in *The House of Mirth: Case Studies in Contemporary Criticism*, ed. Shari Benstock (New York: St. Martin's Press, 1994), 464–82. See also Erlich, *Sexual Education*, 16–49, 50–74.

82. For a discussions of Veblen's influence on *The House of Mirth*, see Montgomery, *Displaying Women*; Merish, "Engendering Naturalism"; J. Michael Duvall, "The Futile and the Dingy: Wasting and Being Wasted in *The House of Mirth*," in *Memorial Boxes and Guarded Interiors: New Essays on Edith Wharton and Material Culture*, ed. Gary Totten (Tuscaloosa: University of Alabama Press, 2007), 159–83; Ruth Bernard Yeazell, "The Conspicuous Wasting of Lily Bart," *English Literary History* 59 (1992): 713–34.

83. Elizabeth Ammons, editor's note, in Wharton, *House of Mirth*, 30.

84. Cotton, "Swine and Goats," 314–18.

85. Elizabeth Ammons, editor's note for "Sarum Rule," in Wharton, *House of Mirth*: "The classic form of Christian liturgy in Latin used in England before the protestant [sic] Reformation and remaining the source of the modern Anglican or Episcopal liturgy" (20).

86. See Carol Singley's careful explication of this imagery in the novel and her discussion of Wharton's use of Hawthorne's "The Celestial Railroad" and Bunyan's *The Pilgrim's Progress*, in *Matters*, 73–77. Also see note 3 above.

87. For a personal memoir of this reform movement, see Jane Addams, *Twenty Years at Hull House; with Autobiographical Notes*, ed. with an intro. by Victoria Bissel Brown (Boston: Bedford/St. Martin's, 1999). For a discussion of these alternative values as they appear in the novel, see Lawrence Buell, "Downwardly Mobile for Conscience's Sake: Voluntary Simplicity from Thoreau to Lily Bart," *American Literary History* 17 (2005): 653–65.

88. On working girls' clubs in this period, see Eileen Connell, "*The House of Mirth* and the New York City Working Girls' Clubs," *Women's Studies* 26:557–604. Also, Linda S. Watts, "The Bachelor Girl and the Body Politics: The Built Environment, Self-Possession, and the Never-Married Woman in *The House of Mirth*," in Totten, ed., *Memorial Boxes*, 187–207. For an overview of young working women's lives in New York at this time, see Kathy Peiss, *Cheap Amusements: Working Women and Leisure in Turn-of-the-Century New York* (Philadelphia: Temple University Press, 1985).

89. For a discussion of Lily's emotional response to luxurious interiors, see Jean-Christophe Agnew, "A House of Fiction: Domestic Interiors and the Commodity Aesthetic," in *Consuming Visions: Accumulation and Display of Goods in America, 1880–1920*, ed. Simon J. Bonner (New York: W. W. Norton, 1989), 133–55. For more on Agnew's analysis, see e-note.

90. Campbell, *Romantic Ethic*, 36–57, 77–95.

91. For discussions of this novel in relation to *Sister Carrie*, see Merish, "Engendering Naturalism"; Maureen Howard, "*The House of Mirth*: The Bachelor and the Baby," in *The Cambridge Companion to Edith Wharton*, ed. Millicent Bell (Cambridge, UK: Cambridge University Press, 1995), 137–56; and Alan Price, "Lily Bart and Carrie Meeber: Cultural Sisters," *American Literary Realism: 1870–1910* 13 (1980): 238–45.

92. Numerous biographers and critics have noted the parallels between Lily Bart's upbringing and that of Edith Wharton herself. Gloria Erlich, for example, writes, "The Bart family style and values caricature those of the Jones family" (*Sexual Education*, 54). "Lily" was also one of Edith Jones's nicknames as a girl.

93. A story published just before *The House of Mirth* focuses on a young woman whose marriageability, like Lily's, is seen as her family's "last asset." Edith Wharton, "The Last Asset" (1904), in *The Collected Stories of Edith Wharton*, ed. with an intro. by R. W. B. Lewis (New York: Charles Scribner's Sons, 1968), 590–615.

94. For a helpful discussion of the psychological consequences of materialistic values, see Tim Kasser, Richard M. Ryan, Charles E. Couchman, and Kennon M. Sheldon, "Materialistic Values: Their Causes and Consequences," in *Psychology and Consumer Culture*, ed. Kasser and. Kanner, 11–28. See also introduction in this volume, note 30 and e-note 30 for related sources.

95. Thomas Cole's "The Voyage of Life" is a series of four paintings from 1840 depicting the stages of man's life in a religious allegory beginning with his setting out on the river of life as a child, enduring various threats and challenges as a mature adult, and ending with his being ushered in the divine afterlife by a guardian angel. Tremendously popular, Cole's allegory was strongly reminiscent of Bunyan's own allegory of spiritual pilgrimage. Lily's disdain for these images and the values they represent sheds an ironic light on her own psychological and moral journey on the river of life, which ends not with her induction into heaven but with her fatal wreck in a "dingy" boarding house.

96. McCracken, "Diderot Unities," 118–29.

97. The parallels between Wharton's memories of her father and her portrayal of Mr. Bart have often been noted. See for example, Erlich, *Sexual Education*, 54.

98. On Lily's artistry and self-fashioning, see Cynthia Griffin Wolff, "Lily Bart and the Beautiful Death," *American Literature*, 46, no. 1 (March 1974): 16–40; Emily J. Orlando, "Picturing Lily: Body Art in *The House of Mirth*; or, Her Body Becomes Her Art," in *Edith Wharton and the Visual Arts* (Tuscaloosa: University of Alabama Press, 2007), 55–86; Elaine Showalter, "The Death of the Lady (Novelist): Wharton's *House of Mirth*," *Representations* 9 (Winter 1985): 133–39. See e-note 80 above for more sources.

99. Elizabeth Kowaleski-Wallace, in *Consuming Subjects: Women, Shopping, and Business in the Eighteenth-Century* (New York: Columbia University Press, 1997), perceptively analyzes the intersecting constructions of woman as commodity, as producer of herself as commodity, and as the marketer of that commodity (111–43). See e-note for more details.

100. For a discussion of prostitution and *The House of Mirth*, see Margit Stange, "Lily Bart at the Point of 'Modification,'" in *Personal Property: Wives, White Slaves, and the Market in Women* (Baltimore, MD: Johns Hopkins University Press, 1998), 54–71. Many critics discussing Lily's self-commodification and the marriage market also deal with the theme of prostitution. See Lee, *Edith Wharton*, 202; and sources listed in e-note 80.

101. See Edwards, *A Treatise on the Religious Affections* (1746). His discussion of grace as "Consent to Being in General" may be found in *The Nature of True Virtue*.

102. This quotation is from a diary Wharton kept during Walter Berry's final illness in 1927. It is quoted in Lee, *Edith Wharton*: "October 4: I don't believe in God, but I believe in his saints. Then — ?" (655). The original source is housed in the Edith Wharton Collection, Yale Collection of American Literature, Beinecke Rare Book and Manuscript Library, Yale University.

103. See e-note for Hermione Lee's summary assessment of Wharton's "skeptical agnosticism."

104. See e-note 53 on this issue in Wharton's own life.

105. Anne McClintock, *Imperial Leather: Race, Gender, and Sexuality in the Colonial Contest* (New York: Routledge, 1995), 154. For discussions of this novel that also draw on McClintock's insights, see e-note.

106. Ibid., 152–53. See also Mary Douglas, *Purity and Danger: An Analysis of Concepts of Pollution and Taboo* (Baltimore: Penguin, c. 1966, 1970) and Adeline Masquelier, ed., *Dirt, Undress, and Difference: Critical Perspectives on the Body's Surface* (Bloomington: Indiana University Press, 2005), esp. the introduction, which discusses Mary Douglas's work and its influence, 1–33.

107. McClintock, *Imperial Leather*, 153. See introduction in this volume, e-note 39, for a quotation from Marx on the commodity fetish.

108. McClintock, *Imperial Leather*, 153.

109. Ibid., 161–62.

110. Ibid., 161.

111. See introduction in this volume, e-note 22, for scholarship on the "separate spheres."

112. McClintock, *Imperial Leather*, 164–65.

113. Ibid., 165.

114. Ibid. In *Sentimental Materialism: Gender, Commodity Culture, and Nineteenth-Century American Literature* (Durham and London: Duke University Press, 2000), Lori Merish agrees with McClintock's overall analysis. See e-note for her argument.

115. See note 80 above on Lily's self-fashioning as a commodity for the marriage market.

116. The comment on a "futile" shape references Veblen's *The Theory of the Leisure Class*. For a discussion of this issue in the novel, see Duvall's "The Futile and the Dingy" and other sources cited in note 82. In *Sentimental Materialism*, Lori Merish provides a valuable overview of how the gendering of consumption helps to produce and police class boundaries (see e-note 114). On the class relationships displayed in the novel's opening scene, see Kaplan, "Crowded Spaces," 88–103.

117. See my earlier discussion of consumer goods serving as a "map" to the "territory" of social and cultural relationships in chap. 1 in this volume and in chap. 1, note 30.

118. Theorists on this issue of women and the body tend to see women as more "burdened by natural immanence" than men. See, for example, Susan Bordo, *Unbearable Weight*, 1–42. See also Simone de Beauvoir, *The Second Sex*, trans. and ed. H. M. Parshley (1949; rpt. New York: Knopf, 1952) and Sherry B. Ortner and Harriet Whitehead, eds., *Sexual Meanings: The Cultural Construction of Gender and Sexuality* (Cambridge, UK: Cambridge University Press, 1981). As anthropologists have often noted, across cultures female imagery

tends to be polarized between "virgin" and "whore," a binary symbolizing the separation of the sexual, mortal body from the asexual, immortal spirit. For more on this issue, see e-note.

119. Alcott, "Experiments," *Little Women*, 135–48.

120. Alcott, *Little Women*, 601.

121. On this issue see Jennifer Fleissner, "The Biological Clock: Edith Wharton, Naturalism, and the Temporality of Womanhood," *American Literature* 78 (2006): 519–48.

122. However, if economic security is a necessary condition for happiness and self-realization, as Abraham Maslow claims, it is a not a sufficient one. Hence Thoreau's dictum that clothes, while necessary to preserve the vital heat, should not be used to define the person whose heat is thus preserved. As we have seen, Alcott modified this Transcendental dictum, allowing clothing not to define but to express the individual, and saw this self-expression as both natural and healthy, with its frustration a source of distress and its realization, within the individual's economic means, a matter of social connection and creativity.

123. Fitzgerald, *Great Gatsby*, 157. For a discussion of consumer desire and acquisition as a form of "terror management," a strategy for escaping the painful awareness of human vulnerability and mortality, see Sheldon Solomon, Jeff Greenberg, and David Shepherd, "Lethal Consumption: Death-Defying Materialism," in *Psychology and Consumer Culture*, ed. Kasser and Kanner, 127–46. An important source for their analysis is Ernest Becker, *The Denial of Death* (New York: Free Press, 1973).

124. Judith Fetterley, "'The Temptation to be a Beautiful Object': Double Standard and Double Bind in *The House of Mirth*," *Studies in American Fiction* 5 (1977): 199–211.

125. On the role of materialistic behavior in providing an escape from painful emotions and fears, see these additional essays in *The Psychology of Consumer Culture*, ed. Kasser and Kanner: Deborah Du Vann Winter, "Shopping for Sustainability: Psychological Solutions to Overconsumption," 69–87; Jeffrey Kottler, Marilyn Montgomery, and David Shepherd, "Acquisitive Desire: Assessment and Treatment," 149–68; and Ronald J. Faber, "Self-Control and Compulsive Buying," 169–87.

CHAPTER 3. *Lily at the Crossroads*

1. For a discussion of Wharton's use of Bunyan's *Pilgrim's Progress* and Hawthorne's "The Celestial Railroad," see Singley, *Matters*, 67–88; esp. "Railroads and Pilgrims," 73–77.

2. Some analyses of Selden's character include: Erlich, *Sexual Education*, 50–74; Kim, "Lamarckism," 187–210; Wolff, *Feast of Words*, 112–33; Linda Wagner-Martin, *The House of Mirth: A Novel of Admonition* (Boston: G. K. Hall, 1990), 30–40; David Holbrook, *Edith Wharton and the Unsatisfactory Man* (London: Vision, 1991), 21–37. See also Buell, "Downwardly Mobile," 653–65, for a discussion of Selden's "republic of the spirit" in relation to American ideas about "voluntary simplicity."

3. Campbell, *Romantic Ethic*, 195–201.

4. See Lears, "From Salvation to Self-Realization," 1–38.

5. Wharton's emphasis here on a "more specialized race" has been much noted by critics dealing her interest in evolutionary theory. I will discuss this issue further in chap. 4.

6. See Bourdieu, *Distinction*, 11–96.

7. See e-note for critics on Wharton's treatment of Lawrence Selden.

8. For a thoughtful discussion of Lily's repeated maskings and veilings, see Kress, "Designing Our Interiors," 131–59.

9. Lily's slighting reference to the early fifties suggests her rejection of the sentimental values promoted by women writers in the period, values still shaping books like *Little Women*. Just as Lily would be humiliated if forced to wear the earlier period's "book-muslin dresses" and "gigot sleeves" (much as Lucretia Jones was humiliated by wearing her unfashionable tarlatan dress), she finds no help in the unfashionable values of "true womanhood." And yet, while this advice seems empty, mere "copy-book maxims," Lily's later encounters with Nettie Struther will give her another view of that older discourse.

10. For a sensitive psychoanalytic reading of Lily's troubled relationship to Selden and her "child-like" responses to him, see Lidoff, "Another Sleeping Beauty," 181–207.

11. See Galbus, "Edith Wharton's Material Republic," 1, 3–7, for a careful explication of this dialogue in relation to the ideas expressed in Plato's *Republic*. Also Singley, *Matters*, 164–67. For more on Galbus's and Singley's analyses, see e-note.

12. Henry David Thoreau, "Solitude," *Walden*, 383. For more on this issue, see e-note.

13. For more on this issue, see the discussion in chap. 1 and the related notes 17, 18, and 19.

14. For a discussion of early modern debates about gold and its value — intrinsic or symbolic — see "Idolatry and Political Economy," in Hawkes, *Idols of the Marketplace*, 27–47. See also Walter Benn Michaels, ed., *The Gold Standard and the Logic of Naturalism: American Literature at the Turn of the Century* (Berkeley: University of California Press, 1987).

15. For discussions of Veblen's influence on *The House of Mirth*, see (among others) Montgomery, *Displaying Women*; Duvall, "The Futile and the Dingy"; Yeazell, "Conspicuous Wasting"; Merish, "Engendering Naturalism," 257.

16. On the "waste" of human nature in a society of display, see Duvall, "The Futile and the Dingy," and Yeazell, "Conspicuous Wasting." See also Meg March's acquisitive desire for purple silk as a sign of social status in *Little Women* and chap. 1 in this volume, note 48 and e-note 48.

17. Webb Keane, "Sincerity, 'Modernity,' and the Protestants," *Cultural Anthropology* 17, no. 1 (2002): 65–92.

18. Lionel Trilling, *Sincerity and Authenticity* (Cambridge, MA: Harvard University Press, 1972).

19. Keane, "Sincerity," 83–84.

20. Ibid., 84.

21. Ibid., 74.

22. On these responses to Protestant individualism, see introduction in this volume, notes 22 and 23 and e-notes 22 and 23.

23. On this issue, see Burkitt, "Ethics, Self, and Performativity," in *Social Selves*, 58–84.

24. Harriet Beecher Stowe, *The Minister's Wooing* (1862); rpt. in Harriet Beecher Stowe, *Uncle Tom's Cabin, or, Life among the Lowly; The Minister's Wooing; Oldtown Folks* (New York: Literary Classics of the United States, 1982).

25. For a discussion of the continuation of Calvinist thinking, in secularized form, in Wharton's work, see Singley, *Matters*, 89–126.

26. Keane, "Sincerity," 83.

27. Ibid.

28. On the social construction of taste and cultural "distinction," see Bourdieu, *Distinction*, 11–96.

29. For a discussion of the links between women's business dealings and prostitution, an implied issue here and an important theme through the novel, see Kowaleski-Wallace, *Consuming Subjects*, 111–43. See also chap. 2 in this volume, note 99 and e-note 99; note 100; and e-note 80.

30. Jonathan Edwards, *The Nature of True Virtue*.

31. For a discussion of this opposition see Mikhail Bakhtin, *Rabelais and His World*, trans. Helene Iswolsky (1965; Bloomington: Indiana University Press, 1984), esp. chap. 5, "The Grotesque Body and Its Sources," 303–67.

32. McClintock, *Imperial Leather*, 160–67. On the hidden interdependence of the domestic, leisured lady of "taste" and the women whose labor supported her and whose devalued status provided the necessary opposition and contrast to define her, see Merish, *Sentimental Materialism*, 1–27, esp. 19–21. This devaluation applied most obviously to women of color, but produced a subtle racialization of white working-class women as well. On these issues, see also Sarah Way Sherman, "Party Out of Bounds: Gender and Class in Jewett's 'The Best China Saucer, '" in *Jewett and Her Contemporaries*, ed. Karen L. Kilcup and Thomas S. Edwards (Gainesville: University Press of Florida, 1999), 223–48.

33. Wharton's description of Lily's aesthetic goals are deeply connected to her own love of beauty, a love she felt from earliest childhood and which sustained her work in literature and design throughout her life. See chap. 2 in this volume, note 15 and e-note 15; also note 49.

34. Sir Joshua Reynolds was not only the painter of the portrait Lily selects for her self-presentation in the *tableaux vivants*, he was also the author of *Discourses on Art*, an important work on the uses of classical imagery to represent women. According to Jason Williams, Wharton had a copy of Reynolds's *Discourses* in her library and discussed his ideas in her letters ("Competing Visions," 7–8). For more on classical imagery and women's portraits during this period, see chap. 1 in this volume, note 51 and e-note 51. Virtually every critic writing on *The House of Mirth* has an analysis of this scene. For some examples, see e-note.

35. Singley writes: "This idealized scene is a triumphant moment when Lily's true essence is revealed, not because Lily transfixes the gaze of her observers, but because in selecting her subject, she forgoes the 'advantages of a more sumptuous setting' and overcomes the fear 'that she was risking too much in dispensing with such supports.' . . . Lily appears simply as she is: the portrayal is 'simply and undisguisedly the portrait of Miss Bart'" (*Matters*, 81).

36. Kim writes, "Like an anomalous moment that does not count in an enduring character, the frivolous individual or society will have no dimension in time and thus no real existence" ("Lamarckism," 201). I would argue, however, that although Lily is indeed the product of a frivolous society, she is not herself wholly frivolous; hence, as Wharton explains, the "dramatic significance" and "tragic implication" of her story (*A Backward Glance: An Autobiography* [1933, 1934; rpt. New York: Touchstone, 1998], 207).

37. Kress, "Designing Our Interiors," 135.

38. Ibid., 145.

39. Ibid., 135. Kress's discussion compares Wharton's treatment of this central question with that of her contemporaries, in particular the pragmatist George Herbert Mead.

40. F. Scott Fitzgerald, "Absolution," in *The Short Stories of F. Scott Fitzgerald*, ed. Matthew J. Bruccoli (1924; rpt. New York: Scribner, 1989), 271.

41. See chap. 2 in this volume, note 80 and e-note 80, on Lily's self-fashioning and self-commodification.

42. However, the conditions of *Little Women*'s own production, as we've seen, belie this. Alcott was not Jo, but a more complex, divided person than her fictional heroine. Alcott's pseudonymous publication of sensational stories like "Behind a Mask," some featuring sympathetic confidence women, shows another, disavowed, side of their author.

43. A similarly ironic example from twenty-first-century consumer behavior would be the shopper who purchases an expensive sports utility vehicle named "Escape" or "Liberty" only to put him or herself deeply into debt to pay off the loan, thereby limiting the very freedom the commodity symbolized.

44. See e-note for more on Lily's difficulty "living with her thoughts."

45. This has been an important theme for Wharton critics. See, for example, Gimbel, *Orphancy and Survival*; Boydston, "'Grave Endearing Traditions,'" 31–40; Erlich, *Sexual Education*, 50–74.

46. Alcott, *Little Women*, 18. Jo goes on to ask, "We ought to have our roll of directions, like Christian. What shall we do about that?" and Mrs. March replies, "Look under your pillows Christmas morning and you'll find your guide-book" (18). Needless to say, Lily Bart has neither a guide-book nor a wise mother to help her. For a perceptive reading of this scene between Lily and Gerty, see Lidoff, "Another Sleeping Beauty," 519–32.

47. On the way that identity depends upon self-narration and the deployment of learned discourses, see White and Epston, *Narrative Means*, 1–37.

48. Lee, *Edith Wharton*, 204–5; Buell, "Downwardly Mobile," 661.

49. For a discussion of Dickens and the "Carol Philosophy" of moral and social reform, see Davis, *Lives and Times*, 51–87. For more on Dickens and sentimentalism, see e-note.

50. Henry James, *The Ambassadors*, ed. with an intro. by Leon Edel (1903; rpt. Boston: Houghton Mifflin, 1960).

51. Bunyan, *Pilgrim's Progress*, 61.

52. Ibid., 79–80.

53. Alcott, "Amy's Valley of Humiliation," in *Little Women*, 83–91.

54. Bunyan, *Pilgrim's Progress*, 80.

55. Ibid., 80.

56. Ibid., 133–34.

57. Ibid., 137; internal quotation from Psalms 111:10; Proverbs 9:10.

CHAPTER 4. *Smart Jews and Failed Protestants*

1. For discussions of this issue, as well as comparisons of *The House of Mirth* with other major novels featuring Jewish characters, see e-note.

2. On the issue of appearance and reality in the novel, see Christopher Gair, "The Crumbling Structure of 'Appearances': Representation and Authenticity in *The House of Mirth* and *The Custom of the Country*," *Meddelanden fran Stringbergssallskapet* 43:349–73; rpt. in *Edith Wharton's* The House of Mirth: *A Casebook*, ed. Carol J. Singley (New York: University Press, 2003), 271–97.

3. Gary Levine *The Merchant of Modernism: The Economic Jew in Anglo-American Literature, 1864–1939* (New York: Routledge, 2003), 53–65; Goldman-Price, "'Perfect Jew' and

The House of Mirth," 163–79; Jennie A. Kassanoff, *Edith Wharton and the Politics of Race* (New York: Cambridge University Press, 2004), 37–58; Elizabeth Ammons, "Edith Wharton and Race," in *The Cambridge Companion to Edith Wharton,* ed. Millicent Bell (Cambridge: Cambridge University Press, 1995), 68–86. See this chapter's e-note 1 for more citations.

4. John Higham, *Send These to Me: Immigrants in Urban America,* 2nd ed. (Baltimore, MD: Johns Hopkins University Press, 1984), 95–116.

5. Ibid., 99.

6. Ibid., 99–100.

7. Ibid., 100.

8. Ibid., 100–101.

9. Ibid., 101.

10. Goldman-Price, " 'Perfect Jew' and *The House of Mirth,*" 26.

11. Ibid., 27.

12. According to Hermione Lee, "The ambivalent relation of Jewish financiers to the establishment can be seen in the contrast between a short-lived 'American Society for the Suppression of the Jews' in the 1870s, which demanded that they be 'excluded from all first class society,' and the meteoric rise of the millionaire Jewish financier August Belmont. (Wharton made good use of this in the characters of Simon Rosedale in *The House of Mirth* and Julius Beaufort in *The Age of Innocence*)" (57).

13. Goldman-Price, " 'Perfect Jew' and *The House of Mirth,*" 27.

14. Abraham Cahan, *The Rise of David Levinsky,* ed. Jules Chametzky (1917; rpt. New York: Penguin, 1993); Anzia Yezierska, *Salome of the Tenements,* intro. by Gay Wilentz (1923; rpt. Champaign: University of Illinois Press, 1996).

15. Higham, *Send These to Me,* 106.

16. Ibid., 109.

17. Ibid.

18. C. Ford Worthington, ed., *Letters of Henry Adams,* 2 vols. (Boston, 1938), 1:388–89; quoted in Higham, *Send These to Me,* 109.

19. Henry Cabot Lodge, quoted in Richard Weiss, "Racism in the Era of Industrialization," in *The Great Fear: Racism in the Mind of America,* ed. Gary G. Nash and Richard Weiss (New York: Holt, Rinehart and Winston, 1970), 134; Goldman-Price, " 'Perfect Jew' and *The House of Mirth,*" 29.

20. Goldman-Price, " 'Perfect Jew' and *The House of Mirth,*" 29.

21. Ibid., 29–30. The internal quotation is from William E. H. Lecky, "Israel Among the Nations" (1893), in *Historical and Political Essays* (London: Longmans, Green, 1910) 108. Wharton identified Lecky as one of "the formative influences" of her life (the others included Charles Darwin, Hippolyte Taine, and Herbert Spencer) in a letter to Sara Norton dated 16 March 1908 from 58 Rue de Varenne, Paris; quoted in *The Letters of Edith Wharton,* ed. R. W. B. Lewis and Nancy Lewis (New York: Charles Scribner's Sons, 1988), 135–37.

22. Lecky, "Israel Among the Nations," 115; quoted in Goldman-Price, " 'Perfect Jew' and *The House of Mirth,*" 30.

23. Goldman-Price, " 'Perfect Jew' and *The House of Mirth,*" 30–31.

24. Levine *Merchant of Modernism*; Hillel Levine, *Economic Origins of Anti-Semitism: Poland and Its Jews in the Early Modern Period* (New Haven: Yale University Press, 1991).

25. Gary Levine, *Merchant*, 2.

26. Hillel Levine, *Economic Origins of Anti-Semitism*, 84–5; quoted in Gary Levine, *Merchant*, 2–3.

27. Hillel Levine, *Economic Origins of Anti-Semitism*, 109, quoted in Gary Levine, *Merchant*, 3.

28. Weber, *The Protestant Ethic*, 155–83; Werner Sombart, *The Jews and Modern Capitalism*, trans. M. Epstein (Glencoe, IL: Free Press, 1951).

29. Sander Gilman, *Smart Jews: The Construction of the Image of a Jewish Superior Intelligence* (Lincoln: University of Nebraska Press, 1996), 47; Gary Levine, *Merchant*, 3.

30. Gary Levine, *Merchant*, 3.

31. Ibid.

32. Ibid., 8.

33. Ibid.

34. Ibid.

35. Zygmunt Bauman, "Allosemitism: Premodern, Modern, Postmodern," in *Modernity, Culture, and the Jew*, ed. Bryan Cheyette and Laura Marcus (Stanford: Stanford University Press, 1998), 150–51.

36. Halttunen, *Confidence Men and Painted Women*, 49–50.

37. On Max Weber and "disenchantment," see Peter Homans, "Loss and Mourning in the Life and Thought of Max Weber: Toward a Theory of Symbolic Loss," in *Symbolic Loss: The Ambiguity of Mourning and Memory at Century's End* (Charlottesville: University Press of Virginia, 2000), 225–38. As argued earlier, *Little Women* seems to be a transitional text in this process of disenchantment.

38. Keane, "Sincerity," 83–84.

39. Recent work on the character of Rosedale addresses the issue of his performativity and the challenges it poses to the identities of other characters in the novel. See Meredith Goldsmith, "The Year of the Rose: Jewish Masculinity in *The House of Mirth*," *Modern Fiction Studies* 51 (2005): 374–92; Henry B. Wonham, "Edith Wharton's Flamboyant Copy," in *Playing the Races: Ethnic Caricature and American Literary Realism* (New York: Oxford University Press, 2004), 127–90; Lori Harrison-Kahan., "'Queer Myself for Good and All': *The House of Mirth* and the Fictions of Lily's Whiteness," *Legacy* 21 (2004): 34–49.

40. Halttunen, Confidence Men and Painted Women, 196–97.

41. On the "crisis of representation," see Lears, *No Place of Grace*. On "personality," see Susman, "'Personality' and the Making of Twentieth-Century Culture." See also Goffman, *Presentation of Self*.

42. Andrew R. Heinze, "*Schizophrenia Americana*: Aliens, Alienists, and the 'Personality Shift' of Twentieth-Century Culture," *American Quarterly* 55, no. 2 (2003): 227–56.

43. Alexis de Tocqueville, *Democracy in America*, trans. Henry Reeve, rev. by Francis Bowen, vol. 2. (New York: Vintage Books, 1945), 145–47.

44. See also Burkitt, *Social Selves*, 173–84, for a discussion of the social subject as multiple and destabilized, particularly his discussion of Kenneth J. Gergen's *The Saturated Self: Dilemmas of Identity in Contemporary Life* (New York: Basic Books, 1991) and Zygmunt Bauman's *Liquid Modernity* (Cambridge, UK: Polity Press, 2000).

45. For sources on Karl Barth's critique of liberal Protestantism, see chap. 1 in this volume, e-note 14.

46. Peter Steinfels, "Fighting Modernists: A Decree That Shaped Catholicism," On Belief, *New York Times*, September 1, 2007.

47. Madison Grant, *The Passing of the Great Race, or The Racial Basis of European History* (New York: Charles Scribner's Sons, 1916). On the widespread influence of Grant's ideas on the culture and politics of his time, see Jonathan Peter Spiro, *Defending the Master Race: Conservation, Eugenics, and the Legacy of Madison Grant* (Burlington: University of Vermont Press, 2009).

48. For more on scientific racism and antisemitism, see e-note.

49. Lee, *Edith Wharton*, 271–72. For a discussion of the importance of the Dreyfus affair and its wider implications, see Louis Begley, *Why the Dreyfus Affair Matters* (New Haven: Yale University Press, 2009).

50. Kim, "Lamarckism," 187–210. For additional sources on Wharton and Darwinian theory, see chap. 2 in this volume, note 56 and e-note 56.

51. Kim, "Lamarckism," 191. Claire Preston and Bert Bender are two critics who have addressed Lamarckian influences on Wharton's work, although not to the extent that Kim has done. See Preston, *Edith Wharton's Social Register*; and Bender, "Edith Wharton, from 'The Descent of man' to *The Reef*," in *The Descent of Love: Darwin and the Theory of Sexual Selection in American Fiction, 1871–1926* (Philadelphia: University of Pennsylvania Press, 1996), 314–40.

52. L. J. Jordanova, *Lamarck* (Oxford: Oxford University Press, 1984), 109; quoted in Kim, "Lamarckism," 191.

53. Kim, "Lamarckism," 191.

54. Ibid., 198.

55. Wharton, "Life & I," 1086–87.

56. For more on epigenetics, see e-note.

57. For more on "race" as a socio-historical construct, see e-note.

58. Bourdieu, *Distinction*, 11–96.

59. According to Madison Grant: "Whether we like to admit it or not, the result of the mixture of two races, in the long run, gives us a race reverting to the more ancient, generalized and lower type. The cross between a white man and an Indian is an Indian; the cross between a white man and a negro is a negro; the cross between a white man and a Hindu is a Hindu; and the cross between any of the three European races and a Jew is a Jew" (15–16).

60. Goldman-Price, "'Perfect Jew' and *The House of Mirth*," 163–79; Levine, *Merchant*, 53–65; Kassanoff, *Edith Wharton and the Politics of Race*, 37–58; Ammons, "Edith Wharton and Race," 68–86. In *Our America: Nativism, Modernism, and Pluralism* (Durham, NC: Duke University Press, 1995), Walter Benn Michaels asserts that "the family in Wharton is social, not racial" (111). Michaels also argues that, in *The Age of Innocence*, Wharton is not concerned with genealogical purity, but rather believes that the family can be "strengthened rather than jeopardized by the threat of illegitimacy" (112).

61. According to Carol Singley (*Matters*, 57), one of the books in Wharton's library at her death was Asa Gray's *How Plants Grow* (1858).

62. Edith Wharton, letter to F. Scott Fitzgerald, Pavillon Colombe, St. Brice-sous-Forêt, 8 June 1925, in Wharton, *Letters*, 482.

63. For an excellent, detailed history of Jewish immigrants, their real-life responses to American consumer culture, and their use of consumer goods as inflected by Jewish culture and religious practices, see Andrew R. Heinze, *Adapting to Abundance: Jewish Immigrants, Mass Consumption, and the Search for American Identity* (New York: Columbia University Press, 1990).

64. Halttunen, *Confidence Men and Painted Women*, 33–34; R. W. B. Lewis, *The American Adam: Innocence, Tragedy, and Tradition in the Nineteenth Century* (Chicago: University of Chicago Press, 1955).

65. Fitzgerald, *Great Gatsby*, 75.

66. See Henry Wonham's illuminating discussion of Wharton's use of ethnic stereotypes.

67. Toni Morrison, *Playing in the Dark* (New York: Vintage, 1993), 16–17.

68. For a discussion of the possible collaboration between Rosedale as a businessman and Lily as the aesthetic commodity to which he offers "backing," see Goldsmith.

69. On the theme of market exchange and the risk of transactions, see Gary Levine, *Merchant*; Wai-chee Dimock, "Debasing Exchange: Edith Wharton's *The House of Mirth*," *PMLA* 100 (October 1985): 783–92; and Walter Benn Michaels, "Action and Accident: Photography and Writing," in *The Gold Standard and the Logic of Naturalism*, 217–44.

70. For a thorough discussion of Bunyan's response to the rise of nominalist ideas about values and market exchange, as well as the "anti-essentialist conception of the subject" that accompanied them, see Hawkes, *Idols of the Marketplace*, 213–30.

71. Rosedale's behavior here also recalls Nathaniel Hawthorne's satirical version of Bunyan's allegory "The Celestial Railroad," in which the Satanic train conductor offers to make passengers "more comfortable" by stowing their burdens in the baggage car. See Singley, "Railroads and Pilgrims," in *Matters*, 73–77.

72. Bunyan, 25.

73. Ibid.

74. Ibid., 26.

75. Ibid.

76. Ibid., 26–27.

77. Ibid., 28–29.

78. Ibid., 29.

79. Ibid., 29–30.

80. Ibid., 30.

81. Gary Levine, *Merchant*, 59.

82. Goldman-Price, "'Perfect Jew' and *The House of Mirth*," 34.

83. Gary Levine, *Merchant*, 11.

CHAPTER 5. *Lily in the Valley of the Shadow*

1. For a thorough discussion of the tension between sentimentalism and realism in Wharton's work, see Hoeller, *Wharton's Dialogue*, esp. 1–29 and 96–125.

2. For discussions of *The House of Mirth* in relation to *Sister Carrie*, see Merish, "Engendering Naturalism," 229–70; Howard, "*The House of Mirth*: The Bachelor and the Baby," 137–56; and Price, "Lily Bart and Carrie Meeber," 238–45. See e-note for critics on Dreiser and consumer culture.

3. Dreiser, *Sister Carrie*, 373.

4. Ibid.

5. For a discussion of cultural anxieties about women's tea-drinking and compulsive consumption, see Kowaleski-Wallace, *Consuming Subjects*, 19–69. See also Bonnie Lynn Gerard, "From Tea to Choral: Raising the Dead Lily Bart," *Twentieth Century Literature* 44, no. 4 (1998): 409–27. Dale Bauer has a thorough review of Wharton's preoccupation with addiction: "Wharton's 'Others': Addiction and Intimacy," in *The Historical Guide to Edith Wharton*, ed. Carol J. Singley (Oxford, UK: Oxford University Press, 2003), 115–45. For a comparison of my approach to Bauer's, see e-note.

6. On the "wasting" of Lily's human potential, see Duvall, "The Futile and the Dingy," 159–83; and Yeazell, "Conspicuous Wasting," 713–34.

7. Joanne Dobson, "Reclaiming Sentimental Literature," *American Literature*, 69, no. 2 (June 1997): 263–88.

8. Kete, *Sentimental Collaborations*, 31–32.

9. Ibid., 34. For overviews of recent work on sentimentalism, see Hoeller, "From Agony to Ecstasy," 339–69; Mary Chapman and Glenn Hendler, "Introduction," in *Sentimental Men: Masculinity and the Politics of Affect in American Culture*, ed. Mary Chapman and Glenn Hendler (Berkeley: University of California Press, 1999), 1–16; Cindy Weinstein, *Family, Kinship, and Sympathy in Nineteenth-Century American Literature* (New York: Cambridge University Press, 2004), 194–95.

10. Kete, *Sentimental Collaborations*, 34. See chap. 1 in this volume, note 16, for sources on sentimentalism and deathbed scenes.

11. Harriet Beecher Stowe, *The Pearl of Orr's Island*, with an intro. by E. Bruce Kirkham (1862; rpt. Hartford: The Stowe-Day Foundation, 1979). See introduction in this volume, e-note 20, for more on Stowe, liberal Protestantism, and Christian nurture.

12. Henry James, *The Portrait of a Lady*, ed. Jan Cohn (1881; rpt. Boston: Houghton Mifflin, 2001. For intertextual studies of James and Wharton, see Adeline R. Tintner, "Part 1: Wharton and James," in *Edith Wharton in Context: Essays on Intertextuality* (Tuscaloosa: University of Alabama Press, 1999), 9–90; and Jerome Loving, "The Death of Romance: *The Portrait of a Lady* in the Age of Lily Bart," in *A Forward Glance: New Essays on Edith Wharton*, ed. Clare Colquitt, Susan Goodman, and Candace Waid (Newark: University of Delaware Press, 1999), 100–115.

13. Howells, quoted in Wharton, *A Backward Glance*, 147.

14. For Kete on the role of dead children in sentimental literature, see e-note.

15. For a discussion of the importance of sincerity in sentimental mourning rituals, see Halttunen, *Confidence Men and Painted Women*, 124–52.

16. See also Duvall on "dinginess" and "wasting."

17. In *A Feast of Words*, Cynthia Griffin Wolff writes of Selden, "His moral aesthetic code is deeply flawed. It is a code he can only follow by a series of suppressed hypocrisies; he is as much a parasite on the house of mirth as Lily is" (129). For an equally critical assessment, see Wagner-Martin, *House of Mirth*, 30–40.

18. It is, I think, worth noting that Wharton links this "victory" to a human rather than an otherworldly "renewal," and "renewal" is a word that becomes increasingly insistent in the novel's final pages. Also, for Darwin-influenced theorists, successful reproduction means the

survival of an individual's genes after her death — in evolutionary terms, a kind of biological immortality.

19. See e-note for more on object-relations theory.

20. For sensitive psychoanalytic readings of this scene (and the following scene of Lily's death), see Lidoff, "Another Sleeping Beauty," 519–32; and Erlich, *Sexual Education*, 50–74. While aspects of my own reading have much in common with theirs, I see a stronger link between Lily's drug use and the unfulfilled needs that propel her materialistic behavior. I also cannot agree with Lidoff that Lily is incapable of love, although I do see her as struggling to recognize, express, and act on the love she feels.

21. Merish, "Engendering Naturalism," 257.

22. Gary Levine, *Merchant*, 64.

23. Lee, *Edith Wharton*, 202; Nancy Topping Bazin, "The Destruction of Lily Bart: Capitalism, Christianity, and Male Chauvinism," *Denver Quarterly* 7, no. 4 (Winter 1983): 104. On this issue, see also Robin Beaty, "'Lilies That Fester,'" 97–108.

24. Singley, *Matters*, 78.

25. Hoeller, *Wharton's Dialogue*, x.

26. Ibid., xii.

27. Merish, "Engendering Naturalism," 340.

28. Ibid. See also Boydston, "'Grave Endearing Traditions,'" 31–40.

29. Merish, "Engendering Naturalism," 339.

30. Gary Levine, *Merchant*, 64.

31. For a discussion of the stylistic shift that appears in this passage, see e-note.

32. For a comparison of this reading with that of Sharon Kim, see e-note.

33. See e-note for more attachment theory and contemporary epigenetics' view on "nature and nurture."

34. Leo Tolstoy, *Anna Karenina,* trans. Louise and Aylmer Maude, with an intro. by W. Gareth Jones (1877; rpt. New York: Oxford University Press, 1995).

35. Edith Wharton, "The Bunner Sisters," *Edith Wharton: Collected Stories 1911–1937,* ed. with an intro. by Maureen Howard (1916; rpt. New York: The Library of America, 2001), 236.

36. James Baldwin, "Sonny's Blues" (1957), in *Black Writers of America: A Comprehensive Anthology*, ed. Richard Barksdale and Kenneth Kinnamon (New York: Macmillan, 1972), 731.

37. Stowe, *Pearl of Orr's Island*, 396–97.

38. There have been numerous critical discussions of the novel's "unsaid word." For especially thoughtful examples, see Shari Benstock, "'The Word Which Made All Clear': The Silent Close of *The House of Mirth*," in *Famous Last Words: Women Against Novelistic Endings*, ed. Alison Booth (Charlottesville: University Press of Virginia, 1993), 230–58; and Waid, *Edith Wharton's Letters*, 15–49. For more on this issue, see e-note.

39. For critics on this last scene and the image of Lily Bart's dead body, see e-note.

40. Henry James, "The Beast in the Jungle" (1903), in *Henry James: Major Stories and Essays*, ed. Leon Edel et. al. (New York: Library of America, 1999), 445–90; and Wharton *The Age of Innocence*, 274. For a comparison of the conclusions to *The House of Mirth* and "The Beast in the Jungle," see Singley, *Matters*, 85.

Index

Note: *LW* indicates *Little Women; HM* indicates *The House of Mirth.* An "e" prefixed before a page number indicates e-note location.

Archer, Isabel (fictional character), 247–48
artistic creativity and self-expression,
    39–40, 45–46, 149–50, 152–53
associated objects in systems of consumer
    goods, 105
Auerbach, Nina, 27
authentic self: in Amy's self-presentation,
    42–44; and fashion, 32–33, 39, e10–
    11n39, e11n44; vs. hypocritical material-
    ism in *LW*, 31–33, 35–36, 38, 39; internal
    sources of, 39; Lily's complex elements
    of, 127–29, 142–43, 150–52, 236–38,
    249–51; making choices for, 38, 55;
    Marmee as guide to, 22; material goods
    as symbols of, 62, 124; as modernity's
    goal, 138; obscuring of in modern
    environment, 184; social construction of,
    61; value of, 42; Wharton's, 86–87, 151

Backward Glance, A (Wharton), 74–75,
    78–79, 82
Bakhtin, Mikhail, 149
Baldwin, James, 266
Bart, Lily (fictional character): aesthetic
    sensibility, 106–7, 115, 150, 211, 213;
    anxiety, overwhelming need to escape,
    7, 217, 218–20, 226–27; appearance over
    substance, 93, 104–5, 113–14, 133, 257,
    e24–25n39; aunt/guardian's relation-
    ship to, 95–96; authentic self, 127–29,
    142–43, 150–52, 236–38, 249–51; and
    blackmail, 12, 148–49, 206, 210, 229;
    capability for love, 301n20; charitable
    instincts, 146–47; compartmentalization
    of conscience, 145; complications and
    contradictions of, 74; continuity of
    life vision, 190, 259–60, e24nn32–33,
    e24n38; as con woman, 107, 119–21, 145,
    155–58, 161; core vs. essential self, 14;
    and deathbed sentimentalism, 249–50,
    267; death of, 265–66, e24–25n39;
    descent into self-loathing, 160–61;
    "dinginess" signifier for, 104, 110–21,
    120, 160, 163, 211, 220, 221, 229–30, 258;
    disdain for spiritual pilgrimage allegory,

290n95; divided motives and lack of
    self-awareness, 106–7, 171–73; divided
    self, 74, 107–8, 126, 128–29, 152, 154, 157–
    58, 161, 169, 170, 185–86, 236–37, 261–62,
    263, e24–25n39; emotional attachment
    struggles, 87, 95–96, 102–3, 129, 134–35,
    154–55, 159, 164, 250–51, 253–54, 259–61,
    266–67; essential self, 14, 112–13, 151,
    e24–25n39; failure to obtain grace,
    166–68; fashion's role in identity of, 104,
    114, 145–46, 257; frivolousness of, 74,
    189, 294n36; and Gerty, 99–100, 109,
    114–15, 146, 150, 152, 159–63, 171–72; and
    Gus Trenor, 143–44, 155–57; idolatrous
    materialism of, 7, 100–102, 117, 164, 169,
    173; isolation and death of, e24n32;
    jewel self-representation, 104, 105, 106,
    110–18, 151; lack of emotional literacy,
    100, 104, 109, 129, 152, 161, 259–60; lack
    of financial savvy, 145; moral integrity
    struggle, 93, 108, 165, 171–72, 205, 207,
    209, 211–14, 217, 220, 238, 262–63, 266;
    as ornamental beauty, 93, 104, 113–14,
    133, 257, e24–25n48; overwhelming
    need to escape anxiety, 7, 217, 218–20,
    226–27; parallels with Wharton's life,
    85, 290n92, e19–20n44; and par-
    ents, 86, 102–3, 184; pride of, 217–18,
    222–26, 228, 230–31, 236, 259; and
    prostitution, 12, 106–7, 161, 290n100,
    294n29; and Rosedale, 8, 144–45, 170,
    195–207, 210–14; and Selden, 122–23,
    125–43, 148, 154–55, 164–65, 230–38,
    249–51; self-assessment of, 147–48,
    154; self-production of, 93–109, 106–7,
    108, 141–42, 151, 211, 213; and servant
    class labor, 112–13; slough of despond,
    165; and Struther, 251–56; in *tableaux
    vivants*, 149–54; tragedy of materialism
    for, 2, 73, 258. *See also under* addic-
    tion; commodification; Farish, Gerty;
    self-awareness
Bart, Mr. (fictional character), 102–3
Bart, Mrs. (fictional character), 102–4, 106,
    107

Barth, Karl, 186, e8–9n14

Baudrillard, Jean, 1, 19, 34, 66, 71, 105

Bauer, Dale, e22n5

Bauman, Zygmunt, 183

beauty: artistic creativity and self-expres-
    sion, 39–40, 45–46, 149–50, 152–53; Lily
    as ornamental beauty, 93, 104, 113–14,
    133, 257, e24–25n48; Lily's attachment
    to, 106–7, 115, 150, 211, 213; Wharton's
    love of, 77, 86, 294n33

Bedell, Madelon, 21, 47, 276n8

Bellomont as ultimate vanity fair of *HM*,
    97, 100

Belmont, August, 177, 296n12

Berry, Walter, 87, 287n55

Bhaer, Fritz (fictional character), 56–57

blackmail, 12, 148–49, 206, 210, 229

Blair, Amy, 91–92

"blood" for Wharton as underlying feelings
    and desires, 189–90

body/spirit dualism, Protestant, 12, 88, 108,
    137–39

Bourdieu, Pierre, 11, 67, 125, 190

Breward, Christopher, e11n44

Brodhead, Richard, 22, e14n66

Brooke, John (fictional character), 39

Buell, Lawrence, 163

Bunner Sisters, The (Wharton), 263

Bunyan, John, 3. See also *Pilgrim's Progress*

Burkitt, Ian, 11, 14, 61, 281n57, 297n44

Bushnell, Candace, 92–93

Bushnell, Horace, 23, 50, 273n20, e4n20,
    e5n22

Campbell, Colin, 3, 11, 28–29, 57, 64, 124

capitalism, origins in Puritan asceticism,
    2–3, 30, 181–82

captive self, Lily's, 129

Catholicism. *See* Roman Catholicism

"Celestial Rail-Road, The" (Hawthorne),
    73, 98, 284n3, 299n71

character. *See* moral discourse and
    development

child development, liberal Protestant
    view of, 9–10, 22–23, 273n20, e12n50,

e24n33. *See also* moral discourse and
    development

chloral hydrate, 15, 220, 226–27, 238–39,
    264–65

Christian nurture and sentimentalism:
    child's accessibility to, 9–10, 23; as
    embodied in Gerty Farish, 99, 159,
    163, 223; limitations of, 8, 10, 163; in
    LW, 22–28, 50–52, 140, 184; in moral
    consumerism, 6; Protestant adoption of,
    67–68, 140, 183–84; Struther and Lily,
    251–56. *See also* Bushnell, Horace

Christmas, beginnings of modern, 1–2, 17,
    276n8

class: gendering of consumption and,
    291n116; in *LW,* 67–68; racializing of
    lower classes, 113, 187; servant class,
    111–13, 294n32; shifts in Wharton's New
    York, 75–76. *See also* leisure class

classical representation of women in art,
    152–53, 280n51, 294n34, e12n51

class identity, 67, 112, 283n80

Cole, Thomas, 290n95

commercial gaze, Rosedale's, 174

commodification: debasement of people
    and ideals, 74; inherent moral worth in
    for Lily, 115; Lily as decorative object,
    133; Lily's acceptance of responsibil-
    ity for, 128; and Lily's surface beauty,
    112–14; for marriage market, 12, 93,
    100, 103–5, 106–7, 119–21, e17n68,
    e17n80, e17n99; Marx on, e6–7n39;
    need for sincere home away from, 255;
    Rosedale's market evaluation of Lily,
    206; as trap for Lily, 116–17, 229; and
    Victorian dirt fetish, 110–11; of women
    generally, 36, 290n99, e17n99

Confidence Men and Painted Women
    (Halttunen), 29, 91, 184–85

consumer culture: and audience shifts
    between *LW* and *HM,* 91; as discourse
    with objects, e9–10n30; emergence of,
    3, e2n4; emotional emptiness of focus
    on, 25; *LW* as integral part of today's, 71;
    March girls' attachments, 18–21, 47–62;

and modern Christmas, 1–2, 17, 276n8; modern navigation of, 28–29, 64–66; moral participation in, 6, 25, 31, 37–40, 42–43, 61–62, 64–67, 101; New York in Wharton's time, 76, 89–90; pleasure of anticipation, 101; and Romantic bohemianism, 28, 124–25; and sacramentalism, 29–33; sensational literature as dangerous addiction, 57; subversion of through handmade gifts, 63; Wharton's mother's attachment to, 81–82, 86; women as primary consumers, 4, 291n116, e3–4n15, e18n114; and worldly asceticism, 3, 30, 181–82. *See also* fashion; personal style; signs of happiness

continuity of life visions, 190, 259–60, e24nn32–33, e24n38

con-woman, Lily Bart as, 107, 119–21, 145, 155–58, 161

core vs. essential self, 14, 61. *See also* authentic self; Burkitt, Ian

Cotton, John, 30, 33, 95

creative consumerism, 62, 65

Cressida, Lady (fictional character), 97–99

crisis conversion view of moral development, 66, 67, 140, 183–84, 186

crisis of representation in Victorian era, 29, 185–86

culture of publicity, 90

Custom of the Country, The (Wharton), 86, 93, 194–95

Darwinian theory, 188, e16n56

deathbed scene sentimentality, 239–50, 261–62, 267, 277n16, 282n66

Debord, Guy, 66

De Quincy, Thomas, 272n14, e3n14

dialogic method, 38, 51–52, 89, 101, 109, 127, 140, 273n21, e19n11

"Diderot Effect, The" (McCracken), 34–35

"dinginess" signifier for Lily Bart, 104, 110–21, 120, 160, 163, 211, 220, 221, 229–30, 258

distinction, 68, 105, 124, 125–26, 144, 193

domesticity in *HM*, 255–56, e25n39

Dorset, Bertha (fictional character), 143, 148, 165, 170–71, 201

Dorset, George (fictional character), 220

Douglas, Ann, 6, 273n22, 274n29, e4–5n22

Douglas, Mary, 31, 110, 291n106

Dreiser, Theodore, 65, 219–20

dress reform, Alcott family's views on, e11n40

Dreyfus case, 188

dualism, Protestant, 12, 88, 108, 137–39

economic security and happiness, 4, 292n122. *See also* affluence

education of the will as cultivation of taste, 26–28

Edwards, Jonathan, 23, 147

embodiment: and Catholic sacramentalism, 30; of Christian nurture in Gerty Farish, 99, 159, 163, 223; compensations of women's, 116; Lily as idolatrous materialist, 100–102; merging with spirituality in *LW,* 245

Emerson, Ralph Waldo, 32, 61, 69–70, 136

emotional attachment: and acquisition of tastes and cultural traits, 190, 259–60; as compensation for women's embodiment and labor, 116; as counter to existential threat, 117; and freedom of the will, 108; friendship as Wharton's source of, 87; grief's importance in, 240; importance in identity formation, 17, 24; intimacy, Wharton's treatment of, 109, 134, 154–55, 164, e22n5; and Jo's redemption, 50–51; Lily's struggles with, 87, 95–96, 102–3, 129, 134–35, 154–55, 159, 164, 250–51, 253–54, 259–61, 266–67; material goods as insufficient substitutes for, 86; vs. materialism as theme of *LW,* 17–20; as moral guide, 27, 109; as necessary for child thriving, e24n33; as source of happiness, 17–18, 275n37; as true wealth, 258. *See also* family's role in identity development

emotional literacy: Lily's lack of, 100, 104, 109, 129, 152, 161, 259–60; Lily's lessons from Selden in, 133–34; March girls' training in, 32, 109

envy and fertility (Meg's themes), 21, 25, 33–35, 42

epigenetics, e21n56, e24n33

Episcopalianism, Wharton on, 75

Epston, David, 11, 14, 61, 274n30, 281n57, 295n47

equality, human, 113

essence, social construction of, 182

essential self: Amy's polished and presented, 44–45; character vs. appearance, 113; vs. core self, 14, 61; debate on Lily's, 14, 112–13, 151, e24–25n39; and Lily's sense of class superiority, 112; vs. personality, 11; and Protestant dualism, 12; racial and ethnic identity as source of, 187–88, 189, 209–10; vs. social self, 38. *See also* authentic self

ethics of style, Wharton's interest in, 285n15

evolutionary theory, influence on Wharton, 87, 88–89, 90, e16n56

existential threat, *LW* vs. *HM* on, 117

family's role in identity development: closing of cycle in *LW,* 62–64; failure of in Lily's case, 184; family as cure for emotional emptiness, 25–26; impact of Beth's illness and death, 59–60; vs. individualism, 6, 18, 24–25, 130–31, 137, 140; March girls' moral development, 7, 10, 18, 38, 47–48, 57; for Selden, 123–24; and therapeutic ethos, 8

Farish, Gerty (fictional character): and Lily, 99–100, 146; at Lily's death, 267–68; on Lily's essential self, 150, 152; on Lily's fear of intimacy, 109; Lily's judgment of status of, 114–15; and Lily's tragic self-awareness, 221–23; pressing for true story from Lily, 171–72; as refuge for Lily in her despair, 159–63; on Rosedale, 195; and Selden, 165; Selden on, 142; as sentimental idealist, 8

fashion: Alcott's critique of, e7–8n8, e11n40, e12n48; and authentic self, 32–33, 39,

e10–11n39, e11n44; vs. authentic style, 32–33, 37–38, 43–44, 47–48, 292n122, e10–11n39; classical representation of women in art, 152–53, 280n51, 294n34, e12n51; dress reform, Alcott family's views on, e11n40; and prison of financial obligation, 156; Protestant association with Catholic moral corruption, 3–4; role in Lily's identity, 104, 114, 145–46, 257; studies of, e10n37; Thoreau's utilitarian view of clothing, 281n55; violet color, Alcott's symbolic use of, e12n48; Wharton's interest in, 82, 86

feminization of consumption, 4, e3–4n15

Fisher, Carry (fictional character), 199

Fitzgerald, F. Scott, 65, 117, 193

Franchot, Jenny, 5, 37, 273n19, 280n54, e3n19, e14–15n82

freedom from all material accidents, 130–31, 132, 137–38, 139, 144, 151, 152, 266–67

freedom of the will, and emotional attachment, 108

frivolousness, Lily's, 74, 189, 294n36

Fruitlands community, 25, 62, 131, 277–78n18

Fullerton, Morton, 85

furies, Lily's, 158–60, 209, 226, 239

Galbus, Julia A., e19n11

gendering of consumption and class boundaries, 4, 291n116, e3–4n15, e18n114

gendering of language in *LW,* 24

German men, Alcott on feminine qualities of, 281n64

Gilbert, Daniel, 275n37

Goldman-Price, Irene, 177–78, 179, 180, 192, 210

grace, God's, 23, 29, 263

Grant, Madison, 187–88, 214–15, 298n59

Great Gatsby, The (Fitzgerald), 65, 117, 193

Greek philosophy, 89

grief, and transformation through loss, 23, 166, 240, 243–46, 267–70, e6n3, e14n66, e22n14, e23–24n31

Gryce, Mrs. (fictional character), 96

Gryce, Percy (fictional character), 96, 119–21, 143

Gura, Philip, 273n17, e8n13, e9n15

Haffen, Mrs. (fictional character), 148–49

Halttunen, Karen, 11, 29, 31, 43, 91, 184, 185, 192

happiness: affluence as no guarantee of, 117; and economic security, 4, 292n122; emotional attachment as source of, 17–18, 275n37; Lily's revision of original definition, 261; and limitations of Christian nurture, 8, 10, 163. *See also* signs of happiness

Hassam, Childe, 1

Hawthorne, Nathaniel, 73, 98, 284n3, 299n71

hedonism, modern vs. traditional, 28, 280n49

Heinze, Andrew, 185–86

Higham, John, 176, 178, 182

Hoeller, Hildegard, 255

homelessness and orphancy in Wharton's work, 87

House of Mirth, The (Wharton): Bellomont as ultimate vanity fair, 97, 100; contrasts with *LW,* 8–9, 103, 109, 113, 117, 124, 135, 159; controversy surrounding, 92; as critique of New York high society, 254–55; domesticity in, 255–56; ever-shifting identity discourses, 194; Greek philosophical influence, 89; "inherited tendencies" in, 191–92; as moral cautionary tale, 6–7, 73; overview comparison to *LW,* 2; parallels to *LW,* 90–91, 99–100, 101, 108, 122–23, 124, 125, 127–28, 152, 166, 267; publishing career of, 91, e3n13; racial and ethnic identity in, 190–92, 214–15, e21–22n57; "therapeutic ethos," 9–10; Wharton's biographical strands in, 11–12, 74–75, 86; writing of, 90–91. *See also main characters*

hunger and pleasure, moral choice in, 27–28

Hurstwood, George (fictional character), 219–20

hypocrisy in self-presentation: challenge for Protestantism, 29–30, 91, 94–96, 186; as fashion vs. authentic style, 33; and Haffen vs. Lily, 149; Lily's, 107, 119–21, 145, 155–58, 161; in New York society, 94–99; Rosedale's avoidance of, 215; Selden's critique of, 142–43; Wharton's concern with, 91. *See also* appearance over substance

identity: appearance over substance, 31, 93, 104–5, 113–14, 133, 257, e24–25n39, e24–25n48; class, 67, 112, 283n80; core vs. essential self, 14, 61; divided self, 14, 74, 107–8, 126, 128–29, 152, 154, 157–58, 161, 169, 170, 185–86, 236–37, 261–62, 263, e24–25n39; emotional attachment's importance to, 17, 24; ever-shifting discourses in *HM,* 194; fantasized futures and adult identity, 18–20; fashion's role in, 104, 114, 145–46, 257; freedom of in republic of the spirit, 132; immigration and American crises of, 185–86; Lily's adoption of anti-materialist, 12–13, 266–67; *LW'*s contribution to construction of national, 68; and mercurial identity of Alcott, 70; modernity crisis of, 184; nature vs. nurture, 136–37, 191–92, 257, e24n33; Protestant individualistic self, 6, 8, 137–38, 141, 250; sacraments' role in formation of, 4; as signified by consumer desires in *LW,* 19; social construction of, 67–70, 110–11, 183–86, 203; spiritual, 186–87; Wharton on, 9, 86, 89, 136–37, 191–92, 257, e24n33. *See also* essential self; family's role in identity development; racial and ethnic identity; self-construction; self-production

idolatrous materialism: addiction to, 7, 32, 100–101, 117, 145–46, 219–20, 222, e22n5; defined, 117; in Jewish stereotype, 8; Lily's, 7, 100–102, 117, 164, 169, 173; mistaking symbol for substance as sign of quality, 115; in New York society, 94–99; and nominalist economic thinking,

Christmas transformation, 1–2, 17, 276n8; contrasting representational economies, 175; as corrupter of Protestant anti-materialism, 6–7, 8, 194–95; hedonism in, 28, 280n49; immanentism in secular form, 189; Jewish version of materialism in, 183; navigation of consumer culture, 28–29, 64–66; separating self-production from social context, 139–40; weakness of sentimentalism in, 187

Moffatt, Elmer (fictional character), 194–95

Montgomery, Maureen, 89–90

Moods (Alcott), 54, e13–14n61

moral discourse and development: and child development, 273n20, e12n50; Christian nurture's role, 22–28, 50–52, 140, 184; and compartmentalization of conscience, 145; consumer culture participation, 6, 25, 31, 37–40, 42–43, 61–62, 64–67, 101; crisis conversion view, 66, 67, 140, 183–84, 186; elitism in *LW,* 68; emotional attachment as moral guide, 27, 109; liberal Protestant understanding of, 22–23, 66; Lily's moral integrity struggle, 93, 108, 165, 171–72, 205, 207, 209, 211–14, 217, 220, 238, 262–63, 266; March girls' training, 5–6, 7, 10, 17–20, 26–27, 32, 37–38, 40–48, 50–52, 57, 66–67; as marketplace, e9n23; in New York society, 94–97; passing on through social action, 66–67; and personal style, 5, 33, 211; *Pilgrim's Progress* as agent of discourse, 17–19, 20–21; Puritan-to-Enlightenment shift, 22–23; Rosedale's rise to moral integrity, 213–14; secularization of, 5–6; Selden's lack of moral integrity, 250, e18–19n7; stewardship approach to material goods, 3; utilitarian moral attitude, 66; Wharton's personal issues, 76–78, 87–89

mortality and moral frailty, confrontation with as prerequisite for salvation, 166–68

Mount, the, 90

mourning as catalyst for self-awareness, 23, 166, 240, 243–46, 267–70, e6n3, e14n66, e22n14, e23–24n31

narration's role in self-construction: in *HM,* 7, 14, 161, 163–64, 172, 173, 212–13, 232, 236, 249–50; in *LW,* 10, 11, 38, 52, 61, 246. *See also* Burkitt, Ian; Epston, David; White, Michael

Nature of True Virtue, The (Edwards), 23, 147

nature vs. nurture in identity formation, 136–37, 191–92, 257, e24n33

New York society: hypocrisy in self-presentation, 94–99; old money vs. new money, 93–94, 143; race, definition for New York patricians, 179; repression of feeling through prohibition on expression, 286n48; Wharton's relationship to, 75–76, 87–88, 254–55

Nieriker, Ernest, 70

nominalist economic thinking, 180–82, 192–93, 206

nouveau riche, hypocrisy of, 33, 93–94

object-relations psychology, e24n33

ornamental beauty, Lily's identity as, 93, 104, 113–14, 133, 257, e24–25n39

Otteson, James R., e9n23

Passing of the Great Race (Grant), 187

Pearl of Orr's Island, The (Stowe), 240–45

Peniston, Mrs. (fictional character), 94–95, 114–15, 159, 164

performance vs. sincerity in self-presentation, 92

performative Jew, 183, 185, 186, 187–88

personality, American shift to, 11, 39, 92, 185

personal style: Gerty Farish's creation of, 99–100; influence of inner character on, 125; Lily's lack of financial resources for, 115; manufacturing ability to reflect, 21; March girls' journeys to, 36–38, 42, 44, 62; moral aspects, 5, 33, 211; Rosedale's,

175; Selden's family's, 124. *See also* fashion

philosophy, Wharton's influences, 88–89

Pilgrim's Progress (Bunyan): acknowledgment of frailty as path to salvation, 166–67; as agent of moral discourse, 17–19, 20–21; importance for Alcotts, 276n7; Jewish stereotype in, 207–9; and Lily's self-awareness struggle, 140–41; Lily's slough of despond, 158–59; and *LW,* 49, 58; as model for vanity fair, 3; spiritual transparency, 241; Wharton's use of imagery, 122–23, 158–59, 166, 220, 262–63, 284n3, 290n95

Plato, 89, 273n21, 287n65, 293n11, e8n13, e19n11. *See also* Socratic method

polish and cultivation, 113, 280n50

Portrait of a Lady, The (James), 246–49

poverty as signifier and agent of mortality, 116–17

pride, destructiveness of, 40–42, 217–18, 222–26, 228, 230–31, 236, 259

private vs. public social reform and Alcott, 67

private vs. public spheres and consumer culture, e3–4n15, e4–5n22

prostitution, 12, 106–7, 161, 290n100, 294n29

Protestant anti-materialism discourse: Alcott's reworking of, 2–3; anti-Catholic discourse, 3–4, 5, 31–32, 182, 273n19, 280n54, e4n19, e9n29; family support and moral choice, 6–7; Gerty's relationship to, 123; hypocrisy vs. integrity issue, 29–30, 91, 94–96, 186; vs. Jewish, 181–82; Lily's adoption of, 12–13, 215; March girls' negotiation of, 48; modern impact on, 6–7, 8, 139–40, 194; Selden's relationship to, 7, 123, 124, 131, 137–43; in Stowe's work, 242–43; in the United States, 278n28; and Victorian consumption anxieties, 18; Wharton's reworking of, 2–3; worldly asceticism and accumulation of capital, 2–3, 181–82

Protestant elite and antisemitism, 176, 185, 186, 187, 296n12

Protestant Ethic and the Spirit of Capitalism, The (Weber), 2–3, 180–81

Protestant gaze, 5–6, 37, 46, 56, 140

Protestantism: acceptance of Catholic rituals and icons, 29, 37, 68, 283n82, e14–15n82; body/spirit dualism, 12, 88, 108, 137–39; and Christian nurture, 67–68, 140, 183–84; Christian nurture's dependence on, 184; critique of Jewish legalism, 209; Episcopalianism, 75; individualism in, 6, 8, 137–41, 250, 266–67; inner contradictions of, 141; and literary text as symbol vs. substance, e3n14; Wharton on, 75, 87–88. *See also* liberal Protestantism

public vs. private social reform and Alcott, 67

public vs. private spheres and consumer culture, e3–4n15, e4–5n22

Puritanism: vs. Catholic idolatry, 31–32; hypocrisy problem, 29–30; origins of capitalism in, 2–3, 30, 181–82; severe dualism of, 108; stewardship view of material goods, 6, 30, 61, 132, 133, 147; vestiges in Wharton's family, 75; and Victorian consumption anxiety, 30–31; view of children in, 22; Wharton's early influence from, 74, 75, 76, 89

Rabelais and His World (Bakhtin), 149

race, definition for New York patricians, 179

racial and ethnic identity: anti-Irish sentiment, Alcott's, 280n47, e11n47; Bronson Alcott on, 283–84n88; Jews and Jewishness, 7–8, 169–70, 175–80, 176, 183, 185, 186, 187–88, 207–10, 296n12; racializing of lower classes, 113, 187; as source of essential identity, 187–88, 189, 207–10; Wharton's conceptualizing of, 188–89, 190–94, 214–15, e21–22n57

realism: Alcott's contradictions, 47, 70–71; Wharton's, 2, 90, 218, 239–48, 255–56, 284n1

religious discourse: within Christian nurture, 10; crisis conversion view of moral

in, 92; performativity allowance by Protestantism, 185; Protestant criticism of Catholic-influenced, 5; as sign of Rosedale's Jewishness, 192–93; as untainted by domestic labor, 95; Victorian anxieties over, 11, 29. *See also* fashion; hypocrisy in self-presentation; sincerity in self-presentation

self-production: contrasting elements of, 141; Lily's, 106–7, 108, 112, 141–42, 151, 211, 213, 290n98; and representational economies, 5. *See also* commodification; identity

self-reliance, Selden's aspiration for, 130–31

self-sabotage, Lily's talent for, 121–22, 165

self-sacrifice, lack of reward for in Wharton's work, 238

Send These to Me (Higham), 176

sensational narratives, Alcott's, 54, 281nn58–60, 281n63, e13n58, e13n60

sentimentalism: continuity of life visions, 190, 259–60, e24nn32–33, e24n38; deathbed scene, 233, 239–50, 261–62, 277n16, 282n66; defined, 24, 239–40; and family as center of moral development, 6, 25–26; German legacy in *LW*, 56–57; Gerty and Lily's relationship, 162; grief's salvific consequences, 23, 166, 240, 243–46, 267–70, e6n3, e14n66, e22n14, e23–24n31; immanentism, 6, 23–24, 184, 186, 189–90, 240, e8–9n13, e9n15; influence on Wharton and *HM*, 90–91, e23–24n31; and Lily, 74, 105–6, 190, 259–60, 293n9, e24n32; in *LW*, 24–27, 66; relationship to realism in *HM*, 254–61, 267; secular weakening of, 184; Selden's appearance, 125; and social construction of value, 182; sources for, e5–6nn22–23; Stowe's, 240–45, e4n20; in Struther's offer of help to Lily, 239; Wharton's critique of, 14, 141, 218, 284n1, e16n53. *See also* Christian nurture and sentimentalism

servant class, 111–13, 294n32

sexuality, 84–86, 106, 107, 108, 109

shopping. *See* consumer culture

signs of happiness: association with affluence, 1–2, 100; as insufficient to counter existential threat, 117; Lily's fantasies surrounding, 100, 114–15, 222; Lily's prison within, 93, 100, 104; and *LW* as consumer product, 71; problem of consumer goods as, 34–35; rejection of to attain salvation, 243; and sacramentalism, 29; transformation of into useful experience, 132, 133

sincerity in self-presentation: deathbed scene as catalyst for, 244, 249–50; and home away from commodity culture, 255; importance for Amy's authentic identity, 43–44; and Jewish materialism, 182; Lily's instances of, 213, 221–22, 232–38; Lily's rejection of, 171–72; vs. performance, 92; Protestant insistence upon, 137–39, 184–85; and quality of artistic expression, 153; Rosedale's, 201–3; and standards of taste, 185; Victorian obsession with, 11, 29; Wharton's concern with, 91

Singley, Carol, 73, 75, 88, 89, 98, 151, 254, e16n53

Sister Carrie (Dreiser), 65, 219–20

Smith, Adam, 278n23, e4–5n22, e9n23

social construction: authentic self, 61; of essence, 182; of identity, 67–70, 110–11, 183–86, 203; of value, 182

social context, modernity's attempt to separate self-production from, 139–40

social reform crusades, Alcott's, 67, e11n40, e14n79

social vs. essential self, 38

Socratic method, 38, 51–52, 89, 101, 109, 127, 140, 273n21, e19n11. *See also* Plato

solitude, Wharton and Lily's, e19–20n44

Sombart, Werner, 181

sorrow, transformative power of, 165–66. *See also* mourning as catalyst for self-awareness

Southworth, E. D. E. N., 53, 281n58

Spark, The (Wharton), 88

spiritual identity, turn-of-century anxieties, 186–87

spiritual transparency, in Stowe's Mara Lincoln, 241–42

Spragg, Undine (fictional character), 194–95

Stepney, Jack (fictional character), 144

Stern, Madeleine, 281n63

stewardship view of material goods, 3, 6, 30, 61, 132, 133, 147

Stowe, Harriet Beecher, 240–45, e4n20, e22n14

Strickland, Charles, 67

Struther, Nettie (fictional character), 14, 251–56, 259–60

style, personal. *See* personal style

"surface," Lily's, 112–14, 214, 224–25, 251

Susman, Warren, 11, 92, 185

sylvan being, Lily's, 127–29, 150–51

symbolic vs. functional value of objects, 12, 19, 25, 31, 42, 110–11. *See also* signs of happiness

sympathetic realism, Wharton's, 284n1

tableaux vivants, Lily Bart in, 149–54

taste, cultivation of, 26–28, 185, 190, 259–60

tea, Lily's addiction to, 211, 212, 220, 226, 300n5

Theory of Moral Sentiments, The (Smith), 278n23, e4–5n22, e9n23

therapeutic ethos, 8, 9–10, 274n29, 282n77

Thoreau, Henry David, 4, 32, 33, 130, 281n55, 292n122, e19n12

Tiffany Blue Box, 1, e1nn1–2

Tompkins, Jane, 6, 140, 273n22, e4–5n22

totemism, e10n38

Touchett, Ralph (fictional character), 246–49

tragedy, Wharton's use of, 163–64

Transcendentalism, 5, 6, 23, 24–25, 89, 272n17, 279n33

Trenor, Gus (fictional character), 143, 145–46, 155–57, 175, 191–92

Trenor, Judy (fictional character), 97–98

troubled child self, Lily's, 127–28, 131, 134, 142–43, 154–55, 159–60, 162, 264, 265

urbanization, social anxieties over, 29, 31. *See also* modernity

Valley of Decision, The (Wharton), 89

Valley of the Shadow, Lily's, 262–63

Veblen, Thorstein, 2, 139, 272n16, 289n82

Victorian marketplace and anxieties: acceptance of rituals and icons of Catholicism, 283n82, e14–15n82; agrarian-to-urban shift anxieties, 29, 31; dirt fetish, 110–11, 149; labor and social value, 12, 110–11; Protestant anti-materialism discourse, 18; Puritanism's influence on, 30–31; self-presentation, 11, 29; sensational literature and *LW,* 57; separation of spheres, servants' contradiction of, 111–12; whore and virgin dichotomy, 115–16, 149

violet color, Alcott's symbolic use of, 280n48, e12n48

Von Rosk, Nancy, e24–25n39

"Voyage of Life" (Cole), 290n95

Washburn, Reverend, 78, 87, 286n38

Weber, Max, 2–3, 28, 30, 181

Weinberg, H. Barbara, 1

Wharton, Edith: and Alcott, 2, 73, 79, 90; attitudes about Jews, origins of, 177, 179–80; authentic self of, 86–87, 151; autobiographical aspects of *HM,* 11–12, 74–75, 86; and Berry, 87, 287n55; birth of, 76; "blood" as underlying feelings and desires, 189–90; ethical views of, 287n59; and ethics of style, 285n15; fashion interest of, 82, 86; fondness for father, 82–83; and happy-ending expectation of audiences, 242; interest in religion, 78; library as refuge for, 77–78; love of beauty, 77, 86, 294n33; moral development of, 76–78, 87–89; and New York society, 75–76, 87–88, 254–55; parallels with Lily, 85, 290n92, e19–20n44; philosophy and evolutionary theory, 87, 88–89, 90, e16n56; problems with mother, 77, 81, 83–85; on Protestantism,

75, 87–88; reading and writing, need for, 86–87; religious and social background of, 74–76, 89, e17–18n103. See also *House of Mirth, The*

Wharton, Teddy, 85

Wharton's Dialogue with Realism and Sentimentalism (Hoeller), 255

White, Michael, 11, 14, 61, 274n30, 281n57, 295n47

Whitman, Walt, 88

women: commodification of, 36, 290n99, e17n99; immanence and bodies of, 115–16, 291–92n118

women in society: Alcott's empowerment of, 5; classical representation in art, 152–53, 280n51, 294n34, e12n51; dependence on men for financial security, 8, 255–56; and sentimentalism in *LW*'s time, 24; shopping as gendered female, 4, 291n116, e3–4n15, e18n114; as symbols of affluence for men, 4–5, 7, 272n16; Victorian anxieties about labor of, 12, 110–11; virgin and whore dichotomy, 115–16, 149, 291–92n118

worldly asceticism, 2–3, 30, 181–82

World of Goods, The (Douglas and Isherwood), 31